Language typology and syntactic description

Volume I
Clause structure

Language typology and syntactic description is published under the
auspices of the Center for Applied Linguistics.

Language typology and syntactic description

Volume I
Clause structure

Edited by
TIMOTHY SHOPEN
Australian National University

90 -2267

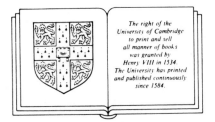

CAMBRIDGE UNIVERSITY PRESS

Cambridge
New York   Port Chester
Melbourne   Sydney

Published by the Press Syndicate of the University of Cambridge
The Pitt Building, Trumpington Street, Cambridge CB2 1RP
40 West 20th Street, New York, NY 10011, USA
10 Stamford Road, Oakleigh, Melbourne 3166, Australia

First published 1985
Reprinted 1986, 1990

Printed in Great Britain by the
Athenaeum Press Ltd, Newcastle upon Tyne.

Library of Congress catalogue card number: 84-20028

British Library cataloguing in publication data

Language typology and syntactic description.
Vol. 1, Clause structure
1. Grammar, Comparative and general-Syntax
I. Shopen, Timothy
415   P291

ISBN 0 521 25700 X hard covers
ISBN 0 521 27659 4 paperback

Contents

Clause and sentence types

3 Speech act distinctions in syntax
JERROLD M. SADOCK
University of Chicago
and
ARNOLD M. ZWICKY
Ohio State University

4 Negation

JOHN R. PAYNE

University of Manchester

5 Passive in the world's languages

EDWARD L. KEENAN

University of California, Los Angeles

6 Information packaging in the clause
WILLIAM A. FOLEY
Australian National University
and
ROBERT D. VAN VALIN, JR
University of California, Davis

Acknowledgements

This work began at a conference on field work questionnaires initiated by Rudolph Troike at the Center for Applied Linguistics (CAL). The participants agreed that the best way to prepare for field work is to develop an idea of what to look for, and this led to the idea of a typological survey that could serve as a reference manual and a textbook for students.

Many people have helped us in the work that we now present. I will name only a few here. Rudolph Troike and John Hammer of CAL, and Alan Bell of the National Science Foundation did much to help in the organization of the project, and the National Science Foundation provided generous financial support without which the work would not have been possible. Diana Riehl of CAL was a reliable and capable intermediary in the complex administration of the project. Carmen Silva-Corvalan and Sandra Thompson deserve special thanks for their work at UCLA, while here in Australia many people provided help. The Australian National University has been very generous in its support of my work. I am grateful to Penny Carter and Julia Harding of Cambridge University Press for the careful work in the production of our books. Three people that have been especially helpful to me in the final stages of the editing are Edith Bavin, Jean Harkins, and above all, Rosemary Butt. My thanks to all.

Timothy Shopen
Canberra, Australia
February 1984

Abbreviations for grammatical terms

The following are abbreviations for grammatical terms used frequently in the glosses for examples. Other abbreviations are explained as they are presented.

ABS	Absolutive	IO	Indirect object
ACC	Accusative	IRR	Irrealis
ACT	Actor	LOC	Locative
AG	Agent	NOM	Nominative
ART	Article	NZN	Nominalization
ASP	Aspect	NZR	Nominalizer
ASSOC	Associative	OBJ	Object
AUX	Auxiliary	OBL	Oblique
BEN	Benefactive	PART	Participle
CL	Classifier	PASS	Passive
COMP	Complementizer	PCL	Particle
COMPL	Completive	PERF	Perfective
COND	Conditional	PL	Plural
DAT	Dative	PREP	Preposition
DECLAR	Declarative	PRES	Present
DEF	Definite	PRO	Pro form
DEM	Demonstrative	PROG	Progressive
DET	Determiner	Q	Question marker
DO	Direct object	REFL	Reflexive
DU	Dual	REL	Relativizer
EMPH	Emphasis	RPRO	Relative pronoun
ERG	Ergative	SG	Singular
FUT	Future	SJNCT	Subjunctive
GEN	Genitive	SUBJ	Subject
HABIT	Habitual	TNS	Tense
IMP	Imperative	TOP	Topic
INCOMPL	Incompletive	VN	Verbal noun
INDIC	Indicative	1	First person
INF	Infinitive	2	Second person
INSTR	Instrumental	3	Third person

Introduction

Clause structure is the first of three volumes comprising the work *Language typology and syntactic description*. The second volume is *Complex constructions* and the third is *Grammatical categories and the lexicon*. Our purpose has been to do a cross-linguistic survey of syntactic and morphological structure that can serve as a manual for field workers, and for anyone interested in relating observations about particular languages to a general theory of language.

In investigating the structure of a language, it is of first importance to know what to look for, to have informed expectations, a working hypothesis about the likely correlations between various aspects of syntax and word formation among the languages of the world. One can never prepare fully in advance for the 'how-to-do-it', the methodology of field work. A great deal of that will depend on an unpredictable interaction of ethos, personality and on-the-spot ingenuity. And indeed, discovery and understanding in science come as unplanned-for gifts of the imagination. One must welcome the particular characteristics of a language that make it a unique cultural artifact, and different from any other, but at the same time, one will understand the workings of the language better, even in its most distinctive traits, the more one knows what languages tend to be like.

There are six chapters in this volume. It begins with two chapters on component parts and relations within the clause. The first is by Paul Schachter on part-of-speech systems. He discusses both content-word and function-word categories. While all languages have verbs and nouns, he shows they may differ from each other in the other categories they possess; nevertheless, he demonstrates certain consistent tendencies in the grouping of notions and functions among the parts of speech.

The second chapter is by Avery Andrews on the major functions of the noun phrase. He distinguishes common grammatical functions for noun phrases and then shows how particular noun phrases operate in the syntax of a language such that they could be said to be part of a system of grammatical relations. He surveys the major variants of these systems.

The four remaining chapters concern clause and sentence types. In the third chapter of the volume, Jerrold Sadock and Arnold Zwicky discuss speech act distinctions in syntax. They consider the sentence types into which the main clauses of a language can be categorized, with concern for both their form and their use.

In the fourth chapter of the volume, John Payne discusses negation. He takes care to establish language-independent criteria for the various ways in which negation has scope within the syntax of sentences, and then surveys the variety of forms that these different kinds of negation can take.

In the fifth chapter, Edward Keenan writes about the passive construction, a means of constructing clauses with the same propositional content as can be expressed by the active but with marked effects of foregrounding and backgrounding. He contrasts it briefly with other foregrounding and backgrounding constructions, and devotes most of the chapter to the place of the passive in the syntactic systems of the world's languages.

The sixth and final chapter is by William Foley and Robert D. Van Valin, Jr with the title 'Information packaging in the clause'. This chapter complements the preceding one on passives in that it gives a broader overview of foregrounding and backgrounding constructions, and the authors develop an essentially functional typology for such constructions.

Note: References to chapters in all three volumes of *Syntactic typology and language description* are preceded by the volume number. For example: chapter 1.2 (chapter 2, this volume), chapter 11.3 (Volume 11, chapter 3).

1 Parts-of-speech systems*

PAUL SCHACHTER

0 Introduction

Parts of speech is the traditional term for the major classes of words that
are grammatically distinguished in a language. While all languages make
parts-of-speech distinctions, there are rather striking differences between languages with regard to both the kind and the number of such
distinctions that they make. A field worker investigating an unfamiliar
language may therefore find it useful to know what generalizations can
be made about parts-of-speech systems. What, for example, can be said
about the ways in which, and the limits within which, parts-of-speech
inventories may differ from one another? Which parts-of-speech distinctions are universal and which language-specific? What are the ways in
which languages that lack a particular part of speech express the
semantic equivalent? And what relations are there between the parts-of-
speech system of a language and the language's other typological
characteristics? It is the aim of this chapter to provide some answers to
such questions.

By way of orientation, the present section sets forth some general
assumptions that underlie the presentation in the rest of the chapter.
First, then, it is assumed here that the primary criteria for parts-of-
speech classification are grammatical, not semantic. As has been amply
demonstrated in the linguistic literature (cf., for example, Fries 1952),
the familiar notional parts-of-speech definitions, such as 'a noun is the
name of a person, place, or thing', fail to provide an adequate basis for
parts-of-speech classification, since there are many cases in which their
applicability or inapplicability is unclear. Grammatical criteria, on the
other hand, are not open to this objection.

The grammatical properties of a word that are here taken to be
relevant to its parts-of-speech classification include the word's distribution, its range of syntactic functions, and the morphological or syntactic
categories for which it is specifiable. Consider, in this connection, the
three words of the sentence:

(1)   Boys like girls

The words *boys* and *like* can be shown to differ in their distributions (**Like boys girls* is ungrammatical), in their functional range (*boys* can function as a subject but *like* cannot), and in their categorizations (*boys* is categorized for number but not for tense, while *like* is categorized for both). Thus these two words are assigned to distinct parts-of-speech classes. On the other hand, the words *boys* and *girls*, having highly similar distributions (cf. *Girls like boys*), functional ranges, and categorizations, are assigned to the same parts-of-speech class. There are, to be sure, cases that are less clearcut than these – cases, for example, involving *partial* similarities of distribution, functional range, or categorization, which may require dividing a parts-of-speech class into subclasses. (For some further discussion, see section 1.0.) But by and large the grammatical properties in question constitute a serviceable basis for parts-of-speech classification.

While it is assumed here that the assignment of words to parts-of-speech classes is based on properties that are grammatical rather than semantic, and often language-particular rather than universal, it is also assumed that the *name* that is chosen for a particular parts-of-speech class in a language may appropriately reflect universal semantic considerations. Thus, although the familiar notional definition of nouns mentioned above does not always provide an adequate basis for deciding whether or not a given word is a noun, once the words of a language have been assigned to parts-of-speech classes on grammatical grounds and it is found that one of these classes includes the preponderance of words that are the names of persons, places, and things, then it is perfectly reasonable to call this class the class of nouns, and to compare the class so named with the similarly named classes of other languages. (On this point, see Lyons 1968:317–19.) Thus the words *boys* and *girls* are assigned to the same parts-of-speech class (and the word *like* to a different class) on language-particular grammatical grounds, but it is on universal semantic grounds that the class to which *boys* and *girls* are assigned is called the class of nouns (while that to which *like* is assigned is called the class of verbs).

Another assumption reflected in this chapter is that all languages make a distinction between *open* and *closed* parts-of-speech classes. Following Robins (1964:230), we can describe open classes as those 'whose membership is in principle unlimited, varying from time to time and between one speaker and another' and closed classes as those 'contain a fixed and usually small number of member words, which are [essentially] the same for all the speakers of the language, or the dialect'. Thus open classes are classes such as nouns and verbs, and closed classes are classes such as pronouns and conjunctions.

That all languages contain open classes is beyond doubt, despite occasional apocryphal reports to the contrary: i.e., reports of languages whose vocabularies consist of only a few hundred words. A more serious question can be raised about the universal status of closed classes. It is certainly true that closed classes play a rather minor role in some languages, and it has in fact sometimes been claimed that there are languages in which they play no role at all. The languages in question are invariably so-called *synthetic* languages: that is, languages that favor morphologically complex words. (Synthetic languages are commonly contrasted with analytic languages, in which words consisting of a single morpheme are the norm. If a scale were established, ranging from highly synthetic languages, such as Eskimo, to highly analytic ones, such as Vietnamese, modern English would be somewhat closer to the analytic than to the synthetic end of this scale.) The relation between a language's position on the synthetic–analytic scale and the role of closed classes in that language is discussed more fully in section 2.0. That section also considers, and rejects, the claim that there are known instances of languages with no closed classes at all.

The distinction between open and closed parts-of-speech classes provides the basic organizing principle of the remainder of this chapter, with open classes being dealt with in sections 1.0–4 and closed classes in sections 2.0–5.

1.0 Open classes

The open parts-of-speech classes that may occur in a language are the classes of *nouns, verbs, adjectives,* and *adverbs*. Typically, each of these classes may be divided into a number of subclasses on the basis of certain distinctive grammatical properties. For example, the class of nouns in English may be divided into such subclasses as common and proper (on the basis of whether or not the nouns occur with articles like *the: the girl* vs. **the Mary*), count and non-count (on the basis of whether or not they occur in the plural: *chairs* vs. **furnitures*), etc. And the class of English verbs may be divided into such subclasses as transitive and intransitive (on the basis of occurrence with objects: *enjoy it* vs. **smile it*), active and stative (on the basis of occurrence in the progressive: *is studying* vs. **is knowing*), etc. Such subclasses are not ordinarily identified as distinct parts of speech, since there are in fact properties common to the members of the different subclasses, and since the label *parts of speech* is, as noted earlier, traditionally reserved for 'major classes'. In any case, the discussion of open parts-of-speech classes in this chapter does not include a systematic account of the subclassification of these classes, but instead offers only a few observations concerning subclasses that are particularly widespread, or that seem particularly interesting from a typological viewpoint.

It must be acknowledged, however, that there is not always a clear basis for deciding whether two distinguishable open classes of words that occur in a language should be identified as different parts of speech or as subclasses of a single part of speech. The reason for this is that the open parts-of-speech classes must be distinguished from one another on the basis of a *cluster* of properties, none of which by itself can be claimed to be a necessary and sufficient condition for assignment to a particular class. And the fact is that languages vary considerably in the extent to which the properties associated with different open word classes form discrete clusters. Typically there is some overlap, some sharing of properties, as well as some differentiation. In English, for example, although nouns, verbs, and adjectives are clearly distinguished from one another in various ways, there are still certain properties that they share. Thus nouns and adjectives, as well as verbs, may be subclassified as active vs. stative on the basis of occurrence in the progressive (compare *John is being a boor/boisterous* and **John is being my brother/tall*). And in certain other languages, as will become clear in the following sections, nouns and verbs, or nouns and adjectives, or verbs and adjectives, may have very much more in common than they do in English. What this means is that there may in some cases be considerable arbitrariness in the identification of two open word classes as distinct parts of speech rather than subclasses of a single part of speech. Thus some rather celebrated questions – for example, whether or not all languages make a distinction between nouns and verbs – may ultimately turn out to be more a matter of terminology than of substance (cf. section 1.2).

In the following presentation of the open parts-of-speech classes, nouns, verbs, adjectives, and adverbs are discussed in turn. In each case, the characteristic grammatical and notional properties of the class are enumerated, with relevant examples. Certain subclasses are also noted, and, where appropriate, there is a discussion of the question of the universality of a particular parts-of-speech distinction (cf. section 1.2), or of the ways in which languages that lack a particular distinction express the semantic equivalent (cf. sections 1.3 and 1.4).

1.1 *Nouns*

The distinction between *nouns* and *verbs* is one of the few apparently universal parts-of-speech distinctions. While the universality of even this distinction has sometimes been questioned, it now seems that the alleged counter-examples have been based on incomplete data, and that there are no languages that cannot be said to show a noun–verb distinction when all relevant facts are taken into account. We shall look further into the matter of languages which allegedly fail to distinguish nouns and verbs at the end of section 1.2, after the characteristic properties of these two parts of speech have been described.

The label *noun* is assigned to the class of words in which occur the names of most persons, places, and things. (As was explained in the introductory section, this type of notional correlation is not the basis for determining membership in a class, but merely the basis for assigning a name to a class established on other grounds. It is therefore not a matter of concern if the class of nouns includes, as it typically does, words that are not the names of persons, places, or things, or if some such names are found in some other class.) The most common function for nouns is as arguments or heads of arguments: for example, as (heads of) subjects or objects, as in the case of the italicized words of:

(2)   The little *boy* was eating *candy*

Nouns may also function as predicates, however, either with an accompanying copula, such as English *be*, (3), or Hausa *ne*, (4), or without any copula, as in Tagalog, (5), or Russian, (6):

(3)   They are *teachers*

(4)   Su   *malamai* ne
        they teachers COP
        'They are teachers'

(5)   Mga *guro*   sila
        PL   teacher they
        'They are teachers'

(6)   Oni *učitelja*
        they teachers
        'They are teachers'

Typical categories for which nouns may be specified, either morphologically or syntactically, are case, number, class or gender, and definiteness. Case marking indicates grammatical functions (such as subject, direct object, and indirect object), as in the following examples from Latin, (7) (in which case is marked morphologically, by suffixation), and Japanese, (8) (in which case is marked syntactically, by postpositions).

(7)   Femin-a   mal-um   puell-ae dedit
        woman-NOM apple-ACC girl-DAT gave
        'The woman gave an apple to the girl'

(8)   Onna   ga   shojo ni   ringo o   ataeta
        woman SUBJ girl   DAT apple OBJ gave
        'The woman gave an apple to the girl'

Number marking distinguishes singular from plural, and, more rarely, dual, as in English *house/houses*; Eskimo *iglu* 'house'/*iglut* 'houses'/*igluk* 'two houses'; or Tagalog *bahay* 'house'/*mga bahay* 'houses'. Class or gender marking partitions the set of nouns into subsets, each of which has its own distinctive marking and/or necessitates a distinctive marking on certain other words which show agreement with nouns. Typically, the classification is in part semantically based and in part semantically arbitrary. Examples include the gender systems of Indo-European languages (e.g. German *der Mann* (the-masculine man) 'the man', *die Frau* (the-feminine woman) 'the woman', *das Mädchen* (the-neuter girl) 'the girl'), the class systems of Bantu languages (such as Swahili, in which most nouns that refer to human beings are in class I, which takes the prefix *m-*, e.g. *mtu* 'person', *mtoto* 'child', *mgeni* 'stranger', but in which some of the other classes have little semantic coherence), and the noun-classifier systems of such languages as Thai (cf. section 2.2, below). Some examples of definiteness distinctions are *a man* vs. *the man*, Norwegian *en mann* 'a man' vs. *mannen* 'the man', and Hebrew *ish* 'a man' vs. *ha-ish* 'the man'.

In most languages some grammatical distinction is made between *common nouns*, which are used to refer to any member of a class of persons, etc. (e.g. *girl, city, novel*) and *proper nouns*, which are used to refer to specific persons, etc. (e.g. *Mary, Boston, Ivanhoe*). The precise character of the grammatical distinction, however, as well as its precise semantic correlates, may show considerable variation from language to language. For example, while common nouns in English differ from (most) proper nouns by occurring with articles, in Tagalog (which has no articles) common and proper nouns take different case markers and topic markers, as the following examples illustrate:

(9)   Malapit *sa*   babae   *ang* bata
        near   OBL woman TOP child
        'The child is near the woman'

(10)   Malapit *kay* Maria *si*   Juan
        near   OBL Maria TOP Juan
        'Juan is near Maria'

Moreover, the Tagalog classes that are distinguished on this basis are not semantically coextensive with the English classes of proper and common nouns. The Tagalog nouns that take the markers of (10) are restricted to those that refer to specific *persons*; nouns that refer to specific *places*, etc. take the other set of markers, although their English equivalents are clearly proper, rather than common, nouns:

(11) Malapit *sa* Maynila *ang* Pasay City
      near   OBL Manila TOP Pasay City
      'Pasay City is near Manila'

Apart from making a distinction between common and proper nouns, languages may make various other kinds of subclass distinctions within the set of nouns: for example the gender distinctions mentioned above, or a distinction between count and non-count nouns, which may be manifested by occurrence vs. non-occurrence in the plural. As was explained in section 1.0, however, such subclass distinctions go beyond the scope of this chapter.

1.2 *Verbs*

Verb is the name given to the parts-of-speech class in which occur most of the words that express actions, processes, and the like. The characteristic function of verbs is as predicates, as in:

(12) The people *danced*
      The student *solved* the problem

In some languages, however, verbs can also occur as arguments as in the following example from Tagalog:

(13) Pinanood ko ang mga *sumasayaw*
      watch   I TOP PL were dancing
      'I watched the ones who were dancing'

      cf. *Sumasayaw*   ang mga tao
          were dancing TOP PL person
          'The people were dancing'

The use of a verb as an argument is to be distinguished from the probably more common use of a verbal *noun* as an argument, as in Akan:

(14) Mehwɛɛ *asaw*   no
      I watched dancing the
      'I watched the dancing'

The verbal noun is a noun which is morphologically related to a verb, but which does not itself occur as a verbal predicate. For example, the verbal noun *asaw* of (14) is related to the verb *saw* 'dance' but could never itself be used as a predicate.

The categories for which verbs may be specified include tense, aspect, mood, voice, and polarity. (As in the case of nouns, the categorization may be manifested either morphologically or syntactically. Only morphological illustrations will be given in this section, however. For some syntactic illustrations, see the presentation of auxiliaries in section 2.3. See also, for further information on tense, mood, and aspect, chapter III.4, and for a detailed treatment of mood 1.3.) Tense marking indicates time relative to the time of the utterance: for example Haya *akaija* 'he came (earlier than a few days ago)', *alaizile* 'he came (within the past few days)', *yaija* 'he came (earlier today), *alaija* 'he will come (in the near future), *aliija* 'he will come (in the distant future). Aspect marking indicates whether the action of the verb is regarded as complete or incomplete, durative or momentaneous, etc.: for example Classical Greek *bebouleûsthai* 'to have already decided', *bouleúesthai* 'to be deciding', *bouleúseasthai* 'to decide (unspecified for completeness or durativeness)'. Mood marking involves distinctions such as indicative (actual) vs. subjunctive (possible) or declarative vs. interrogative: for example, French (*qu'*)*il viendra* '(that) he will come' vs. (*qu'*)*il vienne* '(that) he may come'; Menomini *pi·w* 'he is coming, came' vs. *pi·ʔ* 'is he coming?, did he come?'. Voice marking has to do with the role of the subject in the action expressed by the verb, the most common voice distinction being active vs. passive, as in Latin *videt* 'he sees', *videtur* 'he is seen'. And polarity marking distinguishes affirmative from negative, as in Akan *tu* 'pulls', *ntu* 'doesn't pull'. (In addition to being marked for inherently verbal categorizations, verbs in some languages are marked to indicate certain categorizations (person, number, class) of their subjects and, less frequently, their objects: for example, Latin *video* 'I see', *videmus* 'we see'; Swahili *wa-ta-ni-uliza* (they-future-I-ask) 'they will ask me'; *ni-ta-wa-uliza* (I-future-they-ask) 'I will ask them'.)

In all languages it is possible to subclassify verbs as transitive or intransitive on the basis of whether or not they occur with objects. In some languages the transitive–intransitive distinction entails certain other grammatical distinctions. For example, in Bambara the past tense is expressed by an auxiliary (*ye*) with transitive verbs but by a suffix (*-la*) with intransitive verbs:

(15)   U   ye   a san
        they PAST it buy
        'They bought it'

(16)   U   boli-la
        they walk-PAST
        'They walked'

Many languages also have a subclass of *copulative* verbs, like English *be*, that occur with predicate nominals or adjectives. In other languages, however, there is either no copula at all (as in Tagalog – cf. example (5)) or the copula is not a verb (as in Hausa – cf. example (4)). (For further discussion of non-verb copulas, see section 2.5.) Another widespread subclassification of verbs involves a distinction between *active* verbs, which express actions and the like, and *stative* verbs, which express states and the like. (As was noted in section 1.0, this distinction in English is correlated with occurrence vs. non-occurrence in the progressive.)

To turn now to the question of the universality of the noun–verb distinction, there are, as previously noted, languages with regard to which the legitimacy of such a distinction has been denied. Probably the best-known case is that of Nootka, which has often been cited in the linguistic literature as lacking a noun–verb distinction, on the basis of the analysis of Swadesh (1939). Recently, however, Jacobsen (1976) has re-examined the Nootka data, and has shown that, while the distinction between nouns and verbs in Nootka is less obvious than it is in many other languages, there is nonetheless a reasonably clear distinction to be made.

The following are the kind of examples that have been cited in support of the alleged lack of a noun–verb distinction in Nootka:

(17)   Mamu·k-ma   qu·ʔas-ʔi
        working-PRES(INDIC) man-DEF
        'The man is working'

(18)   Qu·ʔas-ma   mamu·k-ʔi
        man-PRES(INDIC) working-DEF
        'The working one is a man'

As these examples indicate, the notionally noun-like root meaning 'man', *qu·ʔas*, and the notionally verb-like root meaning 'working', *mamu·k*, show, from the point of view of a language like English, rather surprising similarities of function and categorizations. Thus *qu·ʔas* can function not only as an argument, as in (17), but also as a predicate, as in (18), without any accompanying copula. And *mamu·k* can function not only as a predicate but also as an argument (as in (17) and (18) respectively). Moreover, both the notionally noun-like and the notionally verb-like roots may be marked either for the typically nominal category definite (by the suffix -ʔi) or the typically verbal category present (by the suffix -ma).

What Jacobsen points out, however, is that the functional and categorizational ranges of roots like qu·ʔas and roots like mamu·k, although similar, are not identical. For example, while qu·ʔas and other notionally noun-like roots may function as arguments either with or without the suffix -ʔi, mamu·k and other notionally verb-like roots function as arguments only when suffixed. Compare (19) and (20):

(19)   Mamu·k-ma   qu·ʔas
       working-PRES(INDIC) man
       'A man is working'

(20)   *Qu·ʔas-ma   mamu·k
       man-PRES(INDIC)   working

Moreover, some of the apparent similarities between nouns and verbs in Nootka turn out, on careful examination, to be of rather questionable significance. Thus there is evidence that Nootka tense morphemes, such as -ma in (17) and (18), are best analyzed as clitics that attach to the clause-initial word, whatever category this word belongs to. (For fuller discussion, see chapter III.1.) It thus seems clear that Nootka does make a distinction that can be identified as a distinction between nouns and verbs, although this distinction is subtler than that found in English and many other languages.

Nootka is by no means alone, however, in making a fairly subtle distinction between nouns and verbs. Since the characteristic function of nouns is as arguments and that of verbs is as predicates, a functional distinction between nouns and verbs becomes difficult to establish to the extent that nouns occur as predicates and verbs as arguments without any distinctive marking (such as a copula accompanying the predicative nominal or some morpheme indicating nominalization of the verb). Consider in this connection the following examples from Tagalog:

(21)   Nagtatrabaho ang lalaki
       is working   TOP man
       'The man is working'

(22)   Lalaki ang nagtatrabaho
       man   TOP is working
       'The one who is working is a man'

As previously noted, and as further illustrated by (22), predicate nominals in Tagalog are not accompanied by a copula and verbs occur freely as arguments. Thus, from a functional point of view, nouns and verbs appear to be at least as similar in Tagalog as they are in Nootka. (Tagalog does, however, make a more clear-cut distinction in categorization: only verbs are inflectable for aspect.)

Nonetheless, while languages may differ considerably in the extent to which they make a grammatical distinction between nouns and verbs, it seems correct to say that all languages do in fact make some distinction between them. One might, however, wish to say that in some languages, such as Nootka and Tagalog, nouns and verbs have enough in common grammatically for there to be some question about whether to regard them as two subclasses of a single part of speech rather than two distinct parts of speech. Since this seems to be essentially a matter of terminology, it need not concern us further.

1.3 *Adjectives*

While all languages appear to distinguish two open classes, nouns and verbs, only certain languages make a further distinction between these and a third open class, the class of *adjectives*. The major question with which this section will be concerned is how adjectival meanings are expressed in languages that lack an open adjectival class. First, however, the properties of adjectives in those languages in which they do constitute a distinct open parts-of-speech class will be summarized.

The traditional notional definition of adjectives identifies them as the class of words denoting qualities or attributes. This definition has some well-known shortcomings (see, for example, the discussions in Jespersen 1924 and Lyons 1971), but no obviously better notional definition has been proposed. As a result, even in notionally based grammars, adjectives have usually been defined at least in part in functional terms, as words which modify nouns. Among the words which modify nouns, a distinction is sometimes made between *limiting adjectives* and *descriptive adjectives*. However, the so-called limiting adjectives (words such as *some*, *this*, *other*) never constitute an open class, and will not here be treated as adjectives at all (see section 2.2 for a discussion of such words). The present discussion is thus confined to descriptive adjectives.

In addition to functioning as modifiers of nouns (e.g. *tall* in *the tall woman*), adjectives may also function as predicates (as in *The woman is tall*). Like predicate nouns, predicate adjectives may or may not be accompanied by a copula. Thus English uses a copula while Ilocano does not:

(23)   Natayag daydyay babae
        tall   TOP   woman
        'The woman is tall'

A category for which adjectives are often specified is degree, which includes the traditional distinctions positive, comparative, and superlative – for example English *tall/taller/tallest*; Ilocano *natayag* 'tall'/*nataytayag* 'taller'/*katatayagan* 'tallest' – as well as various others: for example *very/too/so/rather tall*. In some languages, adjectives are also marked to indicate the categorizations of the nouns they modify or – when the adjectives are predicates – of the nouns that are their subjects. In Latin, for example, adjectives are marked for the case, gender, and number of nouns they modify (or are predicated of). Thus in:

(24)   Feminae *procerae* homines *proceros* amant
        women tall   men   tall   like
        'Tall women like tall men'

procerae is a nominative feminine plural form agreeing with *feminae* while *proceros* is an accusative masculine plural form agreeing with *homines*.

To turn now to the question of how the notional equivalent of adjectives is expressed in languages which lack an open adjective class, a distinction can be made between two groups of such languages. First, there are languages in which there *is* a class that can be called adjectives, but in which this class is closed rather than open, with anywhere from less than ten members (e.g. Igbo, which has eight) to fifty-odd (e.g. Swahili). And second, there are languages which lack a distinct adjective class altogether. Let us consider each of these groups in turn.

With regard to the first group, Dixon (1977b) has noted a rather striking cross-linguistic consistency in the range of meanings that the closed adjective class is used to express. Specifically, he finds that this class is likely to include words denoting dimensions (e.g. words meaning 'large' or 'small'), color, age, and value (e.g. words meaning 'good' or 'bad'). On the other hand, it is less likely to include words denoting position ('high', 'low'), physical property ('hard', 'soft'), human propensity ('kind', 'cruel'), or speed. A paradigm case in support of Dixon's claim is offered by Igbo (cf. Welmers and Welmers 1969), whose eight adjectives are neatly distributed among the four favored semantic areas (see Table 1.1).

Dixon also suggests that there are some cross-linguistic tendencies, in languages with closed adjective classes, for certain specific types of 'adjectival' meanings to be expressed by verbs and other specific types by nouns. He suggests, for example, that physical properties are more often expressed by verbs than by nouns, while human propensities are more often expressed by nouns than by verbs. This seems, however, to

Table 1.1 *Igbo adjectives*

Dimension		Color		Age		Value	
ukwu	'large'	ojii	'black, dark'	ọhụrụ	'new'	ọma	'good'
nta	'small'	ọca	'white, light'	ocye	'old'	ọjọọ	'bad'

be only a statistical tendency, and counter-examples are not hard to find. Thus Hausa seems to prefer nouns to verbs for expressing adjectival meanings in general, while Bemba seems to prefer verbs to nouns (see examples (25–30) below), although each of these languages sometimes uses the less favored part of speech. In any event, it is clear that nouns and verbs between them must in general take up the slack left by a paucity of adjectives, and it is therefore of interest to see how each of these open classes is used to express adjectival meanings.

To begin with nouns, languages with closed adjective classes often use abstract nouns (equivalent in many cases to English nouns formed with *-ness*: *kindness*, *hardness*, etc.) in possessive constructions to express adjectival meanings. The following are some examples from Hausa, showing the syntactic parallelism between constructions with adjectival meanings and other constructions involving possessive modifiers, (25), and possessive predicates, (26):

(25) mutum mai   alheri   /arziki   /hankali
      person having kindness/prosperity/intelligence
      'a kind/prosperous/intelligent person'

      cf. mutum mai   doki
         person having horse
         'a person having a horse'

(26) Yana da   alheri   /arziki   /hankali
      he is with kindness/prosperity/intelligence
      'He is kind/prosperous/intelligent'

      cf. Yana da   doki
         he is with horse
         'He has a horse'

Some examples involving physical properties are:

(27) itace mai   tauri   /laushi /nauyi
      wood having hardness/softness/heaviness
      'hard/soft/heavy wood'

(28)   Yana da   tauri   /laushi /nauyi
        it is with hardness/softness/heaviness
        'It is hard/soft/heavy'

The expression of adjectival meanings through *verbs* in languages
with closed adjective classes typically involves relativization to express
the equivalent of a modifying adjective. The following examples from
Bemba are representative:

(29)   umuuntu ùashipa   /ùakosa   /ùaceenjela
        person   who is brave/who is strong/who is wise
        'a brave/strong/wise person'

        cf. umuuntu ùalemba
            person   who is writing
            'a person who is writing'

The equivalent of a predicate adjective, on the other hand, is expressed
by a non-relativized verb:

(30)   Umuuntu áashipa /áakosa /áaceenjela
        person   is brave/is strong/is wise
        'The person is brave/strong/wise'

        cf. Umuuntu áalemba
            person   is writing
            'The person is writing'

(As these examples indicate, relativized verbs in Bemba have low tone
on the subject-concord prefix while non-relativized verbs have high tone
on this prefix. In addition, with nouns in the human singular class – but
not those in other classes – there is a segmental difference between the
relative and non-relative subject prefixes.)

A further point to be noted about languages with closed adjective
classes is that, in some of these languages, adjectives occur *only* as
modifiers, and do not occur as predicates at all. One such language is
Hua, as is shown by the following examples (from Haiman 1978):

(31)   a.   Bura fu nupa fu baie
              that pig black pig is
              'That pig is a black pig'

        b. *Bura fu nupa baie
              that   pig black is

To return to the question of how adjectival meanings are expressed in
languages that lack an open class of adjectives, let us now consider this
question in relation to the second group of such languages: i.e.,

languages that have no distinct adjective class at all, either open or closed. Such languages can themselves be divided into two groups: languages in which adjectival meanings are expressed primarily by nouns (hereafter, *adjectival-noun languages*) and languages in which adjectival meanings are expressed primarily by verbs (hereafter, *adjectival-verb languages*).

In adjectival-noun languages, adjectival meanings seem in general to be expressed by nouns that designate an object (or objects) embodying a specified quality. The English equivalent of such nouns often takes the form adjective-plus-*one*(*s*), as the following example from the adjectival-noun language Quechua illustrates:

(32)   Rikaška: hatun-(kuna)-ta
        I saw   big-(PL)-ACC
        'I saw the big one(s)'

A comparison of (32) with (33) illustrates the grammatical similarity in Quechua between nouns with adjectival meanings (such as *hatun* 'big (one)') and other nouns (such as *alkalde* 'mayor').

(33)   Rikaška: alkalde-(kuna)-ta
        I saw   mayor-(PL)-ACC
        'I saw the mayor(s)'

As these examples show, nouns that express adjectival meanings can, like other nouns, be used as verbal objects, in which case they take the accusative suffix *-ta*, and can be pluralized by means of the suffix *-kuna*.

The following Quechua examples further illustrate the grammatical parallelism between nouns with adjectival meanings and other nouns in this adjectival-noun language:

(34)   Chay runa hatun (kaykan)
        that   man big   (is)
        'That man is big'

(35)   Chay runa alkalde (kaykan)
        that   man mayor (is)
        'That man is mayor'

(36)   chay hatun runa
        that big   man
        'that big man'

(37)   chay alkalde runa
        that mayor   man
        'that man who is mayor'

These examples show that nouns with adjectival meanings are not grammatically distinguished from other nouns either in their use as predicates or in their use as modifiers. Thus, in (34) and (35), the predicates *hatun* and *alkalde* both follow the subject and both optionally co-occur with the copulative verb *kaykan*, while in (36) and (37) the modifiers *hatun* and *alkalde* both immediately precede the noun they modify.

Adjectival-verb languages seem to be like languages with closed adjective classes in the way they use verbs to express adjectival meanings. As was noted above, in languages like Bemba, which have closed adjective classes but also use verbs extensively to express adjectival meanings, the usual verbal equivalent of a predicate adjective is a predicate verb in a non-relative construction (cf. example (30)), while the usual verbal equivalent of a modifying adjective is a verb in a relative construction (cf. example (29)). These same equivalents are found in adjectival-verb languages, as the following examples from one such language, Mandarin Chinese, illustrate:

(38)   Neige nühaizi piaoliang
        that   girl   beautiful
        'That girl is beautiful'

(39)   Neige nühaizi liaojie
        that   girl   understand
        'That girl understands'

(40)   piaoliang de nühaizi
        beautiful REL girl
        'a girl who is beautiful, a beautiful girl'

(41)   liaojie   de nühaizi
        understand REL girl
        'a girl who understands, an understanding girl'

Examples (38) and (39) are predications, while examples (40) and (41) are modification constructions. As these examples show, verbs with adjectival meanings, such as *piaoliang* '(be) beautiful', and other verbs, such as *liaojie* 'understand', function in the same way in each of these construction types.

While there are some languages, such as Mandarin, which are clearly adjectival-verb languages, in that they appear to offer no consistent basis for distinguishing verbs with adjectival meanings from other verbs (or, at least, from other stative verbs such as 'understand' or 'know'), there are other languages whose classification as adjectival-verb languages is more problematic. These are languages in which the words that express adjectival meanings have most of the grammatical properties of (other) verbs – especially of stative verbs – but in which these adjectival words also have at least one distinctive property not shared by (other) verbs. One example of such a language is Mojave. In this language, adjectivals and stative verbs are indistinguishable when they are used as predicates. Consider the following examples:

(42) ʔi:pa-č   homi:-k (iðu:m)
      man-SUBJ tall-PRES (AUX)
      'The man is tall'

(43) ʔi:pa-č   su:paw-k (iðu:m)
      man-SUBJ know-PRES (AUX)
      ‚The man knows'

As these examples illustrate, when used as predicates the adjectival stem *homi:* 'tall' and the stative verb stem *su:paw* 'know' take the same tense–aspect suffixes and optionally co-occur with the same auxiliary. (Non-stative verbs also take identical tense–aspect suffixes, but optionally co-occur with a different auxiliary.) Adjectivals are distinguishable from statives (and other verbs), however, when they are used as modifiers. When verbs are used as modifiers, they must appear in a relativized form, which in the relevant cases involves a prefixed k^w-, as in:

(44) ʔi:pa k^w-su:paw-n^y-č   iva:k
      man REL-know-DEM-SUBJ is here
      'The man who knows is here'

(As the gloss indicates, the verb stem in this construction is followed by a demonstrative suffix and a case-marking suffix.) When adjectivals are used as modifiers, on the other hand, the occurrence of the relativizing prefix is optional. Thus the following example is grammatical with or without the prefixed k^w-:

(45) ʔi:pa (k^w-)homi:-n^y-č   iva:k
      man (REL-)tall-DEM-SUBJ is here
      'The tall man is here'

Compare the ungrammatical:

(46) *ʔi:pa su:paw-n^y-č   iva:k
      man know-DEM-SUBJ is here

In the case of such a language, one would probably wish to analyze words with adjectival meanings as a distinguishable subclass of verbs rather than as a distinct part of speech, but this is perhaps an arbitrary choice.

1.4 Adverbs

Apart from nouns, verbs, and adjectives, there is one other open part-of-speech class that is attested in certain languages: the class of *adverbs*. The label *adverb* is often applied to several different sets of words in a language, sets that do not necessarily have as much in common with one another, either notionally or grammatically, as, say, the subclasses of nouns or verbs that may occur in the language. For example, all of the italicized words of (47), which cover a considerable semantic and grammatical range, would ordinarily be identified as adverbs in a grammar of English:

(47)   *Unfortunately*, John walked *home extremely slowly yesterday*

A question may thus be raised as to whether there is sufficient similarity among the various types of 'adverbs' that may be recognized in a language to justify their being assigned to a single parts-of-speech class. I shall assume here that this question can, in general, be answered affirmatively, and that, for example, the italicized words of (47) can justifiably be assigned to a single parts-of-speech class, although they must obviously also be assigned to separate subclasses. (The subclass designations for these words would be 'sentence adverb' (*unfortunate-ly*), 'directional adverb' (*home*), 'degree adverb' (*extremely*), 'manner adverb' (*slowly*), and 'time adverb' (*yesterday*). Some subclasses of adverbs may be closed rather than open, but since the class as a whole is open, it seems convenient to deal with the entire class in the present section.)

The usual functional definition of adverbs identifies them as modifiers of verbs, adjectives, or other adverbs (see, for example, Curme 1935). In order to extend this definition so as to include sentence adverbs like *unfortunately* (which are in fact modifiers of entire sentences), and to allow for certain other possibilities (such as adverbs that modify entire verb phrases), we can say that adverbs function as modifiers of constituents other than nouns. The notional range of adverbs varies with the type of constituent modified. Sentence modifiers, for example, commonly express the speaker's attitude toward the event being spoken of; modifiers of verbs or verb phrases commonly express time, place, direction, manner, etc.; and modifiers of adjectives and adverbs commonly express degree.

Given the wide functional and notional range of adverbs, it is not surprising to find that there are no categorizations that are common to the entire class. In most cases, in fact, adverbs are not specified for any categories at all, although there are some exceptions. (Manner adverbs, for example, are sometimes specifiable for degree, as in *John worked hard/harder/hardest.*)

Some cross-linguistic observations may be made about the morphology of certain classes of adverbs. In many languages, manner adverbs are derivable from adjectives by means of fairly productive processes of derivational morphology. Thus in French many manner adverbs – as well as sentence and degree adverbs – are formed by adding the suffix *-ment* to the feminine singular form of an adjective: for example *lentement* 'slowly' (cf. *lente* 'slow (feminine singular)'), *malheureusement* 'unfortunately' (cf. *malheureuse* 'unfortunate (feminine singular)'); *activement* 'actively' (cf. *active* 'active (feminine singular)'). And in Turkish many manner adverbs are formed by *reduplication* of adjectives: for example *yavaş yavaş* 'slowly' (cf. *yavaş* 'slow'), *derin derin* 'deeply' (cf. *derin* 'deep'); *acɨ acɨ* 'bitterly' (cf. *acɨ* 'bitter').

There is also a cross-linguistic tendency for manner adverbs – or a subset of manner adverbs – to have certain phonological properties that distinguish them from other words. For example, in Hausa many adverbs are high-tone monosyllables of the form obstruent-vowel-obstruent – for example *kaf* 'completely', *kas* 'specklessly', *kat* 'with a snapping sound' – an otherwise rare pattern in this language. This phenomenon has received special attention in African linguistics, where the term *ideophone* has gained currency as the label for 'a word, often onomatopoeic, which describes a predicate, qualificative or adverb in respect to manner, colour, sound, smell, action, state or intensity' (Doke 1935:119). But the phenomenon is, as noted by Courtenay (1976), by no means confined to African languages, and is attested, for example, in Australian languages as well. (Courtenay also notes that in some languages the peculiar phonological properties that distinguish ideophones from other words are not confined to adverbs. According to her analysis of Yoruba, for example, this language has ideophonic nouns, verbs, and adjectives, as well as adverbs. It seems, however, that while *all* adverbs in Yoruba are ideophonic, only relatively few nouns, verbs, and adjectives are.)

Before turning to consider how adverbial meanings are expressed in languages that lack a distinct open parts-of-speech class of adverbs, we should note that, even in languages *with* such a class, adverbial meanings are often expressible in other ways as well. In English, for example, phrases consisting of a preposition plus a noun or noun phrase can be used to express a wide range of adverbial meanings: time (*at dawn*), place (*in school*), direction (*to church*), manner (*with ease*), etc. And there are also expressions involving adjectives that paraphrase certain adverbs: for example *it is unfortunate that* (cf. *unfortunately*), *in a careless manner* (cf. *carelessly*). Not surprisingly, similar use is made of nouns and adjectives to express adverbial meanings in many languages in which there is no open adverbial class. (Some of the languages in question have a small, closed class of adverbs; others do not.)

In Arabic, for example, according to Bateson (1967), many adverbial meanings are expressed by nouns or adjectives (which Bateson considers a subclass of nouns) in the accusative case. Relevant examples are *ɣadan* (next day: accusative) 'tomorrow' (cf. *ɣadu* 'next day'); *yoman* (day: accusative) 'daily' (cf. *yom* 'day'); *sariɛan* (swift: accusative) 'swiftly' (cf. *sariɛ* 'swift'). In Tagalog, which lacks distinctive manner adverbs, the meaning equivalent of such adverbs is regularly expressed by adjectives preceded by the marker *nang*: *nang mabilis* (marker 'quick') 'quickly'; *nang malakas* (marker 'loud') 'loudly'; *nang bigla* (marker 'sudden') 'suddenly'; etc. There are also languages in which the meaning equivalent of a manner adverb is regularly expressed by an adjective without any special marking. One such language is Trique, in which, according to Robert Longacre (personal communication), the class of adjectives simply does double duty, modifying verbs as well as nouns.

In some languages, the meaning equivalent of certain adverbs is expressed by *verbs*. This is particularly common in the case of comparative and superlative degree adverbs (e.g. English *more* and *most*), whose equivalent in a good many languages is expressed by a verb meaning 'surpass', as in the following Hausa examples:

(48)   a. Ya   fi   ni hankali
          he(PERF) surpass me intelligence
          'He is more intelligent than I am'

       b. Ya   fi   su   duka hankali
          he(PERF) surpass them all   intelligence
          'He is the most intelligent of them all'

(There are also, of course, languages in which the comparative and superlative are expressed by affixes on adjectives, as in English *smarter*, *smartest*.) Some other examples of verbs expressing adverbial meanings are to be found in the following sentences from Akan:

(49)   a. Ɔtaa   ba   ha
          he pursue come here
          'He often comes here'

   b. Ohintaw kɔ hɔ
      he hide go there
      'He goes there secretly'

The constructions in (49) are so-called *serial verb constructions* (see Schachter 1974 for some discussion).

Finally, it may be noted that in heavily synthetic languages, it is common for a wide range of adverbial meanings to be expressible by verbal affixes. Eskimo, for example, has a large set of suffixes with adverbial meanings that can occur between a verb root and an inflectional suffix. A few examples of such suffixes are: *-nirluk* 'badly', *-vluaq* 'properly', *-luinnaq* 'thoroughly', *-yumaaq* 'in the future', *-kasik* 'unfortunately', *-qquuq* 'probably'. And a similar situation obtains in Yana, where there are verbal suffixes such as *-ʔai* 'in the fire', *-xui* 'in(to) the water', *-sgin* 'early in the morning', *-ca(a)* 'at night', *-xkid* 'slowly', and *-ya(a)gal* 'quickly' (from Sapir and Swadesh 1960).

2.0 Closed classes

Languages differ more from one another in the closed-class distinctions they recognize than in the open-class distinctions. This is true both of the *number* and of the *type* of classes recognized. Thus there are languages which have been claimed (not quite correctly, as we shall see) to have no closed classes at all, while there are others that distinguish a dozen or more closed classes. And there may be no universally attested closed classes comparable with the universally attested open classes of nouns and verbs. (One closed class that is perhaps universal is the class of interjections – cf. section 2.5.) Nonetheless, it is apparently the case that, however diverse the closed-class systems of different languages may be, all languages do in fact have closed, as well as open, parts-of-speech classes.

Before we take a closer look at the kinds of closed parts-of-speech classes that occur, let us first consider the question of the correlation between the prominence of closed classes in a language and another typological feature: the position of the language on the analytic–synthetic scale. As was noted in the introduction to this chapter, languages may differ very greatly in the degree of morphological complexity they tolerate in words. Thus there are heavily analytic languages, in which there are few or no words that contain more than a single morpheme. And there are also heavily synthetic languages, in which polymorphemic words are the norm.

Not surprisingly, closed word classes tend to play a more prominent role in analytic languages than they do in synthetic languages. This is because much of the semantic and syntactic work done by the members of closed word classes in analytic languages is done instead by *affixes* in synthetic languages. We have already seen that, in some heavily synthetic languages, affixes may even do service for certain *open* word classes (cf. the Eskimo and Yana examples of affixal equivalents of adverbs cited at the end of the preceding section). The use of affixes in place of closed word classes is, however, a good deal more common – a claim that is substantiated in detail in the sections that follow. Therefore, by and large, the more use a language tends to make of morphologically complex words, the less use it will tend to make of closed word classes, and the fewer distinct types of closed classes it will tend to recognize.

It might therefore be expected that there would be some heavily synthetic languages that would make no use of closed classes at all. And in fact there have been claims to this effect with regard to at least one such language – witness the following quotation from Sapir (1921:119): 'In Yana the noun and verb are well distinct ... But there are, strictly speaking, no other parts of speech.' However, subsequent investigation seems to have persuaded Sapir that, in addition to nouns and verbs, Yana does have a 'relational proclitic' (which is a kind of case marker, marking non-subjects) and a small set of articles (Sapir and Swadesh 1960) – words which, in the terminology of this chapter, would be assigned to the closed class of *noun adjuncts* (cf. section 2.2, below). And it also seems likely that Yana has (or, rather, *had*, since the language is now extinct) some interjections. Still, this is certainly a very meager inventory of words belonging to closed classes, and it is safe to say that no analytic language could possibly manage with such an inventory.

In the discussion of closed word classes that follows, these classes are dealt with under the following headings: pronouns and other pro-forms (section 2.1), noun adjuncts (2.2), verb adjuncts (2.3), conjunctions (2.4), and other closed classes (2.5). These headings merely constitute a convenient framework for discussion, and are not claimed to have any theoretical status. In each case, the discussion of the closed classes in question will be accompanied by some discussion of the counterparts of these classes (if any) in languages in which the classes are not attested.

2.1 *Pronouns and other pro-forms*
This section surveys the various types of pro-forms that occur in languages and some of the ways in which languages that lack a particular pro-form type may express the semantic equivalent. The term *pro-form*

is a cover term for several closed classes of words which, under certain circumstances, are used as substitutes for words belonging to open classes, or for larger constituents. By far the commonest type of pro-form is the *pronoun*, a word used as a substitute for a noun or noun phrase. Various subtypes of pronouns may be distinguished, among them *personal*, *reflexive*, *reciprocal*, *demonstrative*, *indefinite*, and *relative*. These subtypes are discussed in turn below. (There are also *interrogative pronouns*, but these are best considered together with other interrogative pro-forms – pro-adverbs, pro-verbs, etc. – and the discussion of them is thus deferred until later in the section.)

Personal pronouns are words used to refer to the speaker (e.g. *I*, *me*), the person spoken to (*you*), and other persons and things whose referents are presumed to be clear from the context (*he*, *him*, *she*, *her*, *it*, etc.). While personal pronouns in some languages occur in essentially the same sentence positions as other nominal expressions, it is rather common for them to show distributional peculiarities. This is true, for example, of direct-object personal pronouns in English, which must immediately follow the verb in some cases where other types of direct objects need not, as illustrated in (50).

(50)   Turn it on
         *Turn on it

         cf. $\begin{cases} \text{Turn the radio on} \\ \text{Turn on the radio} \end{cases}$

And it is more strikingly true of other languages in which personal pronouns are *clitics* whose distribution may be consistently distinct from that of non-clitic nominals. (For further discussion of clitics, cf. section 2.5.) For example, object personal pronouns in French, both direct and indirect, normally precede the verb while non-pronominal objects normally follow it, as in (51).

(51)   a. Jean le leur   donnera
            Jean it to them will give
            'Jean will give it to them'

         b. Jean donnera le pain   aux   enfants
            Jean will give the bread to the children
            'Jean will give the bread to the children'

Similarly in Tagalog, personal-pronoun agents and topics normally follow the first constituent of the sentence, while other agents and topics normally follow the verb. For example:

(52)   Hindi ko   siya   nakita
        not   I(AG) him(TOP) saw
        'I didn't see him'

   cf. Hindi nakita ni Pedro si   Juan
       not   saw   AG Pedro TOP Juan
       'Pedro didn't see Juan'

It is quite common for the equivalent of personal pronouns, particularly of subject and object pronouns, to be expressed by affixes on the verb. The following examples of pronominal affixes are from Swahili and Quechua respectively:

(53)   Ni-li-wa-ona
        I-PAST-you-see
        'I saw you'

(54)   Maqa-ma-nki
        hit-me-you
        'You hit me'

Commonly such pronominal affixes may co-occur with non-affixal pronouns when a pronominal subject or object is being emphasized; compare (55) with (54):

(55)   Qam noqata maqamanki
        you me   hit me you
        '*You* hit *me*'

There are languages in which, while personal pronouns do occur, they are often avoided in favor of certain nouns which are considered to be more polite. In Malay, for example (cf. Winstedt 1914), a speaker under certain circumstances will use some self-depreciating noun (e.g. *hamba* 'slave') to refer to himself and some honorific noun (e.g. *tuan* 'master', *dato* 'grandfather', *nenek* 'grandmother') to refer to his addressee. (This situation led Robins (1964) to suggest that in Malay 'the nearest equivalents of the English pronouns are members of an open class' (p. 230). It seems, however, that while self-depreciating and honorific nouns are often used in place of pronouns, there are also undeniable personal pronouns in Malay – *aku* 'I', *kamu* 'you', etc. – which may be used under appropriate circumstances.)

Finally it should be mentioned that in some languages the equivalent of a particular English personal pronoun may be expressed by the *absence* of any overt form in a particular context. In the Japanese sentences in (56) and (57), for example, there are no overt equivalents of 'he', 'her', and 'I'.

(56)   John wa Mary o   sitte-imasu ga, amari yoku wa sirima-sen
         John TOP Mary OBJ knows   but really well TOP knows-not
         'John knows Mary, but he doesn't know her very well'

(57)   Gohan o   tab-tai
         rice   OBJ eat-DESIDERATIVE
         'I want to eat rice'

Reflexive pronouns are pronouns which are interpreted as coferential with another nominal, usually the subject, of the sentence or clause in which they occur. In English the reflexive pronouns are formed with *-self* or *-selves*:

(58)   John shaved *himself*
         John and Bill shaved *themselves*

It happens that in English *-self/-selves* pronouns are also used to indicate emphasis, as in:

(59)   John *himself* shaved Bill

In many languages, however, the reflexive and emphatic structures are formally unrelated, and the latter do not involve pronouns. Note, for example, the following Tagalog sentences:

(60)   Inahit   ni John ang *sarili niya*
         shaved AG John TOP self   his
         'John shaved himself'

(61)   Inahit   ni John *mismo* si   Bill
         shaved AG John EMPH   TOP Bill
         'John himself shaved Bill'

(The emphatic *-self/-selves* forms and their non-pronominal counterparts in other languages should perhaps be considered a type of *discourse marker* – cf. section 2.2.)

Some languages which have distinct reflexive and non-reflexive third person pronouns do not make such a distinction for the other persons, but instead use the same first and second person pronouns both reflexively and non-reflexively. Note the following examples from French:

(62)   a. Ils   *me* voient
            they me see
            'They see me'
         b. Je *me* vois
            I   me see
            'I see myself'

(63)   a. Ils *te* voient
             they you see
             'They see you'

        b. Tu *te* vois
             you you see
             'You see yourself'

(64)   a. Ils *les* voient
             they them see
             'They see them'

        b. Ils *se* voient
             they REFL see
             'They see themselves'

There are also languages in which an invariable form is used for the reflexive, regardless of the person or number of the nominal with which it is coreferential. This is true, for instance, of Japanese, as the following examples illustrate:

(65)   Taroo wa *zibun* o   mamotta
        Taroo TOP REFL   OBJ defended
        'Taroo defended himself'

(66)   Boku wa *zibun* o   mamotta
        I   TOP REFL   OBJ defended
        'I defended myself'

(These examples, as well as some of those cited below, are from Faltz 1977.)

In a good many languages, reflexive forms are analyzable as a head nominal modified by a pronominal possessive agreeing with the subject. Often the head nominal also occurs as a common noun meaning 'head' or 'body'. For example, Fula reflexives, as in (67), are formed with *hoore* 'head', while Akan reflexives, as in (68), are formed with *ho* 'body'. There are also languages such as Malagasy, (69), that use a common noun *without* a modifying possessive:

(67)   Mi gaañi   *hooreqam*
        I wounded my head
        'I wounded myself'

(68)   Mihuu *me ho*
        I saw   my body
        'I saw myself'

(69)   Namono *tena* Rabe
         killed   body Rabe
         'Rabe killed himself'

In languages that do not have reflexive pronouns or reflexively interpreted nouns or noun phrases, reflexive meanings may be expressed by verbal affixes, as in the following examples from Tswana (where the reflexive affix is *-i-*) and Lakhota (where it is *-ic'i-*):

(70)   Ke-tla-*i*-thêk-êla   selêpê
         I-FUT-REFL-buy-BEN axe
         'I shall buy an axe for myself'

(71)   Ophe*ic'i*thon
         'He bought it for himself'

         cf. Ophet^{h}on
             'He bought it'

Reciprocal pronouns, like reflexive pronouns, are interpreted as coreferential with a co-occurring nominal, but are used to express mutual actions, conditions, etc. The English reciprocal pronouns are *each other* and *one another*, as in:

(72)   They helped *each other*
         They helped *one another*

Reciprocal and reflexive formations are often closely related. In Akan, for example, the reciprocal is formed by a kind of doubling of the reflexives:

(73)   Wohuu wɔn ho   wɔn ho
         they saw their body their body
         'They saw each other'

         cf. Wohuu wɔn ho
             they saw their body
             'They saw themselves'

There are, in fact, some languages in which there is regularly the possibility of ambiguity between reciprocal and reflexive meanings because the same forms can be used to express both. A case in point is French, as the following example illustrates:

(74)   Ils   *se*   flattent
         they REFL/RECIP flatter

         'They flatter $\begin{cases} \text{themselves'} \\ \text{each other'} \end{cases}$

An unambiguously reciprocal meaning may, however, be conveyed by adding to (74) the phrase *l'un l'autre* 'one another', as in:

(75)   Ils   se   flattent l'un   l'autre
        they REFL/RECIP flatter   the one the other
        'They flatter one another'

Languages that lack reciprocal pronouns, like those that lack reflexive pronouns, typically express equivalent meanings through the use of special affixes on the verb. In Ilocano, for example, reciprocal verbs contain the prefix *ag-* and the infix *-inn-* (which is inserted after the first consonant of the verb stem): for example *agsinnakit* 'hurt one another' (cf. *sakit* 'hurt'), *agtinnulong* 'help one another' (cf. *tulong* 'help').

Demonstrative pronouns are pronouns like English *this, that, these,* and *those* in:

(76)   *This* resembles *that*
        Do you prefer *these* or *those*?

Such pronouns are treated in depth in chapter III.5 and will only receive brief mention here. Demonstrative pronouns are widely attested. There are, however, languages in which demonstrative and third person personal pronouns are not distinguished. This is the case, for example, in Southern Paiute (cf. Sapir 1930), where words consisting of a demonstrative morpheme followed by a third person morpheme do double duty as demonstrative and personal pronouns: for example *aŋa* (*a-* (that) + *-ŋa* (3rd person singular animate)) 'that one, he'; *iŋa* (*i-* (this) + *-ŋa*) 'this one, he', *arï* (*a-* + *-rï* (3rd person singular inanimate)), 'that one, it', etc. (In addition to demonstrative pronouns, many languages have morphologically related demonstrative *articles*. For some discussion of these, see section 2.2.)

Indefinite pronouns are pronouns like English *someone, something, anyone, anything.* In many languages (including English) these forms are rather transparently analyzable as consisting of two morphemes, one expressing the meaning of indefiniteness, the other the meaning 'person' or 'thing': for example Akan *obi* (*o-* (human prefix) + *bi* (indefinite stem)) 'someone', *ebi* (*e-* (non-human prefix) + *bi*) 'something', or French *quelqu'un* (*quelqu'* (some) + *un* (one)) 'someone', *quelque chose* (*quelque* (some) + *chose* (thing)) 'something'.

Some languages have distinct indefinite-subject pronouns which are used to indicate an unspecified human subject. The English equivalent may have *they, you, one, people,* etc. according to the context. Some examples, from French, (77), and Hausa, (78), respectively, are:

(77) a. *On* dit qu'il pleut
          INDEF says that-it rains
          'They say that it's raining'

      b. *On* ne sait   jamais
          INDEF NEG knows never
          'You/One never can tell'

(78) a. Kada   *a*   yi haka
          shouldn't INDEF do thus
          'You/One shouldn't do that'

      b. Yana so   *a*   zo
          he is wanting INDEF come
          'He wants people to come'

Relative pronouns are pronouns like English *who* and *which* in:

(79)   The man *who* wrote that was a genius
       The book *which* he wrote was brilliant

Many languages do not have relative pronouns, but instead make use of *personal* pronouns in forming relative clauses, as in the following example from Akan:

(80)   Mihuu obi   a   ɔwɔ aka   *no*
        I saw someone REL snake has bitten him
        'I saw someone whom a snake had bitten'

    cf. Ɔwɔ aka   no
       snake has bitten him
       'A snake has bitten him'

Another common way of forming relative clauses involves *deletion* of the relativized nominal from the relative clause, as in the following example from Tagalog:

(81)   Sino ang bata-ng   pumunta sa   tindahan?
       who TOP child-LINK went   OBL store
       'Who is the child who went to the store?'

For still other relativization strategies, see chapter II.3.

To turn now from pronouns to pro-forms of other types, the following types of pro-forms are discussed in turn below: *pro-sentences, pro-clauses, pro-verbs, pro-adjectives, pro-adverbs,* and *interrogative pro-forms.* This listing is not intended to be exhaustive. For example, it is argued in Schachter (1978) that the italicized words of sentences like (82) should be identified as *pro-predicates:*

(82)   Jack fell down, but Jill *didn't*
        Jill isn't crying, but Jack *is*

But this parts-of-speech type does not seem to be common enough to warrant discussion here.

Pro-sentences are words like English *yes* and *no*, which are used in answering questions, and which are understood as equivalent to affirmative and negative sentences respectively. (For example, in answer to *Is it raining?*, *Yes* is equivalent to *It's raining* and *No* to *It isn't raining.*) While most languages have such pro-sentences, they are not universal. In Mandarin Chinese, for example, the affirmative answer to a polar question is whatever verb occurred in the question, while the negative answer is *bu* 'not' optionally followed by this verb, as illustrated in (83).

(83)   Ni qu ma?   Qu/Bu (qu)
        you go Q   go /not (go)
        'Are you going?'   'Yes'/'No'

There are also languages, however, which have a *larger* set of pro-sentences than English does. One rather common phenomenon is for *yes* to have two different equivalents, according to whether the question being answered is in the affirmative or in the negative. The following examples are from French:

(84)   Il vient?   Oui
        he comes   yes
        'Is he coming?'   'Yes'

(85)   Il ne vient pas?   Si (, il vient)
        he NEG comes not   yes (he comes)
        'Isn't he coming?'   'Yes (, he's coming)'

Another common phenomenon is the occurrence of a set of distinctive pro-sentences that are used in answer to existential questions (ones equivalent to English questions with *Is(n't) there ... ?*, etc.). For example, in Tagalog the usual equivalents of *yes* and *no* are *oo* and *hindi* respectively:

(86)   Umuulan ba?   Oo /Hindi
        is raining Q
        'Is it raining?'   'Yes'/'No'

In answer to existential questions, however, the existential pro-sentences *mayroon* and *wala* are used instead:

(87)   Mayroon ba-ng pagkain?   Mayroon/Wala
        EXIST   Q-LINK food
        'Is there any food?'   'Yes' /'No'

(As the question in (87) shows, *mayroon* is also used as an existential marker (cf. section 2.5) in non-pro-form sentences. The same is true of *wala*, which occurs as a negative existential marker.)

One common type of *pro-clause* is the question tag: a word with the force of a question, which is appended to another clause. Some question tags are used to form *alternative* questions, others to form *confirmation* questions. Alternative questions are equivalent to certain English questions with *or* (e.g. *Is it raining or not?*), and quite commonly it is a word meaning 'or' that is used as an alternative-question tag, as in the following example from Hausa:

(88)   Ana   ruwa, *ko*?
        one is rain   or
        'Is it raining or not?'

Confirmation questions are questions in which the speaker is asking for confirmation of a statement to which the question tag is appended. An example, from Tagalog, is:

(89)   Umuulan, *ano*?
        is raining CONFIRMATION TAG
        'It's raining, isn't it?'

In a good many languages, the equivalent of a question tag is expressed by a fixed idiomatic formula: for example French *n'est-ce pas* (literally 'is that not') or German *nicht wahr* (literally 'not true'). (In English the formula equivalent to a question tag is not fixed, but varies with the preceding statement: cf. *You haven't eaten, have you?*; *John left, didn't he?*; etc.)

Another type of pro-clause is the *so* or *not* of English sentences like:

(90)   John says that it will rain, but I don't think *so*
        John says that it will rain, but I think *not*

(*So* and *not* in such cases are substitutes for *that* clauses: cf. *I don't think that it will rain, I think that it won't rain*.) In some languages, the same words that are used as pro-sentences meaning 'yes' or 'no' can be used as pro-clauses. Thus in French, *oui* 'yes' and *non* 'no' occur in constructions like:

(91)   a. Je crois   que *oui*
           I believe that yes
           'I believe so'

b. Il dit que *non*
he says that no
'He says not'

Pro-verbs, pro-adjectives, and *pro-adverbs* are words which substitute
for verbs (or verb phrases), adjectives (or adjective phrases), and
adverbs (or adverb phrases) respectively. In Mandarin Chinese (cf.
Chao 1968), there are pro-verbs such as *lai* 'do it', *tzemme* 'do this',
nemme 'do that'. An example, using the most common of these, *lai*, is:

(92)   Ni buhui   xiu   zhe jigu,   rang wo *lai*
        you know how(NEG) repair this machine let   I   do it
        'You don't know how to repair this machine; let me do it'

An example of a pro-adjective is the *le* of a French sentence such as
(93).

(93)   Jean est grand, mais je ne *le*   suis pas
        Jean is tall   but I NEG PRO ADJ am not
        'Jean is tall, but I'm not'

And an example of a pro-adverb is English *thus* or its (more commonly
used) Akan equivalents *sɛɛ* 'this way' and *saa* 'that way, the same way':

(94)   Menoa no *sɛɛ*,   na ɔno nso noa   no *saa*
        I cook it this way, and he too cooks it that way
        'I cook it this way, and he cooks it the same way'

Interrogative pro-forms are words like English *who, what, where,
when*, etc., as these are used at the beginning of questions. The set of
interrogative pro-forms often cuts across other parts-of-speech classes.
Thus in English there are interrogative pronouns (e.g. *who, what*),
interrogative adverbs (e.g. *where, when*), and interrogative articles (e.g.
which in *which book* – cf. section 2.2 for a general discussion of articles).
And some other languages have interrogative pro-forms with no English
counterparts. In Tagalog, for example, the interrogative root *ano* 'what'
(which is also used as a confirmation-question tag) occurs in various
formations with adjective-forming and verb-forming affixes. Some examples of the resultant interrogative adjectives and verbs are
(INVOL = Involuntary):

(95)   a. *Napakaaano* nila?
           very what   they
           'What are they very much like?'

        cf. Napakataas nila
            very tall   they
            'They are very tall'

b. *Nagano*   ka?
   (PERF ACTIVE) what you
   'What did you do?'

   cf. Nagsalita   ka
       (PERF ACTIVE) speak you
       'You spoke'

c. Naano   ka?
   (PERF INVOL) what you
   'What happened to you?'

   cf. Natalisod   ka
       (PERF INVOL) trip you
       'You tripped'

It appears that all languages have interrogative pro-forms, but that the types of interrogative pro-forms that occur vary considerably from language to language, partly in conformity with the language's overall parts-of-speech system. Thus a language that lacks adverbs in general will naturally enough not have interrogative adverbs. For example, in Yana, which evidently has no adverbs, the equivalents of English *when, where,* etc. are all expressed by verb stems:

(96)   a. Beema'a-wara-nʒa-n?
          where-PERF-I-Q
          'Where am I?'

       b. Beeyauma-s aik nisaayau?
          when-FUT   his going away
          'When will he go away?'

2.2 *Noun adjuncts*

This section discusses several classes of words that typically form phrasal constituents with nouns. In most cases, these words, here labeled *noun adjuncts*, have clear semantic import, conveying some information about the referent of the phrasal constituent that is not expressed by the noun itself: for example the role of the referent in the action expressed by a co-occurring verb, or whether the referent is singular or plural. In some cases, however, the noun adjuncts appear to be semantically empty and merely to be required under certain circumstances by the syntax of the language. (This seems to be true, in particular, of certain *classifiers* – see below.) Four general classes of noun adjuncts will be distinguished here: *role markers, quantifiers, classifiers,* and *articles.* These classes are discussed in turn below.

Role markers include *case markers, discourse markers,* and (other) *adpositions* (i.e., *prepositions* or *postpositions*). Case markers are words that indicate the syntactic and/or semantic role (e.g. subject and/or agent) of the noun phrase to which they belong. Discourse markers are words that indicate the discourse role (e.g. topic) of the associated noun phrase. If the role marker precedes the noun, as in the following example from Tagalog, it may be called a preposition:

(97)   Ipinansulat *ni* John *ng* liham *kay* Mary *ang* makinilya
        wrote with AG John OBJ letter IO   Mary TOP typewriter
        'John wrote Mary a letter on the typewriter'

And if the role marker follows the noun, as in the following example from Japanese, it may be called a postposition:

(98)   Type   *de*   *wa* John *ga*   Mary *ni* tegami *o*   kaita
        typewriter INSTR TOP John SUBJ Mary IO letter   OBJ wrote
        'John wrote Mary a letter on the typewriter'

There are certain adpositions that are clearly not discourse markers, but that are not ordinarily identified as case markers: for example the postposition *de* in (98), and the words indicating various locative relations in the following examples from English and Akan respectively:

(99)   It's *on/under/beside* the table

(100)   Ɛwɔ pon no *so/ase/nkyɛn*
        it is table the on/under/beside
        'It's on/under/beside the table'

The distinction between case-marking and other adpositions seems to be a somewhat arbitrary one, however, based in part on the traditional identification of only certain types of grammatical or semantic roles with the label 'case'. (It is also true, however, that in some languages locative and other adpositions must be distinguished from case-marking *affixes* which occur in the same phrase. For example, in Latin 'on the table' is *super mensam*, which consists of the preposition *super* 'on' and a case-marked form, the accusative, of the noun *mensa* 'table'. In such cases the adposition shows the relation of a noun (phrase) to some larger syntactic unit while the affix shows its relation to the adposition.)

A certain correlation is known to exist between the general word-order type of a language and the occurrence in the language of prepositions as opposed to postpositions. In particular, Greenberg (1963:62) has claimed that verb-initial languages are always preposition-al while verb-final languages are almost always postpositional (cf. (97) and (98) above). In verb-medial languages the situation is less clear-cut. While the majority of such languages are prepositional (cf. (99)), there are also a good many that are postpositional instead (cf. (100)).

In languages that do not use role markers to indicate the grammatical, semantic, or discourse roles of nouns, or that use markers for some such roles but not others, the roles in question may be indicated by word order or by affixation. English, for example, uses word order to distinguish subjects from objects (compare *The boy loves the girl* and *The girl loves the boy*) while Latin uses case-marking suffixes. Compare (101) and (102).

(101) Puellam puer amat
girl(ACC) boy(NOM) loves
'The boy loves the girl'

(102) Puella puerum amat
girl(NOM) boy(ACC) loves
'The girl loves the boy'

There are also languages in which the affixes that indicate the role of a noun or noun phrase may appear on a *verb* rather than on the noun or noun phrase itself. In Swahili, for example, the affix *-i-* on a verb expresses the equivalent of the benefactive preposition *for*, as in (103).

(103) Ni-li-m-p-*i*-a chakula mwanamke
I-PAST-her-give-for-∅ food woman
'I gave food for the woman'

cf. Ni-li-m-p-a chakula mwanamke
I-PAST-her-give-∅ food woman
'I gave the woman food'

(See also the Tagalog example (97), above, in which the affix *ipinan-* on the verb *ipinansulat* indicates that the topic noun phrase *ang makinilya* is to be interpreted as playing the role of an instrument.)

Finally, it may be noted that certain discourse roles are sometimes indicated by the use of special syntactic constructions or by intonation. Thus the English equivalent of the Akan focus marker *na* of (104) is the so-called cleft-sentence construction, while the English equivalent of the Akan contrast marker *de* of (105) is intonational:

(104) Kwame na ɔbɛyɛ adwuma no
Kwame FOCUS he will do work the
'It's Kwame who will do the work'

(105) Kwame de, ɔbɛkɔ, na Kofi de, ɔbɛtena
Kwame CONTRAST he will go and Kofi CONTRAST he will stay
ha
here
'*Kwame* will go but *Kofi* will stay here'

The next group of noun adjuncts to be considered, the *quantifiers*, consists of modifiers of nouns that indicate quantity or scope: for example numerals, and words meaning 'many', 'much', 'few', 'all', 'some', 'each', etc. In some languages a quantifier is required if plurality is to be explicitly indicated. Tagalog, for example, uses the quantifier *mga* in this way:

(106)   Nasaan ang *mga* pinggan?
         where TOP PL dish
         'Where are the dishes?'

And Vietnamese appears to have some fifty different pluralizers (which, however, also carry some more explicit quantifier meaning: 'all', 'all (vague)', 'many', 'a few', etc. – cf. Binh 1971:113–14). In such languages the explicit indication of plurality is generally optional. Thus if *mga* is deleted from (106), the resultant sentence can still be interpreted as meaning 'Where are the dishes?', although it could also mean 'Where is the dish?'.

There are a number of languages in which quantifiers, or at least certain quantifiers, vary in form according to the semantic properties of the nouns they modify. Thus the Akuapem dialect of Akan has two distinct forms for certain numerals, according to whether the noun modified is human or non-human: for example *nnipa baanu* (people two) 'two people' vs. *mmoa abien* (animals two) 'two animals'. And in Japanese there are semantically conditioned variants such as *sannin* 'three (of humans)', *sanba* 'three (of birds)', *sanbon* 'three (of cylindrical objects)', *sanmai* 'three (of thin flat objects)', etc. (The Japanese examples are bimorphemic, each consisting of the quantifier morpheme *san-* 'three' plus a classifier morpheme: cf. the discussion of classifiers below.)

The range of meanings expressed by a distinct parts-of-speech class of quantifiers varies considerably from language to language, and languages that have such a class may nonetheless have other means for expressing particular quantity or scope meanings. One such means involves nouns of quantity or scope in attributive phrases, as in Hausa *mutane da yawa* (people with abundance) 'many people', or in possessive-like constructions, as in Akan *nnipa no nyinaa* (people the wholeness) 'all the people' (cf. *nnipa no ntade* (people the clothes) 'the people's clothes'). Another involves *verbs* of quantity, such as Akan *dɔɔso* 'be enough/much', as in:

(107)   Wɔnoaa   aduan a   ɛdɔɔso
         they cooked food   REL it is enough
         'They cooked enough/a lot of food'

It is, of course, very common for plurality to be expressed by affixes on nouns, whether by suffixation, as in English *houses*, *fingers*, or by prefixation, as in Ilocano *balbalay* 'houses', *ramramay* 'fingers' (where the plural prefix is a reduplication of the first three segments of the noun stem – cf. *balay* 'house', *ramay* 'finger'). Less common, but attested in certain synthetic languages, is the use of noun affixes to express other quantifier meanings: for example Yana *hanmau-* 'many', as in *hanmauyaa* 'many people'.

The next group of noun adjuncts to be considered is the *classifiers*. These are words which are required by the syntax of certain languages when a noun is also modified by a numeral. (In some languages, such as Mandarin Chinese, classifiers are also required when nouns are modified by demonstratives, or by one of certain non-numerical quantifiers. In Thai, on the other hand, classifiers are obligatory only with a subset of numerals, those expressing 'small definite numbers' – cf. Adams and Conklin 1974.) The closest English analog to classifiers are the words that follow the numerals in expressions like *two heads of lettuce* or *three ears of corn*. But while in English only a relatively small group of nouns are not directly modified by numerals, in languages with classifiers this is true of all nouns. Thus in English one says *two boys*, *three dogs*, *four houses*, etc. But in Thai the equivalent expressions must all have classifiers: *deg sɔɔŋ khon* (boy two classifier) 'two boys', *maa saam tua* (dog three classifier) 'three dogs', *baan sii laŋ* (house four classifier) 'four houses', etc.

The number of classifiers found in a language may be quite large. Thus Warotamasikkhadit (1972) lists over sixty classifiers that occur in Thai, and acknowledges that the listing is incomplete. In some cases a given noun may co-occur with one of two or more different classifiers, in which case each classifier usually has a distinct meaning. Thus in the Thai examples *kluay sii kɔɔ* (banana four classifier) 'four banana trees (in a cluster)', *kluay sii wii* (banana four classifier) 'four bunches of bananas', *kluay sii bai* (banana four classifier) 'four bananas', the meaning difference is obviously conveyed by the distinct classifiers.

As the examples from Thai have suggested, the classifier or classifiers that may occur with a given noun are selected by that noun. Thus the classifier *khon* is selected by *deg* 'boy' while the classifier *tua* is selected by *maa* 'dog'. But although the selection of classifiers is in part semantically based (thus *khon* is used only for humans), there is not always any obvious semantic basis for the selection of a particular classifier by a particular noun, and 'sometimes native speakers themselves are not sure which classifier is to be used in agreement with a certain noun' (Warotamasikkhadit 1972:23). Evidently the situation is rather similar to that found in the inflectional grammatical-gender systems of Indo-European or Bantu languages, where there are some generalizations that can be made about the semantic correlates of the genders, but where there are also many cases in which the gender classification appears to be semantically arbitrary (cf. section 1.1, above).

The last group of noun adjuncts to be considered is the group of *articles*. Under this heading I wish to include, in addition to the words usually identified as definite and indefinite articles (e.g. English *the*, *a*), words that are sometimes identified as demonstrative adjectives or modifiers (e.g. *this* in *this man*, *that* in *that woman*). The reasons for grouping the demonstrative modifiers together with the (other) articles are both syntactic and semantic. Syntactically, demonstrative and other articles usually constitute a single distributional class, occurring in the same position in relation to the noun and other elements of the noun phrase, and not co-occurring in a single noun phrase: compare *a small woman*, *this small woman*, Akan *ɔbea ketewa bi* (woman small a) 'a small woman', *ɔbea ketewa yi* (woman small this) 'this small woman'. (There are exceptions, however. For example, in Hebrew the equivalent of the definite article is a prefix, and this prefix can co-occur with a demonstrative: e.g. *ha-ish ha-ze* (the-man the-this) 'this man'.) And semantically, demonstrative modifiers are like definite articles in being reference indicators. (Thus *this* often indicates that the referent of the following noun is close at hand, just as *the* often indicates that the referent of the following noun is assumed to have already been established.) In a good many languages, in fact, there are single words which may be translated 'the' or 'that' according to the context: for example German *die Frau* (the/that woman) 'the/that woman'; Akan *ɔbea no* (woman the/that) 'the/that woman'. (While the demonstrative modifiers are here grouped with the articles, for the reasons just indicated, it is also true that they usually have a close relation, both semantically and morphologically, to the demonstrative *pronouns* discussed in section 2.1.)

Articles may or may not show agreement with the nouns they modify. In Akan, for example, although nouns and (certain) adjectives are inflected for number, the definite article and demonstrative *no* is invariable: cf. *ɔbea ketewa no* (woman small the/that) 'the/that small woman', *mmea nketewa no* (women plural-small the/that) 'the/those small women'. In German, on the other hand, the definite article and demonstrative *der/die*, etc. varies in form with the number, gender, and case of the noun it modifies: *der Mann* (the/that-nominative-singular-masculine man) 'the/that man', *die Frau* (the/that-nominative-singular-feminine woman) 'the/that woman', *das Buch* (the/that-nominative-singular-neuter book) 'the/that book', etc.

Languages that do not have articles may express equivalent meaning morphologically. For example, in Yuma, the demonstrative suffixes -*va*, -*n*^{y}, and -*sa* are placed between the noun stem and the case marker: e.g. *ʔa·ve-va-c* (snake-this-nominative) 'this snake', *ʔa·ve-n*^{y}-*c* (snake-that-nominative) 'that snake', *ʔa·ve-sa-c* (snake-that(distant)-nominative) 'that (distant) snake'. Similarly, in Tonkawa, a meaning of definiteness is expressed by a suffix -*ʔa·* before the case suffix on a noun, while a meaning of indefiniteness is expressed by the lack of this -*ʔa·*: for example *k*^{w}*a·n-ʔa·-la* (woman-the-nominative) 'the woman'; *k*^{w}*a·n-la* (woman-nominative) 'a woman'.

The morphological indication of definiteness may be tonal rather than affixal. Thus in Bambara definiteness is expressed by a low final tone on the noun: for example *káfè* 'the coffee' (cf. *káfé* 'coffee' – the falling tone at the end of *káfè* results from the addition of a low final tone to an inherently high tone). There are also languages in which the definite–indefinite distinction is, in some instances at least, expressed by the case system. Thus in Southern Lappish (cf. Wickman 1955) a definite direct object is in the accusative case while an indefinite direct object is in the nominative case, as in the following example:

(108) a. jüktie treæwgəjd'ə dojtəmə
           when skis(ACC)   one has made
           'when one has made the skis'

       b. jüktie treæwgah dajtθjh
           when skis(NOM) they make
           'when they make skis'

2.3 Verb adjuncts

This section is concerned with two classes of words that form phrasal constituents with verbs: *auxiliaries* and *verbal particles*. (The label *auxiliaries* seems preferable to the perhaps more common *auxiliary verbs* from a cross-linguistic point of view, since it allows for the inclusion of non-verbs in the class. While most auxiliaries are probably derived from verbs historically, and many can reasonably be identified as a subclass of verbs synchronically, there are also cases – such as the Hausa examples cited below – where a synchronic analysis of auxiliaries as verbs seems questionable.)

Auxiliaries are words that express the tense, aspect, mood, voice, or polarity of the verb with which they are associated: i.e., the same categorizations of the verb as may be expressed by means of affixes (cf.

section 1.2). English examples of auxiliaries expressing tense, aspect, and mood (respectively, future, perfect, and conditional) are:

(109)   John *will* understand
        John *has* understood
        John *would* understand

English also offers examples like the following of auxiliaries expressing voice (passive) and polarity (negative), in combination with tense:

(110)   John *was* understood
        John *won't* understand

Some representative examples from other languages are:

Bambara

(111)   a. U *ye*   a san
           they PAST(AFFIRM) it buy
           'They bought it'

        b. U *ma*   a san
           they PAST(NEG) it buy
           'They didn't buy it'

        c. U *bɛ*   a san
           they PROG(AFFIRM) it buy
           'They are buying it'

        d. U *lɛ*   a san
           they PROG(NEG) it buy
           'They aren't buying it'

Hausa (in this language a subject-pronoun morpheme and an auxiliary morpheme regularly combine to form a single word, the ordering of the two morphemes varying with the auxiliary used; HABIT = Habitual):

(112)   a. *Za*-ta   tafi
           FUT-she go
           'She will go'

        b. Ta-*kan*   tafi
           she-HABIT go
           'She goes'

        c. Ta-*na*   tafiya
           she-PROG going
           'She is going'

        d. *Ba*-ta   tafiya
           PROG(NEG)-she going
           'She isn't going'

And *Kannada* (examples from Upadhyaya and Krishnamurthy 1972):

(113)   a. Baritta *iddiini*
            writing I(PROG)
            'I am writing'
        b. Baritta *irtiini*
            writing I(PROG HABIT)
            'I am writing'

In some languages sequences of two or more auxiliaries are allowed, in which case their order in relation to one another is generally fixed, as in the following examples from English and Tera (the latter from Newman 1970):

(114)   John *must have been* sleeping

(115)   Ali *kə   ka   da*   nji ƚu
        Ali SJNCT HABIT DISTANT eat meat
        'Ali should regularly eat meat (there)'

In other languages, such as Bambara (cf. (111)), only one auxiliary may occur in each clause.

Greenberg (1963) has noted a correlation between the position of an inflected auxiliary in relation to the verb and other word-order properties of the language. Stated in general terms, this correlation is to the effect that the position of an inflected auxiliary in relation to the verb will generally be the same as the position of the verb in relation to an object. Thus in languages where the verb precedes the object (e.g. English), an inflected auxiliary generally precedes the verb, while in languages where the verb follows the object (e.g. Kannada), an inflected auxiliary generally follows the verb. (Greenberg's own generalization is somewhat narrower than this: namely, 'In languages with dominant order VSO, an inflected auxiliary always precedes the main verb. In languages with dominant order SOV, an inflected auxiliary always follows the main verb' (p. 67). Greenberg thus does not propose a generalization about SVO languages. The data that he cites, however, show that, in almost all cases, inflected auxiliaries precede the verb in SVO, as in VSO, languages.)

It should be noted that Greenberg's word-order generalization applies only to *inflected* auxiliaries, so examples like those in (111) do not constitute an exception to it. (That is, while Bambara is a SOV language in which the auxiliary precedes the main verb, Greenberg's generalization is irrelevant to Bambara since the auxiliary is uninflected in this language.) There is, however, one well-known systematic exception to Greenberg's word-order generalization, having to do with so-called 'verb-second' languages, such as German. These are languages which show sov order in subordinate clauses, but in main clauses place a tense-bearing verb immediately after the initial constituent: cf. the position of the non-auxiliary verb *hat* 'has' in the following German examples:

(116)   a. Ich weiss, dass er zu viel   Arbeit *hat*
         I   know that he too much work   has
         'I know that he has too much work'

         b. Er *hat* zu viel   Arbeit
         he has too much work
         'He has too much work'

         c. Heute *hat* er zu viel   Arbeit
         today has he too much work
         'Today he has too much work'

In such languages, auxiliaries follow the verb in subordinate clauses, thus conforming to Greenberg's generalization. In main clauses, however, a tense-bearing auxiliary immediately follows the initial constituent and thus precedes the non-tense-bearing verb. Note the position of the auxiliary *wird* 'will' in the following examples:

(117)   a. Ich weiss, dass er zu viel   Arbeit haben *wird*
         I   know that he too much work   have   will
         'I know that he will have too much work'

         b. Er *wird* zu viel   Arbeit haben
         he will too much work   have
         'He will have too much work'

         c. Heute *wird* er zu viel   Arbeit haben
         today will he too much work   have
         'Today he will have too much work'

In languages that lack auxiliaries, the equivalent meanings are often expressed by verbal affixes. Some examples from Tagalog, all involving the verb base *luto* 'cook', are: *magluluto* 'will cook', *nagluluto* 'is cooking', *nagluto* 'has cooked', *nakakapagluto* 'can cook', *niluto* 'was cooked'. It is also possible, of course, for a language that does have auxiliaries to have such verbal affixes as well. Thus English uses an auxiliary to express the future tense (*will cook*) and an affix to express the past tense (*cooked*). Negation, like the other categorizations that may be expressed by auxiliaries, may be expressed affixally (as in Akan *n-kɔ* (negative-go) 'doesn't go' – cf. *kɔ* 'goes'), but is also very commonly expressed by a distinct parts-of-speech class of *negators* (cf. section 2.5, below).

The second class of verb adjuncts to be discussed, the verbal particles, is a closed class of uninflected words that co-occur with certain verbs. Examples from English are the italicized words in:

(118) John woke *up*, turned *off* the alarm, and switched the light *on*

In some cases the verbal particles may have clearly distinguishable locative or directional meanings, for example:

(119) John kept his head *up/down*
       John carried the package *in/out*

In other cases, however, the particle forms an idiomatic lexical unit with the verb and does not carry any separable meaning: for example *up* in *wake up, give up, hurry up*; *down* in *break down, calm down, write down*.

Some examples of particles from languages other than English (respectively, German, Akan, and Ga'anda – the last from R. M. Newman 1971) are:

(120) a. Er stand sehr früh *auf*
          he stood very early on
          'He got up very early'

       b. Er sah den Wagen *an*
          he saw the car   at
          'He looked at the car'

(121) a. Kofi gyee   Kwame *so*
          Kofi received Kwame on
          'Kofi answered Kwame'

       b. Kofi daa Kwame *ase*
          Kofi lay Kwame under
          'Kofi thanked Kwame'

(122) a. ə ɓənnda   wanɓəɓa *in*
          PERF they send medicine along
          'They sent medicine along'

       b. Ni   xiy pirsh *kadə*
          I(FUT) buy horse away
          'I will sell a horse'

In some languages, some or all of the verbal particles also occur as (and are historically derived from) adpositions (cf. section 2.2). Thus English *up* and *down* and German *auf* and *an* also occur as prepositions, while Akan *so* and *ase* also occur as postpositions. In other languages, however, for example Ga'anda, the verbal particles are entirely distinct from adpositions.

While the particles are, in general, selected by the particular verbs with which they occur, and while they often join with the verbs in forming idiomatic units, the verbs and particles are, as the examples cited above have shown, not necessarily adjacent to one another. The syntactic rules of a language may specify that a verb and an associated particle may or must be separated from one another under certain circumstances. In English, for example, the object of a transitive verb may in most cases come between the verb and the particle, as well as after the particle:

(123)   John *looked* two words *up*
         John *looked up* two words

In German, if the verb is in clause-final position, the particle is prefixed to it, as in:

(124)   Ich weiss, dass er sehr früh *auf-stand*
         I   know that he very early up-stood
         'I know that he got up very early'

But if the verb follows the initial constituent of the clause (as it regularly does if the clause is a main clause and the verb is tense-marked – see above), the particle follows the verb, and is separated from it by other constituents of the verb phrase, as in (120). Similarly in Akan and Ga'anda a transitive verb and a particle are separated by the object of the verb (cf. (121) and (122)).

2.4 *Conjunctions*

Conjunctions are words that are used to connect words, phrases, or clauses. Two general classes of conjunctions, *coordinating* and *subordinating*, are traditionally distinguished. The coordinating conjunctions are those that assign equal rank to the conjoined elements. (English examples are *and*, *or*, and *but*.) The subordinating conjunctions are those that assign unequal rank to the conjoined elements, marking one of them as subordinate to the other. (English examples are *whether*, *that*, *although*, etc.) These two classes of conjunctions are discussed in turn below.

Coordinating conjunctions generally occur *between* the elements that they conjoin. There is often evidence, however, that the conjunctions are more closely associated structurally with one of the conjuncts than with the other. One type of evidence to this effect is phonological, having to do with the points within a conjoined structure at which a pause (often reflected in writing by a comma) is possible. In some languages, such as English, there is a potential for pause immediately *before* a coordinating conjunction but not immediately *after* one, while in others, such as Japanese, just the opposite is true – compare (125) and (126):

(125)   John, (and) Bill, and Tom came
       *John and, Bill and, Tom came

(126)   John to,   Bill to,   Tom ga   kita
       John and Bill and Tom SUBJ came
       'John, Bill, and Tom came'
       *John, to Bill, to Tom ga kita

Thus in languages like English, coordinating conjunctions can be characterized as *prepositional*, since they form structural units with the conjuncts they precede, while in languages like Japanese, they can be characterized as *postpositional*, since they form structural units with the conjuncts they follow.

It appears that the prepositional or postpositional character of the coordinating conjunctions that occur in a language are quite systematically associated with the language's general word-order characteristics. Specifically, non-verb-final languages generally have the prepositional type of conjunction, verb-final languages the postpositional type. Further evidence to this effect is to be found in the positions of correlative – or paired – coordinating conjunctions, such as English *both–and* and *either–or*. In non-verb-final languages, such as English (see (127)) and Hausa (see (128)), correlative conjunctions typically precede each of the conjuncts, while in verb-final languages, such as Japanese (see (129)) and Turkish (see (130)), they typically *follow* each of the conjuncts:

(127)   *Both* John *and* Bill like Mary

(128)   *Da* Audu *da* Bello sun   ci   abinci
       and Audu and Bello they(PERF) eat food
       'Both Audu and Bello have eaten'

(129)   Michiko *to*   Michika *to*   ga   gakusei desu
       Michiko and Michika and SUBJ student are
       'Both Michiko and Michika are students'

(130)   Šapkanɨ *da* paltonu   *da*   giy
       your hat and your coat and wear
       'Wear both your hat and your coat'

(As examples (128–30) suggest, correlative coordinate conjunction in most languages involves repeating the *same* conjunction, whether before each conjunct, as in Hausa, or after each, as in Japanese and Turkish. Correlative conjunction in English is thus somewhat atypical.)

Languages may vary quite markedly in the types of constituents that they allow to be connected by means of coordinating conjunctions. In English, a very wide range of constituents may be connected in this way: nouns and noun phrases, verbs and verb phrases, adjectives, adverbs, prepositions, clauses, etc. In a good many other languages, on the other hand, coordinating conjunctions (or at least those that are the translation equivalents of *and*) are used primarily, or exclusively, to connect nouns and noun phrases. This is true of Hausa and Japanese, for example (although these languages do have ways of expressing the *semantic* equivalent of verb phrase conjunction, etc. – see below).

In this connection, it is interesting to note that in many languages 'and' and 'with' are expressed by the same word, as in the following Hausa and Japanese examples:

(131)   a. John *da*   Bill sun   zo
           John and Bill they(PERF) come
           'John and Bill came'

        b. John ya   zo   *da*   Bill
           John he(PERF) come with Bill
           'John came with Bill'

(132)   a. John *to*   Bill ga   kita
           John and Bill SUBJ came
           'John and Bill came'

        b. John ga   Bill *to*   kita
           John SUBJ Bill with came
           'John came with Bill'

If, as such examples suggest, the 'and' conjunction in these languages has developed historically from a prepositional or postpositional noun adjunct (cf. section 2.2), it is not surprising to find that it is used primarily for conjoining nominals.

Let us now consider some of the alternatives to coordinating conjunctions that languages may use to express the semantic equivalent. One such alternative is simple concatenation of the conjuncts, as in the following examples of verb-phrase coordination from Akan and Hausa respectively:

(133)   Nnipa no dii nam nomm bia
        people the ate meat drank beer
        'The people ate meat and drank beer'

(134) Audu ya   tafi ofishinsa ya   yi aiki
       Audu he(PERF) go office his he(PERF) do work
       'Audu went to his office and worked'

While such concatenative constructions are especially common for conjoining verbs and verb phrases, they are by no means restricted to this function. There are, for example, a good many languages that use concatenation for noun-phrase coordination as well, either as an alternative to coordinating conjunctions (as in Japanese and Turkish) or as the sole coordination strategy (as in Lahu – cf. Matisoff 1973).

Some other coordination strategies that do not involve conjunctions are illustrated by the following examples, from Akan and Japanese respectively:

(135) Yɛ-ne   wɔn abom   bio
       we-be with them have united again
       'We and they have united again'

(136) John wa asa   okite,   kao o   aratta
       John TOP morning getting up face OBJ washed
       'John got up in the morning and washed his face'

Example (135) (taken from Christaller 1875) involves the coordination of nominals. In this example the equivalent of *and* is expressed by the verb *ne*. The fact that *ne* is properly analyzed as a verb is clear from the forms of the pronouns that precede and follow it: *yɛ-* is a form which occurs elsewhere strictly as a *subject* pronoun prefixed to a verb, while *wɔn* is a form which occurs elsewhere strictly as an *object* pronoun following a verb. The sentence structure in (135) involves serial verbs – cf. Schachter (1974) – and may be compared with that of a sentence like:

(137) Yɛ-de   wɔn aba
       we-take them have come
       'We have brought them'

Example (136) (from Kuno 1973) involves verb-phrase coordination, and is similar to the concatenative constructions cited above (e.g. (133–4)), except that the first verb in (136) is a dependent form, the gerundive *okite* 'getting up' (cf. *okita* 'got up').

Let us turn now to the subordinating conjunctions. These are words that serve to integrate a subordinate clause into some larger construction. Like their coordinating counterparts, subordinating conjunctions may be prepositional or postpositional, with the prepositional type common in non-verb-final languages, the postpositional type common in verb-final languages. The following examples, from non-verb-final

Tagalog and verb-final Uzbek respectively, are thus quite typical. (The subordinating conjunctions in these examples are *complementizers* (COMP) – see below.)

(138)   Itinanong ko *kung* nasaan sila
     asked   I   COMP where   they
     'I asked where they were'

(139)   Ula Hasan gayergæ ketkæn *dep*   suradi
     they Hasan where   went   COMP asked
     'They asked where Hasan had gone'

Three classes of subordinating conjunctions can be distinguished on the basis of their functions: *complementizers, relativizers,* and *adverbializers.* These are discussed below in turn.

Complementizers mark a clause as the complement of a verb (cf. (138–9)), noun (140), or adjective (141):

(140)   I question the claim *that* the earth is flat

(141)   I am afraid *that* I must leave

A good many languages have a complementizer that is rather transparently derived from the verb meaning 'say'. This is true, for example, of *dep* in (139), and it is also true of *sɛ* in the following example from Akan:

(142)   Ɛyɛ nokware *sɛ*   mihuu no
     it is truth   COMP I saw him
     'It's true that I saw him'

(As (142) shows, complementizers that are derived from verbs meaning 'say' are by no means restricted to indirect quotation.)

One common alternative to the use of a complementizer is simply not to mark the subordinate status of a complement clause, as in (143) or its Hausa equivalent, (144):

(143)   He said it was raining

(144)   Ya   ce ana   ruwa
     he(PERF) say there is rain
     'He said it was raining'

Another alternative is to mark the subordinate status of the complement clause by nominalizing it: for example, by using a nominalized verb form and marking the complement subject as a possessive, as in the following English and Uzbek examples:

(145)   John anticipated Mary's winning the prize

(146)   Ula Hasanni gayergæ ketkænini suradi
       they Hasan's where   his going asked
       'They asked where Hasan had gone'

(The nominalization construction of (146) alternates with the complementizer-marked clause of (139).)

Relativizers are markers of relative clauses. Some examples, from Hausa and Akan respectively, are:

(147)   Na   ga mutumin *da* ya   yi aikin
       I(PERF) see the man REL he(PERF) do the work
       'I saw the man who did the work'

(148)   Ɔbarima *a*   minim no te   hɔ
       man   REL I know him lives there
       'A man whom I know lives there'

Note that relativizers are not the same as relative pronouns (which are discussed in section 2.1). Relativizers merely mark the clause in which they occur as relative, while relative pronouns in addition have some nominal function within the clause. If we compare the relativizers of (147) and (148) with the relative pronouns in their English translations, we can see that Hausa *da* and Akan *a* have no nominal function, while *who* and *whom* function as subject and object respectively of the relative clauses in which they occur.

Languages that do not use relativizers to mark relative clauses may use relative pronouns or special relative verb forms, as in the Quechua example in (149) (from Weber 1976), or may simply leave the relative clause unmarked, as in the Japanese example in (150) or its English translation:

(149)   Maqa-ma-q runa fiyu
       hit-me-REL man bad
       'The man who hits me is bad'

(150)   Kore wa watakusi ga   kaita hon   desu
       this TOP I   SUBJ wrote book is
       'This is a book I have written'

Adverbializers mark clauses as having some adverbial function, such as the expression of time, purpose, result, etc. (See chapter II.4 for a detailed typology of adverbial clauses.) In some languages, many of the words that serve as adverbializers also serve as prepositional or postpositional noun adjuncts (cf. section 2.2), as the following English, Japanese, and Hausa examples illustrate:

(151)   John left *after* $\begin{cases} \text{Sally arrived} \\ \text{the game} \end{cases}$

(152)   Ressya ga   tuku $\left.\begin{array}{l} \\ \end{array}\right\}$ *made* kore o   site-kudasai
        Ohiru

        train   SUBJ arrive $\left.\begin{array}{l} \\ \\ \end{array}\right\}$ until this   OBJ do-please
        noon

        'Please do this until $\begin{cases} \text{the train arrives'} \\ \text{noon'} \end{cases}$

(153)   *Da* $\begin{cases} \text{sun} \\ \text{dare} \end{cases}$ ZO $\left.\begin{array}{l} \\ \end{array}\right\}$ zamu   yi rawa

        at $\begin{cases} \text{they(PERF) come} \\ \text{night} \end{cases}$ $\left.\begin{array}{l} \\ \end{array}\right\}$ we(FUT) do dancing

        'As soon as they come $\left.\begin{array}{l} \\ \end{array}\right\}$ we'll dance'
        'At night

In some languages, an adverbializer in a subordinate clause may be optionally paired with another conjunction occurring in the main clause. English, for example, can pair *if* and *then*, as in:

(154)   If John goes, (then) Bill will too

In Vietnamese, there are many such optional pairings, as in the following examples (from Binh 1971):

(155)   *Vi*   anh   mach   thay   giao,   (*ma*)
        because older brother report teacher (therefore)

        Ba phai phat
        Ba PASS punish
        'Because you reported him to the teacher, Ba was punished'

(156)   *Khi*   toi den,   (*thi*)   Ba di roi
        when I   arrive (then) Ba go already
        'When I arrived, Ba had already gone'

(157)   *Tuy*   Ba noi   nhanh (*nhung*) toi cung-van heiu
        although Ba speak fast   (but)   I   still   understand

        duoc
        possible
        'Although Ba talked fast I could still understand him'

There are also cases where an adverbializer in a subordinate clause is *obligatorily* paired with a conjunction in the main clause. In counterfactual conditional sentences in Hausa, for example, the counterfactual conjunction (CF) *da* must appear in both the antecedent clause and the consequent clause (at least if the latter has a perfect-aspect predicate):

(158)   *Da* an   tambaye su,   *da* sun   yarda
        CF one(PERF) ask   them CF they(PERF) agree
        'If they had been asked, they would have agreed'

Various alternatives to the use of adverbializers are discussed in chapter II.4. These include simple juxtaposition of clauses and the use of special subordinate verb forms. Additional examples of the latter are provided by the following Eskimo sentences (from Harper 1974):

(159)   Qiu-ga-ma   isiqpunga
        cold-because-I I am coming in
        'Because I'm cold, I am coming in'

(160)   Audla-ru-vit   quviasutjanngittunga
        go away-if/when-you I will be unhappy
        'If/When you go away, I will be unhappy'

2.5 *Other closed classes*
This section surveys some of the more widespread closed parts-of-speech classes not discussed in previous sections. The classes to be surveyed are: *clitics*, *copulas* and *predicators*, *existential markers*, *interjections*, *mood markers*, *negators*, and *politeness markers*. They are discussed below in the listed order.

Clitics are words that occur in a fixed position in relation to some other sentence element. (If the fixed position is before the other element, the clitics are sometimes called *proclitics*; if after, they are sometimes called *enclitics*.) In some languages, clitics regularly follow the first word of the clause in which they occur. This is true, for example, of Tagalog, as is illustrated by the position of the clitic *daw* 'they say' in the following sentences:

(161)   a. Darating *daw*   si   Pedro bukas
           will arrive they say TOP Pedro tomorrow
           'They say Pedro will arrive tomorrow'

        b. Hindi *daw*   darating si   Pedro bukas
           NEG   they say will arrive TOP Pedro tomorrow
           'They say Pedro won't arrive tomorrow'

        c. Bakit *daw*   hindi darating si   Pedro bukas?
           why   they say NEG   will arrive TOP Pedro tomorrow
           'Why do they say Pedro won't arrive tomorrow?'

(The placement of clitics in Tagalog is actually somewhat more complex than these examples suggest: cf. Schachter and Otanes 1972:429–35.) In other languages, clitics occupy a fixed position in relation to a verb. In French, for example, clitics immediately precede the verb that governs them, except that they follow an affirmative imperative. Note the position of the clitic *y* 'there' in the following French sentences:

(162) a. Elle *y*   reste aujourd'hui
          she there stays today
          'She is staying there today'

       b. Il faut   *y*   rester aujourd'hui
          it is necessary there to stay today
          'It's necessary to stay there today'

       c. Restez-*y* aujourd'hui
          stay-there today
          'Stay there today'

In addition to having a fixed position in relation to other sentence elements, clitics also generally have a fixed, or partly fixed, position in relation to one another. Thus the three clitics in the French example in (163) must occur in the order shown, while the four in the Tagalog example in (164) allow the order variation shown, but no other:

(163) Personne *ne   nous en*   donne
       no one   NEG us   some gives
       'No one gives us any'

(164) Nagtatrabaho *ka na* $\begin{Bmatrix} ba & daw \\ daw & ba \end{Bmatrix}$ roon?

       are working   you now $\begin{Bmatrix} \text{Q} & \text{they say} \\ \text{they say} & \text{Q} \end{Bmatrix}$ there

       'Do they say you are working there now?'

Since the class of clitics is positionally defined, it may cut across parts-of-speech classes that are defined on a functional basis. For example, the class of clitics in French includes the negator *ne*, the object and reflexive pronouns, *y* 'there', and *en* 'from there, some, etc.', and the class of clitics in Tagalog is even more heterogeneous, as is clear from examples such as (164) and (165):

(165) Hindi *pa man lamang tuloy*   *siya* nakakapagalmusal
       NEG yet even just   as a result he   can have breakfast
       'As a result, he hasn't even been able to have breakfast yet'

Given this kind of heterogeneity, there is little of a systematic character that can be said about the types of elements that are likely to show clitic behavior, and thus about the probable counterparts of these elements in other languages. It may be noted, however, that clitics are likely to be phonologically light words, relatively short and/or unstressed, and that, cross-linguistically, personal pronouns (which are usually phonologically light) seem to show more of a tendency to cliticize than any other single type of element. (For further discussion of clitics, with emphasis upon their differentiation from affixes, see chapter III:3.)

Copulas are words used to indicate the relation between a subject and a predicate nominal or adjective. Many languages use a subset of *verbs*, the copulative verbs (cf. section 1.2), to indicate this relationship. This is true, for example, of English, which has copulative verbs like *be*, *become*, etc. In other languages, however, the copulas are clearly not verbs, and have quite distinct grammatical properties. In Hausa, for example, verbs precede their objects and are inflected for tense–aspect. Copulas, on the other hand, follow the predicate nominal and are uninflected except for gender, as in the following examples:

(166)   a. Ita yarinya *ce*
        she girl   COP
        'She is a girl'

      b. Shi yaro *ne*
        he boy COP
        'He is a boy'

(*Ce* is the copula used with feminine singulars, *ne* the one used in all other cases.)

In some languages a distinction is made between copulas and what may be called *predicators*. The latter are used to mark predicate nominals when there is no overt subject. In Bambara, for example, the predicator *don* is distinguished from the copulative verb *ye*:

(167)   Alamisadon *don*
       Thursday   PREDICATOR
       'It's Thursday'

(168)   Bi   ye   Alamisadon *ye*
       today PRES Thursday   be
       'Today is Thursday'

In other languages, however, the same words predicate nominals with and without subjects. Compare the following Hausa example with (166):

(169)   Audu *ne*
       Audu COP
       'It's Audu'

As was noted in section 1.2, there are languages that do not use copulas (or copulative verbs) to indicate the relation between a subject and a predicate nominal or adjective. In such languages the relation is indicated by juxtaposition, as in the following Ilocano examples:

(170)   a. Ina   daydyay babae
        mother that   woman
        'That woman is a mother'

       b. Napintas daydyay babae
        beautiful that   woman
        'That woman is beautiful'

There are also languages that use juxtaposition to express the relation in the *present*, but for non-present times use a tense-marked copulative verb, as in the following Swahili examples:

(171)   a. Hamisi mpishi
        Hamisi cook
        'Hamisi is a cook'

       b. Hamisi $\left\{\begin{array}{l}\text{alikuwa}\\\text{atakuwa}\end{array}\right\}$ mpishi

        'Hamisi $\left\{\begin{array}{l}\text{was}\\\text{will be}\end{array}\right\}$ a cook'

Emphasis markers are words that emphasize a predicate. (Words that emphasize a *nominal* are here called *contrast markers*, and are included in the category of *discourse markers* treated in section 2.2 – cf. example (105).) Examples, from Vietnamese and Thai respectively, are:

(172)   Ong Ba *co*   xem quyen truyen ay
       Mr Ba EMPH read book story   that
       'Mr Ba *did* read that novel'

(173)   Naarii, kin Kaaw *sia*
       Nari   rice eat   EMPH
       'Nari, *do* eat your rice'

The usual English equivalent of an emphasis marker is a stressed auxiliary verb, as in the translations of (172) and (173), but in colloquial English *so* and *too* are sometimes used as emphasis markers:

(174)   I am *so/too* telling the truth

Languages that do not have emphasis markers may be able to express the semantic equivalent by means of stress, and even in languages *with* emphasis markers this means may be available. Thus in Thai, according to Warotamasikkhadit (1972), the use of the emphasis marker *sia*, as in (173), is equivalent to placing emphatic stress on the verb.

Existential markers are words which are equivalent to English *there is/are*, etc. Examples, from Hausa and Spanish respectively, are:

(175)   *Akwai* littafi a kan   tebur
        EXIST book at top of table
        'There is a book on the table'

(176)   *Hay* muchos libros en la biblioteca
        EXIST many   books in the library
        'There are many books in the library'

Some languages also have distinct negative existential markers, as in the following Hausa example:

(177)   *Babu*   littafi a kan   tebur
        EXIST(NEG) book at top of table
        'There isn't a book on the table'

Languages that do not have existential markers often use verbs meaning 'be (located)' to express equivalent meanings, as in the following examples from Akan and Japanese:

(178)   Sika   bi   wɔ   me foto mu
        money some is located my bag in
        'There is some money in my bag'

(179)   Yama   ni ki ga   aru
        mountain on tree SUBJ is
        'There are trees on the mountain'

It is also quite common for there to be a close relation between existential and *possessive* constructions. For example, a word-by-word translation of the French existential idiom *il y a* is 'it there has', and in Tagalog the same words are used as existential and possessive markers:

(180)   a. Mayroon-g
          Wala-ng   } libro sa mesa

        EXIST/POSS-LINK
        EXIST/POSS(NEG)-LINK } book on table

        'There { is / isn't } a book on the table'

b. Mayroon-g
    Wala-ng   } libro ang bata

EXIST/POSS-LINK   }
EXIST/POSS(NEG)-LINK } book TOP child

'The child { has / doesn't have } a book'

Interjections are words, often of an exclamatory character, that can constitute utterances in themselves, and that usually have no syntactic connection to any other words that may occur with them. English examples are *ah, aha, bah, oh, wow*, etc. The class of interjections of a language often include words which are phonologically distinctive. For example, English words must in general contain at least one vowel sound, but interjections like *hmm, pst*, and *shh* are vowelless. And in many languages clicks (sounds produced with a velaric air stream) can occur in interjections (as in English *tsk-tsk*), but not elsewhere.

Although there are a good many linguistic descriptions that fail to mention interjections, it seems likely that all languages do in fact have such a class of words. In the case of extinct languages, interjections may not be attested in the written records because of the generally informal, colloquial character of this word class. In the case of modern languages, the omission of interjections from a linguistic description probably just signifies that the description is incomplete.

Mood markers are words that indicate the speaker's attitude, or that solicit the hearer's attitude, toward the event or condition expressed by a sentence. One common type of mood marker is the *request marker*, as exemplified by English *please*. Some others are illustrated by the Japanese examples of (181) (from Kuno 1973), and the Tagalog examples of (182):

(181)   a. Kore wa hon desu *yo*
           this TOP book is   STATEMENT
           '(I am telling you that) this is a book'

      b. Kore wa hon desu *ka*?
           this TOP book is   Q
           'Is this a book?'

      c. John wa baka   *sa*
           John TOP foolish STATEMENT
           '(It goes without saying that) John is a fool'

(182)   a. Mabuti *ba* ang ani?
           good   Q TOP harvest
           'Is the harvest good?'

b. Mabuti *kaya*   ang ani?
   good   Q(SPECULATIVE) TOP harvest
   'Do you suppose the harvest will be good?'

c. Mabuti *sana* ang ani
   good   WISH TOP harvest
   'I hope the harvest is good'

(The Tagalog mood markers of (182) all also belong to the class of *clitics* – see above.) In languages that do not use mood markers, the semantic equivalent may be expressed in a wide variety of ways: for example by word order and intonation (as in English statements and questions), by verb inflections (cf. section 1.2) or auxiliary verbs (cf. section 2.3), by explicit attitudinal expressions (e.g. *I hope, do you suppose*), etc.

Negators are words like English *not*, which negate a sentence, clause, or other constituent. As was noted above, some languages have distinctive existential negators. In Tagalog, for example, the existential negator is *wala* (cf. (180)), while the general negator is *hindi* (cf. (165)). It is also quite common for languages to have distinctive *imperative/optative* negators: for example Tagalog *huwag*, as in (183).

(183)   a. *Huwag* kayo-ng umalis
           NEG   you-LINK leave
           'Don't leave'

        b *Huwag* siya-ng pumarito
           NEG   he-LINK come here
           'He shouldn't come here'

In some languages negation is regularly expressed by a *pair* of negative words. This is true, for example, of standard French, where negation requires the negative clitic *ne* plus some other negative word, as in (184).

(184)   a. Jean *ne*   veut *pas* manger
           Jean NEG wants not to eat
           'Jean doesn't want to eat'

        b. Jean *ne*   veut *rien*   manger
           Jean NEG wants nothing to eat
           'Jean doesn't want to eat anything'

It is also true of general negation in Hausa, in which low-tone *bà*

precedes and high-tone *bá* follows the constituent being negated, thus
very neatly indicating the scope of the negation. For example:

(185)   a. *Ba* Halima ta   yi *ba*
           NEG Halima she(PERF) do NEG
           'It's not the case that Halima did it'

        b. Halima *ba*-ta   yi *ba*
           Halima NEG-she(PERF) do NEG
           'Halima didn't do it'

        c. *Ba* Halima *ba* ta   yi
           NEG Halima NEG she(PERF) do
           'It's not Halima who did it'

Languages that do not use negators may express negation by means of
a verbal affix, as in Akan *ɔ-n-kɔ* (he-negative-go) 'he doesn't go' or
Tonkawa *yakp-ape-n-o* (strike-negative-progressive-3rd person-present-
declarative) 'he is not striking him'. There are also languages in which
negation is expressed by an auxiliary verb – cf. section 2.3 for examples.

The last closed parts-of-speech class to be discussed is the class of
politeness markers. These are words which are added to sentences to
express a deferential attitude toward the person addressed. In Tagalog,
for example, there are two politeness markers, *po* and *ho*, either of
which may be added to any sentence the speaker wishes to render
polite. (*Po* is more polite than *ho*; to borrow the terminology of Kuno
(1973), *po* may be called 'superpolite'.) In some other languages, such
as Japanese, the expression of politeness involves, instead of markers, a
special polite vocabulary: for example *ee* 'yes (polite)', *hai* 'yes (superpolite)' vs. *un* 'yes (informal)'; *boku* 'I (polite or informal)', *watakusi* 'I
(polite or superpolite)' vs. *ore* 'I (informal)'. (Japanese also has a special
polite *affix*, *-mas-*, which is added to a verb in polite speech: e.g.
ake-mas-u (open-polite-present) 'open (polite)' vs. *ake-ru* (open present) 'open (informal)'.) The use of special polite forms for 'you' is
particularly common: for example Spanish *usted* 'you (polite singular)',
ustedes 'you (polite-plural)' vs. *tú* 'you (informal singular)', *vosotros*
'you (informal-plural)'.

This concludes our survey of closed parts-of-speech classes, as well as
of parts-of-speech classes in general. While certain minor classes have
been ignored, the great majority of the parts of speech encountered in
the languages of the world have been covered, and on the basis of the
material presented here, the field worker investigating an unfamiliar
language should be reasonably well-prepared for whatever parts-of-
speech system he or she meets.

NOTE

* My thanks to Sharon Klein and Jean Mulder for their help in gathering the data on which this chapter is based. My thanks also to the following for sharing their knowledge of languages cited in the chapter: George Bedell, Kent Bimson, Eser Erguvanli, Aryeh Faltz, Barnabas Forson, Talmy Givón, Charles Li, Pamela Munro, Jørgen Rischel, Jilali Saib, Sukari Saloné, Michiko Shintani, John Soper, Michika Takaichi, Sandra Thompson, Alan Timberlake, and David Weber.

2 The major functions of the noun phrase

AVERY ANDREWS

0 Introduction

In this chapter we will discuss the major functions of noun phrases (NPS) in the languages of the world. We can think of NPS as having three basic kinds of functions: semantic, pragmatic, and grammatical. Semantic and pragmatic functions are aspects of the meaning of sentences, grammatical functions aspects of their structure.

Semantic functions, also called semantic roles, are the ways in which the meaning of a sentence specifies the referent of an NP to be participating in the situation which the sentence refers to. Consider (1):

(1)   The farmer kills the duckling

Here the verb *kill* indicates that we have a situation in which one entity kills another. It provides two semantic roles, 'killer' and 'killed', taken by the referents of the preverbal NP *the farmer* and postverbal NP *the duckling*, respectively. In order for the sentence to be true, the referents of these NPS must act or be acted upon in accord with these roles. Semantic roles are thus an aspect of the relation between sentences and the situations they refer to.

Language is used not merely to depict the world, but to communicate in it: its users are part of the world they talk about. There is therefore a further aspect of meaning, involving factors other than what a sentence refers to, which contributes to determining when the sentence may be used. This aspect of meaning, called pragmatics, involves such things as the hearer's presumed ignorance or knowledge of various features of the situation being talked about, what the speaker wishes to put forward as the topic of conversation, and so on. Properties of this sort that pertain to NP are the pragmatic functions.

In English, for example, (1) has the variants shown in (2):

(2)   a. It is the farmer that kills the duckling
        b. It is the duckling that the farmer kills

The sentences of (2) designate precisely the same kind of situation as (1). But (2a) presumes that the hearer knows that somebody or something kills the duckling, but not who or what; and (2b) presumes that the hearer knows that the farmer killed somebody or something, but not who or what. (1), on the other hand, in its most straightforward articulation, with neutral intonation, does not presume knowledge on the part of the hearer of any event of killing. These sentences thus give their NPs the same semantic roles, but different pragmatic functions. We will say that (2a) 'focuses' the subject of *kill* (treats it as new information and as the unique entity filling the role of the subject), and that (2b) does the same with the object of *kill*.

The semantic roles and pragmatic functions of the NPs in a sentence may be called their 'semiotic functions', since they have to do with the meaning of the sentence. Semiotic functions are ultimately signaled by 'overt coding features' such as word order, case marking and cross-referencing (agreement). But it is difficult to provide a coherent account of how this occurs in terms of a direct connection between coding features and the semiotic functions they express. Rather it seems better to posit an intervening level of grammatical structure: the coding features indicate the grammatical structure of the sentence, and the grammatical structure determines the semiotic functions.

The grammatical functions of NPs are the relationships in this grammatical structure which participate in determining the semantic roles and pragmatic functions of NP. For example, in (1) we recognize the grammatical functions of subject (preverbal NP) and object (postverbal NP). There is a principle associated with the verb *kill* which assigns the 'killer' role to the subject and the 'killed' role to the object. The semantic role of an NP is thus determined jointly by the verb and the grammatical function of the NP. The structural positions of *the farmer* and *the duckling* in (2a) and (2b) respectively, likewise assign to them the pragmatic function of focus.

Grammatical functions are also involved in principles governing the form of sentence structure. A familiar example is the principle of subject–verb agreement in English, whereby a present tense verb with a third person singular subject takes a special form ending in /-z/. Thus if the subject of (1) is pluralized, the form of the verb must change, but pluralizing the object does not have this effect:[1]

(3)   a. The farmers kill(*s) the duckling
       b. The farmer kill*(s) the ducklings

The grammatical function of subject is thus involved in this constraint on the form of English sentences.

The relationships between semiotic functions, grammatical functions, and coding features may be represented in Figure 2.1.

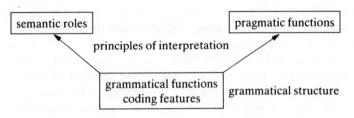

Figure 2.1. The relationship between semiotic functions, grammatical functions, and coding features

Principles of grammatical structure govern the distribution of grammatical functions and their expression in terms of coding features: on the basis of grammatical structure, principles of interpretation govern the assignment of semantic roles, pragmatic functions, and other aspects of meaning not considered in this chapter (such as 'modal structure', Jackendoff 1972, and other logical scope relations).

In this chapter we will be primarily concerned with the grammatical functions of NPS in clause structure. But since the task of the grammatical functions is to express the semantic and pragmatic ones, we will want to survey these briefly first. Therefore the first section of the chapter will be devoted to the preliminaries of semantic roles, coding features and pragmatic functions. Then in section 2 we will present a basic classification of grammatical functions into three types, 'core', 'oblique' and 'external', and discuss the latter two. Finally, in section 3 we will discuss the core grammatical functions.

But before proceeding, I will discuss further the notions of grammatical structure and grammatical function. There are at least two fundamentally contrasting views of the nature of grammatical functions in sentence structure.

In one, the 'relationally based' view, grammatical functions are treated as labels of relations in a network. On this approach, the essential sentence structure of (1) might be something like (4):

(4)

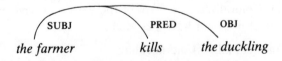

Here *the farmer* bears the grammatical relation SUBJ, *duckling* the grammatical function OBJ, and the verb *kills* the grammatical function PRED. The overt form of the sentence would be determined by principles for realizing such networks, which would determine the linear order on the basis of the network of grammatical relations.

The second is the 'configurational' view, in which grammatical functions are defined in terms of the arrangement of phrases or similar compositional units. In conventional phrase-structure theory, for example, (1) would get a structure like (5):

(5)

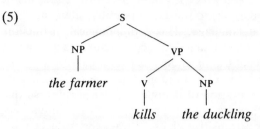

In the theory of Chomsky (1965), subject would be defined as 'NP under s', object as 'NP under VP'.

The relational view is adopted in various forms in relational grammar and its offshoot arc pair grammar (Johnson 1977, Perlmutter 1980, Johnson and Postal 1980, Postal 1982); in lexical-functional grammar (Bresnan 1982a) and many other theories (including those referred to as 'functional grammar'). The configurational view is adopted in classical transformational grammar (Chomsky 1965) and certain of its offshoots, such as the various versions of the extended standard theory. Dowty's (1982) account of grammatical relations in Montague grammar can also be put into this category. See Moravcsik and Wirth (1980) and Pullum and Jacobson (1982) for illustration of a variety of contemporary accounts.

The issues involved in deciding between these and other theories of the formal nature of sentence structure are complex and difficult, but fortunately have little significance for basic descriptive work on languages. Therefore in this chapter we will not advocate any specific position on the exact nature of sentence structures and grammatical functions, although the discussion will be most easily understood in terms of the relational view.

The most important thing to keep in mind is that sentence structures and grammatical functions are abstract intermediaries between semantic roles, pragmatic functions, and the overt coding features that express them. They are postulated because they help to explain the principles that govern the form and meaning of sentences.

In the literature, the term 'grammatical relation' is used as a virtual synonym of 'grammatical function'. However, we will differentiate them slightly here. A grammatical function will be any relationship which it might be useful to recognize which is definable over the sentence structures of a language under study, regardless of the extent to which it is important for the grammatical principles of that language. On the other hand, a grammatical relation in a language will be a grammatical function that is generally significant for the workings of the grammatical principles of that language, and which it would therefore be reasonable (although not necessarily correct) to posit as a primitive element in the sentence structures of the language. This terminological distinction, although novel, is useful for discussing sentence structures in a language without making controversial claims about their nature.

Thus, in English, subject and object are grammatical relations, since they are relevant for the operation of many grammatical rules, so that one could plausibly view them as primitive concepts of English sentence structure. But 'subject of a transitive clause' ('transitive subject') and 'subject of an intransitive clause' ('intransitive subject'), although they are grammatical functions (since they are definable within any reasonable theory of English sentence structure), do not qualify as grammatical relations in English, since they are not the relationships that are relevant for the operation of grammatical rules.

1 Preliminaries

1.1 *Semantic roles*

In the most basic kind of sentence structure, there is a verbal element that denotes a type of situation, which usually implies various roles, that is, ways of participating in that situation. Thus we have seen that *kill* denotes a situation with 'killed' and 'killer' roles, among others. The element that defines the type of situation and the roles we call a 'predicate', the NPs filling the roles we call 'arguments'.

The predicate needn't be a single verb. Sometimes the predicate is a complex consisting of several verbs, or a verb plus a nominal or adverbial element. (6a) illustrates a two-verb predicate from the Papuan language Barai (Foley and Olson 1985), (6b) a verb + noun predicate from the Dravidian language Malayalam (Mohanan 1982), and (6c) verb + (adverbial) particle predicate from English. The complex predicate in each example is italicized:

(6) a. Fu fase isema *fi   isoe*
        he letter wrongly sat write
        'He wrongly sat writing a letter'

     b. Kuṭṭi ammaye *salyam   ceyṭu*
        child mother   annoyance did
        'The child annoyed the mother'

     c. The guards *beat* the prisoners *up*

Languages also have 'minor sentence types' in which a non-verbal element is the predicate, or where there is no overt predicate word, the predicate being understood from the syntactic structure of the sentence as a whole. We illustrate this possibility with some examples from Russian:

(7)   a. Kniga na stole
          book   on table
          'The book is on the table'

       b. U menja kniga
          of me   book
          'I have a book'

In addition to a main predicate, a sentence may have additional, subsidiary predicates. In the sentence *John made Mary happy*, for example, the principal predicate is the verb *made*, and the adjective *happy* is a subsidiary predicate applying to *Mary*. In spite of these possibilities, we will generally refer to the main predicate simply as 'the verb'.

A predicate defines a set of highly specific roles, such as 'killer' and 'killed'. Examining the nature of the relations between these roles and grammatical relations, we find that it is far from arbitrary: there are always far-reaching regularities and generalizations, statable in terms of semantically definable classes of roles. Thus it is no accident that *kill* expresses the killer as subject and the killed as object: *kill* is one of a large class of verbs in which one participant, possibly exercising his will, does something to another which significantly affects that other. When two-participant verbs in English meeting this description are in their active form (we will discuss passives later), they always have the acting, 'Agent', argument as subject, and the acted upon, or 'Patient', argument as object.

I will use the term 'semantic role' to refer both to the specific roles imposed on NPS by a given predicate, such as 'killer' and 'killed', and to the more general classes of roles, such as 'Agent' and 'Patient'. Semantic roles are important in the study of grammatical functions since grammatical functions usually express semantic roles in a highly systematic way.[2]

In our subsequent discussion we will first examine the Agent and Patient roles, and the intimate connection they have with the basic grammatical forms of all languages. Then we will survey a variety of other semantic roles which it is useful to recognize.

1.1.1 *Agent and Patient*

I will define an Agent as a participant which the meaning of the verb specifies as doing or causing something, possibly intentionally (i.e. because (s)he wants to). The intention is qualified as possible because most verbs taking a causing or active participant (*kill* and *hit* in English, for example) are consistent with that participant acting intentionally, but do not require it to.[3] Therefore the subjects of verbs such as *kill*, *eat*, *smash*, *hit*, *kick*, and *watch* are Agents, while the objects of these verbs are not.

A Patient will be defined as a participant which the verb characterizes as having something happen to it, and as being affected by what happens to it. The objects of *kill*, *eat* and *smash* are clearly Patients, while those of *watch*, *hear* and *love* are clearly not. The objects of *hit* and *kick* are intermediate in status, because although something obviously happens to them, they are less clearly affected by it. In most languages, NPS with these roles behave like Patients, and can be considered as marginal instances of this role.

But sometimes their grammar is significantly different. For example in Northwest Caucasian languages such as Abkhaz and Adyge, verbs like *hit* take a different NP-marking strategy than verbs like *kill* (Catford 1976), showing that the object of *hit* is not a true Patient.

Agent and Patient play a fundamental role in all languages. The class of two-argument verbs taking an Agent and a Patient (e.g. *kill*, *eat*, *smash*) is important enough to be given a name: we shall call them 'primary transitive verbs' (PTVS).

Languages always seem to have a standard way or small set of ways in which they normally express the Agent and Patient of a PTV. If an NP is serving as argument of a two-argument verb, and receiving the morphological and syntactic treatment normally accorded to an Agent of a PTV, we shall say that it has the grammatical function A; if it is an argument of a verb with two or more arguments receiving the treatment normally accorded to the Patient of a PTV, we shall say that it has the grammatical function O. A sentence is called 'transitive' if it has A and O functions in its syntactic structure, 'intransitive' if one or both functions is missing. These definitions are with respect to the possibly abstract syntactic structure of the sentence: the NPS needn't appear in the overt, visible form. An NP in an intransitive sentence that is receiving the treatment normally accorded to the single argument of a one-argument predicate will be said to have S function.[4]

A, S and O are important because languages always seem to use PTVS as a grammatical model for a great many other types of verbs. In English and most other languages, for example, the verb *see* expresses the seer as an A and the seen as an O even though it is clear that seers are not Agents, and things seen not Patients. The fact that so many verbs seem to use PTVs as a syntactic model makes it difficult, and, fortunately, unnecessary to be absolutely precise about drawing the boundaries of the class.

A, S and O are grammatical functions, not grammatical relations, though often one of them coincides with a grammatical relation in a language. In English, for example, O can be identified with the grammatical relation object, but neither A nor S can be identified with subject, A comprising transitive subjects, S intransitive subjects, neither of which would be reasonable to posit as grammatical relations for English. But since in any reasonable theory of English sentence structure A and S would be structurally definable as transitive and intransitive subject, respectively, they are grammatical functions in English.

Although A, S and O cannot in general be regarded as grammatical relations, they are closely associated with them, and they are further-more associated with the syntactically most 'active' ones, those most important in the grammatical system of a language. Hence identifying A, S and O is the first step in working out the system of grammatical relations in a language.

Most often, one finds one grammatical relation associated with A and S, and another with O. The former sort of grammatical relation we will call 'subject', the latter 'object'.[5] This usage of 'subject' and 'object' is only one of many that are in circulation, but it picks out the subject and object in most instances where there is no serious controversy about the use of the terms. We will sometimes speak of 'standard subject and object' to distinguish the present usage from various plausible extensions.[6] A, S and O and their connections with grammatical relations will be further discussed at the beginning of section 3.

1.1.2 *Other semantic roles*

Besides Agent and Patient, a number of other semantic roles are also important for grammar. Semantic roles in general may be divided into two rough classes: Participatory and Circumstantial roles. Participatory roles are borne by what one would think of as actual participants in the situation implied by the verb. Agent and Patient are the quintessential Participatory roles. Circumstantial roles are borne by entities that do not really participate, but instead form part of the setting of the event. Benefactive, the person for whom something is done, is a typical Circumstantial role.

Aside from Agent and Patient, some of the other more important

Participatory roles are Directional, with Source and Goal subtypes; 'Inner' Locative (giving the location of a participant, rather than of the event or state as a whole), Experiencer (a participant who is characterized as aware of something); Recipient (a participant who 'gets' something), Theme[7] (a participant which is characterized as being in a state or position, or changing its state or position), Causer (a participant who causes something, but does not act intentionally), and Instrumental (a participant that the Agent uses to act on the Patient). Note that the Theme and Patient roles are closely related, though not identical: unlike Patients, Themes needn't be acted upon by anything, and it is sometimes appropriate to regard as Patients certain arguments, such as things that are hit or kicked, which may be regarded as affected by what is done to them, but do not necessarily undergo a consequent change of state.

Examples of these roles are given below:

(8)   a. Tiger snakes$_{\text{Theme}}$ inhabit Australia$_{\text{Inner Locative}}$

     b. George$_{\text{Agent \& Theme}}$ walked from/to the store$_{\text{Source/Goal}}$

     c. I$_{\text{Experiencer}}$ love Lucy

     d. Frederika$_{\text{Causer}}$ annoys me$_{\text{Experiencer}}$

     e. Bruce$_{\text{Agent}}$ handed Darlene$_{\text{Recipient}}$ a steak$_{\text{Theme}}$

     f. Bill$_{\text{Agent}}$ prodded the snake with a stick$_{\text{Instrumental}}$

     g. The earth$_{\text{Causer}}$ attracts the moon$_{\text{Theme}}$

     h. The car$_{\text{Theme}}$ is expensive

Note that not every NP in these examples has a semantic role of one of the categories that we have named. No presently known system of semantic roles can be comprehensively applied in a convincing manner.

Aside from Benefactive some other important Circumstantial roles are 'Outer' Locative (the place where something is done), Reason (reason why something is done), Circumstantial Comitative (something that accompanies a participant, but does not itself participate), and Temporal. These are illustrated below:

(9)   a. Susan caught a lizard in the garden$_{\text{Outer Locative}}$

     b. Bruce barbecued a steak for Darlene$_{\text{Benefactive}}$

     c. Alvin shot up a sign for fun$_{\text{Reason}}$

     d. Shirley went diving with a speargun$_{\text{Circumstantial Comitative}}$

     e. Jack ate a sausage during the race$_{\text{Temporal}}$

The distinction between Participatory and Circumstantial roles is closely related to a distinction between 'complements' and 'adjuncts' that will be introduced in section 2.2.

There are of course many (probably infinitely many) more semantic roles that might be significant for the grammar of a language. The ones discussed here are merely some of the more recurrent ones. There are many types of roles that we have not discussed at all. It should also be pointed out that, in accord with most of the literature, we have paid little attention to the problem of *defining* the semantic roles, having contented ourselves with rather vague characterizations.

1.2 Coding strategies

There are three basic techniques which languages use to code syntactic functions: order and arrangement, NP-marking (case marking), and cross-referencing (agreement). We consider each in turn.

1.2.1 Order and arrangement

This strategy is familiar from English. It is the order of the NPs in (1) relative to the verb that indicates which is the subject and which the object. English is an example of what we will call a 'determinate' word-order system, one in which grammatical principles to a considerable extent prescribe the order of NPs. In such systems we find a 'basic' order, with various alternative orders systematically related to it. Since the workings of such systems are familiar from English, there is no need to discuss them here.

We also find systems in which there is a preferred order, but where a great deal of variation is possible as long as ambiguity is not introduced (though some languages seem to tolerate surprising amounts of ambiguity). Thus in Dakota (Van Valin 1977, 1985) the preferred order is Subject–Object–Verb (SOV). If the semantics of the verb is not sufficient to determine which NP takes which role, this order must be followed. Hence changing the order of NPs in (10) changes the meaning:

(10)   a. Wičhása ki mathó wą kté
           man   the bear a   killed
           'The man killed a bear'

        b. Mathó wą wičhása ki kté
           bear   a   man   the killed
           'A bear killed the man'

But if there is only one semantically plausible choice for subject, the relative order of NPs becomes free (though NPs and other constituents must remain in front of the verb):

(11)   a. Wičhása ki   ix?é wą wąyáke
           man   the rock a   saw
        b. Ix?é wą wičhása ki   wąyáke
           rock a man   the saw
        'The man saw a rock'

In Dakota syntax, it does not seem to be sensible to try to describe the order possibilities in terms of a basic order and specific alternatives. Rather the order is free, subject to an sov preference, especially when needed to prevent ambiguity. This sort of system we will call 'fluid', as opposed to the highly determinate word-order system of languages like English.

Apart from the determinate/fluid distinction, languages also differ in whether word order is a normal means for marking grammatical relations, or whether it is invoked only under rather special circumstances, if at all. English and Dakota fall into the first category, Warlpiri, to be discussed in the next subsection, into the second.

Fluidity seems to be characteristic of many languages of diverse word-order types. The main difficulty in assessing the extent to which word order in a language is fluid stems from the fact that elicitation of sentences from informants will tend to produce the normal word order. Observation of normal language use will often reveal a much wider range of orders in the appropriate contexts.

1.2.2 NP-marking

No language makes exclusive use of ordering to code grammatical relations, and many make very little use of it for this purpose. A strategy which every language uses to some extent, and some use almost exclusively, is NP-marking. In the NP-marking strategy, the syntactic function of the NP is indicated by a morphological marker on the NP. This marker may take the form of an inflectional ending (see chapter III.3 for discussion of inflection), or be a morphologically autonomous element, in which case it is often called a 'particle', a preposition (if it precedes the NP), or a postposition (if it follows). Both the inflectional endings and the morphologically autonomous elements are often called 'case markers'. There are no generally accepted conventions governing the application of the terms 'particle', 'pre/postposition' and 'case marker' to morphologically autonomous NP-markers.

In English the principal use of NP-marking is with verbal arguments introduced by prepositional phrases. Thus the sentences of (12) are virtual paraphrases:

(12)   a. Bobby spoke to the meeting about the proposal

        b. Bobby spoke about the proposal to the meeting

To marks its NP as the addressee of *speak*, *about* marks its NP as the subject matter. Although the former order is preferred, both are possible, and it is clear that order does not mark the roles of these NPs.

Many languages make far more extensive use of NP-marking, using it to mark almost all NP functions, including subject, object, or their counterparts. One example of this is Tagalog, which will be discussed below. Here we shall discuss an even more extreme example, Warlpiri (Hale 1973, 1976, 1978, 1979; Nash 1980).

In English, principles of order and arrangement not only indicate the functions of NPs, but the NPs themselves are also identified in terms of such principles, in that the constituent parts of NPs appear in a definite order, which may be described by phrase-structure rules, as explained in any reasonable introduction to generative grammar. In Warlpiri both the functions and the constituency of NPs are usually indicated by NP-marking.

The one major principle of word order for Warlpiri simple clauses involves the 'auxiliary element'. This expresses the verbal categories of tense and mood (and also carries person-and-number markers for some of the verbal arguments, as we shall see in the next subsection), and comes in first or second position (see Hale 1973:311–14 for discussion), depending on its phonological shape. The order of all other elements is free. Furthermore, there is no requirement that the constituents of an NP be contiguous: they must merely share the same endings.[8]

The following three strings are therefore fully synonymous, and may be regarded as three versions of the same sentence:[9]

(13)   a. Kurdu-ngku ka   maliki   wita-ngku wajilipi-nyi
           child-ERG   PRES dog(ABS) small-ERG chase-NONPAST

       b. Wajilipi-nyi ka wita-ngku maliki kurdu-ngku

       c. Maliki ka kurdu-ngku wajilipi-nyi wita-ngku

       'The small child is chasing the dog'

The auxiliary *ka* indicates that the tense is present. It is supplemented by the tense-ending on the verb, which shows non-past tense. The 'ergative' ending *-ngku* on *wita* 'small' and *kurdu* 'child' marks these as comprising one NP that bears A function. The absence of any ending on *maliki* shows that this belongs to a different NP, which can bear O function (and S as well, as we shall see). This unmarked form is called the 'absolutive'. The endings thus indicate how the NP components are to be grouped together, and what function the resulting NPs are to have. There are twenty-one more arrangements of the words of (13) with the auxiliary in second position, and they are all grammatical and mean the same thing as (13).

There are two further observations worth making. First, -ngku is not a subject marker, because it does not normally mark the s function. Rather, single arguments of one-argument verbs are normally in the absolutive case:

(14)   Ngarrka ka   purla-mi
        man(ABS) PRES shout-NONPAST
        'The man is shouting'

If we assume that case marking directly reflects grammatical relations, we would have to deny that Warlpiri had a subject relation: rather, we would have to say that it had one grammatical relation covering A function, and another covering o and s functions. In fact, although they are not directly marked by the case forms, Warlpiri does seem to have subject and object grammatical relations, as we shall see in 3.2.1–3.

The second observation is that Warlpiri can group the members of an NP into a single overt constituent, and in this case the ending need only appear on the last word of the NP:

(15)   a. Wita kurdu-ngku ka   maliki   wajilipi-nyi
           small child-ERG   PRES dog(ABS) chase-NONPAST
           'The small child is chasing the dog'

        b. Wita   ka   kurdu-ngku maliki   wajilipi-nyi
           small(ABS) PRES child-ERG   dog(ABS) chase-NONPAST
           'The child is chasing the small dog'

The position of ka after wita kurdu-ngku in (15a) indicates that these two words form a constituent, and that they are therefore taken together as an NP despite the difference in endings. In (15b), where ka appears between wita and kurdu-ngku, these two words do not form a constituent, so wita has to be construed with maliki, and the sentence means 'The child is chasing the small dog'.

Warlpiri requires a somewhat more abstract kind of analysis than what we have so far required for English: English NPs can be identified as units in a 'surface constituent structure' directly reflected in the linear order of elements. In Warlpiri we need at least two levels of analysis: overt constituent structure, relevant for auxiliary placement and a few other phenomena, and a deeper level at which 'functional' units such as

NPS are recognized even if their constituent elements are scattered throughout the overt structure.

NP-marking systems are traditionally classified into the two major types of 'nominative–accusative', and 'ergative–absolutive'. Nominative–accusative systems have a 'nominative' case associated with the A and s functions, and an 'accusative' associated with o function. Ergative–absolutive systems are those such as Warlpiri, which have an absolutive' associated with o/s and an 'ergative' associated with A. It is also useful to establish the term 'dative' to refer to NP-marking that is associated with Recipients. These terms will subsequently be used freely in glosses and discussion. See chapter III.3 and below for further discussion of the structure of NP-marking systems.

1.2.3 *Cross-referencing*

In cross-referencing, also called agreement, various grammatical properties of an NP, such as noun-class (gender), number, person or case are registered on an element bearing some specific syntactic relation to the NP. As mentioned above, the Warlpiri auxiliary cross-references certain grammatical functions by manifesting markers for their person and number. Third person singular ergative and absolutive NPs take no marker, so overt cross-referencing does not appear in examples (13–15). But first or second person, and dual (DU) or plural NPs take non-null markers, as illustrated in example (16):

(16)   Nya-nyi   ka-rna-palangu   wawirri-jarra
        see-NONPAST PRES-1SG(SUBJ)-3DU(OBJ) kangaroo-DU(ABS)
        (ngajulu-rlu)
        (I-ERG)
        'I see two kangaroos'

The clitic *rna* cross-references a first person singular A, *palangu* a third person dual o. The cross-referencing system in fact treats A and s alike as opposed to o, and thus forms part of the evidence that Warlpiri has standard subjects and objects. It will be discussed further in 3.2.1.

The cross-referencing markers in Warlpiri and most other languages do not function primarily to code the grammatical function of NPs. In (16), for example, the markers are redundant because the functions are already coded by the markers on the NPs themselves. Furthermore, in examples such as (13–15), where A and o are both third person singular, the markers are both zero, and thus provide no information about the functions of the NPs at all.

Rather the primary function of cross-referencing markers is as substitutes for (or perhaps as forms of) pronouns.[10] Thus in (16), the A pronoun *ngajulu-rlu* 'I-ERG' is optional, and the meaning doesn't change if it is omitted. The o *wawirri-jarra* 'two kangaroos' is also optional, but if it is omitted the sentence means 'I saw them two'. A sentence such as *nya-nyi ka-rna* would mean 'I saw him/her/it': the absence of any o cross-reference markers indicate that the o is third person singular.

Thus cross-referencing in Warlpiri (and most other languages that have it) is not a major part of the system coding the syntactic functions of overt NPS. But since cross-reference markers often serve as substitutes for NPS, they are an important part of the system which specifies what entities take what roles in the situation denoted by the predicate. Since grammatical functions of NPS and the devices coding them are also part of this system, cross-referencing systems should be investigated together with NP function coding systems.

Occasionally, however, cross-referencing does provide the principal signal for a grammatical relation of an overt NP in a sentence. A good example is provided by Ancient Greek. Ancient Greek had case marking and very free word order (at least in writing). There is a participial construction in which the subject of the complement is suppressed when it is identical to some NP in the main clause. But the information is not lost as to what the subordinate clause subject is, because the participial verb form that the construction uses is marked for the gender (see below), number and case of the matrix NP to be understood as the subject. This information, especially the case information, is usually sufficient to identify what is to be understood as the subject of the complement.

It is thus the case marking on the participle that disambiguates the following pair of sentences:

(17)   Klearchos   ape:nte:se Philippo:i   apio:n
        Klearchus(NOM) met   Philip(DAT) leaving(NOM)
        'Klearchus met Philip while Klearchus was leaving'

(18)   Klearchos   ape:nte:se Philippo:i   apionti
        Klearchus(NOM) met   Philip(DAT) leaving(DAT)
        'Klearchos met Philip while Philip was leaving'

Both nominals are masculine singular, so indication of these categories is omitted from the glosses. The nominative marking on the participle in (17) indicates that the subject of this participle is to be understood as the nominative of the matrix sentence, *Klearchos*, while the dative on the participle in (18) indicates that this participle's understood subject is to be the matrix dative, *Philippo:i*.

This is an unusually straightforward example of cross-referencing marking grammatical relations. Usually, when it manages to do this, it does so by means of complex interactions with other strategies and principles. An interesting example of this is the 'inverse person-marking' system of Algonquian languages, discussed for Plains Cree in Wolfart (1973) and chapter 1.6, section 2.2.

The categories most often involved in cross-referencing are person, number, case and 'noun class'. The first three have already been illustrated. As for the last, many languages divide their nouns into classes or 'genders', which are sometimes based on semantic features, such as humanness, sexual gender, animacy, shape, etc., and sometimes arbitrary to a greater or lesser extent. In Ancient Greek, for example, the noun classes (masculine, feminine, neuter) reflect sexual gender fairly faithfully for adult humans, and are therefore called genders, but are largely arbitrary elsewhere. For further discussion of these and other categories involved in cross-referencing, see chapter III:3.

1.3 *Pragmatic functions*

Pragmatic functions involve a great variety of considerations, about which there is, furthermore, considerable controversy. Some of the notions that have figured in recent discussions include: (a) what the hearer is presumed to be already conscious of vs. what he isn't ('given' vs. 'non-given'); (b) what the sentence is about ('topicality'); (c) whether an NP has or doesn't have a referent uniquely identifiable to the hearer ('definiteness'); (d) whether the speaker is referring to a particular instance of an entity as opposed to any instance of it ('specificity'); (e) what is 'foregrounded' as important vs. what is 'backgrounded' as secondary; (f) the point of view taken by the speaker on the situation under discussion ('empathy', or 'perspective'); (g) inherent 'salience properties' of NPS, such as animacy, humanness, or first-personhood.

In this chapter we will for the most part restrict our attention to givenness, definiteness, and topicality. For further discussion of these and the other pragmatic factors the reader is referred to chapter 1.6, Prince (1978, 1979), and to the papers in Li (1976) and Givón (1979b).

In terms of givenness and topicality, there are two principal articulations of the sentence: topic–comment, and focus–presupposition. We will first consider these, and then briefly examine a third type, 'presentational' articulation.

1.3.1 *Topic–comment articulation*

In topic–comment articulation there is usually one NP, the topic, which indicates what the sentence is about. The remainder of the sentence, the comment, provides information about the topic.

By definition, topics are given, that is, presumed to be in the consciousness of the hearer by virtue of the preceding discourse or already shared knowledge.[11] There is a different pragmatic function, 'presentational', whereby a new entity may be introduced and commented upon. Topics furthermore seem always to be definite. The reason for this is presumably because it is pointless to make a comment about the referent of an NP if the NP doesn't manage to identify a specific referent to the hearer.

There are two principal kinds of topics: those whose topicality is predictable from the immediately preceding discourse, and those whose topicality is not. For an illustration of the two types, consider the following story:

(19)   Once upon a time there was a king with two sons. The older son expected to take over the kingship. *He* spent his time travelling with the army and working with the secret police. As for *the younger*, he concentrated on studying philosophy at the university.

The italicized pronoun *he* in the third sentence is expected to be topic, since its referent is also the topic of the immediately preceding sentence. *The younger* in the fourth sentence represents a new, unexpected topic. The switch in topic is registered by the *as for* construction, which seems to register that some entity introduced previously in the discourse is being made the new topic. We shall call these two types 'expected topic' and 'switch topic'. In many languages the subject grammatical relation is associated with the topic (expected or switch) function. There are various indications of this, the simplest of which is a general tendency for subjects to be definite.

Keenan (1976a) observed that in some languages, such as Malagasy and Kinyarwanda, the subject must be definite.[12] Thus the following sentence from Kinyarwanda (Kimenyi 1980:59) has only (a) as a gloss, not (b):

(20)   Úmwáana a-ra-lir-a
        child   3SG-PRES-cry-ASP

        a. 'The child is crying'
        b. *'A child is crying'

Patientive direct objects are not constrained to be definite (though certain other kinds of objects are, as discussed by Kimenyi).

In English, of course, there is no *requirement* that subjects be definite, as witnessed by the grammaticality of (20b) in English. But there is nonetheless a very strong *tendency* for subjects to be definite. Thus Givón (1979a:51–3) reports that in a sample of a variety of types of narrative written English, 91% of subjects were definite, versus 56% of (direct) objects. These facts can be explained in terms of requirements or tendencies that subjects be topics.[13]

As we shall see in section 3.2 below, such a tendency does not appear to be a universal property of subjects, though it is a common one. In Warlpiri, for example, there is no tendency apparent for subjects to be definite.

On the other hand so-called 'topicalization' constructions are frequently (but not always) associated with switch-topic functions (Chafe 1976:49, Duranti and Ochs 1979:401). The *as for* construction above is one example. Some others of these constructions with their standard names are given below, with the topicalized NPs italicized:

(21) a. Topicalization:
        Spaghetti on toast I find to be an absolutely revolting way to begin the morning
      b. Left-dislocation:
        Word-processors, I sometimes think they should be recycled into Space Invaders machines
      c. Right-dislocation:
        I can't believe they're for real, *the maniacs who pay $100 a gram for cocaine*

The functions of these constructions are all undoubtedly different, although the current literature does not clearly spell out how.

1.3.2 *Focus–presupposition articulation*

In this kind of articulation, the body of the sentence, the presupposition, represents a situation with which the hearer is presumed to be familiar. The focus NP gives the identity of a participant presumed to be unknown to the hearer. The *it*-cleft construction of (2) is a typical example of focus–presupposition articulation. English has two other means of expressing this, the *wh*-cleft construction, and 'contrastive stress' on the focus:

(22) a. A bear is what the man killed
      b. The man killed *a bear*.

Again, these constructions differ in their usage. See Prince (1978) for a discussion of the differences between *it*-cleft and *wh*-cleft constructions. To see a difference between stressing and the other constructions, observe that (22b) is a more natural answer than (22a) or the *it*-cleft *it's a bear that the man killed* to the question *what did the man kill?*

Topic–comment articulation can be superposed on focus–presupposition articulation: in a sentence such as *George is looking for bears*, *George* might be topic, and **bears** focus. The comment would be *is looking for bears*, the presupposition *George is looking for X*.

1.3.3 *Presentational articulation*

Not all sentences have topic–comment or focus–presupposition articulation. One of the most important of the other types is presentational sentences, which introduce a new entity into the discourse. English has certain constructions dedicated to this function, such as the expletive *there* constructions: *once there was a king with three children*. English sentences can also be presentational without using special presentational constructions: *a king with three children lived in a valley*, or *a person is standing outside the door*.

Languages with a restriction that subjects be definite frequently use explicitly presentational structures in order to introduce an entity whose semantic role is normally expressed with the subject function. In Kinyarwanda, for example, the indefinite subject counterpart to (20a) 'A child is crying' would treat the indefinite NP as complement of the existential element *hari*, with the body of the clause appearing as a relative clause (Kimenyi 1980:60):

(23)   Ha-ri úmwáana ú-rir-a
        it-be child   he-(REL)cry-ASP
        'There is a child who is crying/A child is crying'

Similar devices for the treatment of indefinite subjects are quite common (Kuno 1971).

Presentational sentences can be used to introduce an entity and comment on it with a relative-clause-like structure, as in (23), or an English sentence such as *Once there was a king who lived in a valley . . . .* Such clauses have a topic–comment structure inside them, with the introduced NP serving as the topic for a comment made by the relative clause.

2.0 Types of grammatical function

We will distinguish three fundamental types of grammatical function: core, oblique and external,[14] which may be thought of as constituting successive layers of clause structure. The first division is between the external functions and the others, which we will call internal.

External functions give the appearance of being essentially outside of the basic clause structure, and are each associated with a fairly specific pragmatic function. The *it*-cleft construction of (2) and the various topicalization constructions of (21) exhibit typical external functions. An external function never itself has an association with any specific semantic role, although the NPS bearing them often (but not always) acquire a semantic role by other means.

The internal functions have close associations with semantic roles, though they may be associated with pragmatic functions as well. Subject, object and the various prepositional phrases in (8) and (9) bear typical internal functions. Note that by saying that internal functions are associated with semantic roles we do not mean that they have them as invariant properties. Subject in English is associated with the semantic role of Agent, but many subjects are not Agents; the preposition *to* is often associated with the semantic role Recipient, but not always.

Among internal functions, A, s and o have a special status, because they almost always have a variety of properties which set them off from most of the other grammatical functions. In English for example, with the exception of personal pronouns, A, s, and o are unmarked NPS, with functions coded by order relative to the verb, while most other functions are coded by prepositional NP-marking.

In English, not only do NPS with A, s and o functions differ in appearance from prepositionally marked NPS, they also differ in various aspects of their syntactic and semantic behavior. Two important properties are that they tend to express a wider range of semantic roles, and that they tend to be 'targetted', that is, singled out for special treatment, by various rules of syntax which appear to function in terms of specific grammatical relations rather than in terms of semantic roles or clearly definable pragmatic functions. This property will be further illustrated in section 3. Rules involving PPS, on the other hand, tend to apply to a wide range of constituents, including non-PPS, with restrictions being statable in terms of semantically specifiable rather than formal categories.

In most other languages there is a similar distinction between a small class of grammatical relations expressing A, s and o (and sometimes other) functions, which behave somewhat like subject and object in English, and a larger class, which behave like English PPS. We thus divide the internal function into two categories, calling the former class of grammatical functions 'core', the latter, 'oblique'. Thus the core functions are by definition A, s, o and whatever other grammatical functions are sufficiently like them to be plausibly grouped with them and opposed to the others, which are the oblique functions.

Languages in which the core/oblique distinction corresponds to that
between bare NPS and those with a marker are not uncommon. Some
additional examples are Jacaltec (Craig 1977), Bahasa Indonesia
(Chung 1976), Dakota (Van Valin, 1985), Malagasy (Keenan 1976a)
and the Bantu languages, some of which will be discussed below.

In other languages, there does not seem to be a significant syntactic
distinction between marked and unmarked NPS. In Japanese (Kuno
1973), Russian (Comrie 1979), and Tagalog (Schachter 1977), for
example, all NPS are marked. In other languages, such as Warlpiri, some
NPS are unmarked, but the marked NPS include some which are by
definition core (A in Warlpiri). Furthermore the syntactic behavior of
the marked NPS is not significantly different from that of the unmarked
ones.

Nonetheless, something corresponding to the core/oblique distinction in English seems to exist in most such languages. One set of cases,
commonly called 'syntactic' cases, code the core functions, another,
commonly called 'semantic' cases, mark the oblique functions. NPS with
'syntactic' cases tend to express a wide range of semantic functions and
to be targetted by rules sensitive to grammatical function, while NPS with
'semantic' cases tend not to have these properties.

In general, the properties of core NPS suggest that they should be
viewed as bearing 'abstract grammatical relations': structural relationships which are not necessarily directly reflected by coding features,
and do not necessarily correlate precisely with semantic roles, pragmatic
functions, or other aspects of meaning. By contrast, the grammatical
function of obliques, such as the PPS in (8, 9), can for the most part be
identified with their semantic roles.

Most of the typological work on grammatical functions has been
directed to core functions, external and oblique functions being largely
ignored. Therefore we will provide short discussion of these two types in
the remainder of this section, and then discuss core functions and the
grammatical relations associated with them in section 3.

2.1 *External functions*

As we observed above, external functions give the appearance of being
essentially external to clause structure, and are each closely associated
with a specific pragmatic function. But the grammar of a language does
not specify any associations between external functions and semantic
roles, and, for some external functions, their bearer needn't bear any
semantic role in the sentence at all.

Suppose Jim's wife, Harriet, has left him. If some of the couple's
former friends were discussing Jim, one of them might say:

(24)   Speaking of Jim, what's Harriet been up to lately?

In English, such constructions have a fairly minor place in the system of the language, but in many languages they are the predominant form of sentence in ordinary usage. Such languages were called 'Topic Prominent' by Li and Thompson (1976), and seem to be especially characteristic of Southeast Asia.

We illustrate typical instances of such constructions with examples from Chinese, Lahu (Tibeto-Burman), and Japanese, with the Topic (which appears in initial position) italicized:

(25)   a. Chinese (Li and Thompson 1976):
      Nèi-chang huǒ xìngkui   xīaofang-duì laí   de kuài
      that-CL   fire fortunate fire-brigade come PCL quick
      'That fire, fortunately the fire-brigade came quickly'

    b. Lahu (Li and Thompson 1976):
      Hɔ   ɔ̄   na-qhɔ̀ yì   ve yò
      elephant TOP nose   long PCL DECLAR
      'Elephant, noses are long'

    c. Japanese (Kuno 1973:65)
      Nihon wa Tokyo ga   sumi-yoi
      Japan TOP Tokyo NOM easy-to-live-in
      'As for Japan, Tokyo is comfortable to live in'

These examples cannot be adequately glossed in English, since their nearest counterparts use the *as for* and *speaking of* constructions, which, as noted above, carry a switch-topic force that is absent in (25). Chafe (1976:50) characterizes the function of the Topic in these constructions as that of setting 'a spatial, temporal or individual framework within which the main predication holds'.

External functions whose bearers needn't have a semantic role in the accompanying clause will be called 'free'. Free external functions always seem to introduce topics, functioning more or less as described by Chafe. Furthermore they always place an NP at the beginning of the sentence, with (Lahu, Japanese, English) or without (Chinese) accompanying morphological material.

Other external functions require their bearer to have a semantic role in the clause (of course this is also possible for free topics). We call these 'bound'. In English the *it*-cleft, *wh*-cleft, topicalization and left- and right-dislocation constructions are bound external functions. Observe the contrast below:

(26)   a.   As for American self-confidence, Columbia gave people a lift

         b.   *American self-confidence, Columbia gave people a lift

         c.   *It was American self-confidence that Columbia gave people a lift

In all of these examples, the clause fails to assign a semantic role to the initial NP. The result is acceptable in the case of the *as for* construction, but not in the case of the others.

Bound external functions have a wider range of pragmatic effects than free ones, such as indicating focus–presupposition or presentational articulation. They are coded syntactically by means of two basic techniques.

The first is that morphological material is attached to the NP bearing the function (and perhaps elsewhere as well), but the NP is left in its normal position in the sentence structure. An interesting example of this is provided by the Dravidian language Malayalam (Mohanan 1982).

Malayalam is an SOV language with NP-marking by case marking and postpositions, and consequently fairly free word order (but, unlike Warlpiri, major constituents, such as NPs, are not broken up). There is a 'cleft' construction in which the verb is suffixed with *at* 'it', and the clefted NP is suffixed with a form of *aa* 'be'. The normal word order is the same as in a non-clefted sentence. Below we give a sentence in normal word order, with four clefted variants, the cleft NPs being italicized:

(27)   Kuṭṭi   iṇṇale   ammakkə   aanaye   koṭuṭṭu
       child(NOM) yesterday mother(DAT) elephant(ACC) gave
       'The child gave an elephant to the mother yesterday'

(28)   a. *Kuṭṭiy-aanə* iṇṇale   ammakkə   aanaye
         child(NOM)-is yesterday mother(DAT)   elephant(ACC)
         koṭuṭṭ-atə
         gave-it
         'It is the child that gave an elephant to the mother yesterday'

       b. Kuṭṭi   *iṇṇaley-aanə* ammakkə   aanaye
         child(NOM) yesterday-is   mother(DAT)   elephant(ACC)
         koṭuṭṭ-atə
         gave-it
         'It is yesterday that the child gave an elephant to the mother'

       c. Kuṭṭi   iṇṇale   *ammakk-aanə* aanaye
         child(NOM) yesterday mother(DAT)-is elephant(ACC)
         koṭuṭṭ-atə
         gave-it
         'It is the mother that the child gave an elephant to yesterday'

d. Kuṭṭi   iṇṇale   ammakkə   *aanayey-aan*
child(NOM) yesterday mother(DAT) elephant(ACC)-is
koṭuṭṭ-atə
gave-it
'It is the elephant that the child gave to the mother yesterday'

It is also possible to cleft the verb, although this does not concern us
here. The elements of all of these sentences could be freely reordered.

The second alternative is to put the external function NP at the
beginning or the end of the sentence, perhaps accompanied by additional material, and perhaps with certain changes within the sentence. The
left- and right-dislocation structures of (21b, c), repeated here for
convenience, illustrate the simplest sort of case:

(21)   b. Left-dislocation:
           Word-processors, I sometimes think they should be recycled
           into Space Invaders machines

        c. Right-dislocation:
           I can't believe they're for real, the maniacs who pay $100 a
           gram for cocaine

The external NP acquires its semantic role by virtue of being coreferential
with a pronoun in the clause structure, which is otherwise unaltered.
(26b) illustrates the necessity for such a coreferential NP to exist in the
left-dislocation construction; the reader can construct similar examples
for right dislocation.

The cleft constructions illustrate the addition of extra material to the
external NP, together with the commonest sort of deformation of the
accompanying clause, the creation of a 'gap'. In the position in
the clause where one would expect the NP bearing the semantic role
of the external NP to appear, there is nothing. Below we illustrate some
of the places where gaps can appear, representing the omitted NPS
with an underlined space:

(29)   a. It was Kristin that __ shot JR
        b. It was JR that Kristin shot __
        c. It is JR that you should deal with __ in Dallas
        d. It is JR that Cliff thinks __ paid for the revolution
        e. It was a country in Southeast Asia that JR said he had been
           financing the construction of hospitals in __

We see gaps being subject, object, object of a preposition, subject of a
subordinate clause, and object of a preposition in a subordinate clause.

There are many more possibilities, though they are far from being unconstrained. In English, the topicalization and *wh*-cleft constructions (21a, 22a) also involve a gap.

Various further deformations of the accompanying clause are possible. In Modern Icelandic, there is a topicalization construction in which an NP is put in initial position, leaving a gap, and the usual svo order is altered by putting the verb in front of the subject (Thrainsson 1979:59–65):

(30)   a. Normal word order:
Ólafur   lofaði   Maríu   þessum   hring
Olaf(NOM) promised Mary(DAT) this(DAT) ring(DAT)
'Olaf promised Mary this ring'

   b. *þessum hring* topicalized:
þessum   hring   lofaði   Ólafur   Maríu
this(DAT) ring(DAT) promised Olaf(NOM) Mary(DAT)
'This ring Olaf promised Mary'

Cleft-type constructions (those with focus–presupposition articulation) frequently involve relative-clause-like structures, and therefore have features associated with relative clauses. In Kinyarwanda, for example, verbs in relative clauses have special tones, and this is one of the ways that a cleft construction will differ from a plain construction (Kimenyi 1980:70–3):

(31)   a. Umukoôbwa y-a-haa-ye   úmwáana íkárámu
girl   she-PAST-give-ASP child   pen
'The girl gave the child the pen'

   b. N'-iíkárámu umukoôbwa y-a-haá-ye   úmwáana
be-pen   girl   she-PAST-(REL)gave-ASP child
'It is the pen that the girl gave the child'

Although the external functions have various kinds of effects on the form of the sentences they appear in, it is clear that they are essentially independent of the system of internal grammatical relations that primarily express semantic roles, and are in effect 'superposed' on it. This has led to their being called 'overlay' functions in relational grammar (Perlmutter 1980).

Sentence-level intonational and stress features, operating either alone or in conjunction with syntactic mechanisms, may also be employed to express bound external functions. In English, for example, we can impose focus–presupposition articulation simply by stressing the focus, as illustrated in (22b) above. Stress is frequently used as a focus marker.

I am not aware of its being used to mark Topics, except in contrastive constructions, such as *speaking of Mary and Jim,* **Mary** *will* **like** *this dish, but* **Jim** *will* **hate** *it.*

Although I have stated that NP with bound external functions must have semantic roles, I have said little about how they acquire them. Consideration of the examples above suggests two possibilities.

In the case of the Malayalam focusing construction of (28) and the English stress-marked focusing construction of (22b), it seems clear that the NP with focus function simultaneously bears an external and an internal function, and acquires its semantic role by virtue of the latter. On the other hand NPS with free external functions may be most plausibly treated as getting their semantic role (if they have one) not by themselves bearing an internal function but by virtue of being coreferential to another NP that does. Note that this internal NP needn't be a pronoun: *As for the king, that august personage was becoming uneasy about the activities of his eldest son.*

This leads to the appealing suggestion that NPS with bound external functions obligatorily bear an internal function, and thereby obligatorily acquire a semantic role, while NPS with free external functions do not bear an internal function, and therefore only have a semantic role if they happen to be coreferential to an NP that does bear an internal function. In cases where the external function is coded by position, such as the topicalization, dislocation and cleft constructions of (21, 22a, 29, 30), the position of the NP would be determined by its external function, the position associated with the internal function being empty or occupied by a pronominal filler.

Unfortunately, the available evidence is not consistent with this scheme. In Icelandic, for example, alongside of the topicalization construction of (30b), there is a left-dislocation construction:

(32)   Left-dislocation:
   a. þessi   hringur,   Ólafur   lofaði   Maríu
      this(NOM) ring(NOM) Olaf(NOM) promised Mary(DAT)
      honum
      it(DAT)
      'This ring, Olaf promised it to Mary'

   b. Kjarnorkuslysið,   margir menn fórust *(í því)
      the nuclear accident(NOM) many people died   in it(DAT)
      'The nuclear accident, many people died *(in it)'

Both are bound functions, but Zaenen (1980) argues in effect that topicalization involves a single NP with both an external topic function and an internal function, while left-dislocation involves one NP with a topic-like external function that is coreferential to another with an internal function.

One indication of this is the case marking: in topicalization the preposed NP appears with the case appropriate to the internal function whereby it acquires its semantic role. Thus, since the NP that is the Theme of *lofa* 'promise' is normally dative (as is the Recipient as well), the preposed NP in (30b) is dative. This suggests that the preposed NP in this construction actually bears the internal function normally borne by the Theme of *lofa*.

In left-dislocation, on the other hand, the preposed NP appears in the nominative, regardless of the case that would normally be borne by an NP with its semantic role. This case appears instead on a pronoun, which appears in a normal clause-internal position. This suggests that it is the pronoun rather than the preposed NP that bears the internal function. But left-dislocation is nonetheless a bound function like topicalization, as revealed by (32b), which is bad if a clause-internal pronoun coreferential to the preposed nominative is lacking.

For further discussion of the syntax and the pragmatic import of these and other topicalization-like constructions in Icelandic, see Thrainsson (1979) and Zaenen (1980).

Thus bound external functions may well occur in two varieties: those whose bearers have an internal function as well, and those whose bearers are obligatorily coreferential to an NP with an internal function. See Cinque (1977) for additional relevant discussion.

The position is also unsettled for free external functions. Although the *wa*-marked NP in the Japanese example (25c) is clearly bearing a free topic function, some of the examples in Kuno (1973) suggest that *wa*-marked NPs may bear internal functions. Consider (33) (Kuno 1973:55):

(33)   Boku ni   wa nihongo   ga   nigate desu
        I   DAT TOP Japanese-language NOM bad   be
        'As for me, I am not good at Japanese'

Ni (Dative) marks the Incompetent role of *nigaru* 'be bad at'. Since it appears on the *wa*-marked NP, it seems likely that this NP bears an internal function responsible for the appearance of *ni* as well as the external function marked by *wa*.

Furthermore, in many cases there is no clear indication of whether an NP with an external function bears an internal function as well or is merely coreferential with one that does. The topicalization and *it*-cleft constructions of English fall into this category. The present typology is therefore based on the observationally transparent free/bound distinction.

Ascertaining what external functions a language has is fairly straightforward: determining their use is a far more difficult matter, as indicated in the discussion of pragmatic functions in section 1.3 above. It is usually fairly easy to tell the difference between an external function and an internal one, although there are occasional difficult cases. See chapter 1.6 for further discussion of external functions.

2.2 *Oblique functions*

In this section we examine oblique grammatical functions. We will first investigate English, showing that English obliques fall into two main classes: complements and adjuncts. The distribution of complements is governed by potentially idiosyncratic specifications on verbs (or other predicators). Adjuncts on the other hand appear whenever they would be semantically appropriate. In fact, we shall see that it is reasonable to think of the complement/adjunct distinction as overlapping the core/oblique distinction, with the class of complements comprising all core NPS and some obliques. Adjuncts, on the other hand, always seem to be oblique, in that they do not seem to exhibit behavioral similarities to A, S and O.

Then we will look at obliques in Warlpiri, to illustrate something of the behavior of obliques in a case-marking language. Finally we will briefly summarize the dimensions of typological variation in systems of oblique grammatical functions.

2.2.1 *Obliques (PPS) in English*

English oblique NPS are found in prepositional phrases (PPS). English PPS are not homogeneous but seem to fall into classes which can be defined in terms of the way in which their form and distribution is or is not determined by the verb. As stated above, the two principal classes are what we shall call 'complements' and 'adjuncts'. The distribution of adjuncts is free, subject to the requirement that the sentence make sense. The Circumstantial roles of 1.1.2 are often introduced by adjuncts. Thus in English any verb which is semantically suitable may take a locative phrase, or a benefactive phrase with the preposition *for*. But distribution of complements is subject to idiosyncratic restrictions imposed by verbs. To see the nature of these restrictions, let us examine the nature of the constructions associated with verbs of giving, such as *give*, *hand*, *present*, etc., in which an Agent transfers a Theme from his own custody to that of a Recipient.

Such verbs take six patterns of association between their semantic roles and the grammatical relations that express them, illustrated below. (a) and (b) are the major patterns, (c) minor, and (d–f) extremely minor:

(34)　a. Susan handed Paul the shovel
　　　b. Susan handed the shovel to Paul
　　　c. They supply us with weapons
　　　d. Cheech laid a joint on Chong
　　　e. Geraldine foisted six kittens off on(to) Jock
　　　f. J.R. bestowed many favors (up)on Afton

(34b–f) illustrate various oblique constructions, while (34a), with two bare NPS after the verb, illustrates something we haven't discussed yet, a 'double object' construction. In 3.3.1 below we will argue that the first postverbal NP here is the direct object, while the second bears another core grammatical relation, 'second object'.

There is considerable systematicity in the relations between semantic roles and their overt expressions in (34). In the double-object and *with* constructions, Recipients are the first or sole objects. Otherwise they are the objects of goal prepositions such as *to*, *on*, *upon* and *onto* (the latter three frequently being optional alternants). Themes, on the other hand, are either second objects or objects of with.

But there is also considerable idiosyncrasy. *Hand*, and a great many other verbs, appear in patterns (a) and (b), but not the others. *Supply* appears with (c) and (b), and maybe (a) for some speakers, but not with (d–f). *Equip*, on the other hand, appears only in (c). None of the verbs taking any of (a–c) take any of (d–e), except *fob off*, which takes (c) and (d, e), with substantially different meanings: *Fred fobbed Jack off with a scratched record* vs. *Fred fobbed a scratched record off on(to) Jack* (in the first sentence, Fred is getting rid of Jack, in the second, of a record).

There are, furthermore, idiosyncratic restrictions on whether some of these obliques are optional or obligatory. The *with* phrase can be ellipsed with *supply*, but not *provide*, with the object retaining the Recipient role:

(35)　a. We supply Iran (with weapons)
　　　b. We provide Iran *(with weapons)

Similarly, *to*-objects are usually optional but with some verbs they are obligatory:

(36)　a. Susan passed the shovel (to Paul)
　　　b. Susan handed the shovel *(to Paul)

On this basis it seems appropriate to include core NPS as complements together with obliques whose distribution is subject to lexical control.

Although the choice of prepositions in the complement PPs of transfer verbs has a semantic rationale, the preposition is clearly not making an independent contribution to the meaning, since one cannot vary the choice of preposition independently to vary the meaning. But there are PPs which appear to be complements where the preposition does seem to make an independent contribution to meaning. The verb *put*, for example, takes an obligatory directional phrase in *in(to)* or *on(to)* (and most other goal PPs), while *move* takes an optional directional PP in *into* and *onto*, but not *in* or *on*:

(37)   a. Cally put the key *(*on(to)* *the table*/*in(to)* *the box*)
       b. Cally moved (the computer) (*onto*/*on the table)

The *on/in* components here indicate spatial relationships, while the possibilities for omitting or including *to* seem more arbitrary. (*On/in* is of course acceptable with *move* when the PP is an Outer Locative rather than a Directional).

These PPs seem clearly to be complements rather than adjuncts, but they resemble adjuncts in that the preposition is a partially independent bearer of meaning. It seems appropriate to think of the PP as a whole as being a complement to the verb, rather than of the NP within it as being one.

We therefore classify English PPs into adjuncts, and two types of complements. In the first kind of complement, which we will call 'P-objects', the verb determines the choice of preposition, and the NP within it functions as an argument of the verb. In the second type, which we will call 'P-complements', although the verb may constrain the choice of preposition, it does not determine it completely. Rather the preposition expresses meaning to some extent independently from the verb, and the PP as a whole functions as complement.[15]

Although in many cases it is clear whether one is dealing with a complement or an adjunct, there are also doubtful (perhaps intermediate) cases. For example, almost any verb which is semantically appropriate may take an instrumental *with*-PP, suggesting that these are adjuncts:

(38)   a. The old man walks with a stick

       b. I write papers with a word-processor

       c. Jimmy poked Owen with a stick

But Matthews (1981:18) notes that the verb *go* does not take instrumental *with*: *He went with a stick* means merely that he went carrying a stick with him, not that he used it to go. It is not clear whether this restriction can be made to follow from the meanings of *go* and instrumental *with*. Therefore it is unclear whether instrumentals should be regarded as complements or adjuncts.

Drawing the complement/adjunct distinction may require considerable knowledge of a language and deep insight into its semantics. The core/oblique distinction, on the other hand, is usually relatively obvious. For this reason the latter rather than the former distinction is emphasized in this study.

Oblique grammatical functions are typically more tightly tied to specific semantic roles than are the core grammatical relations. In the case of the adjuncts and P-complements, the NP-marker of the oblique grammatical function specifies the semantic role to a considerable degree independently of the verb, while the P-object markers are also more tightly tied to given semantic roles than are subject or object. Objects, for example, can be Themes or Recipients, while *with*-objects can be Themes but not Recipients; *to*-objects Recipients but not Themes.

2.2.2 Obliques in Warlpiri

Warlpiri cases (NP-markers) can be divided into two main groups: the 'syntactic' cases (ergative, dative and absolutive) and the 'semantic' cases (all the rest). The latter can be further divided into three subgroups: local semantic, non-local semantic, and 'derivational semantic'. The syntactic cases code core functions, which will be reviewed for Warlpiri in section 3. The local and non-local semantic cases express oblique functions, with the local semantic cases expressing primarily spatial notions, the non-local cases non-spatial ones (the local cases do have some non-spatial uses). The 'derivational' cases seem for the most part to form modifiers of NPs rather than complements to the verb, and are therefore largely beyond the scope of this chapter.

Table 2.1 presents some of the most important cases. The listing for the non-local semantic cases is incomplete, since the boundary of this category is unclear.

Table 2.1 *Warlpiri cases*

Local semantic		Non-local semantic		Syntactic	
Locative (at):	-rla/ngka	Instrumental:	-rlu/ngku	Ergative:	-rlu/ngku
Allative (to):	-kurra	Causal:	-jangk	Dative:	-ku
Elative (from):	-ngurlu	Considerative:	-wana wana	Absolutive:	-ø
Perlative (along):	-wana				
Comitative (with):	-rlajinta				

The form of some of these endings is affected by a vowel harmony rule converting *u* to *i* after stems in *i*, so that we get *maliki-ki* 'dog-DAT', *wati-ngki* 'man-ERG', and *yuwarli-ngirli* 'from the house'.

The local semantic cases primarily indicate the spatial notions of location at (or on, or in), motion to, motion from and motion along, and motion or position together with:

(39) a. Lungkarda   ka   ngulya-ngka nguna-mi
          bluetongue(ABS) PRES burrow-LOC lie-NONPAST
          'The bluetongue skink is lying in the burrow'

      b. Nantuwu   ka   karru-kurra parnka-mi
          horse(ABS) PRES creek-ALL   run-NONPAST
          'The horse is running to the creek'

      c. Karli   ka   pirli-ngirli   wanti-mi
          boomerang(ABS) PRES stone-ELATIVE fall-NONPAST
          'The boomerang is falling from the stone'

      d. Pirli   ka-lu-jana   yurutu-wana   yirra-rni
          stone(ABS) PRES-they-them road-PERLATIVE put-NONPAST
          'They are putting stones along the road'

      e. Maliki   ka   nantuwu-rlajinta parnka-mi
          dog(ABS) PRES horse-COMITATIVE run-NONPAST
          'The dog is running along with the horse'

Hale (1982) provides a detailed account of the semantics of these cases.

The Warlpiri case system makes fewer distinctions than the systems of prepositions of English, but similar effects are achieved by other means. There are, for example, adverbial particles which, although not syntactically bound to a local case-marked NP, nonetheless refine the locative concept expressed. *Kulkurru*, for example, specifies *between*-ness:

(40) Maliki   ka   nguna-mi   yuwarli-jarra-rla kulkurru-jarra
      dog(ABS) PRES lie-NONPAST house-DU-LOC   between-DU
      'The dog is lying between the two houses'

Without *kulkurrujarra*, the sentence could be interpreted as meaning merely that the dog was near the houses.

Occasionally the local cases are used idiomatically, in ways not fully explicable in terms of their basic meanings. For example the verb *manyu-karri-mi* 'play-stand-NONPAST', meaning 'to play a game', takes the locative case on the game played. This may co-occur with a locative designating the place where the event takes place:

(41)   Ngarrka-patu ka-lu   kardi-ngka
        man-PL(ABS) PRES-they card-LOC
        manyu-karri-mi   karru-ngka
        play-stand-NONPAST creek-LOC
        'The men are playing cards in the creek'

These usages are reminiscent of idiomatic P-objects in English.

The non-local semantic cases are for the most part minor in the structure of the language. The 'true' instrumental expresses the instrument used by an Agent to act on a Patient. It *only* appears with transitive verbs taking an ergative Agent and absolutive Patient, not with intransitives (or with a category we shall discuss below of two-argument verbs not taking an ergative). See examples (42a) and (42b). There is another method for expressing the instrumental relation, and this one may be used with either transitives or intransitives. It involves one of the 'derivational semantic' cases, the proprietive -*kurlu* 'with'. Used in apposition to a nominal, it means that that nominal is in possession of the entity denoted by the nominal to which -*kurlu* is attached, like *with* in 'the man with an axe'. But like *with*, the meaning of -*kurlu* can be extended to indicate not only possession but use. See examples (42c) and (42d):

(42)   a.   Wawirri   kapi-rna kurlarda-rlu panti-rni
              kangaroo(ABS) FUT-I   spear-INSTR spear-NONPAST
              ngajulu-rlu
              I-ERG
              'I will spear the kangaroo with a spear'

        b.   *Purlka   ka   watiya-rlu warru-wapa-mi
              old man(ABS) PRES stick-INSTR around-walk-NONPAST

        c.   Ngarrka-ngku ka   warlu   paka-rni
              man-ERG   PRES firewood chop-NONPAST
              warlkurru-kurlu-rlu
              axe-with-ERG
              'The man is chopping firewood with an axe'

        d.   Purlka   ka   watiya-kurlu warru-wapa-mi
              old man(ABS) PRES stick-with   around-walk-NONPAST
              'The old man is walking around with a stick'

(42c) could be interpreted with only the sense of possession for -*kurlu*, not use, to give 'The man with an axe is chopping firewood' (with some other instrument) and so also (42d), 'The old man with a stick is walking around'. The instrumental sense is nevertheless the usual one in sentences such as these expressing an action where the use of the object in question is a pragmatic likelihood.

The ending listed as causal is also widely used as elative, and preferred as such by some speakers. But it also indicates the cause for the situation designated by the sentence, or a potentially causal prior event:

(43)   Ngarrka-patu ka-lu   warrki-jangka mata nguna-mi-lki
         man-PL(ABS) PRES-they work-CAUSAL tired lie-NQNPAST-now
         'The men are lying down tired now after work'

It can also indicate the material out of which something is made: for example from wood in 'they are making boomerangs from wood'. The 'considerative' (CONS) is applied to an NP denoting something that is given in exchange for something else:

(44)   Japanangka-rlu ka-ju   karli   yi-nyi
         Japanangka-ERG PRES-me boomerang(ABS) give-NONPAST
         miyi-wanawana
         food-CONS
         'Japanangka is giving me a boomerang in exchange for food'

This illustrates nicely that a serious account of semantic roles must go considerably beyond the simple Agent, Patient, Source, Goal, etc., categories that were introduced in 1.1. above.

The uses of the cases we have considered so far mostly involve qualifications of some facet of the action of the verb: the path taken by some participant (and thereby, in some sense, of the 'action'), or additional participant. They thus express participatory semantic roles (c.f. 1.1.2), and function analogously to the oblique complements (P-objects and P-complements) of English. The exception is the causal use of -*jangka*, which provides the background for the event, and is thus a circumstantial adjunct.

The principal circumstantial case is the locative, which can place an event in space (already illustrated in (41)) or in time:

(45)   Ngapa   ka   wanti-mi   wajirrkinyi-rla
         water(ABS) PRES fall-NONPAST greentime-LOC
         'Rain falls in the "green" season'

These uses of the locative correspond to adjuncts in English.

A striking difference between the obliques in Warlpiri and English is in the way in which the complement/adjunct distinction is drawn. Aside from the occasional idiomatic uses, as with *kardi-ngka* 'card-LOC = with cards' in (41), a Warlpiri semantic case always seems to be usable wherever its meaning would make sense. Idiosyncratic restrictions such as those discussed for English in 2.2.1 are quite rare. Most usages of Warlpiri oblique cases thus behave like adjuncts in English. The idiomatic usages might be taken to be P-objects, so there would be a few representatives of this category, but there seems to be nothing whose grammatical behavior corresponds to that of P-complements. It may be that this impression is a consequence of our insufficient knowledge of Warlpiri, and that more study might reveal the familiar categories, but at the moment it seems that in Warlpiri the complement–adjunct distinction is much more closely aligned with the core–oblique distinction than it is in English.

The semantic cases in Warlpiri have one final property which distinguishes them strongly from the syntactic cases. Warlpiri nominals are frequently 'doubly case marked', with first a semantic case marker, and then a syntactic one. For example, with the verb *wajilipi-nyi* 'to chase', an allative may appear either without further case marking, or followed by the ergative marker. In the former the allative NP (ALL) specifies the position of the chasee, but not necessarily that of the chaser. In the latter, it indicates the final position of both chaser and chasee (cf. Granites 1976):

(46)   a. Kurdu-ngku ka   maliki   ngurra-kurra wajilipi-nyi
           child-ERG   PRES dog(ABS) camp-ALL   chase-NONPAST
           'The child is chasing the dog to the camp'
           (Dog, but not necessarily child, arrives at camp)

        b. Kurdu-ngku ka   maliki   ngurra-kurra-rlu wajilipi-nyi
           child-ERG   PRES dog(ABS) camp-ALL-ERG   chase-NONPAST
           'The child is chasing the dog to the camp'
           (Both child and dog arrive at camp)

There are quite a variety of other circumstances under which the semantic case markers can be followed by another case marker.[16] Generally the doubly case-marked NP serves in some way as a modifier of another NP, with its first case marker indicating the semantic relation by virtue of which the modification relation exists (in (46) the allative marker indicates that the modifier NP represents the destination of the modified NP), with the second case marker being an agreement marker, manifesting the case of the modified NP. Double case marking never happens with the ergative or dative first, strongly suggesting that there is an essential difference between the two types of cases.

2.3 *Typological variation*

The principal dimensions of typological variation in systems of oblique grammatical functions appear to be the extent of lexically governed idiosyncrasies in their distribution (substantial in English, apparently much less so in Warlpiri), and in the variety of notions expressed by the markers in the systems.

The former topic will be largely beyond the scope of field work, except in languages where such idiosyncrasies are highly pervasive. The latter is however highly relevant to the field worker. A brief review of the notions commonly expressed in case-marking systems is given in chapter III:3.

A particularly interesting tendency in this domain is for certain groups of notions but not others to be expressed by the same marker in many different languages. Thus sometimes one finds the same NP-marker coding the Locative, Goal and Source roles (*sa* in Tagalog; see 3.5 below), sometimes one finds Locative and Goal expressed by the same marker, with a different one for Source (Yidiɲ; see Dixon 1977a) and sometimes, as in Warlpiri, different markers are used for all three roles. But one doesn't seem to find one marker used for Locative and Source, with a second for Goal; or one for Source and Goal, with a different for Locative. Tendencies such as these, found world-wide, are surveyed for Australian languages in Blake (1977). They are obviously of considerable relevance to the question of how people conceive of events and classify the roles of their participants.

3.0 Core grammatical functions

In this section we examine core grammatical functions in detail. As discussed at the beginning of section 2, core grammatical functions are those expressing A, S and O; and any others that behave like these rather than like obliques. The essential property of core functions appears to be that they are associated with grammatical relations: structural relationships, possibly structural primitives, which are significant for the functioning of grammatical principles, but are often abstract with respect to coding features, semantic and pragmatic properties, or both.

We begin in section 3.1 by reconsidering the A, S and O functions and their role in providing definitions for core grammatical relations. We will discuss the reasons for defining A and O in terms of the Agent and Patient of a PTV, some of the issues that arise in identifying A, S and O in languages, and the nature of the relationship between these grammatical functions and grammatical relations such as subject and object. In the remaining subsections we will discuss various grammatical relations, their properties, and methods for identifying them.

In 3.2 we will examine 'subject', the most widely discussed and studied grammatical relation. We will illustrate typical evidence for postulating an abstract grammatical relation such as 'subject', and present some of the properties of subjects that are frequently useful in identifying them. In 3.3 we will discuss some of the other grammatical relations that appear in languages that do have subjects, such as object, indirect object, and others. In 3.4 we discuss 'syntactically ergative' languages, in which there does not appear to be a standard subject grammatical relation, but instead one grammatical relation for o and s functions, and another for A. In 3.5 we discuss languages in which the evidence bearing on grammatical relations suggests the existence of two 'superposed' systems of grammatical relations. Finally, in 3.6, we will discuss the phenomenon of 'split s' marking, in which there are two normal morphosyntactic treatments for the single argument of an intransitive verb. We shall see that in most such cases there appears to be one subject grammatical relation, in spite of the differences in morphosyntactic treatment.

3.1 A, s *and* O

The notions of A, s and o are fundamental to our typology of interior functions because they are the prototype core functions, and are the basis of the definitions of subject and object. A and o are in turn specified in terms of the notion of Primary Transitive Verb (PTV) defined in 1.1.1: an A is an NP in a transitive sentence receiving the treatment normally accorded to the Agent of PTVs; an o is an NP in a transitive sentence receiving the treatment normally accorded to the Patient of a PTV.

The category of PTVs thus occupies the central position in our typology, and, implicitly at least, in most others. What singles them out for special attention is that in all languages, PTVs are the semantic category of verbs which receives the most uniform grammatical treatment, and which is most widely used as a grammatical model for verbs of other semantic categories.

Thus in English, the Agent of a PTV will normally be expressed as a preverbal NP eliciting number agreement and being nominative if it is a pronoun; the Patient of a PTV as a postverbal NP not eliciting number agreement and being accusative if it is a pronoun (the complicating factor of passive sentences will be discussed below). By contrast, other broad semantic classes are considerably less uniform in their treatment. We have already seen the various treatments accorded to verbs of giving in English; for another example, observe that verbs of emotion may be divided into two classes, one with the Experiencer as subject and the Object of Emotion as object; the other with the Object of Emotion as subject and the Experiencer as object:

(47)   a. Mary likes/detests/enjoys Bill
         b. Bill pleases/amuses/disgusts Mary

In most such cases, we can usually find a semantic basis for the split in grammatical treatment, but the relevant semantic parameters are often very subtle,[17] and tend to vary from language to language.

Although the treatment of PTVs does tend to be uniform in a given language, it is not in general the case that there is only one grammatical treatment available for their Agent and Patient arguments: there are usually a number of options.

In English, for example, PTVs can appear in active sentences, with the Agent a preverbal bare NP and the Patient a postverbal bare NP, or in passive sentences, with the Patient a preverbal bare NP and the Agent a postverbal NP marked by the preposition *by* (the verb forms are also affected). The Agent is furthermore obligatory in the active, but optional in the passive:

(48)   a. The guard killed the prisoner
         b. The prisoner was killed (by the guard)

These shifts in position are associated with other changes. If the Agent is a pronoun, it will be nominative in (48a) and accusative in (48b) (*he killed the prisoner, the prisoner was killed by him*), and vice versa if the Patient is a pronoun (*the guard killed him, he was killed by the guard*). A present tense verb form will agree with the subject in (48a) but with the object in (48b) (*the guard is/*are killing the prisoners, the prisoners are/*is being killed by the guard*). English thus provides two quite different morphosyntactic treatments for the Agent and Patient of a PTV.

But passive sentences appear not to present the *normal* treatment of Agent and Patient for PTVs. Passives are considerably rarer than actives in normal language use. Givón (1979a:58) finds passives to comprise between 4% and 18% of sentences (the less educated the register, the rarer are passives). He furthermore finds the overwhelming majority (70–90%) of passives to have the Agent omitted. Passives with both Agent and Patient expressed are thus quite rare. Furthermore, passives are typically used only when called for by some specific exigency of communication (for discussion of the functions of passives, see chapter 1.6 and Givón 1979a). Therefore in English we may say that an A is a

preverbal NP which elicits agreement in the present and is nominative if
it is a pronoun, while an o is a postverbal NP not eliciting agreement,
which is accusative if it is a pronoun. The treatment of Agents and
Patients in passive sentences may be disregarded in characterizing A and
o in English.

Furthermore, and crucially for our claim that the class of PTVs receives
a uniform grammatical treatment, both active and passive forms are
options for all PTVs. The active is the primary option, the passive the
secondary. One could in fact build passives into the definition of A and
o, by stipulating that verbs with A and o functions should have passive
counterparts, though it is not clear that there would be any point in
doing this.

But we can't always disregard one set of alternative treatments of A, s
or o on the basis that they are secondary rather than primary. In Hindi,
for example, Agents of PTVs are in the nominative (unmarked) case with
non-perfective verbs, but bear the (postpositional) instrumental case-
marker *ne* with past/perfective verbs. Furthermore, Patients of PTVs may
appear in the nominative or with the dative marker *ko*, the dative being
typically used with animate (especially definite) Patients, but not with
Patients which are inanimate/indefinite.[18]

(49)   a. Jamīl   laṛkī ko jagāegā
           Jamil(NOM) girl DAT will-wake-up
           'Jamil will wake up the girl'

        b. Jamīl ne   laṛkī ko jagāyā
           Jamil INSTR girl DAT woke-up
           'Jamil woke the girl up'

        c. Jamīl   khānā   khaū:nga:
           Jamil(NOM) food(NOM) will-eat-up
           'Jamil will eat up the food'

        d. Jamīl ne   khānā   khāyā
           Jamil INSTR food(NOM) ate-up
           'Jamil ate up the food'

Aside from the NP-marking, agreement is also affected: a PTV will agree
(in gender and number) with the Agent if this is nominative. If it isn't,
but the Patient is, the verb will agree with the Patient. If neither the
Agent nor the Patient is nominative, the verb will agree with nothing.
See Kachru, Kachru and Bhatia (1976) for discussion.

It would be quite arbitrary to choose one or another of the two
treatments of the Agent as primary (note that as required by the
semantic uniformity of the class of PTVs, all PTVs take both treatments of

A and both of o, each under the appropriate circumstances). Even if one of them turned out to be commoner in actual usage, we would still simply have two normal treatments for the Agent, the choice depending on tense/aspect. Similarly for the Patient, except that the choice between the two treatments is governed by definiteness and animacy instead of tense/aspect.

In such cases we will say that both treatments of the Agent are A, and both treatments of the Patient are o. In the case of Hindi, it seems reasonably clear that both nominative and instrumental A bear the same grammatical relation, subject (Kachru, Kachru and Bhatia 1976; Pandaripande and Kachru 1976). We cannot make such an argument for nominative and dative o, since there do not seem to be grammatical phenomena which require treating these two forms as having a single grammatical relation. But neither are there any which argue against it, so we may provisionally treat both *ko*-marked and unmarked o as bearing the same grammatical relation, object.

In general, it always seems to be possible to postulate one grammatical relation associated with A function, and it is usually possible to find one other that is associated with o, although frequently, as in Hindi, the facts are merely consistent with there being a single grammatical relation associated with o function, rather than strongly motivating this. There are however some possible instances, such as Mandarin Chinese, of languages with two grammatical relations with o function (3.3.1).

Although A typically bears one grammatical relation, o another, it is not the case that everything that bears these grammatical relations is A or o, respectively. In Hindi, for example, certain predicates appear to take their subjects in the dative case:

(50)   a. Lərke ko əpne dost   yad   ae
          boy   DAT self's friends(NOM) memory came
          'The boy remembered his friends'

       b. Maryam ko əpna   bhai   milā
          Maryam DAT her own brother(NOM) met
          'Maryam met her own brother'

The predicates in these examples also take a second argument in the nominative case, which the verb agrees with (*yad* 'memory' in (50a) is not an argument, but part of a compound predicate with *ae* 'came').

There is a reasonable amount of evidence that the datives here are subjects (Kachru, Kachru and Bhatia 1976; Tunbridge 1980), in spite of their case.[19] Given this, it is probably best to treat the nominatives as the objects, though there is little positive evidence for this.[20]

Nonetheless, we will not consider the dative subjects in (50) to be A, nor the nominative NPS to be o, though these latter may well be objects. We want A, S and O to be categories that are observationally fairly immediate, rather than being dependent on the sometimes rather sophisticated syntactic argumentation that is required to establish grammatical relations when these are not reflected in a simple way by coding features.

That the NPS in (50) are not A and o follows from our definitions, since the fact that the subjects in (50) are dative and the objects obligatorily nominative (*ko* is impossible with them, even though they are animate and definite) means that they are *not* receiving the morphosyntactic treatment normally accorded to the Agent and the Patient of a PTV, in spite of having the grammatical relations that these normally do.

As with Agents and Patients of PTVs, there are frequently multiple realizations for the single arguments of one-argument verbs; s functions would comprise those realizations which it is appropriate to regard as normal, or 'basic'. But there is a difference in that the class of one-argument predicates is not homogeneous in the way that PTVs are.

In Modern Icelandic, for example, the normal treatment for the single argument of a one-argument verb is to appear as a preverbal nominative NP eliciting verb agreement (in person and number):

(51)   a. við   dönsuðum
           we(NOM MASC PL) danced(1PL)

       b. þeir   dóu
           they(NOM MASC PL) died(3PL)

But some one-argument verbs take their single arguments as genitive, dative or accusative NPS (the case determined more or less idiosyncratically by the verb) whose basic position appears to be the preverbal position that is also basic for uncontroversial nominative subjects, and whose syntactic behavior is like that of subjects in most respects, with the exception that it doesn't trigger verb agreement:[21]

(52)   a. þá   vantar   peninga
           them(ACC MASC PL) lacks(3SG) money(ACC)
           'They lack money'

       b. mér   líkar   vel við henni
           me(DAT) likes(3SG) well with her(DAT)
           'I like her'

In this case, the oblique subject constructions are quite clearly in the minority, so that we can identify s function as a nominative subject in an intransitive sentence. But the class of one-argument predicates is not homogeneous in that there is not a uniform set of possible treatments for the single argument of all its members.

There are other instances of non-uniformity in which there are two morphosyntactic treatments of the single argument of a one-argument predicate which are sufficiently common that neither can be convincingly established as s. These are the so-called 'split s' systems first reviewed in Dixon (1979). Usually, the two treatments are roughly apportioned along lines of agentivity. One example of this is provided by Eastern Pomo (McClendon 1978).

In this language, there is one set of nominal forms (which I gloss 'A') for agentive arguments, of transitive or intransitive verbs, and another for Patient-like arguments (glossed 'o'), whether of transitive or intransitive verbs (McClendon 1978:3,7):

(53)   a. mí·p̓ káluhuya
          he(A) went-home
          'He went home'

        b. mí·pal xá·   ba·kú·ma
          he(o) in-the-water fell
          'He fell in the water (accidentally)'

        c. mí·p̓ mí·pal šá·ḵa
          he(A) him(o) killed
          'He killed him'

McClendon describes various other differences between Agent and Undergoer s whereby the former group with A, the latter with o.

We therefore clearly have two morphosyntactic treatments, though it is not clear whether we have two grammatical relations (see the discussion in 3.6 below). In this kind of case we will say that both treatments represent s function, with s_A and s_O subtypes.

A, s, and o functions, thus established, are taken as the basis for the identification of core grammatical relations: subject is the grammatical relation, if there is one, that is associated with A and s function; object the grammatical relation, if there is one, that is associated with o function. In cases where it is not clear that these definitions are satisfied by any grammatical relation, there tends to be controversy about what grammatical relations are present. We will discuss the treatment of a number of such cases below. The core functions in a language, if there are any, are those that are sufficiently similar to A, s and o to merit being grouped with them and opposed to the obliques.

The motivation for establishing these or other definitions with similar effects is that the grammatical relations that they pick out tend to have similar properties cross-linguistically. For example, subjects have a greater tendency to be cross-referenced than do NPS with other grammatical relations, and are more likely to be suppressed in complex sentence constructions. Objects, on the other hand, as illustrated above for Hindi, tend to have case markers which mark humanness, animacy, specificity and related concepts as well as objecthood *per se*.[22] While the reasons for uniformities such as these are far from clear, they make it possible and desirable to establish cross-linguistic terminology for grammatical relations.

On the basis of these preliminaries, we will now examine core grammatical relations in greater detail.

3.2 *Subjects*
Here we consider subjects: their properties and the means whereby they may be identified. In many languages, such as English, a subject grammatical relation may immediately be recognized on the basis of the coding features in ordinary main clauses. In other languages, coding features do not provide a clear indication of which NPS are subjects, or even whether subjects exist at all. It is then necessary to consider more subtle aspects of grammatical structure.

At the outset we must note that there are no properties which in all languages are always exhibited by subjects and only exhibited by them. There may be some properties that are universally restricted to subjects,[23] but there are certainly none that they always have. Rather, we find properties that are exhibited by subjects in a wide range of languages, and which may be plausibly argued to be restricted to subjects in some of them.

Here we will for the most part confine our attention to properties which subjects frequently have and which frequently distinguish them from NPS with other grammatical relations. These properties are thus the ones that are commonly useful diagnostics for subjecthood. In the first subsection we will briefly consider the coding features of subjects in ordinary main clauses; in the subsequent subsections we will consider some of their other grammatical properties.

3.2.1 *Subjects and coding features in ordinary main clauses*
In a great many languages, the coding features of ordinary main clauses clearly mark a subject grammatical relation. In English, subjects of ordinary main clauses are primarily marked by the coding feature of preverbal position. They are also indicated to a limited extent by case marking and cross-referencing. In Ancient Greek, subjects of ordinary

main clauses occupy no definite position, but are for the most part clearly marked by nominative case,[24] which always and only appears on the subjects of finite clauses. Furthermore, verbs agree with their subjects in person and number via a more extensive system than operates in English. A great many other languages are similar in representing grammatical relations fairly consistently by coding features.

But coding features frequently fail to give a clear indication of grammatical relations, or give inconsistent indications. In Hindi, for example, A may be nominative or instrumental, o nominative or dative as seen in (49). ss on the other hand are nominative. So, in terms of NP-marking, sometimes s looks like A, sometimes like o, and sometimes like neither. Cross-referencing does not clarify matters: the verb agrees with nominative s; and with A if it is nominative, otherwise with o if it is nominative, otherwise with neither. Furthermore, since the verb follows A and o rather than coming between them, word order gives no indication of whether s is to be given the same grammatical relation as A or as o.

In Hindi the vagaries of A-marking are conditioned by tense/aspect; those of o-marking by animacy/specificity. Both of these phenomena are extremely common. Another form of inconsistency in coding of grammatical relations and functions are the so-called 'split ergative' systems found in many Australian languages. In these systems some nominals (including singular common nominals) behave as in Warlpiri, having a marked 'ergative' form expressing A function opposed to an unmarked 'absolutive' expressing o/s function. Others, usually including first and second person pronouns, have a nominative expressing A/s function and an accusative expressing o function. Frequently there is also a third group (often including non-singulars, personal names, third person pronouns, etc.) having distinct ergative, absolutive and accusative forms for all three of A, s and o (for such nominals the accusative is furthermore sometimes optional). Systems of this kind from the Australian languages Diyari and Yidiɲ will be exemplified in 3.2.4 and 3.4 below. See also chapter III.3, Comrie (1978), Dixon (1979), Silverstein (1976).

It is also possible for different coding features to give different indications of grammatical relations. This happens in Warlpiri. We have already seen in 1.2.2 that Warlpiri NP-marking assigns ergative case to NPs with A function, and absolutive to NPs with o or s function. Case marking thus does not reflect a subject grammatical relation. But the cross-referencing system does.

The NPs that are cross-referenced are those with the cases labeled as 'syntactic' in 2.2.2: ergative, absolutive and dative. Cross-referencing of absolutive and ergative NPS has already been illustrated in example (16) in 1.2.3, repeated below for convenience. (54) illustrates cross-referencing of a dative; (55) illustrates the failure of cross-referencing to apply with a semantic case, the allative:

(16)   Nya-nyi   ka-rna-palangu   wawirri-jarra
        see-NONPAST PRES-1SG(SUBJ)-3DU(OBJ) kangaroo-DU(ABS)

        ngajulu-rlu
        I-ERG
        'I see two kangaroos'

(54)   Ngaju ka-rna-ngku nyuntu-ku wangka-mi
        I(ABS) PRES-I-you you-DAT   talk-NONPAST
        'I am talking to you'

(55)   Ngaju ka-rna nyuntu-kurra parnka-mi
        I(ABS) PRES-I you-ALL   run-NONPAST
        'I am running toward you'

The form of the markers is not determined directly by the case of the NP being cross-referenced. Rather, it seems to be determined primarily by a subject–object distinction in grammatical relations quite similar to that found in English.

There are two sets of cross-reference markers, one for subjects, and another for objects. The cross-referencing is for number (singular, dual, plural) and person (first, second and third, with an inclusive–exclusive distinction in the first person dual and plural; see chapter III.3, for discussion of these inflectional categories), with a limited case-distinction in the object markers. The subject set is used to cross-reference NPS with A or S function, whether their case is ergative or absolutive:

(56)   a. Ngaju ka-rna purla-mi
           I(ABS) PRES-I shout-NONPAST
           'I am shouting'

        b. Nyuntu   ka-npa   purla-mi
           you(SG ABS) PRES-you shout-NONPAST
           'You are shouting'

        c. Ngajulu-rlu ka-rna yankirri   wajilipi-nyi
           I-ERG   PRES-I emu(ABS) chase-NONPAST
           'I am chasing an emu'

The object suffixes cross-reference NPS with O function, which are absolutive, and also NPS in the dative case. Examples of absolutive object cross-referencing are:

(57) a. Ngarrka-ngku ka-ju   ngaju   pantu-rnu
      man-ERG   PRES-me me(ABS) spear-NONPAST
      'The man is spearing me'

    b. Ngaju   ka-npa-ju   nyuntulu-rlu nya-nyi
      me(ABS) PRES-you-me you-ERG   see-NONPAST
      'You see me'

    c. Ngajulu-rlu ka-rna-ngku nyuntu   nya-nyi
      I-ERG   PRES-I-you   you(SG ABS) see-NONPAST
      'I see you'

Dative objects are cross-referenced by the same markers as are used for absolutives, except in the third person singular, where -*rla* is used instead of zero. Dative objects will be discussed in 3.3.2.

There are various additional principles which determine the form of cross-referencing in examples more complex than these (those involving plurals, for example). They are developed in great detail in Hale (1973), and needn't be considered here. But these complications do not alter the basic point that the systems of NP-marking and cross-referencing give conflicting testimony as to what the basic grammatical relations of A, S and O are.

Further evidence from Warlpiri, to be reviewed in 3.2.2 and 3.2.3 below, indicates that A and S should be grouped together and opposed to O, so that it is the cross-referencing pattern presented here rather than case marking which is the valid indicator of the grammatical relations in Warlpiri.

A final sort of discrepancy between coding features and grammatical relations arises in certain languages in which the coding features are for the most part indicative of the grammatical relations, but where there are certain instances in which they fail. In Modern Icelandic, for example, S and A clearly bear a subject grammatical relation coded by preverbal position, nominative case, and verb agreement, but there are certain verbs (illustrated in (52)) which appear to take oblique subjects, which don't trigger agreement. These have the positional properties of subjects,[25] but neither of the other two coding features.

In fact, some verbs appear to take not only non-nominative subjects, but also what are perhaps nominative objects, which elicit optional verb agreement:

(58)   Mér   líka/líkar þeir
      me(DAT) like(PL/SG) them(MASC NOM PL)
      'I like them'

In such examples there is substantial evidence that it is the preverbal dative rather than the postverbal nominative that is the subject (see the references in note 21). Given this, it seems most straightforward to treat the postverbal NP as an object, in spite of its case-marking and cross-referencing properties.

Coding features thus do not always provide a reliable guide to grammatical relations. Positional properties are probably the most reliable, followed by cross-referencing, with NP-marking being generally the least reliable. Furthermore, when the coding features consistently indicate the presence of a subject grammatical relation, further grammatical properties always seem to confirm its existence (or at least do not contradict it). That is, when word order, NP-marking and cross-referencing (whichever of these are present in a language) are mutually consistent in treating A and S alike as opposed to O, we don't find various other principles of sentence structure treating O and S alike as opposed to A.[26] But even in such languages, the coding properties may only be usual rather than invariant properties of subjects, with some subjects lacking them, and some non-subjects exhibiting them.

3.2.2 *Subject ellipsis*
Perhaps the commonest property of subjects that is useful for identifying them is their tendency to be optionally or obligatorily ellipsed in various kinds of grammatical constructions, especially multi-clause sentence structures. A highly typical example from English is provided by adverbial clauses introduced by the conjunction *while*.

These clauses take two forms. In one, *while* is followed by an ordinary clause structure with a subject and a tensed verb. In the other, the subject is omitted and the verb put in the (gerund) *-ing* form, which does not show agreement:

(59)   a. The student watched the guard while he killed the prisoner

   b. The student watched the guard while killing the prisoner

When the verb is tensed, the subject must be included; when it is in the *-ing* (gerund) form it must be omitted:

(60)   a. *The student watched the guard while killed the prisoner

   b. *The student watched the guard while he/his/him killing the prisoner

Omission of a non-subject NP will not satisfy the requirement, as the reader can easily verify for himself. The subject relation thus functions in the principles governing the form of *while*-constructions.

It is also involved in a principle governing their interpretation. In

(59a) we could understand the *while*-clause subject as referring to the guard, the student, or some third person. In the absence of wider context, we tend to interpret it as referring to some NP within the sentence, and from our knowledge of the world we tend to assume that it refers to the guard rather than to the student.

But the interpretation of (59b) is not so free. Here we would normally understand the student rather than the guard to be killing the prisoner, in spite of the oddity of this situation. There seems to be a principle to the effect that a *while* + gerund construction is interpreted as if it had a subject coreferential to the subject of the matrix clause.[27]

On the basis of (59, 60) alone one might venture an alternative account, in which it is the Agent rather than the subject of the *while* + gerund that is suppressed, and that it is understood as being the same as the Agent rather than the subject of the main clause. On this kind of account, we would have a direct connection between overt form and semiotic categories, without an intervening level of grammatical relations.

This possibility may be discounted on the basis of sentences such as *John felt apprehensive while falling to his death*, in which the overt and 'understood' subjects are not Agents, and even more strongly by examples in which the *while* + gerund construction is combined with the passive construction:

(61)   a. The student watched the guard while killing the prisoner

       b. The student watched the guard while being killed by the prisoner

       c. The student was watched by the guard while killing the prisoner

       d. The student was watched by the guard while being killed by the prisoner

It is the subject of the matrix that is understood as the subject of the gerund, regardless of the semantic roles involved.

It also seems that no well-defined pragmatic notion such as topicality is the conditioning factor, although this is hard to show conclusively, since pragmatic functions are generally more elusive and less well understood. For example, in a sentence such as *A guard tortured the prisoner while watching television* it seems pretty clear that *the prisoner* can be the Topic. Nonetheless, the principles for the interpretation of the *while* + gerund construction continue to operate as before.

Phenomena such as these illustrate the need for a level of syntactic structure at which abstract grammatical relations such as subject are defined, which are distinct from semiotic concepts, and which are significant for the functioning of grammatical rules.

From a theoretical point of view, there are three major possibilities for the analysis of *while* + gerund constructions. The first is that the gerund has no subject in syntactic structure, but that the principles of semantic interpretation treat it as if it had a subject coreferential with that of the matrix (main) clause. Second, the gerund might have a subject in the syntactic structure which is coreferential with the matrix subject, but does not appear in the overt form of the sentence. The third possibility is that the theory of sentence structure characterizes the NP in matrix subject position as the subject of both the main clause and the gerund.

The choice between these possibilities is a complicated question, which does not concern us here. What matters here is that whatever approach is taken, it is clear that the notion of subject plays a central and obvious role in the description of the constructions: it is the subject of the subordinate clause that is obligatorily omitted, and the subject of the matrix that obligatorily serves as its 'controller', that is, as the NP that is understood as the subject of the subordinate clause.

Constructions of this sort are quite widespread across languages, including many in which coding features do not reflect grammatical relations in a straightforward way. Malayalam (Mohanan 1982) uses the *-konta* construction, an equivalent to the *while* + gerund construction, to show that certain datives, equivalent to the Hindi dative subjects of (50), behave like non-controversial nominative subjects in controlling and undergoing obligatorily ellipsis, and should therefore be regarded as subjects. This assignment of grammatical relations is corroborated by further facts (involving reflexive pronouns) which will be reviewed in 3.2.5. Other datives, expressing the Recipient of verbs of giving, do not behave like subjects in the *-konta* and other constructions, and are therefore to be regarded as having a different grammatical relation, indirect object (3.3.2).

In Warlpiri, another counterpart of the *while* + gerund construction provides evidence for a subject grammatical relation in that language. The relevant constructions are 'infinitival' subordinate clauses (adverbial or relative in sense), in which no auxiliary appears, but an 'infinitival complementizer' is attached to the verb, which then appears finally in the infinitival phrase, not being freely reorderable within it (there is, however, a possibility of nominals within the infinitive phrase 'leaking' out of it into the matrix, Hale 1979).

Many of the infinitival complementizers require suppression of the complement subject, imposing various conditions on what it may be understood as being coreferential with. One of these is the complementizer *kurra*, expressing action simultaneous with that of the main verb, and imposing the condition that the complement subject be coreferential with a non-subject argument of the matrix:

(62) a. Ngaju-rlu ∅-rna yankirri   pantu-rnu, ngapa
         I-ERG   AUX-I emu(ABS) spear-PAST water(ABS)
         nga-rninyja-kurra
         drink-INF-while
         'I speared the emu while it (not I) was drinking water'

      b. Ngarrka ∅-rna nya-ngu wawirri   panti-rninyja-kurra
         man(ABS) AUX-I see-PAST kangaroo(ABS) spear-INF-while
         'I saw a man spear a kangaroo'

      c. Ngaju ka-rna-ngku mari-jarri-mi   nyuntu-ku,
         I(ABS) PRES-I-you grief-being-NONPAST you-DAT
         murumuru nguna-nyja-kurra-(ku)
         sick   lie-INF-while-(DAT)
         'I feel sorry for you while you are lying sick'

      d. Karli   ∅-rna nya-ngu pirli-ngirli
         boomerang(ABS) AUX-I see-PAST stone-ELATIVE
         wanti-nyja-kurra
         fall-INF-while
         'I saw the boomerang fall from the stone'

The infinitival verbs of (62a, b) would take ergative subjects if finite, those of (62c, d), absolutive. The examples also illustrate a variety of semantic roles for the omitted subject and its controller.

It is crucial to the argument that -*kurra* requires rather than merely permits omission of the subject: since NPS can be rather freely omitted in Warlpiri, if a complementizer merely permits an omitted argument in its clause to be understood as coreferential with one in the matrix, without requiring omission and understood coreference, we could say that the omitted argument was just an anaphoric pronoun, ellipsed by the usual principles, which happened to be coreferential with an NP in the matrix. There would then be no syntactic phenomenon specifically associated with the subject of a -*kurra* complement (of course, in a language such as English, where NPS are in general not freely omissible, optional ellipsis would be significant).

It is also important that the phenomenon involves a variety of semantic roles. If, for example, only Agents were obligatorily suppressed in this construction, one could claim that the principle referred to

Agent, a semantic role, rather than to a grammatical relation in sentence structure.

Warlpiri does not seem to impose syntactic conditions on the controller of ellipsis in these constructions. Rather the restrictions seem to be primarily semantic in nature (Nash 1980), though more investigation would be required to support firm conclusions.

The Warlpiri and English constructions we have discussed so far are both adverbial in nature, but subject ellipsis can be an optional or obligatory feature of virtually any kind of subordinate or coordinate clause construction in some languages. English non-finite (participial) relative clauses require ellipsis of the subject (which is understood as coreferential with the head):

(63)   a.   People reporting their neighbors to the authorities will be rewarded

       b.   People reported by their neighbors to the authorities will be investigated

(64)   a.   *People their neighbors(') reporting will be investigated

       b.   *People their neighbors(') reported by will be investigated

English has other strategies of relativization that can be used on non-subjects, but in some languages, such as Malagasy (Keenan and Comrie 1977), relativization of any sort is possible only for subjects.

Complement and coordinate clauses can also be useful in arguing for a subject grammatical relation, although probably not as often as adverbial clauses. In Icelandic both can be used to argue for the subjecthood of the preverbal obliques of (52).

There are in Icelandic a considerable number of verbs taking infinitival complements introduced by the complementizer að. These complements require the subject to be missing, and only omission of the subject will satisfy the requirement:

(65)   a.   Ég   vonast til   að sjá hann
          I(NOM) hope   toward to see him(ACC)
          'I hope to see him'

       b.   *Ég vonast til að ég(NOM)/mig(ACC) sjá (hann)

But the putative oblique subjects like those of (52) do basically satisfy the requirement that a subject be ellipsed, though the results are not always tremendously acceptable (Thrainsson 1979:301–4, 469):

(66)   Ég   vonast til   að vanta ekki peninga
        I(NOM) hope   towards to lack   not   money (cf. (52a))
        'I hope not to lack money'

Serbo-Croatian (Perlmutter 1971:16) may be cited as an example of a language in which only subjects can control the ellipsis of complement subjects (of infinitives).

In coordinate clauses in many languages it is possible to omit an NP in one conjunct if it is coreferential with one in another conjunct and if the two NPs have the same grammatical relation in their respective conjuncts. Icelandic is one of those languages. We find that an oblique subject of a coordinated clause may be omitted under coreference with the subject of a preceding conjunct (Rognvaldsson 1982), but this is not possible for an object:[28]

(67)　a.　Ég　　sá　stúlkuna　　og　líkaði vel　við　henni
　　　　　I(NOM) saw the girl(ACC) and liked well with her(DAT)
　　　　　'I saw the girl and liked her' (cf. (55b))

　　　b.　*Ég　　sá　stúlkuna　　og　hún　　heyrði
　　　　　I(NOM) saw the girl(ACC) and she(NOM) heard [me]
　　　　　'I saw the girl and she heard me'

(objects can however be omitted upon coreference to preceding objects, see Thrainsson 1979:470). Likewise, only a subject, including oblique subjects, may control the ellipsis of the subject of a coordinate clause:

(68)　a.　þeim　　　líkar maturinn　　　og　borða mikið
　　　　　them(DAT) likes the food(NOM) and eat　a lot
　　　　　'They like the food and eat a lot'

　　　b.　*þeir　　sjá stúlkuna　og　　　heyrir þá
　　　　　they(NOM) see the girl(ACC) and [she] hears them(ACC)
　　　　　'They (masc) see the girl and she hears them'

Although NPs without the normal coding features of subjects often partake of many of the grammatical properties of subjects, and may therefore be plausibly regarded as subjects, they frequently do not acquire all of the properties of subjects. In Hindi, for example, although the dative subjects of (50) control ellipsis in a construction equivalent to the *while* + gerund construction (the *-kər* construction, see Kachru, Kachru and Bhatia 1976), they may not themselves be ellipsed. In such cases we consider the shared grammatical properties to be indicative of a common grammatical relation. This shared relation accounts for the similarities between the putative oblique subjects and non-controversial ubjects; the overt case difference is responsible for the differences.

3.2.3 *Coding features in non-main clauses*
It frequently happens that the coding features of subjects are different in subordinate clauses than in main clauses. One of the commonest instances of this is when subjects of subordinate clauses acquire special

case-marking. In English, for example, the subject of a gerund can be accusative or genitive, but not nominative, which is the normal case for subjects:

(69)   a. Him/*he running Ewing Oil is difficult to imagine
         b. His/*he running Ewing Oil would upset a lot of people

Another is the Ancient Greek 'circumstantial participle' construction discussed in 1.2.3. If the subject of the participle is not coreferential with any NP in the matrix, it is expressed in the genitive instead of the nominative, which is the normal case for subjects:

(70)   Ape:nte:sa Philippo:i   Klearchou   apiontos
         I-met   Philip(DAT) Klearchus(GEN) leaving(GEN)
         'I met Philip while Klearchus was leaving'

Cross-referencing is also affected: finite verbs in Greek agree with their subjects in person and number, while participles agree in gender, number and case (and infinitives, which take accusative subjects, don't agree at all).

Special NP-marking in subordinate clauses is usually restricted to subjects, although it sometimes involves other core grammatical relations such as object.[29]

Sometimes subordinate-clause coding features provide useful arguments for subjecthood. This happens in Warlpiri. Instead of requiring subject ellipsis, some non-finite clause constructions permit the subject to be expressed, and some of these permit or require a special case-marker on that subject. One of these complementizers is *-rlarni*, which means that the action of the complement is contemporaneous with that of the matrix. Below are some examples with this complementizer:

(71)   Ngarrka-ngku ka   karli   jarnti-rni, ...
         man-ERG   PRES boomerang(ABS) carve-NONPAST
         'The man is carving the boomerang, ...'

         a. ... kurdu-ku/-∅   purla-nyja-rlarni
             child-DAT/(ABS) shout-INF-while
             '... while the child is shouting'

         b. ... kurdu-ku/-ngku maliki   wajilipi-nyja-rlarni
             child-DAT/-ERG dog(ABS) chase-INF-while
             '... while the child is chasing the dog'

         c. ... karnta-ku/-ngku kurdu-ku miyi   yi-nyja-rlarni
             woman-DAT/-ERG child-ERG food(ABS) give-INF-while
             '... while the woman is giving food to the child'

The subject takes either its normal case-marking, or the dative (Nash (1980:233–4) suggests that the former is found with younger, the latter with older speakers). Furthermore the subject must be initial in the *-rlarni* complement, regardless of its case-marking. If, for example, *kurdu-ku* were placed after *maliki* in (71b), it would have to be interpreted as a Beneficiary, so the meaning would be 'The man is carving the boomerang, while somebody is chasing the dog for the child'.

The *-rlarni* construction, in sharp contrast to main-clause constructions, expresses the subject grammatical relation directly in terms of both case-marking and linear ordering: the subject may be marked dative instead of its usual case (regardless of whether that is ergative or absolutive), and the subject must be initial in the complement. These additional phenomena complete the case for the existence of subjects in Warlpiri.

3.2.4 *Switch reference*
The third grammatical test for identifying subjects that we will discuss involves what are called 'switch reference' systems. These are systems in which the verb of a clause bears a marker which indicates, among other things, whether the subject of that clause is the same or different from that of some other clause with a coordination or subordination relationship.

Austin (1981a, b) uses switch reference to argue for subjects in the Australian language Diyari. Grammatical relations are not directly reflected by coding features in Diyari because, like many other Australian languages, Diyari has a split ergative case-marking system in which different sorts of nominals have different systems of case forms for the core grammatical relations A, S and O. First and second person non-singular (dual and plural) pronouns have a nominative (A/S) and an accusative (O); singular common nouns and masculine proper names have an ergative (A) and an absolutive (O/S), while all other nominals have distinct forms for all three functions: ergative (A), absolutive (S) and accusative (O).

Most complex sentence constructions have switch-reference marking, expressed as an affix on the verb of one of the clauses. The affix indicates the type of construction, and whether the subjects of the two clauses are the same or different. One of these constructions is the 'relative clause', a type of subordinate clause which further specifies either some participant in the main clause (an 'NP-relative' interpretation, Hale 1976), or the time of the clause (a 'T-relative' interpretation). If the subject (A or S NP) of the subordinate clause is the same as that of the main clause, *-na*

is added to its verb; if the subjects are different, *-nani* is added. It is the
A/S function rather than the case forms that are relevant for the
switch-reference system.

(72) is an assortment of subordinate clauses with same subject (ss)
marking, (73) an assortment with different subject (DS) marking. Note
that the subordinate clause corresponds to a considerable range of
subordinate clause types in English, including relative clauses, *when*-
clauses, conditionals, and complement clauses. A shared subject may or
may not be deleted in the subordinate clause.

(72)   a. ŋawu ṭika-na   / ŋawu yaṭa-ḷa   ŋana-yi
          he(ABS) return-REL(SS) he(ABS) speak-FUT AUX-PRES

          yiŋkaŋu
          you(SG LOC)
          'If he comes back he'll talk to you'

     b. ŋaṭu kanṭa   kuḻʸakuḻʸa ṭayi-na   / ŋaṇi piṭi-yi
          I(ERG) grass(ABS) green(ABS) eat-REL(SS) I(ABS) fart-PRES
          'When I eat green grass, I fart'

     c. winṭa ŋaṇi pali-na   / ŋaṭu kana ŋakaṇi
          when I(ABS) die-REL(SS) I(ERG) person me(DAT)

          ŋamalka-yi ŋaka
          have-PRES there(LOC)
          'When I die, I will have my people there'
          (*ŋakaṇi* is here functioning as a possessive modifier of *kana*
          'person')

(73)   a. kanʸtʸi mindi-ya ŋani   / ŋaka-lda ŋawu wakaṛa-ŋaṇi
          can   run-PAST she(ABS)   there-LOC he(ABS) come-REL(DS)
          'She could have run (the distance) if he had come back
          again'

     b. ṭanali   nina   ŋayi-yi / nina   waraṛa-na
          they(PL ERG) he(ACC) see-PRES he(ACC) leave-PART

          wanti-nani
          AUX-REL(DS)
          'They see him after he had been left (for a long time)'

     c. ŋaṇi ŋiŋki·ya wakaṛa-na   / ŋaṭu nana   wiḻa
          I(ABS) here-LOC come-REL(SS) I(ERG) she(ACC) woman(ABS)
          ŋayi-yi / yinda-ŋaṇi
          see-PRES cry-REL(DS)
          'When I come here I see that woman crying'

In (72a), there are coreferential NPS in s function in the two clauses, so ss-marking appears. In (72b) the main clause s is coreferential with the (preceding) relative clause A, so again ss-marking appears, even though the coreferential nominals differ in their case forms. In (72c), the relative clause s is coreferential with the matrix A, so again ss-marking appears. In this example note also that the o NP consists of two components, one a pronoun with accusative case-marking, and the other a common noun with absolutive case-marking (no affix).

In (73a), the matrix and relative clause contain no coreferential NPS, so DS-marking appears. In (73b) there are coreferential NPS, but they are os in both clauses (it is understood that the people who see him are different from those who left him). In (73c) there are two relative clauses, the first with a temporal interpretation with s coreferential with the matrix A, the second interpreted as a perception complement, with s coreferential with matrix o. So the first relative clause has ss-marking, the second DS-marking.

Switch reference in this and other types of subordinate clauses provides evidence that Diyari has a subject grammatical relation comprising A and s functions, in spite of the completely ambiguous testimony of the NP-marking system.

3.2.5 *Reflexivization*

Many languages have special pronouns, called reflexive pronouns, that are used when an NP is to be coreferential with an NP bearing a certain structural relationship to it. In many languages, such pronouns are used when an NP is to be coreferential with the subject of a clause that contains it.

One such language is Malayalam (Mohanan 1982). Malayalam has free word order, expressing grammatical relations by NP-marking. NPS in A function are nominative, o are accusative if animate, nominative if inanimate. In this language, the reflexive possessive pronoun *swantam* requires an antecedent which is a subject (either of the clause immediately containing *swantam*, or of some higher one):

(74)   a. Raajaawə swantam bhaaryaye ṇulli
            king(NOM) self's   wife(ACC) pinched

        b. Swantam bhaaryaye raajaawə   ṇulli
            self's   wife(ACC)   king(NOM) pinched
        'The king pinched his own wife'

(75)   *Raajaawine swantam bhaarya   ṇulli
         king(ACC)   self's   wife(NOM) pinched
        'His own wife pinched the king'

These examples show that reflexivization depends on the grammatical relations rather than on linear order.

Like English, Malayalam has a passive construction in which the argument expressed as an object in the active is expressed as the subject, and the argument expressed as the subject in the active is expressed as an instrumental (with the ending -aal). The interaction of reflexivization with passivization shows it to be dependent on grammatical relations rather than semantic roles such as Agent and Patient:

(76) a. Raajaawə swaṇṭam bhaaryaal   ṇullappeṭṭu
          king(NOM) self's   wife(INSTR) pinch(PAST PASS)
          'The king was pinched by his own wife'

      b. Swaṇṭam bhaaryaal   raajaawə   ṇullappeṭṭu
          self's   wife(INSTR) king(NOM) pinch(PAST PASS)
          'The king was pinched by his own wife'

      c. *Raajaawinaal swaṇṭam bhaarya   ṇullappeṭṭu
          king(INSTR)   self's   wife(NOM) pinch(PAST PASS)
          'His own wife was pinched by the king'

As mentioned in note 19, it is common for South Asian languages to have constructions in which the subject is in the dative case instead of the nominative. Malayalam is a typical example. Certain Malayalam verbs take such dative subjects as a lexical property. Also certain derivational affixes, such as the desiderative -aṇam, impose the requirement that the verb derived by adding -aṇam take a dative subject (if a verb V means 'to X', the verb V-aṇam means 'to want to X'). Reflexivization provides one of the arguments that these datives are indeed subjects, since they, but not dative Recipients with ordinary verbs of giving, can antecede swaṇṭam.

(77) a. Raajaawinə swaṇṭam bharryaye ṇull-aṇam
          king(DAT)   self's   wife(ACC) pinch-DESIDERATIVE
          'The king$_i$ wants to pinch his$_i$ wife'

      b. Raajaawinə swaṇṭam bhaaryaye iṣṭam-aanə
          king(DAT)   self's   wife(ACC) liking-is
          'The king$_i$ likes his$_i$ wife'

      c. *Raajaawə makalkkə   swaṇṭam bhartaawine koṭuttu
          king(NOM) daughter(DAT) self's   husband(ACC) gave
          'The king gave his daughter$_j$ her$_j$ husband'

In a similar fashion, reflexivization also provides evidence for dative subjects in Hindi (Kachru, Kachru and Bhatia 1976).

3.2.6 *Other properties of subjects*

There are a number of other typical properties of subjects which are of considerable interest, although not as useful as the ones above for identifying them in doubtful cases. Perhaps the most important of these is the tendency, already observed in 1.3.1, for subjects to be topical or definite.

Van Valin and Foley (1980:339) have proposed a typological division between languages such as English, Malagasy, and Kinyarwanda, where subjects tend to be or must be definite, and languages such as Warlpiri, Dakota (Van Valin 1977), Enga (Li and Lang 1979) and Choctaw (Heath 1977, Davies 1981), where no such tendency is discernible.

Languages where there is an association between subject and topicality have constructions such as passives to vary the semantic role of an NP with a given grammatical relation. Languages without this association tend to lack such constructions. As a result, the associations between semantic roles and grammatical relations are more consistent: Agents can be expected to be subjects, and Patients can be expected to be objects (though not conversely). We can thus refer to the two types of languages as 'Topic–subject' and 'Agent–subject' languages.

Topic–subject languages also frequently have special constructions to introduce agentive participants into a discourse in the 'presentational' pragmatic articulation, such as the English *there-* and Kinyarwanda *hari*-constructions discussed in 1.3.3. Such constructions are typical properties of subjects in Topic–subject languages, but are lacking in Agent–subject languages, presumably because in these languages there is no reason for the subject not to be presentational.

It is not clear whether one can conclude from the presence of constructions such as passives that a language is a Topic–subject language. I do not know if Malayalam is, for example. There are various things that the formal apparatus of a passive construction might be used for besides providing alternate pragmatic articulations for the arguments of verbs.

In conclusion of this discussion of subjects, I emphasize that the properties I have discussed here are merely a representative collection, rather than an exhaustive one, and are limited to properties that are most likely to be useful for identifying subjects. There are various other common subject properties (such as the 'indispensability' and 'independent reference' properties discussed in Keenan 1976c) that are not so useful for this purpose, and are therefore not discussed here.

3.3 *Other core grammatical relations*

In this subsection we discuss some of the other core grammatical relations that are commonly found in languages that have subjects. These grammatical relations are commonly called 'objects': direct objects, indirect objects, and so forth. Objects are generally more problematic than subjects because there are fewer grammatical processes applying exclusively to specific types of objects. It can therefore be difficult to tell whether variations in the coding features of object-like NPS reflect differences in their grammatical relations.

The most important type of object, and the only one that appears to be universal, is the direct object. These are discussed in 3.3.1 together with the highly similar second objects. In 3.3.2 we consider indirect objects, and in 3.3.3 certain other less commonly found grammatical relations.

3.3.1 *Direct objects and second objects*

In this chapter, we define direct object as the grammatical relation associated with o function. In most languages one can plausibly maintain that there is one such; in a few it seems that there may be two.

English and Warlpiri are languages in which it is entirely clear that there is only one grammatical relation associated with o function. This is also fairly clear in Hindi, even though, as noted in 3.1, there are two morphosyntactic treatments for Hindi o, one with accusative case and one with nominative. There appear to be in Hindi no reasons to analyze the two treatments as involving different grammatical relations, and similarly in most other languages with multiple treatments for o. In Mandarin Chinese, however, there may well be two grammatical relations associated with o function, and hence two direct object grammatical relations.

In Mandarin, o can have two clause-internal manifestations (they can also be placed clause-initially as a form of topicalization). They can follow the verb with no marker, or they can come between it and the subject with the prepositional NP-marker *ba*:

(78)   a. Tā mai le   shū   le
          he buy ASP book ASP
          'He has bought a book'

       b. Tā bǎ shū   mai le
          he BA book buy ASP
          'He has bought the book'

The actual function of *ba* is obscure and a long-standing subject of debate. Li and Thompson (1978:231) characterize *ba* as marking definite direct objects, though this is a considerable oversimplification.

Li and Thompson (1981) provide a more detailed treatment, in which various additional factors are considered, such as the way in which the o is affected (traditionally, the *ba*-construction is said to be used when the object is 'disposed of').

That the two sorts of o have different grammatical relations is suggested by the fact that they differ in both NP-marking and position, and even more strongly by the fact that it is possible to have NPs in both positions in one sentence (Li and Thompson 1981:470–2):

(79)   a. Wǒ bǎ tā bǎng le liǎng zhi jiǎo
           I   BA he tie up ASP two CL foot
           'I tied up his/her two feet'

        b. Tā bǎ táizi dǎ   le là
           he BA table apply ASP wax
           'She/he waxed the table'

This appears to happen to verbs which can be regarded as having two Patients, with the Patient in whose fate one is more interested occupying the *ba*-marked preverbal position, the less interesting 'accessory' Patient the postverbal position.

It is not clear that either of the two object positions should be regarded as the 'normal' treatment for o as opposed to the other. On the other hand it does seem likely that they have different grammatical relations. So Mandarin might be an example of a language with two 'direct object' grammatical relations instead of just one, although one would want to investigate further before accepting this conclusion. In any event, Mandarin is an extreme example of a language with multiple forms of expression for o.

Given that a direct object grammatical relation has been identified, the question arises of which NPs bear it. There are two sorts of problems, the first arising in languages with rich NP-marking systems, the second arising in systems that code NP functions by linear order.

When grammatical relations are coded by NP-marking, it almost always happens that a large number of two-argument verbs take non-subject arguments in some case not normally found on o. In Warlpiri, we have noted verbs taking non-subject arguments in the dative and locative cases (examples (54) and (41), respectively). In Icelandic, we have seen a two-argument verb with a nominative non-subject (58), and datives and genitives are also common:

(80)   a. þeir   hjálpuðu mér
           they(NOM) helped   me(DAT)
           'They helped me'

b. þeir   biðu   mín
they(NOM) waited-for me(GEN)
'They waited for me'

In the case of Warlpiri, we will conclude in 3.3.2 that the datives are not direct objects, but indirect objects. On the other hand I have argued that the putative oblique objects of (80) are direct objects, primarily on the basis that in passive sentences they move into subject position and acquire the typical grammatical properties of oblique subjects (Andrews 1982):

(81)   a. Mér   var hjálpað
           me(DAT) was helped
           'I was helped'

        b. Min   var vitjað
           me(GEN) was visited
           'I was visited'

        c. Ég vonast til   að vera hjálpað/vitjað
           I   hope   toward to be   helped/visited (cf. (65–6))
           'I hope to be visited'

Icelandic postverbal nominatives do not undergo passivization, so we cannot produce a positive argument that they are direct objects (i.e. that they have the same grammatical relation as o). This seems however to be the most straightforward analysis. Object-like NPS with similarly dubious status are very commonly encountered, and one cannot always expect to find evidence that will clearly indicate what their grammatical relations are.

In systems that code grammatical relations by order, problems in the identification of direct objects are frequently raised by 'double object' constructions such as that of *Susan handed Paul the shovel*, mentioned in 2.2.1 above. In this construction, after the verb *handed* appear two bare NPS, *Paul* and *the shovel*. As far as position indicates, either could be the direct object, since both are bare and postverbal. But passivization gives an indication: we find that the first object may be passivized, the second not:

(82)   a.   Paul was handed the shovel (by Susan)

        b.   *The shovel was handed Paul (by Susan)

We can only passivize the Theme if the Recipient is expressed as an (oblique) *to*-object, as in *The shovel was handed to Paul (by Susan)*. We therefore identify the first object as the direct object, and treat the second as a different grammatical function, which we will call 'second object'.

In English there is no clear corroborating evidence for this decision.[30] But in certain other languages we do find two or more concurrent indications that one of the two NPS in a double object construction is the direct object. Furthermore, the direct object always turns out to be the NP with a Recipient-like semantic role.

One such language is the Bantu language Chi-Mwi:ni[31] (Kisseberth and Abasheikh 1977). The general form of Chi-Mwi:ni sentence structure is not unlike that of English, subjects and objects being unmarked, and appearing in svo order, followed by obliques with prepositional NP-marking. There is furthermore a passive rule like that of Malayalam, which puts an extra affix on the verb but does not add an auxiliary. Among the differences is that Chi-Mwi:ni has a rich agreement system with subjects triggering obligatory and objects optional cross-referencing on the verb.

o are distinguished from s, a and obliques by the two properties of triggering optional cross-referencing on the verb (the cross-reference marker appearing between the tense marker and the stem, unlike the obligatory subject cross-reference marker, which precedes the tense marker) and being able to undergo passivization. These two properties are illustrated below (Kisseberth and Abasheikh 1977:192–3):

(83)　　a. Nu:ru ∅-chi-łes-ełe　　　chibu:ku
　　　　　Nuru　he(s)-it(o)-bring-ASP book
　　　　　'Nuru brought the book'

　　　　b. Chibu:ku chi-łes-el-a　　　na Nu:ru
　　　　　book　　it(s)-bring-ASP-PASS by Nuru
　　　　　'The book was brought by Nuru'

There are double object constructions, like those of English, in which two NPS appear postverbally without NP-marking. The simplest constructions of this sort occur with verbs taking a Theme and a Goal/Source (which may be a Recipient or Loser, or simply something to which something is applied, such as a cart that is oiled). We will refer to these non-Theme arguments as 'Recipients', though their range of semantic roles is wider than that indicated by this term.

In a double-object construction, both of the properties characteristic of o accrue to the Recipient (which normally occupies the immediately postverbal position), but not to the Theme (Kisseberth and Abasheikh 1977:192–3):

(84)   a. Nu:ru ∅-m-ɫet-el-ele   mwa:limu chibu:ku
          Nuru he(s)-him(o)-bring-DAT-ASP teacher book
          'Nuru brought the book to the teacher'

       b. Mwa:limu ∅-ɫet-el-el-a   chibu:ku na Nu:ru
          teacher   he(s)-bring-DAT-ASP-PASS book   by Nu:ru
          'The teacher was brought the book by Nuru'

(85)   a. *Nu:ru ∅-chi-ɫet-el-ele   mwa:limu chibu:ku
          Nuru he(s)-it(o)-bring-DAT-ASP teacher book

       b. *Chibu:ku chi-ɫet-el-el-a   mwa:limu na Nu:ru
          book   he(s)-bring-DAT-ASP-PASS teacher   by Nuru

Note that the presence of a Recipient object is signalled by the affix *el*,
glossed DAT (it is generally called the 'applied' affix in Bantu linguistics).

It seems clear that the Recipient in the double-object construction
should be viewed as the syntactic direct object, since it monopolizes the
properties of a sole object. The Theme in these constructions would
then bear a different grammatical relation, which we might again call
'second object'. A similar situation, involving five 'object properties', is
described in Bahasa Indonesia by Chung (1976).

Sometimes, however, syntactic properties such as passivizability fail
to give a clear verdict in double-object constructions. This is illustrated
by another Bantu language, Chichewa (Trithart 1977, 1979). (86) below
is an instance of a double-object construction similar in appearance to
that in the Chi-Mwi:ni example (84). But unlike Chi-Mwi:ni, either NP
may trigger cross-referencing. Furthermore, either may passivize
(Trithart 1977:31–4):

(86)   a. Jóni a-ná-$\begin{Bmatrix} zí \\ wá \end{Bmatrix}$ pats-a   amá'í áké nthóchí

          John he-PAST-$\begin{Bmatrix} \text{them} \\ \text{her} \end{Bmatrix}$ give-INDIC mother his bananas
          'John gave his mother the bananas'

       b. Amá'í áké a-ná-$\begin{Bmatrix} zí \\ {*}wá \end{Bmatrix}$ pats-idw-a   nthóchí

          mother his she-PAST-$\begin{Bmatrix} \text{them} \\ {*}\text{her} \end{Bmatrix}$ give-PASS-INDIC bananas
          (ndi Joni)
          (by John)
          'His mother was given bananas by John'

c. Nthóchí zi-ná-$\left\{\begin{array}{l}zí\\ {}^*wá\end{array}\right\}$- pats-idw-a amá'í áké

bananas they-PAST-$\left\{\begin{array}{l}they\\ {}^*her\end{array}\right\}$ give-PASS-INDIC mother his
(ndí Jóni)
(by John)
'Bananas were given by John to his mother'

The two objects are not entirely equivalent, however: in the passive sentences the verb may show object agreement only with the Theme, not with the Recipient, regardless of which comes to occupy subject position. A number of other processes which 'elevate' the Theme over the Recipient block object agreement with the Recipient in Chichewa (but not in all Bantu languages: see Kinyarwanda (Kimenyi 1980), for example). Another point worth noting is that object agreement with the passive subject is not accepted by all informants, and is not at all usual in Bantu languages or any others.

In Chi-Mwi:ni it is quite clear that the Recipient should be identified as the direct object, while in Chichewa this is not clear at all. In fact, it is not clear that the various objects in Chichewa should be viewed as having distinct grammatical relations: it might well be appropriate to say that in (86a) there were two NPs bearing the object relation, with the differences in their behavior described directly in terms of semantic roles. This situation is not uncommon in Bantu.[32]

In fact in English the monopolization of passivizability by the first object is not as complete as suggested above. If the Recipient is a pronoun, it seems to be possible to passivize the Theme:

(87) a. No explanation was given them
       b. The job was offered him
       c. Fake documents were given him

Oehrle (1975:177) finds such examples scattered throughout English writing and broadcasting, and finds that the postverbal dative is almost always a pronoun. For other instances in which second objects have a partial assumption of object properties, see the discussion of second objects in Icelandic in Andrews (1982) and Levin and Simpson (1981).

Thus the two NPs in a double-object construction may behave as if they had quite different grammatical relations, the same grammatical relation, or somewhere in between. It would appear that the typology of grammatical relations must provide for a family of direct-object-like relations which may behave more or less like a direct object. It is a striking typological generalization that if the NPs behave differently, it is the one with the Recipient-like semantic role that behaves like a direct object.

Passivization and cross-referencing are the most widely available tests for direct-objecthood, although various other phenomena, such as causativization (see chapter iii:6) and reflexivization occasionally provide evidence as well. See Chung (1976, 1978), Harris (1981:48–52) for interesting examples of argumentation for objecthood.

3.3.2 *Indirect objects*

The double object constructions discussed above are a common option for three-argument verbs, such as verbs of giving, especially in languages that code grammatical functions by position. Another common option is to express one of the three arguments as an oblique, leaving two core arguments. The third possibility, frequently found in languages that code grammatical functions primarily by NP-marking, is to use an additional core grammatical relation, 'indirect object'.

We will define 'indirect object' as a core grammatical relation distinct from direct object that expresses the Recipient of a verb of giving (though it may be used in other ways as well). We thus view it as a syntactic concept distinct from, although related to, semantic concepts such as Recipient. All languages can express the Recipient concept. We shall see, however, that many lack indirect objects.

A language that can be argued to have indirect objects is Warlpiri. Warlpiri verbs of giving and related notions take their Agent as an ergative subject, their Theme as an absolutive, and the Recipient or related role, such as Loser, as a dative. These datives are cross-referenced on the auxiliary by the ordinary object markers except for the third person singular, which is cross-referenced by *-rla*:

(88)   a. Ngaju-ku ka-npa-ju   karli   yi-nyi
          me-DAT   PRES-you-me boomerang(ABS) give-NONPAST

          nyuntulu-rlu
          you-ERG
          'You are giving me a boomerang'

       b. Ngajulu-rlu kapi-rna-rla karli
          I-ERG   FUT-I-him   boomerang(ABS)

          punta-rni   kurdu-ku
          take away-NONPAST child-DAT
          'I will take the boomerang away from the child'

The most straightforward account for the case marking is to view the absolutive as being the direct object (that is, having the grammatical relation expressing o function), and the dative as having a different but related grammatical relation, 'indirect object'.

We also find verbs taking a dative object without an accompanying absolutive, such as *wangka* 'speak to', *parda* 'wait for'.[33] These cross-reference in the same way as those of (88):

(89)   a. Ngaju ka-rna-ngku nyuntu-ku wangka-mi
           I(ABS) PRES-I-you   you-DAT   talk-NONPAST
           'I am talking to you'

    b. Ngarrka ka-rla   kurdu-ku parda-rni
          man(ABS) PRES-him child-DAT wait for-NONPAST
          'The man is waiting for the child'

It seems reasonable to view these datives as bearing the indirect object relation also. A Warlpiri verb thus must have a subject,[34] and may have a direct object, and indirect object, or both.

In English, Bantu, and many other languages, on the other hand, we do not seem to find a grammatical relation like 'indirect object', at least superficially.[35] In these languages, Recipients are expressed either as direct objects, usually in a double-object construction, or as obliques. For example, the *to*-object construction in English gives no evidence of being anything other than an ordinary oblique prepositional phrase. There is no reason to set up a special indirect object relation borne by it, but not by other kinds of PP.

Likewise in many Bantu languages, such as Chichewa. As an alternant to (86a) we have a construction where the Theme is the direct object and the Recipient is marked by the Preposition *kwa*. Furthermore, it assumes the behavior typical of obliques in Chichewa, not being cross-referenceable, for example:

(90)   Joní a-ná-$\begin{Bmatrix} zí \\ *wa \end{Bmatrix}$ pats-a   nthóchí kwa ámá'í ake

        John he-PAST-$\begin{Bmatrix} them \\ *her \end{Bmatrix}$ give-INDIC bananas to   mother his

        'John gave the bananas to his mother'

It can be difficult to judge whether a Recipient is being expressed as an indirect object or as an oblique. Aside from cross-referencing, relativization very often provides a basis for distinguishing indirect objects from obliques: in a number of languages, such as Basque and the Dravidian language Tamil, subjects, objects and putative indirect objects can be relativized by deletion (Keenan and Comrie 1977) while NPS that are clearly obliques cannot do this. For further discussion of indirect objects, see Faltz (1978).

Curiously, indirect objects seem not to occur in the same language with double-object constructions – if a language has a double-object construction, any grammatical functions expressing Recipients other than direct object seem to be clearly oblique. This fact deserves an explanation, though I will not suggest one here.

3.3.3 *Other core relations*
Aside from subject, object and indirect object, various other core grammatical relations can appear. One of them, second object, has already been observed. Some Bantu languages can have as many as three 'objects' in one sentence, as in the following examples from Kinyarwanda (Kimenyi 1980:106):

(91)   a. Umugabo y-a-he-er-eye   abagóre ábáana ibitabo
        man   he-PAST-give-BEN-ASP women children books
        'The man gave the books to the children for the women'

    b. Umugóre y-a-he-eesh-eje   umwáana amáta
       woman   she-PAST-give-INSTR-ASP child   milk
       inkoongooro
       wooden cup
       'The woman is giving the child milk in a wooden cup'

In (91a) the Recipient, Theme and Beneficiary are expressed as unmarked, postverbal NPS which Kimenyi shows to share a wide variety of properties with direct objects; while in (91b) the Recipient, Theme and Instrumental are so expressed. The presence of Beneficiary and Instrument as core NPS is registered by the morphemes glossed BEN and INSTR on the verbs of the two examples. The correct assignment of grammatical relations to examples like these is far from clear, but it would seem that we have either two or more NPS bearing one grammatical relation in the same sentence, or at least two additional core grammatical relations closely related to 'direct object'.

Another example of an unusual core grammatical relation is provided by Warlpiri. Any Warlpiri verb may be supplemented by what Hale (1973) calls an 'adjunct dative', but which we will call a supplementary dative, to avoid confusion with the terminology of this chapter. A supplementary dative is a dative which expresses various semantic roles, but is cross-referenced as an indirect object. If associated with a verb with no special marking, the supplementary dative is interpreted as a Beneficiary:

(92) a. Ngarrka-ngku ka-rla   kurdu-ku karli
       man-ERG   PRES-him(DAT) man-DAT   boomerang(ABS)
       ngurrjuma-ni
       make-NONPAST
       'The man is making a boomerang for the child'

     b. Ngarrka-ngku ka-rla-jinta   kurdu-ku miyi
       man-ERG   PRES-3SG(DAT)-3SG(DAT) child-DAT food(ABS)
       karnta-ku   yi-nyi
       woman-DAT give-NONPAST
       'The man is giving food to the child for the woman'

(92b) shows that the supplementary dative can co-occur with an indirect object, and is thus a distinct grammatical relation.[36] *Jinta* is the form assumed by the second of two cross-reference markers, both referring to a third person singular dative (Hale 1973:336).

That the supplementary dative can be cross-referenced suggests that it is a core grammatical relation, in spite of the fact that it expresses a semantic relation expressed by an adjunct in English. There are further facts which corroborate its core status in Warlpiri.

The interpretation of the supplementary dative may be altered by adding to the verb one of a number of so-called 'preverbs' (which have a variety of additional functions in Warlpiri). Thus with the preverb *marlaja*, the adjunct dative indicates the entity who brings about the situation designated by the sentence. With the preverb *piki(-piki)*, the dative represents an entity of which some participant is in danger:

(93) a. Kurdu-ngku ka   miyi   nga-rni
       child-ERG   PRES food(ABS) eat-NONPAST
       'The child is eating food'

     b. Kurdu-ngku ka-rla   karnta-ku   miyi
       child-ERG   PRES-her(DAT) woman-DAT food(ABS)
       marlaja-nga-rni
       CAUSE-eat-NONPAST
       'The woman brought about the circumstance that the child is eating food'

(94) a. Ngarrka-ngku ka   yujuku   nganti-rni
       man-ERG   PRES humpy(ABS) build-NONPAST
       'The man is building a humpy'

     b. Ngarrka-ngku ka-rla   warlu-ku piki-nganti-rni
       man-ERG   PRES-it(DAT) fire-DAT   DANGER-build-NONPAST
       yujuku
       humpy(ABS)

'The man is building a humpy in danger of fire (either man or humpy is in danger)'

Since the semantic role of the supplementary dative is determined by the form of the verb, its status as a core grammatical relation is confirmed.

Supplementary datives are probably best viewed as the results of a lexical process which derives from one lexical item another with an additional argument whose semantic role is determined by which preverb, if any, is added.

It is quite common for Benefactives to be added by a lexical operation of this sort, although the Warlpiri technique is unusual. More commonly, the Benefactive takes on the appearance and at least some of the properties of a direct object. In English, for example, we can express a Benefactive as a *for*-adjunct or as what looks like a direct (first) object:

(95)   a. Bruce barbecued the steak for Darlene

        b. Bruce barbecued Darlene the steak

Although the benefactive object in (95b) looks like a direct object, it is behaviorally somewhat different, since for most speakers it cannot passivize: *Darlene was barbecued the steak by Bruce* (Fillmore 1965). It is not clear whether we should think of benefactive objects as having a differential grammatical relation than ordinary direct objects, or whether the differences are simply a consequence of the semantic role of the Benefactives.

In many Bantu languages, Benefactives can only be expressed as derived object-like NPS, benefactive adjuncts being absent. Furthermore, the benefactive objects take on object properties more readily than in English, being freely cross-referenced, passivized, etc. Similar processes also add arguments with a wide range of other semantic roles, such as Instrument, Locative, Reason, etc. Example (91) illustrates supplementary Benefactives and Instruments (coded by the addition of -*er*- and -*eesh*- respectively, to the verb) in Kinyarwanda. See Trithart (1977, 1979) and Kimenyi (1980) for further exemplification and discussion.

There is considerable further variety in the sorts of core grammatical relations that a language may have. These examples give an impression of the sorts of things that are possible.

3.4 *Syntactic ergativity*
In most well-described languages with an ergative case-marking system, such as Warlpiri, the syntax is predominantly organized along subject–object lines (Anderson 1976). But there are also languages in which the

syntax is organized along absolutive–ergative lines, with rules targetting o/s but not a/s.

The most famous instance of this type is the Australian language Dyirbal (Dixon 1972). We will here look mainly at Dyirbal's southerly neighbor Yidiɲ (Dixon 1977a). Although this language is much less extreme as an exemplar of syntactic ergativity, it is instructive in that it illustrates the rather common situation in which the evidence for postulating specific grammatical relations is relatively scanty. We will supplement the relatively detailed account of Yidiɲ with some discussion of relevant features of Dyirbal. The languages are concisely described and compared in Dixon (1977b).

Yidiɲ, like Warlpiri and most other Australian languages, has free word order (though there are strong preferences), relying entirely on NP-marking to code syntactic functions. Under certain circumstances, the components of an NP may be split (Dixon 1977a:268–71), but the phenomenon is far more restricted than in Warlpiri (or Dyirbal, which is similar to Warlpiri in this respect). The NP-marking system is of the split ergative type, with different categories of nominals having different systems of case forms.

The three relevant categories are common nominals (nouns and adjectives), pronouns, and deictics. Common nominals inflect ergatively, taking an ergative form in A function, an absolutive form in o/s function. Pronouns (restricted to first and second persons) take an accusative in o function and a nominative in a/s function. Deictics (comprising demonstrative and interrogative/indefinite pronouns, the former also serving as third person pronouns) have two stems: 'human' and 'non-human'. Humans may only be referred to by a human stem, while non-humans may be referred to by either, the use of the human stem being more likely the more humanlike the referent of the NP. Human deictics take an ergative A form, an accusative o form, and an absolutive s form. Non-human deictics inflect like common nominals, except that for some there is an optional accusative.

Some examples illustrating case marking for personal pronouns and common nouns are the following:

(96)   a.   ŋayu   maŋga:-n^y
              I(NOM) laugh-PAST
              'I laughed'

       b.   bun^{y}a   maŋga:-n^y
              woman(ABS) laugh-PAST
              'The woman laughed'

   c. ŋan^{y}a-n^y bun^{y}a:-ŋ   wuɾa:-n^y
     I-ACC   woman-ERG slap-PAST
     'The woman slapped me'

   d. ŋayu   bun^{y}a   wuɾa:-n^y
     I(NOM) woman(ABS) slap-PAST
     'I slapped the woman'

   e. Wagud^{y}a-ŋgu guda:ga wawa:-l
     man-ERG   dog(ABS) see-PAST
     'The man saw the dog'

The evidence for syntactic ergativity in Yidiɲ comes from the subordinate clause constructions of the language. These are similar in function to the relative clauses of Diyari, having what from the English point of view are a variety of relative and adverbial interpretations. There are four morphological types of subordinate clauses, 'dative', 'causal', 'purposive' and 'apprehensional', each with a different ending on the subordinate verb. The first three types are quite similar in their behavior, while the apprehensional clauses are somewhat different.

There is no switch-reference system in Yidiɲ. But there is in the dative, purposive and causal subordinate clauses a near requirement that if the matrix and subordinate clauses contain coreferential NPs (about 85% do in Dixon's texts (Dixon 1977a:323)), this NP should have o/s function in both clauses. This requirement is absolute for clauses with a relative interpretation, that is, for those in which the coreferentiality is essential to the function of the clause, though it is occasionally violated by those with adverbial interpretations (Dixon 1977a:323–49). Furthermore, the coreferential NP in the subordinate clause may only be ellipsed if it is in o/s function (Dixon 1977a:332–3, 341).

Thus we can use the dative subordinate clause construction (DATSUB, signaled by the verbal suffix -n^{y}unda), which expresses simultaneous action, to combine (96a) and (96c) to yield either (97a) or (97b):

(97)   a. ŋayu   manga:-n^y (ŋan^{y}a-n^y) bun^{y}a:-n   wuɾa-n^{y}unda
       I(NOM) laugh-PAST I-ACC   woman-ERG slap-DATSUB
       'I, who was slapped by the woman, laughed'

    b. ŋan^{y}a-n^y bun^{y}a:-n   wuɾa-n^y / (ŋayu) manga-n^{y}unda
       I-ACC   woman-ERG slap-PAST I(NOM) laugh-DATSUB
       'I, who was laughing, was slapped by the woman'

In (97a) the matrix coreferential NP is s and the subordinate is o; in (97b) the matrix coreferential NP is o and the subordinate one is s. s–s and o–o combinations are also possible. In these examples the matrix and subordinate coreferential NPs differ in case form, since the NP is a personal pronoun. The same results would obtain, with the same case forms in both clauses, if the coreferential NPs were common nominals. (97a) and (97b) also illustrate optional omission of the subordinate clause NP; it is also possible to omit the main clause NP, or, rarely, both.

If one of the coreferential NPs is A, the clauses cannot normally be combined as they are. Rather a rule similar to the passive of languages like English, must be used to convert the A to s function, except, very rarely, when the clause is adverbial in sense, and the coreferentiality is 'accidental'.

All transitive verbs have a so-called 'antipassive' form, derived by adding the suffix *-d^{y}i-n* (the *-n* represents the conjugation class of the antipassivized verb). The role normally expressed as A is then expressed as s, while the role normally expressed by o is expressed by an NP in the dative or locative case, the choice determined by 'humanness' in the same way as the choice between human and non-human deictic stems: NPs referring to humans must be dative, while those referring to non-humans may be either dative or locative, but are more likely to be dative the more like humans they are (Dixon 1977a:110–12). This alternation extends to many but not all uses of the dative and locative case forms.

The antipassive construction is illustrated below, where (98a) is the antipassive of (96e), and (98b) is the antipassive of (96d):

(98)   a. Wagu:d^{y}a gudaga-nda/-la wawa:-d^{y}i-n^{y}u
          man(ABS) dog-DAT/-LOC   see-ANTIPASS-PAST
          'The man saw the dog'

      b. ŋayu   bun^{y}a:-nda   wuṛa:-d^{y}i-n^{y}u
          I(NOM) woman-DAT   slap-ANTIPASS-PAST
          'I slapped the woman'

In the change from (96e) to (98a), the Agent changes its case from ergative to absolutive, since it is a common noun, but the pronominal Agent of (96d, 98b) has no case change, since it takes the nominative form for both A and s functions.

Antipassives appear to be virtually exact paraphrases of the corresponding non-antipassive constructions. Questions, for example, will often be answered in the antipassive simply for the sake of injecting grammatical variation into the discourse (Dixon 1977a:118). Like passives in English, however, antipassives appear to be secondary constructions in that they have greater morphological complexity in the verb, and are not used without a definite reason (one might answer a question in the antipassive to vary the style, but wouldn't ask it that way out of the blue).

The antipassive permits us to get the effect of combining (96a) and (96d), in which the shared NP is s in one clause and A in the other. (96d) is converted to its antipassive form (98b), and we get the sentences of (99) as a result:

(99)   a.   ŋayu   maŋga:-nʸ / (ŋayu) bunʸa:-nda
            I(NOM) laugh-PAST   I(NOM) woman-DAT
            wuṛa:-dʸi-nʸunda
            slap-ANTIPASS-DATSUB
            'I, who was slapping the woman, laughed; I laughed while
            slapping the woman'

       b.   ŋayu   bunʸa:-nda wuṛa:-dʸi-nʸu   / (ŋayu) maŋga-nʸunda
            I(NOM) woman-DAT slap-ANTIPASS-PAST   I(NOM) laugh-DATSUB
            'I, who was laughing, slapped the woman; I slapped the
            woman while laughing'

The purposive and causal subordinate clauses, which I will not illustrate here, behave in exactly the same way. In these three types, we have a strong preference (though there are a few counterexamples) for a shared NP to be in o/s function in both the subordinate and matrix constructions. Furthermore this requirement must be met if the clause is to be interpreted as an NP-modifier, or if the subordinate clause instance of the NP is to be deleted (Dixon doesn't state whether deletion of the matrix NP obeys this condition). The syntactic rather than semantic character of these principles is revealed by the fact that the antipassive, which turns an A into an S, permits an Agent NP to come to satisfy them.

These principles treat o and s equivalently, and therefore motivate establishing a grammatical relation, which we shall call 'absolutive', expressing o and s functions. For A function we would propose another grammatical relation, 'ergative'.

In Yidiɲ there is very little further corroboration for this analysis.[37] But in Yidiɲ's southerly neighbor Dyirbal, the case for o-s identification is much stronger. All of the complex sentence constructions of the language (two to four, depending on how one counts) provide evidence for treating o and s as having one grammatical relation and there are various morphological phenomena that do as well.[38]

Symptomatic of the difference between the two languages are the differences in their sentential coordination constructions. One of the most characteristic features of Dyirbal discourse is that long sequences of coordinate clauses tend to be strung together in a 'topic chain' in which all the conjuncts have a shared NP in o/s function, that is, with the absolutive grammatical relation (Dixon 1972:130–2).

In Yidiɲ on the other hand, one does not find these long topic chains:

coordinations (expressing simultaneous action) of two or three clauses containing a shared NP are reasonably common, but not the sequences of up to a dozen or more clauses that one finds in Dyirbal (Dixon 1977a:388). Furthermore the shared NP is not always constrained to have the absolutive grammatical relation. Rather, if it is a common nominal, it must be in the absolutive case in both clauses; if it is a pronoun it must be in the nominative in them (Dixon 1977a:388–92). Thus, if the shared NP is a pronoun, it will have A/S function in both clauses; if it is noun or adjective, o or s function.[39]

We thus have a *prima facie* case, strong in Dyirbal, but weaker in Yidiɲ, that these languages have an essentially different sort of syntactic organization to that found in standard 'subject oriented' systems such as English, with no subject grammatical relation (as defined in this paper), but instead an 'absolutive' grammatical relation comprising o/s function. There are two reservations which we must make, however.

In the first place, this analysis claims that languages such as Yidiɲ and Dyirbal are fundamentally different in character from most other languages, including Australian ones such as Warlpiri and Diyari. In the case of Dyirbal, this conclusion is fairly easy to accept, because of the unusually large number of phenomena treating o and s alike as opposed to A, and the absence of clear instances of syntactic rules treating A and s alike.

But in Yidiɲ the evidence for o–s identification is relatively slight. Furthermore, in many other languages with ergative case marking the evidence for identification of s with either A or o is similarly scanty,[40] and in some cases perhaps even contradictory, as we shall discuss immediately below. Thus Dixon (1977a:393) observes that participants in a conference session devoted to whether various Australian languages had A–s identification or o–s identification were frequently doubtful of the correct treatment of their languages, often changing their minds in the course of preparing final versions of their papers.

Of course there is no guarantee that fundamental and structurally important features of languages will always be highly evident on the basis of the often highly incomplete evidence available to field workers. But one must be suspicious of a structural dichotomy as elusive as the one between subject–object and ergative–absolutive appears to be in many cases.

The second reservation concerns whether Dyirbal, Yidiɲ, or similar languages might have some principles which do treat A and s alike, thereby suggesting the more usual subject–object organization, instead of or in addition to the absolutive–ergative organization. It has been a tacit assumption of the discussion so far that each NP of a sentence can be viewed as having only one grammatical relation. From this assumption we should expect that there might be a number of rules treating o and s alike, or a number of rules treating A and s alike, but not both.

For if a language did have both sorts of rules, we would want to postulate both a subject grammatical relation comprising A and s functions, and an absolutive grammatical relation comprising o and s functions. s NPS would then be both subjects and absolutives, violating the assumption.

Dixon claims that Yidiɲ in fact has two constructions identifying A and s. The first is the imperative: imperatives require a second (or occasionally a first) person pronoun in s or A (s/A) function (Dixon 1977a:370–1). s and A imperatives are illustrated below:

(100)   a. (nʸundu) guwa gali-n
        you(SG)   west go-IMP
        '(You) go west!'

        b. (nʸundu:ba) bunʸa   wawa
        you(PL)   woman watch(IMP)
        '(All of you) watch the woman!'

The second involves a number of particles whose grammar treats s and A alike (Dixon 1977a:372–82, 387). For example the particle *gana:ŋgar* indicates that the referent of the s/A NP was the first to perform a certain action:

(101)   a. ɲayu   gana:ŋgar gali:-nʸ
        I(NOM) first   go-PAST
        'I went first'

        b. ɲayu   gana:ŋgar gunda:-l
        I(NOM) first   cut-PAST
        'I was the first person to cut [that tree]'

On this basis we might draw the conclusion that Yidiɲ had 'inconsistent' syntactic organization, suggesting the presence of both a subject and an absolutive grammatical relation.[41]

It seems quite possible, however, that the phenomena involving A/s may be described directly in terms of semantic roles. They would then be irrelevant for the determination of grammatical relations.

The semantics of imperatives would cause them to tend to have second person NP as the 'agentive', or 'controlling' participant (though other persons might well also be possible, depending on the details of the semantics of imperatives in the language). It furthermore seems to be the case that such participants are only expressed as s or A: there is nothing comparable to the English passive, which converts an A to an oblique. Hence, if we merely say that imperatives have second (or, under certain circumstances, first) person agentive participants, we have accounted for the phenomenon without recourse to an A or s category. Furthermore, this fact about imperatives would very likely follow simply from the meaning of the construction, without requiring any actual statements in the syntax at all, although to be sure of this one would have to know considerably more than we are ever likely to about the semantics of the Yidiɲ imperative.

These considerations are reinforced by the fact that there are no special rules, such as cross-referencing or obligatory ellipsis, applying to the s/A. It is merely represented by a pronoun, optionally ellipsable as are all NPS in Yidiɲ.

Consider by contrast the formal properties of imperatives in English. We have imperatives of actives, such as *go away!* or *eat your supper*, with missing agentive A/s subjects and what are formally at any rate imperatives of passives, such as *be arrested!*, with omitted patientive s subjects. Although one can debate whether the passive imperatives with suppressed non-Agent subjects have precisely the same kind of meaning that ordinary imperatives do, it seems fairly evident that both sorts should be formally described as instances of the same sentence structure, with a missing subject, understood to be the addressee. The syntactic notion of subject thus plays a role in the description of the phenomenon.

The Yidiɲ particles don't give clear evidence for the same reason as imperatives. *gana:ŋgar* seems to assert that the Agent was the first to perform the action, and similarly with the other particles. To get a clear case for reference to an s or A syntactic function, rather than to an agentive semantic role, one would have to show that *gana:ŋgar* could be used in sentences such as 'the tree was the first to fall down (non-agentive s)' or 'I was the first to cut the tree down (A)', but not 'the tree was the first to be cut down by me' (o). The available evidence does not seem to settle the question. Dixon's characterization of the meanings of the particles does however seem on the whole to suggest a semantic solution, since the ones involving s and A seem to describe actions by conscious participants rather than mere events. See Wierzbicka (1981) for further discussion.

Dixon's arguments that A and s sometimes act as if they represented a single grammatical relation thus are not compelling. To argue that two syntactic functions comprise a single grammatical relation we have to show that identifying them makes sense out of a syntactically conditioned phenomenon. This criterion is clearly met in the case of o-identification with the subordinate clause constructions, but not by the imperative and particle constructions that Dixon adduces for the A–S identification.

Other publications that are known to me which attempt to demonstrate syntactic inconsistency in 'ergative' languages fail for essentially the same reason: failure to demonstrate that there is a syntactic phenomenon that depends on grammatical structure rather than semantic roles or morphological features such as case. Perhaps the most suggestive are studies of certain Eskimo dialects, such as Woodbury (1977), Johnson (1980), Payne (1982), though it is difficult to assess these in the absence of a full-length investigation of Eskimo syntax.

It is thus quite possible that 'syntactically ergative' languages lack a subject grammatical relation as defined in this chapter. Their nearest equivalent to a subject would be the absolutive relation, since it is the absolutive that is predominantly involved in cross-clausal syntactic phenomena in these languages. This sort of grammatical relation has been called a 'pivot' by Dixon (1979).

From a formal point of view, furthermore, it is quite possible that the subject and absolutive grammatical relations are the same: many writers, including Dixon (1972), have treated Dyirbal as a language in which the NP with o/s function was formally the subject in terms of its position in sentence structure (Dixon was assuming the Chomsky 1965 definitions of grammatical relations introduced in connection with (5)). There are other possibilities, however, one of which will be introduced in the next subsection.

3.5 *Superposed systems*

We have been assuming implicitly that each NP in a sentence has only one grammatical relation. But in 3.2.6 we noted that the subject grammatical relation in many languages has a dual allegiance, being associated both with the semantic role of Agent and the pragmatic function of Topic. It is not unreasonable to imagine that there might be languages in which there are two superposed systems of grammatical relations, one system aligned to semantic roles, the other to pragmatic functions. Here, following Schachter (1976, 1977), we will argue that Tagalog and similar languages of the Philippine family are in fact of this type.

Tagalog has verb-initial order, with NPs appearing in free order after the verb, with their functions marked by prepositional NP-markers (there is also a topicalization construction, discussed in chapter 1.6, in which any NP may be placed in front of the verb). Verbs are traditionally considered as taking three types of 'core' arguments, called by Schachter and Otanes (1972) 'actor', 'object' and 'directional', which we will ultimately claim to be subject, direct object and indirect object. The first two are marked by *ng* (pronounced [nəŋ]), the latter by *sa*, unless they are 'topic', as will be discussed below. The traditional names for these types of argument are semantically suggestive, but not fully accurate: actors needn't be Agents, and directionals needn't be Directional. There are also various sorts of adjuncts: Benefactives, Outer Locatives, Instrumentals, etc.

One of the arguments (or, more rarely, one of the adjuncts) must be chosen to be what is sometimes called the 'focus', and sometimes the 'topic'. We shall see shortly that the latter term is more appropriate in the present context, and so will be used here. The topic bears the marker *ang* instead of the marker that would otherwise appear, and is obligatorily understood as being definite. Although we call it 'topic', and it certainly is topical, the precise nature of its pragmatic function is not clear. See chapter 1.6 and Schachter (1976, 1977) for discussion. The type of argument or adjunct that is chosen as the topic is indicated by focus affixes on the verb. Below is illustrated an array of topic choices for the verb *alis* 'take out', which has actor, object and directional arguments, and here appears with a benefactive adjunct as well (AF = Actor Focus, OF = Object Focus, DF = Directional Focus, BF = Benefactive Focus, DIR = Directional):

(102) a. Mag-a-alis   ang babae ng bigas sa sako para sa
          AF-FUT-take out TOP woman OBJ rice   DIR sack BEN

          bata
          child
          'The woman will take some rice out of a/the sack for a/the child'

       b. A-alis-in   ng babae ang bigas sa sako para sa
          FUT-take out-OF ACT woman TOP rice   DIR sack BEN

          bata
          child
          'A/the woman will take the rice out of a/the sack for a/the child'

       c. A-alis-an   ng babae ng bigas ang sako para sa bata
          FUT-take out-DF ACT woman OBJ rice   TOP sack BEN   child
          'A/the woman will take some rice out of the sack for a/the child'

       d. Ipag-a-alis   ng babae ng bigas sa sako ang bata
          BF-FUT-take out ACT woman OBJ rice   DIR sack TOP child
          'A/the woman will take some rice out of a/the sack for the child'

In these examples the choice of determiners in the glosses is significant, and is governed by two principles, the one already mentioned that the topic is always understood as definite, and another to the effect that non-topic objects (but not actors or directionals) are always understood as indefinite.

A popular form of analysis for these constructions is to treat them as passives (see Schwartz 1976 and Bell 1976 for exemplification from various Philippine languages). The actor–topic form (102a) is taken as the primary form with the actor as subject, the others as secondary 'passives', with the actor 'demoted' from the subject relation, and some other NP serving as subject.

That the topic bears a subject-like grammatical relation is made clear by the fact that it is targetted by certain principles which target subjects in various languages: relativization, and a 'quantifier launching' process, discussed by Schachter (1976, 1977).

Tagalog relative clauses take the form of sentences with ellipsed topic. The ellipsed topic is understood to be the head NP that the clause is modifying. Hence to relativize on an actor, one uses an actor–topic verb; to relativize on an object, an object–topic verb:

(103)   a. Matalino   ang lalaki-ng b[um]asa ng diyaryo
           intelligent TOP man-REL [AF]-read OBJ newspaper
           'The man who read a newspaper is intelligent'

       b. Interesante ang diyaryo-ng   b[in]asa-∅   ng lalaki
           interesting TOP newspaper-REL [PERF]-read-OF ACT man
           'The newspaper that the man read is interesting'

(104)   a.*Interesante ang diyaryo-ng   b[um]asa ang lalaki
           interesting TOP newspaper-REL [AF]-read TOP man

       b.*Matalino   ang lalaki-ng b[in]asa-∅   ANG diyaryo
           intelligent TOP man-REL [PERF]-read-OF TOP newspaper

The -ng suffix in these examples, glossed REL, is an element with various functions in the grammar: here it is regularly placed on a word in an NP immediately before a relative clause also within that NP. In (103), we see that the topic can be relativized upon: in (104) we see that non-topics cannot be relativized upon. Relativization therefore targets the topic.

The other topic-targetting process is a 'Quantifier Launching' phenomenon. Tagalog quantifiers normally occur within the NP they modify, but for some speakers the quantifier *lahat* may also be placed in an adverbial particle position directly after the verb (Schachter and Otanes 1972:147–8). Such a 'floated quantifier' may modify only the topic, not a non-topic:

(105)   a. ∅-su-sulat   lahat ang mga bata ng mga liham
    AF-FUT-write all TOP PL child OBJ PL letter
    'All the children will write letters'

   b. Su-sulat-in lahat ng mga bata ang mga liham
    FUT-writ-OF all OBJ PL child TOP PL letter
    'The/some children will write all the letters'
    not 'All the children will write the letters'

The topic thus functions as target for a number of grammatical processes.

Although the phenomena of (103–5) show that the topic has a subject-like grammatical relation, there are problems with treating the non-actor-focus forms as passives (although it is possible to put forth something of a case, along the lines of Schwartz 1976). The object-focus and directional-focus forms are extremely common, rather than being relatively rare, as is typically the case with passives. Furthermore, they are not morphologically more complex than the putatively primary actor-focus forms. They merely have different affixes, not additional ones.

The principal difficulty, however, is provided by an argument-ellipsis process which applies to the complements of certain verbs. This process ellipses the actor, regardless of whether it is topic (Schachter 1977:293):

(106)   a. nag-atubili siya-ng h[um]iram ng pera sa banko
    AF-hesitate he(TOP) [AF]-borrow OBJ money DIR bank
    'He hesitated to borrow money from a/the bank'

   b. nag-atubili siya-ng hiram-in ang pera sa banko
    AF-hesitate he(TOP)-REL borrow-OF TOP money DIR bank
    'He hesitated to borrow the money from the bank'

In (106a), the actor of *hiram* 'borrow' is topic as revealed by the actor-topic morphology on the verb, and the absence of an overt *ang*-phrase in the complement. In (106b) the object is topic, but the actor is still ellipsed.

An object or other non-topic can't be ellipsed, even if it is the topic (Schachter 1977:295):

(107)   a. Gusto ni Juang suri-in   siya ng doktor
    want ACT John(REL) examine-OF he(TOP) ACT doctor
    'John wants the doctor to examine him'

   b.* Gusto ni Juang suri-in ng doktor
    want ACT John(REL) examine-OF ACT doctor

Furthermore the process is not restricted to Agents: non-agentive actors of various sorts may be ellipsed, even if they are not topics:

(108) a. Masagwa   ang t[um]a-tanda
           disagreeable TOP [AF]-IMPERF-become old
           'It is disagreeable to become old'

       b. Gusto niya-ng   g[um]anda
           want he/she(ACT)-REL [AF]-beautiful
           'She wants to become beautiful'

(109) a. Gusto ko-ng   t[um]anggap ng gantimpala
           want I(ACT)-REL [AF]-receive OBJ prize
           'I want to be the recipient of the prize'

       b. Gusto ko-ng   ma-tanggap ang gantimpala
           want I(ACT)-REL OF-receive   TOP prize
           'I want to receive the prize'

(110) Ayaw   ko-ng   ma-matay sa Maynila
       not want I(ACT)-REL AF-die   DIR Manila
       'I don't want to die in Manila'

Since this ellipsis process seems to target actors regardless of whether they are topics, actors would appear to bear a grammatical relation that is independent of the topic grammatical relation. Since this grammatical relation expresses A and S functions, it is a subject grammatical relation in the terminology of this chapter.

Independent of the subject grammatical relation is an additional topic grammatical relation, which is to be regarded as an interior function since the semantic role of the topic is coded on the verb stem (furthermore, many verbs are lexically restricted in terms of which of their arguments can be a topic). The topic is not preferentially associated with A/S function, and is thus not a subject according to our definitions (indeed, if anything, it is preferentially associated with O function (Cena MS cited in Payne 1982)).

Since actor turns out to be the subject grammatical relation, it seems appropriate to identify the 'object' with the direct object grammatical relation, and the 'directional' with the indirect object, since Recipients are normally expressed as directionals. These grammatical relations are associated with semantic roles, and so may be called 'role oriented', as opposed to the topic grammatical relation, which is associated with a pragmatic function of topicality, and thus may be called 'topic oriented'.

In Schachter's original discussions of the dual system of grammatical relations in Tagalog, he considers two additional properties of actors: reflexivization, and imperative formation. But he does not devote much attention to demonstrating that the phenomena in question were actually conditioned by grammatical relations, rather than other factors, such as semantic roles. And it appears that the imperative and reflexive phenomena he adduced do not require reference to grammatical relations, and thus do not provide evidence that actor in Tagalog is a grammatical relation. Since we are concerned here with the nature of the evidence for grammatical relations, it is worth examining why Schachter's last two subject properties do not argue for grammatical relations in Tagalog.

Examples such as these show that actors may antecede reflexives whether they are topic or not (Schachter 1977:292):

(111)   a. Nag-alala ang lolo   sa kaniya-ng sarili
           AF-worry TOP grandfather DIR his-REL   self
           'Grandfather worried about himself'

       b. In-alala-∅   ng lolo   ang kniya-ng sarili
           PERF-worry-OF ACT grandfather TOP his-REL   self
           'Grandfather worried about himself'

Schachter also shows that non-actors cannot reflexivize actors, so that the actor, but not the topic, is relevant to reflexivization possibilities.

But to show that actorhood is actually the conditioning factor for reflexivization, and that actor is thus functioning as a grammatical relation, we would have to show that non-actors do not antecede reflexives. This Schachter does not do, and in fact there is no requirement that the antecedent of a reflexive be an actor. In (112a) either the actor or the (directional) Recipient can be understood as the antecedent of the reflexive, which is the possessor of the Theme (object). In (112b) either the actor or the Beneficiary can be understood as the antecedent of the Source (directional) reflexive:

(112)   a. In-i-abot   niya   sa bata ang kaniya-ng sarili-ng
           PERF-OF-hand he(ACT) DIR child TOP his-REL   self-REL

           larawan
           picture
           'He$_i$ handed the child$_j$ a picture of himself$_{i,j}$'

       b. T[um]angap ang Rosa ng sulat para sa bata sa
           [AF]-receive TOP Rosa OBJ letter BEN DIR child DIR

           kaniya-ng sarili
           her-REL   self
           'Rosa$_i$ received a letter for the child$_j$ from herself$_i$/him-her$_j$self'

Bell (1976:30, 157) notes essentially the same facts in the closely related language Cebuano. She suggests that Cebuano reflexivization is governed by a principle referring to semantic roles rather than grammatical relations, the 'Thematic Hierarchy Condition' of Jackendoff (1972) (she also notes some constraints involving surface word order). The same kind of analysis seems indicated for Tagalog. Since Tagalog reflexivization, as opposed to that of Malayalam, seems to function in terms of semantic roles rather than grammatical relations, it does not provide evidence that actor is a grammatical relation independent of topic.

As for imperatives, Schachter notes that an imperative sentence can have the secondary addressee as topic or non-topic, as long as it is actor:

(113)   a. Mag-bigay ka   sa kaniya ng kape
           AF-give   you(TOP) DIR him   OBJ coffee

        b. Bigy-an mo   siya   ng kape
           give-DF you(ACT) him(TOP) OBJ coffee
           'Give him some coffee!'

In (113a) the addressee–actor is topic, in (117b) it isn't (note that the pronouns are morphologically fused with their function markers). Both are good as imperatives.

Schachter says that 'the only ACTORS tolerated in imperative sentences are second-person pronouns' (1977:291). But this statement does not provide evidence that actor is a grammatical relation for the same reason that imperatives do not provide such evidence in Yidiɲ and Dyirbal: the semantics of imperatives are such that one would expect them to occur predominantly with second person subjects, and there is no indication of any syntactic phenomenon involving the actor, especially one which applies on the basis of grammatical relations rather than semantic roles.

In fact the basic syntactic construction of (113), with the verb in a form lacking aspect markers, may be used with non-second person actors with 'hortative' (expressing the sense of 'Let's . . .') and 'optative' (expressing wishes) illocutionary forces (Schachter and Otanes 1972:407–9). There are a number of other imperative, hortative and optative constructions, but none of them produces any more of a case for a syntactic notion of 'actor' covering both topic and non-topic actors.

Complement actor ellipsis thus provides the only clear and presently attested evidence in Tagalog for a subject-like grammatical relation that cross-cuts the topic. Other Philippine languages provide additional evidence for this type of organization of sentence structure. Some, such as Cebuano, have omission of second person actors in imperatives regardless of whether they are topics (Bell 1976, Schachter 1976), thus providing some evidence from imperative constructions; others, such as Kapampangan, have agreement with the actor regardless of whether it is topic (Schachter 1976).

The existence of this 'Philippine type' motivates a revision in the typological division of 'Agent-subject' and 'Topic-subject' languages proposed in 3.2.6. One basic division is between languages which have a core grammatical relation associated with topicality (English, Kinyarwanda, Malagasy, Tagalog) and those which do not (Warlpiri, Diyari, Enga, Dakota). Then the former category may be divided into languages in which the subject grammatical relation is itself the topical grammatical relation (the former Topic-subject class), and those where the topical grammatical relation is distinct from and 'superposed' on the subject (the Philippine type).

The existence of the Philippine type also suggests a tentative reinterpretation of the phenomenon of syntactic ergativity. It has been noted by a number of people that the syntactic properties of absolutives (such as relativizability) are those that tend to be associated with topics. This is especially clear in Dyirbal, with one of the constructions providing evidence for the absolutive relation being actually called a topic chain (Dixon 1972 also comments in various places on the topical pragmatic function of absolutives).

It might then be appropriate to identify the absolutive relation of Dyirbal and Yidiɲ with the topic relation in Philippine languages. Such an identification is suggested by the fact that there is evidence that the object–topic construction is more basic than the actor–topic construction in Tagalog. Object–topic forms appear to be more numerous in ordinary speech (W. Foley, personal communication). Furthermore, and perhaps consequently, they appear to be acquired earlier by children. There are also a number of verbs that have only Patient-focus forms, and others that use the bare stem in Patient-focus, only taking affixes in other focus forms (Cena MS, cited in Payne 1982).

In both Philippine and syntactically ergative languages, a subject grammatical relation would be associated with A/S function, its existence required by universal principles. In Tagalog and other Philippine languages, there are a few grammatical phenomena sensitive to subjecthood; in Dyirbal and Yidiɲ there are none that are known to be (this might be a consequence of our less extensive knowledge of these languages). In both types, the topic grammatical relation would be obligatorily assigned to the direct object, if there is one. Otherwise it is assigned to the s.

Antipassivization 'demotes' the direct object to an oblique, so that the subject becomes the topic. *ng* in Tagalog is thus identified as an instrumental–ergative case marker: it marks the non-Topic subject of a transitive verb, the antipassivized Patient, and Instruments. Although such a treatment is novel within the context of Philippine linguistics, instrumental–ergative cases are reasonably common. In both Yidiɲ and Dyirbal, for example, the instrumental and ergative coincide, and in Dyirbal, the instrumental–ergative may be used on antipassivized Patients (the dative is also an option).

Both sorts of languages have further processes whereby NPS with peripheral semantic roles may be made arguments of the verb. In both Yidiɲ and Dyirbal there is a 'transitivizing' suffix (TRANS) which, when added to a verb, forms a verb taking an additional absolutive argument in a variety of semantic roles, including Instrumental in both languages. In Dyirbal this suffix can be added directly to a transitive verb, so that the sentences of (114) are alternatives:

(114) a. balan   dʸugumbil   baŋgul yaṛaŋgu baŋgu
           CL(ABS) woman(ABS) CL(ERG) man(ERG) CL(INSTR)

           yuguŋgu   balga-n
           stick(INSTR) hit-PRES/PAST

       b. bala   yugu   baŋgul yaṛaŋgu balgal-ma-n
           CL(ABS) stick(ABS) CL(ERG) man(ERG) hit-TRANS-PRES/PAST

           bagun   dʸugumbil-gu
           CL(DAT) woman-DAT
           'The man hit/hits the woman with the stick'[42]

In both languages, the transitivizing affix can be added to intransitive verbs, including antipassives (though with varying semantic force), and in Yidiɲ the only way to apply this affix to a semantically transitive verb is to antipassivize it first. In Dyirbal, we might take the dative case on the semantic object as a sign of covert antipassivization (though the instrumental, which is generally possible on antipassivized objects, is not possible here).

Under the present analyses, these transitivizing affixes are formally similar to the applicational suffixes that register the addition of various object arguments in Bantu. The various additional focus forms in Philippine languages would be treated similarly. The direct object, if present, is demoted to oblique status as an *ng*-phrase, and some other semantic role, such as Directional or Benefactive, or, more rarely, others, is expressed as the object, and therefore the topic.

The collapsing of the syntactically ergative and Philippine types, due essentially to Cena and Payne, obviously needs much further study before it can be accepted. Its most striking prediction is that we should ultimately expect to find evidence for a subject grammatical relation even in syntactically ergative languages, so that these would be syntactically inconsistent in terms of their evidence for grammatical relations. As mentioned at the end of section 3.4, there is some suggestive evidence in this direction, but nothing as yet that is conclusive.

One significant obstacle is that in Yidiɲ and Dyirbal antipassive verbs can be transitivized and vice versa, while in Philippine languages the focusing affixes form a mutually exclusive set. The actor-focus morphology seems to mark coincidence of the subject with the topic, while the patient and peripheral focus affixes seem to indicate that the object–topic has a particular sort of semantic role. Nonetheless, the fact that this analysis unifies two unusual types of languages suggests that it should be taken seriously.

If we adopt it, the typology developed earlier in this subsection needs little further development. Languages which have an interior topic grammatical relation will either identify it with the subject; or with the object if there is one, otherwise the subject. Furthermore all languages will have subjects and objects, though the subject grammatical relation won't necessarily function in grammatical principles. 'Syntactically ergative' languages will simply be those in which grammatical relations are sensitive to an interior topic grammatical relation that preferentially coincides with the direct object.

3.6 *Split s phenomena*

Virtually all languages seem to provide distinct treatments for the Agents and Patients of PTVs, which we have designated as the A and O grammatical functions. From this it is natural to expect that some languages would distinguish between Agent-like and Patient-like single arguments of one-argument predicates, treating the former like A, the latter like O.

Languages of this sort clearly seem to exist. In section 3.1 we discussed Eastern Pomo (McClendon 1978), in which one set of nominal forms is used for A and Agent-like S (s_A), and another for O and Patient-like S (s_O), illustrating these forms in example (53), repeated below for convenience:

(53)   a. mí·ṗ káluhuya
          he(A) went-home
          'He went home'

    b. mí·pal xá·   ba·kú·ma
          he(o) in-the-water fell
          'He fell in the water (accidentally)'

c. mí·p̓ mí·pal šá·k̓a
   he(A) him(O) killed
   'He killed him'

This NP-marking system extends to other nominals as well (with certain complications in the case for proper nouns). There are also suffixes on the verb marking plurality of A/s_A but not o/s_O; and a number of verbs have stem suppletion to indicate plurality of o/s_O but not A/s_A. On the basis of coding features, one would suspect that Eastern Pomo had one grammatical relation associated with A/s_A functions, another with o/s_O.

There are two problems with this view. First, there are certain verbs, primarily verbs of emotion such as 'miss', 'love', 'hate', etc., which take two arguments in the patientive form. There is insufficient evidence to motivate any particular analysis of these verbs, but if we assume that the agentive/patientive NP-marking in Eastern Pomo reflects grammatical relations directly, we will have to allow for two patientive grammatical relations with these verbs.

A more serious problem is a switch-reference system which, although it does provide additional evidence that s_A and s_O should be distinguished, also motivates treating them as different subtypes of one grammatical relation of subject. In this system, consecutive clauses with identical s_A will take same-subject (SS) marking:

(115) a. há· káluhu-y,   si·má· mérqaki·hi
          I(A) went home-ss   went to bed
          'I went home and then went to bed'

       b. há· káluhu-qan,   mí·p̓ mérqaki·hi
          I(A) went home-ds he(o) went to bed
          'I went home and then he went to bed'

Note that in (115a) the subject of the second verb is omitted, since it is indicated to be coreferential with that of the first verb by the ss-marking (-y) on the first verb. McClendon does not explain the function of *si·má·* in this example.

In consecutive clauses in which one s argument is s_A and the other s_O, DS-marking is used, and the pronoun is not omitted in the second clause:

(116) a. há· xá·qákki-qan, wi q̓a·lál tá·la
          I(A) took a bath-ds I(o) got   sick
          'I took a bath and got sick'

       b. wi q̓a·lálma-qan, há· kʰúyhi qóyuhù
          I(o) got sick-ds   I(A) not   come
          'I got sick, that's why I didn't come'

This shows that s_A and s_O are different in their syntactic behavior as well as their overt form.

The evidence that they bear a common grammatical relation is that if two s_O are in consecutive clauses, ss-marking is still used:

(117)   mí·pal kʰí   kox-qan mu·t̓ít̓ki-y   mu·dála
        he(o) he(a) shot-ds curled up-ss died
        'He$_i$ shot him$_j$, and he$_j$ curled up and died'

For a unified treatment of switch reference, it seems that we want to treat both s_A and s_O as subjects. However we want switch reference to require that the subjects be not only identical in reference, but in the property distinguishing s_A from s_O as well.

As to what this property might be, a natural proposal would be that it is case: A and s_A would have one case which we'll call ergative, o and s_O another case, which we'll call accusative. Subjects will then be nominative (A/s_A) or accusative (s_O), while objects (o) will only be accusative. ss-marking will then require that the subjects be coreferential and have the same case.

On this account, emotion verbs with two patientive arguments fall into an expected type: they have accusative subjects (presumably the Experiencer, though McClendon does not provide information to confirm this) and accusative objects.

Other reasonably well-documented languages with an obvious distinction between s_A and s_O functions turn out the same way: there seems to be grounds for treating both kinds of s as bearing a single grammatical relation, with the agentive/patientive distinction superposed on it. Thus, insofar as the published literature indicates, we do not seem to find complete syntactic identification of A and s_A, or of o and s_O.[43]

It turns out, however, that many languages which superficially have a uniform s function turn out upon deeper analysis to have an s_A/s_O distinction. This was first systematically observed by Perlmutter (1978), who noted that in a number of European languages, intransitive agentive verbs had impersonal passives, while intransitive patientive verbs do not. In Icelandic, for example, the verbs *dansa* 'dance' and *deyja* 'die', take s expressed as preverbal nominative NPS that elicit person and number agreement on the verb. But *dansa* has an impersonal passive, and *deyja* doesn't, in conformity with the principle noted by Perlmutter:

(118)   a. það var dansað mikið í partí-inu
           it was danced much at party-the
           'There was much dancing at the party'

b.*það var dáið mikið í kjarnorkuslysi-nu
it   was died much in nuclear accident-the
'A lot of people died in the nuclear accident'

A very extensive system of differences between two types of superficially identical s has recently been detected in Italian (Burzio 1981, Rosen
1982), although the two classes of verbs don't correspond very well to
agentive/patientive.

The status of 'split s' phenomena is thus presently unsettled. The most
one can say at present is s can be split into A-like and o-like types, but
that there is usually some basis for treating both types as having the
grammatical relation of subject, in spite of their differences. Thus they
do not yet require any revision of our typological proposal that subjects
are always present. Nonetheless it seems likely that a more sophisticated
conception of syntactic structure than has been assumed in this chapter
will be required to make sense out of their properties.[44]

NOTES

1 These and subsequent examples assume the convention that '*' within
parentheses means that the example is bad if the material in the parentheses
is included, '*' immediately preceding parentheses means that the example is
bad if the material within the parentheses is omitted. Hence the verbal
ending is impossible in (3a), obligatory in (3b).

2 Semantic roles first began to be discussed extensively in recent American
linguistics with the work of Gruber (1965, 1976) and Fillmore (1968). See
Chafe (1970b), Jackendoff (1972, 1976, 1978), Longacre (1976a) and Ostler
(1979) for some more recent discussions. Some writers, such as Gruber and
Jackendoff, refer to semantic roles as 'thematic relations'. It might be
appropriate, and would be consistent with the usage of these authors, to
restrict this latter term to broad semantic roles that function in grammatical
principles.

3 However, it is not uncommon to find grammatical constructions which
discriminate systematically between intentional and unintentional action. See
Klaiman (1980), for example.

4 It sometimes happens that there are two standard treatments of single
arguments of one-argument predicates, typically one for Agent-like participants, the other for Patient-like ones. In this case we still call NPs receiving
one of these treatments in intransitive clauses 's', and speak of a 'split s'
system with s_A and s_O subtypes. The concepts of A, s and o here are intended
to be essentially the same as those of Dixon (1979), Comrie (1978) (Comrie
uses P for o). Dixon (1979) provides an extensive discussion of 'split s'
systems, which will be discussed in section 3.6.

5 This concept of 'subject' is a clarification of that of Dixon (1979). The extent
to which it is clearer depends on the precise nature of the theory of sentence
structure one is working in. In a relationally based framework, it is perfectly

clear, since the grammatical relations are primitives, and 'subject' is simply whatever grammatical relation is associated with A/S function. In a theory in which grammatical relations are defined concepts rather than primitives, things are potentially more obscure. In this case, the issues are highly theoretical, and therefore beyond the scope of this chapter.

Note also that there are other concepts of 'subject' in circulation, such as 'what the sentence is about' (Catford 1976, Bavin 1980). The present concept might be described as 'semantically based', as opposed to Catford and Bavin's pragmatically based subject concept.

6 Subject and object are thus viewed as formal concepts of sentence structure, which are named by virtue of their typical alignment with semantic or pragmatic, 'notional' categories. This is an application to grammatical relations of a general view of grammatical categories first clearly formulated by Lyons (1968:166–9).

7 This term, introduced in Gruber (1965, 1976), is not as widely used as the others mentioned here.

8 Mary Laughren (personal communication) informs me that the Warlpiri tend to keep NPs together as single constituents in writing, but to break them up in speech.

9 Warlpiri, like many languages, lacks systematic indication of definiteness. The articles in the translations are arbitrarily chosen as 'the'. This will also be the case in the treatment of other languages, unless there is specific indication that definiteness is relevant.

10 See Givón (1979b) for discussion of the close connections between pronominalization and cross-referencing, which Givón claims to be identity.

11 This formulation is from Chafe (1976).

12 Keenan's concept of subject is different from that of this chapter, so that some of the examples he cites, such as Tagalog, are inappropriate here. Malagasy and Kinyarwanda both have subjects in the present sense.

13 It is of course constraints like these that give rise to the principal alternative notion of subject, essentially 'the grammatical relation associated with the topic function', or 'what the sentence is about'.

14 The notions of external, core and oblique grammatical functions are essentially equivalent to the notions of 'overlay', 'term', and 'oblique' grammatical relations in the theory of relational grammar. Since this chapter is not expounding that theory, we use different terminology.

15 The terms P-object and P-complement were borrowed lexical-functional grammar (Bresnan 1982a) and the associated concepts are essentially the same.

16 For further discussion, see Hale (1978) and Nash (1980).

17 In the case of emotion verbs, for example, it seems likely that when the Object of Emotion appears as the subject, it is interpreted as the Causer of the emotion, at least to a greater extent than when it does not. The case is difficult to argue rigorously, however.

18 These and later Hindi examples are from Tunbridge (1980).

19 Such 'oblique subject' constructions are quite common, especially in South

Asian languages, of which they are an areal feature. For syntactic discussion of other South Asian examples, see Klaiman (1980, 1981a, 1981b), Mohanan (1982) and the papers in Verma (1976). For examples from other areas, see Harris (1981) (Georgian), Cole and Hermon (1981) (Quechua), and Thrainsson (1979) (Icelandic).

20 The only argument I know of is that we can accommodate the agreement in (50) and examples like (49d) under the generalization that a Hindi verb agrees with a nominative object if the subject is case marked.

21 For evidence that these preverbal oblique NPS are syntactic subjects, see Thrainsson (1979), Maling (1980) and Rognvaldsson (1982).

22 The cross-linguistic properties of subjects were first compiled by Keenan (1976c). There is presently no comparable compendium for object properties, but see Moravcsik (1978) and Hopper and Thompson (1980) for relevant discussion.

23 Bresnan (1982b) has proposed that 'raising' (functional control, in the terminology of the paper cited) of complement clause arguments is restricted to subjects, but it is far from conclusively demonstrated that this is true.

24 Neuter nominals have identical nominative and accusative forms, however.

25 Not just in ordinary main clauses, but in more complex constructions as well. See Thrainsson (1979) and Maling (1980).

26 Some lexical processes often treat o and s alike even in languages where the existence of subjects is quite clear. For example, in English, o and s form participant nominalizations in -ee, while A forms them in -er: examiner, examinee; but escapee. But such lexical derivational phenomena have no direct bearing on sentence structure.

27 Note that if while is omitted, we immediately understand the matrix object rather than the matrix subject as the subject of the gerund.

28 Although (67a, 68a) are acceptable, speakers seem to prefer not to use ellipsis when the ellipsed NP or its controller is an oblique subject.

29 For an example of this from the Saibai dialect of the Australian language Kalaw Lagaw Ya, see Comrie (1981).

30 Ziv and Sheintuch (1979) in fact argue that it is the second NP that is the direct object, on grounds which I find unconvincing.

31 Chi-Mwi:ni is regarded as a dialect of Swahili, although standard Swahili behaves differently with regard to these phenomena (see Keach 1980 for a detailed analysis of passivization and agreement in standard Swahili).

32 See Gary and Keenan (1977), Kimenyi (1980), Hawkinson and Hyman (1974), Duranti and Byarushengo (1977), Duranti (1979). It seems very likely that phenomena such as the impossibility of agreement with the Recipient in (86c) are motivated by functional considerations of various kinds. See Trithart (1979) and the last two references above for discussion.

33 Most of these verbs take absolutive subjects, but some take ergative ones. These latter verbs fall into two groups: verbs of seeking ('look for', 'dig for' etc.), and verbs of 'unsuccessful action' ('spear at', etc.) which are productively derived from verbs of normal 'successful' action ('spear', etc.). See Hale (1973:335–6), Nash (1980:197–200).

34 Note that Warlpiri, like other Australian languages, does not use subjectless constructions for meteorological constructions (cf. example (45)).
35 In some accounts of sentence structure (such as relational grammar), these languages might be regarded as having indirect objects at a fairly abstract level, but they appear to be lacking in overt structure.
36 I am indebted to Mary Laughren for telling me about this kind of sentence.
37 The little that there is comes from the apprehensional clause construction. An apprehensional subordinate clause almost always contains an NP in o or s function coreferential with some matrix NP, which can have any function (Dixon 1977a:350–5):

(i) n^{y}undu giyi gali-n / wanda:-nd^{y}i
you(SG) not go-IMP fall-LEST
'Don't go [there], you might fall down'

(ii) n^{y}undu gad^{y}idiga-n   giyara-ŋgu   guba:-nd^{y}i
you(SG) keep a long way off-IMP stinging tree-ERG burn-LEST
'You keep away, lest you get stung by the stinging tree'

The apprehensional clause denotes something undesirable that might happen to the shared NP, which seems to be Patient-like in its semantic role: Dixon provides no examples in which the shared NP is an agentive s, or one derived from an A by antipassive. Hence the relevance of these clauses to grammatical relations is unclear.
38 For example, the suffix -*muŋa* forms from verbs a 'participle' meaning 'one who is habitually s/o of v'. Hence from *d^{y}anay* 'stand' we get *d^{y}anay-muŋa* 'one who stands around a lot'; from *narn^{y}d^{y}ay* 'watch' we get *narn^{y}d^{y}ay-muŋa* 'one who is always being watched'. If we wish to form an agentive participle, we must first antipassivize the verb (the antipassive suffix being -*ŋay*). The antipassive of *narn^{y}d^{y}ay* is *narn^{y}d^{y}a-ŋay*, so 'one who always watches' is *narn^{y}d^{y}a-ŋay-muŋa*. The fact that the antipassive changes the role referred to by the participle indicates that the phenomenon, though lexical in nature, is sensitive to grammatical relations.
39 This constraint suggests that the absolutive of common nouns and the nominative of pronouns should be regarded as the same case. A natural way to achieve this would be to regard them both as nominative, defining nominative as the case expressing s function, and usually other functions as well (what we call absolutives are indeed frequently called nominatives, especially in Caucasian linguistics). Coordinate clauses would then be subject to the constraint that the shared nominal have nominative case. This formulation (and Dixon's original, it seems to me) predicts that if the shared nominal is a human demonstrative, it must be in s function, since human demonstratives are only nominative (under the proposed definition) when in s function, being ergative when A, accusative when o. Dixon does not provide evidence as to whether this is the case.
40 For discussion of two apparently extreme cases from the Caucasus, Archi and Chechen, see Kibrik (1979) and Nichols (1980).

41 Dixon himself does not actually draw this conclusion, formulating his analysis indirectly in terms of the grammatical functions A, S and O.

42 Dyirbal nouns are normally accompanied by a classifier, marking case and the membership of the noun in one of four classes. Definiteness/indefiniteness is not marked in the language. The ergative and instrumental cases are formally identical, though glossed differently here and in Dixon's work.

43 Work in progress by M. Durie (1981) suggests strongly that Achenese, analyzed as a subject/object language by Lawler (1977), does in fact have complete identification of A/S_A and O/S_O functions. The case is difficult to make, however, since under Durie's analysis there are relatively few phenomena that are sensitive to grammatical relations.

44 Thus relational grammarians such as Perlmutter and Rosen claim that S_O are direct objects at a rather abstract level of syntactic structure (the initial stratum), but subjects at a more superficial one (the final stratum). Similar ideas within the framework of Government–Binding theory are applied to Italian by Burzio (1981).

3 Speech act distinctions in syntax*

JERROLD M. SADOCK and ARNOLD M. ZWICKY

1 The notion of sentence type

1.1 *Uses and forms*

The speakers of any language can accomplish a great many communicative tasks with the sentences of their language: they can start a conversation, order someone to do something, narrate a tale, ask for information, promise to do something at some future time, report what they know or have heard, express surprise or dismay at what is going on about them, suggest a joint action, give permission for someone to do something, make a bet, offer something to someone, and so on. For some of these *uses* of sentences a language will have specific syntactic constructions, or even specific *forms*, reserved for just these uses – special particles, affixes, word order, intonations, missing elements, or even phonological alterations (or several of these in concert); when a sentence shows one of these it is to be understood as being used in a specific way. Such a coincidence of grammatical structure and conventional conversational use we call a SENTENCE TYPE.

An illustration: the combination of verb–subject word order and rising final intonation in the following English sentences:

(1) a. Have they finished installing the furnace?

b. Are you tired of plucking penguins?

is associated with one use, that of asking a YES–NO QUESTION (a request that the person you are addressing tell you whether the proposition you have supplied him is true or not). In other words, this particular way of framing a sentence in English is associated with the particular 'pragmatic meaning' of asking a yes–no question. (For a useful discussion of speech acts, see Lyons 1977, chapter 16.)

Now any sentence with a conventionally indicated force can be put to uses other than, or in addition to, the one to which it is conventionally suited – (1a), for example, could serve as a reminder to someone to fix a furnace, particularly if it is plain to the addressee that the speaker knows that the furnace is *not* installed. This use, though, depends on the fact that (1a) is conventionally a question of a certain kind.

When there is a regular association of form and the speaker's use of sentences, we will speak of the form–use pair as a sentence type. We have just seen instances of one of the interrogative, or question-asking sentence types in English. In addition to the yes-no question (with inversion and rising intonation), English has several other interrogative sentence types, among them the INFORMATION QUESTION:

(2)   a. Who can we turn to?

        b. Why are you plucking penguins?

and the ALTERNATIVE QUESTION:

(3)   a. Are you going to empty the wastebaskets, or will I have to do it myself?

        b. Did she jump, or was she pushed?

The conventional forces of these sentences share the following feature: they signal the desire of the speaker to gain information from the addressee. Furthermore, these three types have a syntactic commonality in that they all involve placing a verb before the subject (but see section 3.3).

When there is a set of sentence types with similar and related uses and with a similar syntactic form in a language, we will group them under a single heading. We will also identify sentence types of similar use (but possibly different form) in different languages, so that we will speak of languages other than English as having interrogative sentence types, for instance French, with its yes–no question types:

(4)   a. Pleut-il?   'Is it raining?'
        b. Est-ce qu'il pleut?

1.2 *Minor types*

Besides the large families of sentences with basic communicative functions, languages often include a range of minor types, typically involving forms that have a variety of uses in other sentence types. Among the minor types of this sort in English are the SUGGESTIONS, with various sentential formulae:

(5)   How about getting me a beer?
(6)   What about buying a new lamp for the living room table?
(7)   Why spend your money on such trash?
(8)   Why not resign?
(9)   Let's tour the island

using the words, *how*, *what*, *why*, *about* and *let*, all of which have a variety of uses other than in the formation of suggestions. Minor types of this sort are often overlooked in even fairly detailed language descriptions; sometimes the only ones to be mentioned are the special locutions used for greeting, leave-taking, and other punctuation of discourse, as in the English formulae:

(10)   How do you do?
(11)   Pleased to meet you
(12)   Good morning
(13)   See you later

and perhaps a few completely fixed short interjections, like the English:

(14)   Ouch!
(15)   Damn!
(16)   Wow!

The description of a language should make mention of minor sentence types. We discuss some of the most common ones in section 2.3.

1.3 *Explicit performatives*
Many languages have a particular syntactic construction for performing a large number of acts. In this PERFORMATIVE construction, there is a different verb for each act:

(17)   I command you to open that trunk
(18)   I bet (you) ten dollars you can't sing 'God Save the Queen' backwards
(19)   I (hereby) christen this ship '*Titanic II*'
(20)   I warn you that these pigs are flighty

Note that all of these English examples contain a first person subject and a verb in the present non-progressive form. Such sentences have been termed EXPLICIT PERFORMATIVES – explicit, because the specific act performed (commanding, betting, christening, warning) is referred to by the verb in the sentences, in contrast to ordinary declaratives, imperatives, and interrogatives, which perform their acts implicitly, without a word referring specifically to asserting, requesting, or inquiring.

English is rich in explicit performatives (see J. D. McCawley 1977 for a classification of the verbs involved and Searle 1977 for a classification of the acts performed), but not all languages are. Some (for instance, spoken Tamil, as described to us by K. Paramasivam) have nothing truly comparable to this construction in English.

In languages with explicit performatives, there is not necessarily a close fit between sentence types and performative verbs. There will be many verbs (especially those describing culture-specific acts like christening, excommunication, and marriage) that correspond to no sentence types, major or minor, and there may also be sentence types for which there are no explicit performatives. The latter is essentially the case for the English interrogative types, since most speakers cannot use the appropriate verbs in explicit performatives:

(21)   *I ask (you) when you were born
(22)   *I inquire (of you) whether lead is heavy or not

We conclude that both explicit performatives and sentence types involve a classification of sentence uses, but that the two systems are independent, with explicit performatives involving a LEXICAL classification and sentence types a SYNTACTIC classification.

From a syntactic point of view, explicit performatives show a number of features that recur from language to language. They typically have first person singular subjects and second person indirect objects, and they usually look like positive declarative sentences, as in English. As for tense and aspect, they have a neutral form whose meaning covers present time. In English this is the simple present, but in other languages the appropriate form might be one of several other forms.

1.4 Systems and characteristic forms

The task of collecting the sentence types in a language is made difficult by the fact that the expression of sentence use is closely related to, and easily confused with, other aspects of grammar, in particular negation, emphasis, subordination, modals, and adverbs. Thus, it is not uncommon for a morpheme marking sentences as questions to pattern very similarly to elements with clearly modal or adverbial meaning. For instance, in Tagalog (Schachter and Otanes 1972) the question particle *ba* occurs in the same place in sentences as several other particles, including some translatable as 'for a while, yet' (*muna*), 'only, just' (*lamang/lang*), 'because' (*kasi*) and 'too, either' (*din/rin*); the particles *ho* and *po*, which express respect for the person(s) addressed, also occur in this location.

In untangling sentence types from related phenomena, the following two observations are helpful:

First, the sentence types of a language form a *system*, in at least two senses: there are sets of corresponding sentences, the members of which differ only in belonging to different types, and second, the types are mutually exclusive, no sentence being simultaneously of two different types.[1] Thus, in English we can construct endless examples of corresponding declaratives, yes–no questions, and imperatives:

(23)   You caught the speckled geese
        Did you catch the speckled geese?
        Catch the speckled geese!

(24)   He will eat the beans
        Will he eat the beans?
        Eat the beans!

and there is no sentence that is simultaneously of the declarative type and of the imperative type, or of the yes–no question type and of the imperative type. These facts support our classification of the imperative (lacking a subject and having an uninflected verb) as a sentence type in English, even though it also forms a system with the modals in English, the modals being mutually exclusive with one another and with the imperative:

(25)   *He would can be kind

(26)   a. *Must be kind!

        b. *Should jump!

Notice also that the observation that sentence types form a system argues against counting English negative declaratives as a separate sentence type. They are independent of sentence type since they occur with interrogatives and imperatives, too:

(27)   Didn't you catch the speckled geese?
(28)   Don't catch the speckled geese!

This is not to say that no language could have a special sentence type for issuing denials. Indeed many languages have a special negative sentence type that contains a special indicator of negativity, or formal features different from those of the imperative, or both (see section 3.2.2 below).

Second, sentence types show certain *characteristic forms* across languages (see especially sections 3.1–3). Declaratives are characteristically unmarked (without special elements in them or any special ordering); imperatives characteristically have bare verb stems, without any affixes. English declaratives and imperatives are entirely characteristic, a fact that supports our original decision to class them as sentence types. There are, of course, many uncharacteristic forms in the sentence types of the world's languages (the inversion found in English yes–no questions is not extremely common, for instance), but the characteristic forms aid us in the classification and description of new languages.

2 Overall survey

2.1 *The most frequent sentence types*

It is in some respects a surprising fact that most languages are similar in presenting three basic sentence types with similar functions and often strikingly similar forms. These are the declarative, interrogative, and imperative. As a first approximation, these three types can be described as follows: The declarative is subject to judgments of truth and falsehood. It is used for making announcements, stating conclusions, making claims, relating stories, and so on. The interrogative elicits a verbal response from the addressee. It is used principally to gain information. The imperative indicates the speaker's desire to influence future events. It is of service in making requests, giving orders, making suggestions, and the like.

Despite these similarities we can find important differences in the system of sentence types in various languages. One dimension of difference has to do with the specificity of functions. In English, the declarative is quite vague in that it covers a number of acts, many of which are syntactically distinguished in some other languages. In Blackfoot (Frantz 1971) and Greenlandic (Hoijer *et al.* 1946), on the other hand, the formal features that distinguish the declarative are lacking in negative sentences. Onondaga (Chafe 1970a) has a very general imperative type that occurs in all persons and numbers and covers a wide range of more specific acts. Most languages have an imperative restricted to second person logical subjects that indicates the speaker's wish to influence the addressee's actions.

A second parameter that might distinguish languages involves higher-order affinities among the various basic sentence types. In Blackfoot, for example, questions and denials are both expressed in the non-affirmative mode. In English there seems to be a basic similarity between imperatives and declaratives: both have the subject before the verb – as opposed to questions, where it is usually the case that the subject is postposed.[2] In German, imperatives, questions, and certain wishes are similar and distinguish themselves from declaratives in that the verb is in sentence-initial position.[3]

The significance of these interrelationships among the various families of sentence types is not well understood. It is clear that the prosodic, morphological, and syntactic resources of language are by no means fully utilized in distinguishing different sentence types, so that there are frequently similarities among them, and it is obvious that which types are similar differs to some extent from language to language. These relationships should be noted in any description of the sentence-type system of a language.

2.2 Sentence types and attitude markers

One often needs to distinguish between forms that signal true sentence types, and another kind of form we will call an attitude marker. Lahu (Matisoff 1973) would, at first blush, seem to be a language with a much wider range of sentence types than one ordinarily encounters. On closer examination, though, Lahu appears to have extremely few sentence types and a very large number of particles that indicate attitudes, rational and emotional, toward a proposition. The expression of certain of these attitudes (mild desire, obviousness, desire for agreement, etc.) can quite naturally have the effect of a special sentence type.

For the following reasons, though, the attitudinal particles of Lahu should not be thought of as constituting a system of sentence types:

(a) They are not mutually exclusive. They may be freely combined except where the meaning would be contradictory.

As an example, the particle *mē* indicates polite insistence and thus can freely follow imperative, hortative, declarative, and exclamatory particles ('I insist that you/we go', 'I insist that it is (indeed) my pig', etc.), but may not follow true interrogatives (*'I insist whether he is a sham', *'I insist upon where we build the dam').

(b) They are freely embeddable to a quotative particle, in which case the attitude they signal is attributed to the person quoted and so has nothing to do with the communicative act being accomplished by the speaker.

For example, *hé* indicates doubt about the truth of the proposition it follows. Note that it may occur either inside or outside the scope of the quotative particle *cê* (Matisoff 1973:379):

(29) mâ cɔ̂-câ tù hé   cê
     NEG boil-eat FUT DUBITATIVE QUOTATIVE
     'It is said that he probably wouldn't boil it to eat it'

(30) mâ cɔ̂-câ tù cê   hé
     NEG boil-eat FUT QUOTATIVE DUBITATIVE
     'It is probably said that he wouldn't boil it to eat it'

(c) Their conventional meaning does not deal specifically with speech acts, but their combination with other meaningful elements produces the effect of specifying the speech act type of the clause they occur in.

Thus interjectional *ὲʔ* is 'purely interjectory' after other particles, but when used alone amounts to a 'brusque interrogative' or a 'sharp imperative'.

After eliminating these attitude markers, there remains a residue of conventional speech act indicators with surprisingly ordinary properties. There is an interrogative type, with one particle occurring only with interrogative proforms. There is a special imperative intonation, realized as sentence-final glottal stop, and a unique marker for negating imperatives. Finally, the declarative would seem to be unmarked. The particle *yò* (or the sequence *ve yò*), which occurs in the 'stylistically most neutral' sort of declarative, is not, in fact, restricted to declaratives, but also occurs with interrogatives. Thus (as is the case in some other languages we have investigated) the declarative and interrogative are a supertype and differ in that the interrogative is formed from the declarative by the addition of interrogative forms.

2.3 *Examples of some minor types*
2.3.1 *Exclamations*
In addition to the three major families of types, there are a number of minor types, some of which are reasonably common in the languages of the world. Most prominent of these are the EXCLAMATORY types.

The function of exclamatory sentences is much like that of declarative sentences, except that exclamations are intended to be expressive whereas declaratives are intended to be informative. Both represent a proposition as being true, but in an exclamation, the speaker emphasizes his strong emotional reaction to what he takes to be a fact, whereas in a declarative, the speaker emphasizes his intellectual appraisal that the proposition is true. Because of this close relationship, exclamatory sentences are often similar in form to declarative sentences, as in the English exclamatory type with *so* and *such a*:

(31)   That's *so* tacky!
(32)   She's *such a* good syntactician!

However, since exclamations are, like interrogatives, non-assertive, exclamatory sentences often resemble interrogative sentences in form, as in the English exclamatory type with *how* and *what a*:

(33)   How tacky that is!
(34)   What a good syntactician she is!

(Notice, however, that (33) and (34) lack the inversion found in information questions, even though they have some of the same interrogative words.) English also has an exclamatory type that resembles yes–no questions (see N. A. McCawley 1973):

(35)   Boy, does he ever have beautiful legs!
(36)   Wow, can he knit!

(Again, there are differences between (35) and (36) and questions: the exclamations have a different intonation pattern, they combine with interjections like *boy* and *wow*, and they can occur with non-temporal *ever*.)

The connection between exclamations and interrogatives is by no means limited to English. Elliott (1971:102–4) illustrates the connection with examples from French, Romanian, German, Mandarin Chinese, Russian, literary Japanese, and Turkish. Exclamations can also be expected to combine with a special set of interjections and to occur with some special exclamatory adverbial elements (like the Tagalog clitic *pala*, which expresses mild surprise, or the Chrau (Thomas 1971) sentence-final particle *o'n*, which expresses bewilderment or surprise).

In some languages there are special verbal forms for exclamations. So, in Kapampangan (Mirikitani 1972) there is an auxiliary verb *pala* expressing surprise or delight and an aspect prefix *ka-* that functions as an intensifier, much like English *so* in (31) or *how* in (33). And in Menomini there are two sets of verbal inflections, 'one of *surprise*, where the occurrence is new or unforeseen, and one of *disappointment* at the non-occurrence of something expected' (Bloomfield 1933:176).

Finally, in many languages exclamatory constructions may occur as dependent clauses as well as independent clauses. For instance, in English, exclamations can occur as complements to a large class of psychological predicates:

(37)　I'm amazed at how tacky that is
(38)　It is scarcely surprising what a good syntactician she is

2.3.2 *Imprecatives*

A second family of minor types that occur with some frequency is that of IMPRECATIVES: curses. Imprecatives, like exclamations, are expressive or emotional in tone, but unlike exclamations (whose affinities in form are to declaratives and interrogatives), imprecatives often resemble imperatives. This is true of the English minor types illustrated by the (obscene) examples:

(39)　Screw / Fuck / Shit on } you!

Another source for an imprecative type is a special future tense, used by the speaker to say what terrible events will befall the addressee. Turkish has such a special future form, the (otherwise archaic) suffix *-esi*: 'as a finite verb it occurs only in the base-form, i.e., in the third-person singular, and is employed solely for cursing' (Lewis 1967:115):

(40)   ev-in   yikɨl-asɨ
        house-your be demolished-FUT
        'May your house be demolished!'
(41)   gör-mi-y-esi
        see-NEG-he-FUT
        'May he not see!'

2.3.3 Optatives

Still another family of expressive minor types comprises OPTATIVES, expressions of the speaker's wishes. The name 'optative', however, is often applied to constructions that, properly speaking, do not constitute a separate sentence type. In Karok, for instance, there is an adverb *kíri* that is 'used with indicative verb forms to express wishes' (Bright 1957:361), and in Southern Paiute the combination of the emphasizing clitic *-ya'a-* with a verb suffix indicating unreality yields constructions described as optative (E. Sapir 1930:90, 168); but the construction can also be hortatory. That is, it can also be used to urge or suggest a course of action to be followed by the addressee. Thus it appears that this construction is not specifically an optative, but has just the more general meaning that one would expect from the meanings of the morphemes that make it up. Likewise in Karok, optative notions are expressed by the use of much more general attitude markers (see section 2.2 above).

There are several natural sources for a true optative sentence type: future tenses, conditional or subjunctive moods, and imperative moods. Any one of these might become specialized as an optative during the history of a language. Yet in few of the languages known to us has this specialization occurred. For the most part, the optative use of the relevant construction remains as one of a number of related uses, without any special mark. This is so in Latin (Hale and Buck 1966, Woodcock 1959), where a main clause subjunctive has optative force in the first or third person, but also has the force of a proposal, a suggestion, or an indirect command; and in Turkish, where the conditional base of a verb is used to express wishes (but also remote conditions), and the past form of this base expresses 'hopeless wishes relating to past time' (Lewis 1967:131) (but also unfulfilled conditions).

Greenlandic seems to have a genuine optative, distinct in form from the imperative. Both wishes and requests/commands/etc. are expressed by verb forms with a supporting vowel, but wishes have a characteristic consonant suffix *-l-*, whereas the imperatives lack the suffix. Maidu, too, has a distinct combination of mood and aspect suffixes for a category labeled the 'monitive optative'. This seems to constitute a genuine sentence type, but one better described as (AD)MONITIVE than as optative, on the basis of its meaning: '"possible future event of an unpleasant or undesirable nature," that is, some idea of warning or threat is usually implied' (Shipley 1964:49).

3 The most frequent types and their features

3.1 *Declarative*

3.1.1 *The form of declarative sentences*

3.1.1.1 *Unmarked declaratives*. There are two main ways that languages convey assertions, expressions of belief, reports, conclusions, narratives, assessment of likelihood, expressions of doubt, and the like. The most common way is to do nothing special – to use the most basic and widespread form of clause available in the language. Alternatively, some obligatory formal feature may mark clauses as declarative.

In languages of the first, or unmarked declarative, type, declarative sentences usually have the same form as some dependent clauses. This is true in English, where declarative sentences show the same word order as several sorts of subordinate clauses.

(42)   Pigs *which cannot fly* are numerous
(43)   I believe *that pigs cannot fly*
(44)   *If pigs cannot fly*, then dogs cannot sing

and where neither declarative sentences nor these subordinate clauses contain any special particles or inflections. Even in Karok, which uses participial or nominalized constructions for most subordination, declarative sentences have essentially the same form as adverbial subordinate clauses. Typically, in an unmarked declarative language, sentence types other than the declarative will have forms based on the declarative construction, in the sense that the other types involve the declarative construction *plus* some particle (as in one type of Tagalog questions), or an alteration in the word order of the declarative (as in Kapampangan questions), or an inflection parallel to tense/aspect inflections in the declarative (as in Maidu questions, where the interrogative suffixes are parallel to the suffixes indicating tense in declaratives).

3.1.1.2 *Marked declaratives*. In a fair number of languages, however, declarative constructions do not serve as the basis on which other sentence types are formed; instead, the declarative involves syntactic or morphological marks entirely parallel to the marks for other sentence types. For example, in German the word order in declaratives has the inflected verb in second position in the sentence, while in interrogatives (and imperatives) the inflected verb is sentence initial. These orders both deviate from what we may take to be the most basic word order in the language, namely that which occurs in independent clauses of several kinds; in most subordinate clauses the inflected verb comes at the *end* of the clause:

(45)   a. Declarative: Ich sehe zwei Papageien
                          'I   see   two   parrots'

        b. Interrogative: Sehe ich zwei Papageien?
                          'Do I see two parrots?'

        c. Subordinate: . . . weil ich zwei Papageien sehe
                          '. . . because I see two parrots'

More common than the use of word order to mark the declarative is the use of declarative particles (parallel to particles marking other sentence types) or declarative inflections (parallel to inflections marking other sentence types). Declarative particles may be illustrated, somewhat imperfectly, by sentence-initial $y(r)/r$ in Welsh (Bowen and Rhys Jones 1960). This affirmative particle, absent in embedded clauses, is parallel to the negative particle $ni(d)$ and the interrogative particle a, neither of which can co-occur with $y(r)/r$. However, the particle is used only with periphrastic verbs, so that although the periphrastic verbs are the most common colloquial forms, it is not true that *every* positive declarative sentence is marked with $y(r)/r$. A better, but more complex, example comes from the sentence-final declarative particles of Hidatsa. There are five such particles, indicating five different sentence uses in the declarative range (see the next section); they cannot co-occur with one another or with particles marking questions, optatives, and imperatives, and they do not occur in dependent clauses. Though there happens to be no simple particle expressing merely declarative sentence type, any declarative sentence must have one of these five particles (*ski*, *c*, *wareac*, *rahe* and *toak*).

Languages that mark declaratives inflectionally commonly use these same inflections in questions, but different inflections in imperatives and in dependent clauses. Sometimes negative declaratives are inflected differently from positive declaratives. These points can be illustrated by the declarative markers in Greenlandic Eskimo and Blackfoot, both of which use verbal affixes for this purpose.

In Greenlandic, both positive declaratives and positive interrogatives have the mood sign v (p after consonants) preceding the personal suffixes. Different mood signs are found in the imperative and in dependent clauses. The declarative differs from the interrogative in having different personal suffixes for some person and number combinations. Thus, for the verb *iga* 'to cook' we find,

(46)   Igavoq
        cook(INDIC 3SG)
        'He cooks'

(47)   Igava
        cook(Q 3SG)
        'Does he cook?'

(48)   igammat
        cook(CONJUNCTIVE MOOD 3SG)
        'because he cooked'

Negative declaratives *and* interrogatives (but again, not imperatives or dependent verb forms) have a different mood sign, *l*, which follows the ordinary negative marker *ng:i*. As with positives, the inflections of the declarative and interrogative are partially distinct:

(49)   Iganngilaq
        cook(NEG INDIC 3SG)
        'He doesn't cook'

(50)   Iganngila?
        cook(NEG Q 3SG)
        'Does he not cook?'

(51)   iganngimmat
        cook(NEG CONJUNCTIVE MOOD 3SG)
        'because he didn't cook'

In Blackfoot, there are special inflectional paradigms for declaratives, and related (though not identical) forms appear in questions, while imperatives follow quite a different paradigm: the second person singular affix in declaratives is *kit-*, but in imperatives it is *-t*. Negative sentences have the same paradigm as interrogatives. Verbs in the ordinary declarative paradigms are not used in subordinate clauses; instead, there are quite different paradigms for dependent clauses. Compare the independent first person inclusive – *o?p* – with the corresponding dependent affixes – *o?si* and *o?ki*).

3.1.2 *Putative subtypes of declaratives*
3.1.2.1 *The Hidatsa subtypes.* We have already seen, in our discussion of Hidatsa in section 3.1.1.2, that a language may lack a declarative, in

the sense that it has no single sentence type covering the full range of declarative uses. In Hidatsa the 'declarative' is really a supertype, a class of five different types that can be grouped together on the basis of their *use* and on the basis of their *form*: in optatives and imperatives the subject always follows the mood morpheme, which is then sentence initial, while in the five declarative types the mood morpheme either may or must be last in the sentence, following the verb, Hidatsa being an sov language; questions are marked prosodically rather than by a simple morpheme. Even in languages where the declarative is an ordinary type, certain subtypes may be marked in regular ways. In either case, the various types indicate different attitudes the speaker takes towards the proposition he is expressing, or different degrees of belief in the proposition, or different sources for the proposition – all of these matters that might be indicated by adverbs (like *necessarily* or *of course*), modal auxiliaries (like *must*), explicit complement-taking verbs (like *suppose*), or paralinguistically by expressive intonations or expressive modifications.

A dozen or so declarative subtypes have been suggested in one language or another. We cannot pretend to have a thorough survey of the possibilities, though we will illustrate some of them, beginning with the five in Hidatsa.

Hidatsa has an INDEFINITE type, which comes close to a 'neutral' mention of a proposition. Described by Matthews (1965) as a 'perhaps' mood, the indefinite is used when the speaker doesn't know if the proposition is true and doesn't think the addressee knows either. A second type indicates matters of common belief, what 'everyone knows'; this mood is also used in relating narratives. A third type is reportive or quotative, used for reporting what the speaker has heard from someone else (and is not vouching for himself). The fourth type expresses the speaker's beliefs, desires, and feelings. And the fifth type reports what the speaker knows to be true from first-hand evidence.

The Hidatsa system of sentence-type morphemes must be clearly distinguished from superficially similar sets of morphemes which indicate degree of belief, attitude, emphasis, and the like, but which are not mutually exclusive. For example, Tagalog has clitics *daw* and *raw* which from their meaning could be taken to be markers of a quotative/reportive sentence type. Moreover, *daw* and *raw* are syntactically parallel to the question particle *ba*, all of them occurring as clitics to the first word in the sentence. But *daw*/*raw* and *ba* may co-occur, as in (52) (Schachter and Otanes 1972:414):

(52)   Nagtatrabaho daw ba naman kayo roon?
        'Do they say that you're working there instead?'

We conclude that *daw* and *raw* do not mark a genuine sentence type, but are merely adverbial modifiers. This decision is further supported by the fact that *daw/raw* occur in dependent clauses, where they mark indirect quotations. Thus, Tagalog is much like Lahu, discussed in section 2.2 above: there are a few sentence types, plus a variety of attitude markers.

3.1.2.2 *Inferential.* Closely related to quotative/reportive sentences are INFERENTIAL sentences, in which conclusions or inferences are reported. Turkish has special inferential paradigms for the verb 'to be', plus a past inferential affix for other verbs. The Turkish inferential is also used as a quotative/reportive; the *miş*-past 'conveys that the information it gives is based either on hearsay or on inference from observed facts, but not on the speaker's having seen the action take place' (Lewis 1967:122). It turns out, however, that the Turkish inferential inflections do not mark sentence types (in the narrow sense we are using here) but are, like the Lahu and Tagalog particles, attitude indicators. This can be seen from the fact that the inferential and interrogative inflections co-occur, as in (Lewis 1967:106):

(53)   Evde   miymişim
        house(LOC)   Q-miş-1SG
        'Am I said to be at home?'

3.1.2.3 *Dubitative.* Clearly allied to quotative/reportive and inferential sentences are DUBITATIVE sentences, in which doubt or uncertainty is expressed. The relationship arises because reporting what one has heard and classifying a proposition as an inference are both indirect means of conveying the proposition; if a speaker chooses one of these indirect means instead of a straightforward assertion, he may suggest that he has doubts about the truth of the proposition (Lewis (1967:101) remarks that some grammarians have mistakenly labeled the inferential a dubitative). One language in our sample with a dubitative marker is Yokuts, which has a particle *naʔaṣ* and a verb suffix *-(a)l* which together express uncertainty. The morpheme patterns much like the morphemes marking imperatives and imprecatives. But, as in the last few examples, the mark of the dubitative does not exclude the mark of the interrogative (S. Newman 1944:120):

(54)   ʔangiʔ naʔ naʔaṣ ha·noʔuk ʔama·minwa tawṭa-l
        Q   I   PCL with-what them   kill-DUBITATIVE
        'With what could I kill them?'

This example shows the dubitative *-l* in the last word (and the dubitative particle *na ?as*, which always co-occurs with the dubitative verbal affix) *plus* the sentence-initial interrogative marker *?angi?*. Again, from the fact that the dubitative suffix is not mutually exclusive with the interrogative marker, we conclude that the language has an attitude marker rather than a genuinely separate sentence type.

A particularly interesting way of expressing doubt is the 'non-affirmative mode' of Blackfoot, which when used alone expresses uncertainty and also serves as the most common form for yes–no questions. (In addition, it appears in negative sentences.) Thus, Blackfoot appears to have a dubitative sentence type, parallel to and mutually exclusive with an affirmative type and an imperative type.

3.1.2.4 *Emphatic.* A final class of sentences that writers have treated as a special declarative subtype in various languages is the EMPHATIC class. Emphasis or insistence is clearly *not* expressed by a genuine sentence type in the many languages that have emphatic affixes or particles that can be attached to a variety of different word classes, or that have emphatic prosodic marks that can be associated with a variety of different word classes. In such languages, the emphatic marks regularly co-occur with clear marks for sentence types, as in the English emphatic question

(55)   *Do* you like this cake?

and the English emphatic imperative

(56)   *Give* me that cake!

Other languages have rich sets of emphatic particles acting as sentence modifiers. In Chrau, for example, there are nine emphatic assertion particles, as well as morphemes expressing surprise or bewilderment. Again the emphatic particles are not, in general, mutually exclusive with one another or with some of the other particles. In fact, we know of no language in which emphasis or insistence is truly a matter of sentence type rather than being expressed by simple attitude indicators.

3.2 *Imperative*
3.2.1 *The form of imperative sentences*
3.2.1.1 *General remarks.* All languages we have surveyed have one or more distinct syntactic forms that explicitly convey some subset of requests/commands/orders/suggestions/instructions/entreaties, and so on. It is not logically necessary that an imperative sentence type or types be available in a language. The effect of an imperative sentence could be

obtained by declarative sentences meaning 'I want you to ...' or 'You should/must ...' or 'You will ...', or by interrogative sentences meaning 'Will you ...?' or by other similar devices (see section 5.1). Nevertheless, the activities of requesting, commanding, and the like are so frequent in human social life, and so important to it, that no language (it seems) lacks a form dedicated to them.

There is considerable diversity in the way that this complex of speech acts is manifested. In some languages there are pre- or post-sentential particles and in some there are verbal clitics. Special verb morphology in the verb stem or a special set of personal affixes on verbs is also found. Deletion of the subject is fairly frequent, but at least one language, Yokuts (in which the imperative form is a bare verb stem, plus in some dialects a special suffix), has some special subject pronouns that occur only in the imperative sentence type, although they are not required there. At least one language, Chrau, marks imperatives by intonation.

Despite this diversity there are very striking convergences that show up regardless of genetic or typological distance. There are some very clear implicational universals to be found in the formation of imperatives and some substantive universals or near universals. We will begin with the substantive similarities.

3.2.1.2 *Imperatives in ergative languages.* There are languages in which some syntactic processes follow the ergative–absolutive arrangement; these processes treat the objects of transitive verbs and the subjects of intransitives in the same fashion (as 'absolutives'), whereas the subject of transitives is handled differently (as an 'ergative'). See chapter 1.2 on the major functions of the noun phrase. This suggests the possibility of an imperative construction arranged according to the ergative pattern. In a language with an ergative-style imperative, it could be the absolutive argument that would represent the addressee, whether the verb is transitive or intransitive. Thus the imperative of an intransitive verb like *go* would be a request for the addressee to depart, while the imperative of a transitive verb like *convince* would be a request for the addressee to *be* convinced, that is, to believe something.

Included in our sample are two languages, Dyirbal (Dixon 1972) and Eskimo, that are reputed to be among the most ergative in the world. Yet transitive imperatives in these two languages mean exactly what they do in English.

For example, the Greenlandic verb *iga* 'to cook' has both transitive and intransitive forms. The noun phrase that represents the one doing the cooking is in the absolutive case with the intransitive form, but in the transitive sentence it is the thing being cooked that is represented by the absolutive case argument, while the cook is represented by an ergative.

(57) palasi   igavoq
      priest(ABS) cook(INDIC 3SG)
      'The priest is cooking (something)'

(58) angutip palasi   igavaa
      man(ERG) priest(ABS) cook(INDIC 3SG/3SG)
      'The man is cooking the priest'

Nevertheless, the imperative of either form is a request to do some cooking:

(59) Igagit
      cook(IMP 2SG)
      'Cook (something)!'

(60) Igaguk
      cook(IMP 2SG/3SG)
      'Cook it!'

Thus, although Eskimo is ergative morphologically, and to some extent syntactically, the imperative follows the pattern where it is always *subjects* that are addressees for imperatives, whether the verb is transitive or intransitive.[4] To our knowledge, all languages follow this pattern, and the explanation would appear to be a semantic one, the fact that across languages subject position is the usual one for *agents*. With imperatives one does not request something of someone over which that person does not have direct control. Addressees for imperatives must be subjects, but not just any subjects. Verb forms not ordinarily understood to take agentive subjects tend not to be used in imperatives, and languages resist imperatives such as *Be convinced!* or *Weigh 200 lb!* If they are ever used, they are recognized as unusual, and there must be pragmatic factors to compensate, for example it is thought that the addressee can make himself or herself believe something or weigh a certain weight.

3.2.1.3 *Reduction in affixes.* Of the many varieties of signals for the imperative, by far the most common, characterizing well over half of the languages we have examined, is the use of a verb form with fewer than the normal number of affixes. Over half of the languages surveyed, in fact, employ an entirely affixless verbal base to indicate requests. Two tenses are found in one stage of Latin, but tense distinctions of any kind are extremely rare. Aspect distinctions are somewhat more frequent, but also unusual. Differences in conjugation class are sometimes preserved and sometimes obliterated.

In Danish, for example, a verb belongs to one of several conjugation classes. One of the differences in conjugation has to do with whether a vowel intervenes between the verb and certain suffixes. Thus, *købe* 'to buy' has the past tense *købte*, but *hoppe* 'to hop' has the past tense *hoppede*. In the imperative, this difference is obliterated: *køb* 'buy!' *hop* 'hop!'. (Note that in Swedish, this difference in conjugation class is preserved in the imperative, the respective forms being *köp* 'buy!', but *hoppa* 'hop!'.)

The relative frequency with which these various morphological contrasts are dispensed with in imperatives is thus, to a large extent, reflective of the inherent semantics of the imperative. It is notionally future, so tense contrasts are unlikely. The subject naturally refers to the addressee, so second person inflection of the verb becomes redundant. The archetypical request is to do some task to completion, so indications of aspects are somewhat redundant. Semantic considerations cannot explain the suppression of conjugation-class distinctions, of course, but it remains a fact that this also occurs.

3.2.1.4 *Subject pronouns and concord features.* Languages regularly suppress subject pronouns and/or affixes that agree with the subject, at least in some parts of the imperative paradigm. Especially interesting is the fact that personal suffixes are frequently absent, even in languages that quite strictly mark features of the subject on the main verb. Languages that inflect for mood either have no mood inflection in the imperative or, more often (according to our sample), a special sign for the imperative.

Numerous languages present imperative verb forms without personal suffixes in only certain number, gender, person, and politeness combinations.

In German, the suffixes *-st*, *-t*, and *-en* are the usual second person concord markers for the singular familiar, plural familiar, and polite, respectively. These mark all verbal forms with the sole exception of the imperative, where there is no explicit marking for the second singular familiar. Thus compare the present, past and imperative of the verb *sagen* 'to say':

(61)

	PRESENT	PAST	IMPERATIVE
2SG familiar	sag*st*	sagte*st*	sag
2PL familiar	sag*t*	sagte*t*	sag*t*
2SG/PL polite	sag*en*	sagt*en*	sag*en*

If only some of the forms of an imperative paradigm are devoid of explicit personal markers, it appears that these will always include the second person singular, and – provided the language has such categories – the masculine familiar. Hebrew provides another example. While the four second person imperative forms, the masculine and feminine, singular and plural, are all distinct, the masculine singular is special in that it alone has *no* suffix: Here is the paradigm for the imperative of the verb *jašav* 'to sit':

(62)   MASCULINE   FEMININE
     SG   šev   švi
     PL   švu   ševna

The principles governing the suppression of personal affixes seem to be very much the same as those governing the suppression of subject pronouns, the singular, masculine, familiar being the most likely member of the paradigm not to show up explicitly. But pronouns appear to be more frequently suppressed than affixes. In several languages subject pronouns can be suppressed in cases where verbal affixes with the same features cannot. In German, for example, all subject pronouns may be omitted in imperatives, but as we have seen only the second singular, familiar verb concord is lacking.

The suppression in the imperative of what is ordinarily an obligatory feature of the subject, either a subject pronoun or a verbal concord affix, is an amazingly popular phenomenon. In our sample, only one language, Onondaga, was not described as lacking either some subjects or some concord markers in the imperative.

3.2.1.5 *Dependent imperatives.* Another widespread fact about imperatives is that they tend not to occur as dependent clauses. The handbooks are sometimes rather vague on points such as this, but we found no clear examples of a marker of imperativity functioning as a complementizer. Examples like the English

(63)   We bid you enter

come close, but it seems to us that the resemblance is an accidental convergence. In languages with distinct imperative morphology, the imperative is excluded from dependent clauses.

3.2.1.6 *Object marking.* One final interesting but sporadic tendency should be mentioned. The case marking of objects of imperative sentences is often unusual. Some basically nominative–accusative languages (like Finnish and Southern Paiute) show *nominative* objects in the imperative. Thus in Finnish (Comrie 1975:115) we find

(64) Maija   söi kalan
      Maija(NOM) ate fish(ACC)

but

(65) Syö kala
      Eat fish(NOM)!

3.2.2 *Subtypes of the imperative*

3.2.2.1 *Prohibitives.* A striking fact about imperatives is how frequently negative imperatives are handled differently from negative declaratives. Better-known Western languages like English are, in fact, quite unusual in simply adding the marks of negation that are found in other sentence types to the imperative formula in order to convey a prohibition.

Even English, which appears to form straightforward negative imperatives, has a special form for sentences with the main verb *be*:

(66) Don't be stupid!

Here *do* appears, whereas it fails to in the case of corresponding negative assertions and questions:

(67) *I didn't be stupid
(68) *Didn't I be stupid?

Roughly half the languages we surveyed have a negative marker in sentences with imperative meaning which is not the same as the one found in other sentence types. Such languages have what amounts to a special negative imperative type, which we will refer to as the PROHIBI-TIVE (though some writers use the term VETATIVE).

In Yokuts, for example, the general mark of negation is ʼhɔm, but just in case the verb bears the imperative suffix -ka, another negative, ʼa·ñi, is used.

There are also languages in which sentences with negative imperative meaning are not of imperative form. Thus these languages also display a prohibitive sentence type, but it is not formally related to the imperative. Roughly half of our sample languages have non-imperative prohibitives. Some use a normally dependent form of the verb (an infinitive, as in Greenlandic; or a subjunctive, as in Swahili and Latin); some an indicative paraphrase meaning roughly 'cease doing . . .' (as in Welsh) or 'you will not . . .' (as in Hebrew: see examples (75–6) below); and some a special prohibitive adverbial occurring with indicative verb forms (as in Karok, where the adverb *xayfa t*, glossed 'don't', marks the prohibitive). Some languages have both a non-imperative prohibitive *and* a special negative marker in the prohibitive.

Greenlandic Eskimo provides an example of the use of a non-imperative verb form. It has a negative imperative, but one used only to rescind a previous order. For general prohibitions, a negative infinitive is used. The so-called infinitive form of the Greenlandic verb is a dependent form that is used to express action simultaneous with the action in the main clause. The subject of a transitive infinitive is not marked on the verb, but the object is:

(69)   Attornagu   iserpoq
         disturb(NEG INF 3SG) come in(MOOD 3SG)
         'Without disturbing it, he came in'

So also in prohibitions:

(70)   Una attornagu
         this   disturb(NEG INF 3SG)
         'Do not disturb this'

In Modern Hebrew, there is both a non-imperative verb form and a special negative element. There is a distinct imperative form in Modern Hebrew, but, for most verbs, a second person future form is ordinarily used in the colloquial language:

(71)   šev
         sit(IMP)
         'Sit down!'

(72)   tešev
         sit(2SG FUT INDIC)
         'Sit down!' or 'You will sit down'

The ordinary negative marker is the preverbal adverbial *lo'*, for example:

(73)   Hu lo' yošev
         he not sit(MASC SG PRES INDIC)
         'He is not sitting'

But this negative is ungrammatical with the imperative form:

(74)   *Lo' šev

And while *lo'* is grammatical with the second person future form, this does not produce an imperative sentence. Instead a special negative marker, *'al*, that is used nowhere else, combines with the future for the prohibitive construction:

(75)   Lo' tešev
        not sit(2SG FUT INDIC)
        'You will not sit down'

(76)   'Al tešev
        not sit(2SG FUT INDIC)
        'Do not sit down!'

Similarly, in Onondaga, there is a distinct prohibitive type that makes use of the 'peremptory' verb form, rather than the imperative, and requires the special 'prohibitive particle' *ahkwi*.

Roughly three quarters of the languages we investigated cannot form straightforward negative imperatives, either because they use a non-imperative verb form, or because they use a special negative form, or both. We therefore regard the avoidance of such forms as a typical feature of natural languages.

3.2.2.2 *Other imperative subtypes.* The HORTATIVE is in some languages simply a first or third person form of the imperative, but in most languages in our sample it is formally distinct from the imperative. We might say that in the former case (as in Onondaga), there is only a hortative form – an expression of a desire – whereas in the latter case there is a separate imperative. Further subdivision is found in some languages between the first and third person hortatives.[5] Thus English has the special first person hortative *let's*, but no grammatically special form for expressing desires for actions not involving the speaker or addressee.

Occasionally in some languages imperatives divide formally according to the reason behind their issuance. The action called for by a genuine REQUEST is to be performed for the benefit of the requester whereas it is in the interest of the addressee to carry out an admonition or WARNING. INSTRUCTIONS are to be followed in order to complete some task, and ORDERS or COMMANDS demand compliance simply because of the authority that the orderer has over the recipient of the order.

Military commands in English have a special syntax (as pointed out to us by James Lindholm, personal communication). Each command has two parts, a preparatory part followed by an executive part. The system is arranged such that the executive part of the command contains only redundant information. The correct form of a command to turn right while marching is

(77)   Right flank – march!

and the command to place rifles on the right shoulder is

(78)   Right shoulder – arms!

There will be variation from language to language as to whether uses such as these constitute separate sentence types, and as to whether they comprise subtypes of the imperative or of some other major type. If their syntax is distinct from that of imperatives, commands should be considered a separate sentence type.

Still other distinctions are made, in a few languages, as to the conditions under which the requested action is to be carried out. Thus, Tagalog has a special construction for an 'immediate imperative', a command or request for the immediate performance of the action. And Maidu distinguishes an imperative formed with either $p(i)$ or zero, 'used when the action of the order is to be carried out in the presence of the speaker or when there is no interest in the place of the ordered action', from one formed with *padá*, 'used when the ordered action is to be carried out in the absence of the speaker' (Shipley 1964:51).

Finally, we should point out that most, if not all, languages have devices for distinguishing various degrees of emphasis, peremptoriness, politeness, and formality in imperative sentences, as in the English examples:

(79)   Stand up!
(80)   Please stand up!
(81)   Do stand up!
(82)   You stand up!
(83)   Stand *up*!

While these distinctions need not be a matter of different sentence types in our sense (since they have to do with attitudes as well as with different uses of sentences), they deserve note. Even languages with no morphological marks of politeness or formality (like English) have ways of distinguishing these attitudes, and the full system of attitude marks in imperative sentences can be quite elaborate.

3.3 *Interrogative*

3.3.1 *Subtypes of interrogatives*
The languages we have surveyed all have some grammatical signal indicating that the purpose of a sentence that is so marked is to gain information.[6] And we must distinguish several different information-seeking types, ones that usually have distinct syntactic or phonological properties.

Perhaps the most basic interrogative type, and the most widely distributed, is the YES–NO (or NEXUS) question, one that seeks a comment on the degree of truth of the questioned proposition. Closely related to yes–no questions are ALTERNATIVE questions. These provide a list from which, the speaker suggests, the right answer might be drawn. But the list might consist only of a proposition and its negation:

(84)   Is it raining, or isn't it?

In addition, alternative questions provide a link with information questions in that the alternatives that are suggested can be a list of propositions that differ in some way other than logical polarity. Thus in

(85)   Is it raining, or is it snowing?

the alternatives involve distinct predicates that the speaker implies are mutually exclusive. In

(86)   Did Bill stay, or did Harry?

the propositions (also implied to be mutually exclusive) differ in one argument. The alternatives may also differ in more than one place. In the following example, the alternatives are completely distinct, but the idea of mutual exclusivity is still present.

(87)   Is it raining, or did someone leave the sprinkler on?

Alternative questions must be distinguished from sentences such as (88) which present alternative formulations of essentially the same yes–no question. Instead of requiring the addressee to choose which alternative is true, (88) requires a *yes* or *no* answer: *no* if neither proposition is true, and *yes* otherwise:

(88)   Were you ever a member of the Cub Scouts or were you ever engaged in Scouting activities?

In English, questions such as (88) differ from alternative questions in their intonation. The former have a rising intonation on the first alternative – and on all other non-final alternatives if there are any – but a falling intonation on the final one. If this intonation were delivered with (88), it would create a clash because it would signal a choice between mutually exclusive alternatives when the alternatives in (88) are in fact not so. The normal intonation for questions such as (88) is with a rise on each alternative including the last.

The third important, and very nearly universal, interrogative form is the INFORMATION or QUESTION-WORD question. Here the alternatives are specified not in an exhaustive way by listing, but in an open-ended way by quantification:

(89)   Who suggested eating at this place?
(90)   When will we finish this paper?
(91)   How much is that kangaroo in the window?

The yes–no, alternative, and information questions we have seen so
far are alike in being neutral with respect to the answer the speaker
expects. But most languages have what Moravcsik (1971) calls BIASED
questions, questions that a speaker uses to express his or her belief that
a particular answer is likely to be correct and to request assurance that
this belief is true. Many languages therefore have a three-way distinction among yes–no questions: neutral yes–no questions, those biased in
favor of a positive answer, and those biased in favor of a negative
answer, as in English (arrows indicate rising final intonation):

(92)   Was she pushed? (neutral)
(93)   She was pushed, wasn't she? (positively biased)
(94)   She wasn't pushed, was she? (negatively biased)

Just one of the languages we surveyed, Onondaga, is claimed to have
only biased yes–no questions.

A few languages have a special form for RHETORICAL questions, those
a speaker uses just for rhetorical effect when not only is he sure of the
answer, but he judges that the listener knows that he is sure of the
answer as well. It is not clear that explicitly rhetorical questions should
be considered interrogatives at all, unless they bear formal relations
to ordinary interrogatives. Kleinschmidt (1968:57) mentions a very
restricted rhetorical form in Greenlandic, used mainly in the second
person negative intransitive; it resembles an interrogative in having the
second person suffix used for interrogative rather than the one used for
declaratives. He describes this form as expressing a mild negative
judgment, and it thus appears to be a grammaticized rhetorical question. Example (95) is a declarative, (96) a normal interrogative, and (97)
the rhetorical question.

(95)   Naalanngilatit
         'You do not obey'

(96)   Naalanngilit?
         'Do you not obey?'

(97)   Naalanngippit?
         'Do you not obey?' (that is, 'You should obey')

The biased questions – by suggesting which answer is expected – can
achieve this effect in languages that do not have a special rhetorical
question form.

3.3.2 *The form of yes–no questions*

The most striking property of yes–no questions, one that has been observed by many researchers, is their characteristic rising final intonation contour. It has also been pointed out by several investigators that this intonation pattern is very close to, if not exactly like, that of any non-final disjunct. Nevertheless, it seems to us that this intonation pattern has in many cases become a grammatical feature marking interrogation. There are languages (for example Greenlandic) in which the special intonation is not found; Ultan (1969:54) points out that all such languages are postpositional, though this generalization does not hold in the other direction. There are languages (like Chrau) in which this intonation is in complementary distribution with some other formal marker of interrogation; and others still (for instance, Diola, J. D. Sapir 1965) where the rising intonation is found in both yes–no and information questions. Be that as it may, rising final intonation is one of the most frequently found indicators of interrogative force and is in some languages (Jacaltec, for instance, Craig 1977) the *only* feature that distinguishes yes–no questions from declaratives.

Other characteristics of yes–no questions – in the order of frequency in our sample – are these: a sentence-initial particle, a sentence-final particle, special verb morphology, and word order. And we have found additional phonological distinctions of a prosodic nature. In Hopi, for example, the first word of a yes–no question has special stress, and in Hidatsa, the last vowel of the last word is interrupted by a glottal stop. Many languages display several of these properties at the same time or have alternative devices in this range. In a (non-rhetorical) yes–no question, Yoruba (Bamgbose 1966) has either a sentence-initial particle, *ǹjé,* or a sentence-final particle, *bí* or *dọn,* but not both.

Yiddish marks yes–no questions with three features in concert, a sentence-initial particle, a word-order change from the declarative, and final rising intonation, for example:

(98)   Mojše hot gekojft a hunt
        Moses has bought a dog
        'Moses bought a dog'

(99)   Ci hot Mojše gekojft a hunt?
        Q has Moses bought a dog
        'Did Moses buy a dog?'

Word-order change is frequent in European languages but uncommon otherwise. Invariably, the change is such as to place the verb at or near the beginning of the sentence and is thus impossible in a language whose basic word order has the verb first.

A few languages – good examples are Blackfoot and Greenlandic – use special verb morphology to distinguish questions from statements. In Greenlandic yes–no questions there is a special set of concord affixes when the subject is third person; see examples (46–51). Blackfoot yes–no questions are in the non-affirmative mode, manifested as a set of agreement suffixes different from those in positive assertions.

Finally, a fairly common system involves the use of a mobile interrogative clitic. When the clitic occurs on the verb, a question results that interrogates the whole of the sentence. When it occurs on some other constituent, a question results that interrogates just that constituent, with the remainder of the proposition presupposed. Latin illustrates the style very well. The clitic is -*ne*. It may be suffixed to nearly any word in a simplex sentence:

(100)   Est*ne* puer bonus?
        'Is the boy good?'

(101)   Puer*ne* bonus est?
        'Is it the boy who is good?'

(102)   Bonus*ne* puer est?
        'Is it good that the boy is?'

(The translations are necessarily rough.) Sentence (101) requires for its appropriate use that the discourse already be such as to have established that someone is good, sentence (102) that the discourse be such that qualities of the boy are at issue.

Such FOCUSED yes–no questions therefore resemble biased questions to some extent, in that they display a belief by the speaker that a proposition is likely to be true.

Indeed, in Latin (and, with differences, in Turkish), an interrogative particle associated with a negative adverb forms a positively biased[7] yes–no question. Corresponding to English (103) is Latin (104).

(103)   The boy is good, isn't he?

(104)   Non*ne* puer bonus est?

In fact, negative yes–no questions are often positively biased questions (see Moravcsik 1971 and Pope 1973). But in some languages (such as Japanese, Kuno 1973) they are neutral questions about the negative proposition.

Another frequently found question-like type is the CONFIRMATIVE. Rather than having as their goal the garnering of information, these really amount to statements that carry with them the demand that the addressee express his agreement or disagreement. They bear a close resemblance to biased questions and are probably not distinct from them in many languages. They are commonly formed by appending a tag to a declarative base, and the tag is most often, but not always, negative. Quite often, the tag also contains a predicate with a meaning like 'is' or 'true'. Thus Greenlandic has the tag *ila?*, literally, 'is it so?', French *n'est ce pas?*, literally 'is it not?', German *nicht wahr?*, 'not true?' and so forth.

English distinguishes biased tag questions from confirmatives in that the former have question intonation but the latter do not.

(105)   Coffee is expensive, isn't it?   (biased)

(106)   Coffee is expensive, isn't it   (confirmative)

The English sort of opposite polarity tag with a copied predicate appears to be quite rare.

It is not infrequently the case that the formal indications of yes–no questions resemble those of the antecedent of conditional sentences (the clause in a conditional that is expressed in English with *if*). In Biblical Hebrew, for example, yes–no questions are introduced with the particle *ha?im*. This particle consists of an interrogative indicator, *ha*, and the conjunction *?im*, which is used to introduce antecedents of conditionals. German provides several ways of expressing conditionals, one of which involves placing the verb before the subject – just as is done in yes–no questions.

(107)   Das Buch ist rot
        'The book is red'

(108)   Ist das Buch rot?
        'Is the book red?'

(109)   Ist das Buch rot, so muss es mir gehören
        'If the book is red, it must belong to me'

3.3.3 *The form of information questions*
We turn next to the second major type of question, the information question. These are formed with the use of interrogative proforms and occur either in conjunction with, or independently of, the formal markers of interrogativity in yes–no questions. Inversion and special morphology seem frequently to co-occur with interrogative words, but particles and intonation do so only rarely.

In many languages it is difficult to find any formal arguments that would support the idea that yes–no questions and information questions form a class. Thus the German questions

(110)   Ist er krank?
         'Is he sick?'

(111)   Wer ist krank?
         'Who is sick?'

don't seem to have any particular syntactic similarity at all.[8] The same is true in those languages where information questions differ from yes–no questions by being equational in form: 'in Tagalog and in Menomini . . . the [information question] is always an equational sentence, e.g. Menomini [awɛːʔ pajiat¿] "who the-one-who-comes?", that is, "Who is coming?"' (Bloomfield 1933:176). In contrast, special interrogative verb morphology characterizes both yes–no and information questions in Greenlandic:

(112)   Piniarpoq   'He is hunting'
(113)   Piniarpa?   'Is he hunting?'
(114)   Kina piniarpa?   'Who is hunting?'
         (*Kina piniarpoq?)

Here the two types are closely related.

A few languages (Hopi, for example) might lack information questions entirely, using instead indefinite statements ('Someone came') or indefinite yes–no questions ('Did someone come?') to achieve the same effect.

The number of question words is extremely variable, but, as Ultan (1969:53) points out, one contrast which is almost always present, even in languages that do not otherwise make use of the distinction in grammar, is that between personal and impersonal (English *who* and *what*), with Lithuanian and Khasi exceptions in not showing such a contrast. Most languages have pronominal interrogatives, many have pro-adverbial interrogatives (English *when, where, how*). A few have interrogative pro-verbs (Southern Paiute *aɤan·i* – 'to do what? to act how? to have what happen to one?' – and *an·ia* – 'to say what?') – and a few have interrogative pronumerals (Latin *quot* 'how many?' and *quotus* 'the how manyth?'). It would be theoretically possible for a language to get by with a single morpheme for information questions, a nominal modifier glossed as 'what?', so that all or nearly all information questions would involve periphrasis (*what person*? for 'who?', *at what time*? for 'when?', etc.). As it happens, the smallest system of such morphemes known to us is the Yokuts system, with three interrogative stems (glossed 'who', 'who, what', and 'where'), while systems of a dozen or more forms are not uncommon.

As they interrogate part of a proposition, information questions always present the rest of the proposition as old or presupposed information. Thus, *Who killed Cock Robin?* presupposes that someone killed Cock Robin, and *When did you beat your wife?* presupposes that you beat your wife at some time. The new information is the request for the identity of the interrogated part of the sentence. The interrogated part of the sentence can thus be called the 'focus' of the sentence, but it is also what the sentence is about, so the term 'topic' is used as well. Interrogative proforms are often found in focus or topic position, which for many languages is sentence-initial position. In Diola, Karok, and Greenlandic, however, the interrogative occurs in the same syntactic position as a non-interrogative form. In languages with distinct positions for topic and focus, such as Hungarian, the interrogative is in the position of focus. The topic in a Hungarian sentence is initial, while the focused element (including an interrogative word) stands immediately before the verb:

(115)　A　teát　　hogy parancsolod?
　　　　the your tea how you would order
　　　　'How would you like your *tea*?'

A number of languages stress the new information/old information dichotomy in information questions by using their cleft construction to focus the interrogated constituent, the same cleft construction used in declarative sentences. Hausa (Kraft and Kirk-Greene 1973) is like many West African languages in allowing *only* clefted information questions. One cannot ask *Who killed Cock Robin?* but only *Who was it who killed Cock Robin?* And in West Africa at least, it appears that languages constrained to clefted information questions allow only clefted answers to information questions as well.

Semantically, information questions are like alternative questions in specifying a range in which the answer is to be found. Interrogative words indicate either all by themselves, or with the help of syntactic features of the question in which they occur, which part of the proposition the asker is interested in knowing about. That is, they help to determine whether it is the subject, object, verb, or some other element of the proposition that the addressee is requested to supply so as to yield a true proposition. But interrogative words also typically limit the field that the asker expects the unknown to be part of. Thus *who* indicates that the asker wants the addressee to identify a person, *when* indicates a time, *where* a place, and so on. Such words as *whoever*, *whenever*, and *wherever* perform these functions as well, but do not indicate interrogation. Many languages, however, do not formally distinguish interrogatives and indefinites such as these. There is also a strong tendency for interrogatives and relative pronouns to be related, or identical, or at least to overlap to a large extent, as they do in English.[9]

3.3.4 *Dependent interrogatives*

In a great many languages there are dependent clauses with the unmistakable form of information questions (though not necessarily with every formal characteristic of information questions). The most common functions for such DEPENDENT INTERROGATIVES are as complements of verbs of asking, saying, and knowing:

$$(116) \quad \text{Marlene} \begin{Bmatrix} \text{asked} \\ \text{announced} \\ \text{realized} \end{Bmatrix} \begin{Bmatrix} \text{whose handwriting she was} \\ \text{puzzling over} \\ \text{why it was so hard to read} \\ \text{how many hours she had} \\ \text{spent typing} \end{Bmatrix}$$

The complements in (116) clearly have the form of English information questions – they have question words in them, moreover question words located at the beginning of the clause – though they lack one property of information questions, inversion.[10]

A syntactic description of a language should include some account of dependent interrogatives: whether they occur; if so, which ones occur and which syntactic contexts they occur in; and what differences there are between independent and dependent interrogatives.

Dependent yes–no questions also occur, but there are languages (like English) in which the meaning of a dependent yes–no question is supplied by a special dependent information question:

$$(117) \quad \text{Marlene} \begin{Bmatrix} \text{asked} \\ \text{announced} \end{Bmatrix} \text{whether there would be wine (or not)}$$

In English, neither the inversion nor the intonation of independent yes–no questions carries over to dependent clauses. Instead, there is an information-question construction related to disjunctive coordination in the language.

There are sometimes affinities between the form of dependent interrogatives and the antecedents of conditionals even when independent questions do not display them (see section 3.3.2). Thus English allows *if* in place of *whether* in sentences like (117). *If*, of course, is the word that introduces the antecedent clause in conditional sentences.

4 Sentence fragments

4.1 *Free constituents*

In English, an extremely wide range of effects can be obtained simply by uttering a noun phrase and accompanying it with any of a variety of paralinguistic effects, facial expressions, and gestures. Uttering a noun phrase like

(118) Some whiskey
(119) The goblins
(120) Six of those pink ones with the little sprinkles on top
(121) All of you with beards
(122) Lord Threshingham

could convey a request, an order, an offer, a warning, a threat, or an expression of dismay or delight; (118), (119), (120), and (121) could be used to identify certain objects, to supply an appropriate designation for those objects, or simply to call those objects to someone's attention; (121) and (122) could be used to catch the attention of some person or persons, or to address them during a conversation; all could be used to answer a question or to express disbelief in what one has heard or doubt that one has heard correctly; and so on. Probably every language can use free noun phrases for many effects (though not necessarily the same range as in English). The question is: What is the nature of these associations between form (isolated noun phrase) and use?

The question is a very complex one, and we do not propose to give a full answer to it here. We *do* want to point out, however, that many of these effects are surely obtained from the nature of the context in which a noun phrase is uttered. Someone hearing something like (119) is obliged to figure out why the speaker of (119) should be mentioning the goblins at all, and to do this he uses his knowledge of where he and the speaker are, what their relationship to one another is, and what has been going on between them. Without this contextual information, there are many possible interpretations, while in some contexts only one would be reasonable. For the most part, then, we are inclined to say that (118–22) are simply noun phrases, with a variety of uses in context, and that a syntactic description of English would have to say little more than that noun phrases can appear in isolation (a related question is discussed in section 5.1 below).

In some cases, however, there is more to be said. VOCATIVE uses of noun phrases – those in which someone is called or addressed – have many special properties in English and in other languages: only certain noun phrases can be used vocatively, and these may occur either as free constituents or in combination with other constituents, but in the latter case there are restrictions on where they can occur (Zwicky 1974). In some languages, the head noun in a vocative phrase takes a special inflectional form (Latin nominative *servus* '(a/the) servant', but vocative *serve* 'O, servant!'). While vocatives can scarcely be said to make up a special sentence type, since they are not sentences and since they combine with sentences, still they are syntactically special constructions with special uses and require description in every language in which they occur.

In another class of cases, certain free noun phrases show some evidence of syntactic specialness in association with a special use. This is so for the Greenlandic 'verbal participle', a nominal form meaning 'the one who/which ...'; the verbal participle, but not other nearly synonymous noun phrases, can be used in isolation as a declarative with an overtone of wonder, pity or surprise (Kleinschmidt 1968:68). Free noun phrases in English can also function as requests, and, like requests, they can occur with a following *please* (see Sadock 1970:235).

(123)   A beer, please
(124)   The left shoulder, please

Here and in similar cases, a careful description of a language should note that certain sentence fragments seem to belong to one or another of the families of sentence types in the language (in Greenlandic the verbal participle construction is an exclamatory subtype of the declarative family, in English the free noun phrase is, among other things, a request subtype of the imperative family).

These matters are made more difficult still by the fact that the effects associated with free noun phrases are determined in part by the intonation patterns of those noun phrases, and it is notoriously difficult to decide which aspects are meaning-bearing in the same sense that individual morphemes like *poodle* are, and which aspects are essentially paralinguistic, conveying emotional tone or affect in a non-discrete and loose fashion. We have adopted a conservative position here, so as to avoid recognizing a large number of sentence types distinguished from one another by fine shades of meaning.

A final point to be made is that noun phrases are not the only possible free constituents, even in English. English also has free prepositional phrases used with imperative or exclamatory force, as in

(125)   Near the window!
(126)   On the stairs!
(127)   Onto the table!

and other languages can be expected to have additional examples.

4.2 Answers to questions

4.2.1 *Question particles*

One important class of sentence fragments that we did not discuss in the previous section is that of answers to questions (both yes–no questions and information questions). All the noun phrases in (118–22), said with the intonation of ordinary declarative sentences, could be answers to information questions. So could a number of other constituent types, for instance,

(128)   With a fish knife
(129)   Because she liked penguins
(130)   Walk all the way to Westwood
(131)   Very carefully
(132)   Standing up in a hammock

For yes–no questions in English there are two morphemes, *yes* and *no*,[11] whose primary function in the language is to serve as positive and negative answers, respectively, to such questions; hence like (118–22) they are essentially declarative in force. Of course, yes–no questions can be answered with other positive and negative adverbs, like *sure*, *absolutely*, *of course*, *not at all*, and *absolutely not*, as well as by adverbs and other constructions that give less than a definite answer, like *perhaps*, *maybe*, *I guess*, and *so I've heard*. But *yes* and *no* have a special status, being syntactically quite distinct from the ordinary adverbs in English. Some languages may not treat answer words as a special class. There may also be special short responses to imperative sentences, like the positive response *OK* in English:

(133)   Is Katmandu the capital of Nepal? $\begin{Bmatrix} ?OK \\ Yes \end{Bmatrix}$ (, it is)

(134)   That's a lovely wallaby on the porch. $\begin{Bmatrix} ?OK \\ Yes \end{Bmatrix}$ (, I agree)

(135)   Give me a dumpling tomorrow. $\begin{Bmatrix} OK \\ Yes \end{Bmatrix}$ (, I will)

We turn now to some brief general comments on answers to questions, from a cross-linguistic point of view.

4.2.2 *Yes/no and agree/disagree systems*

There are basically three systems for short answers to yes–no questions: YES/NO SYSTEMS, AGREE/DISAGREE SYSTEMS, and ECHO SYSTEMS.[12] English has a typical yes/no system, with a positive particle accompanying, or standing for, a positive answer, and a negative particle accompanying, or standing for, a negative answer:

(136)   Q: $\begin{Bmatrix} \text{Have} \\ \text{Haven't} \end{Bmatrix}$ you seen the flying pig?

A: $\begin{Bmatrix} \text{Yes} \quad [= \text{I have}] \\ \text{Yes, I have} \end{Bmatrix}$

$\begin{Bmatrix} \text{No} \quad [= \text{I haven't}] \\ \text{No, I haven't} \end{Bmatrix}$

(The peculiarity of plain *yes* as an answer to a negative question will be treated below.) Japanese has a typical agree/disagree system, with a positive particle used when the answer agrees with the question in polarity (positive vs. negative) and a negative particle used when the answer disagrees with the question in polarity (examples from Pope 1973:482, but see Kuno 1973, ch. 23 for further complications):

(137)   Q: Kyoo wa atui desu ka?   'Is it hot today?'
         A: Hai, kyoo wa atui desu   'Yes, it's hot today'
            Iie, atuku wa arimasen   'No, it isn't hot today'

(138)   Q: Kyoo wa atukunai desu ka?   'Isn't it hot today?'
                                              [i.e., 'Is it true that it
                                              is not hot today?']

         A: Iie, kyoo wa atui desu   'No, it's hot today'
            Hai, soo desu ne.   'Yes, it isn't hot today'

One complication in these question-answering systems arises from the fact that questions are often biased (see section 3.3.2). Thus the English question *Isn't it raining?* can be used not just to ask whether it is not raining, but simultaneously to indicate that the speaker guesses that it is. A simple positive answer could be very confusing. It could either be interpreted as a positive response to the question itself ('Yes, it is not raining') or as agreement with the speaker's guess ('Yes, you're right; it is raining'). Many languages therefore provide a special positive answer that clears up this potential confusion. German *doch* (instead of *ja*), French *si* (instead of *oui*) and Icelandic *ju* (instead of *já*) all are used to signal unambiguously that a positive answer to the negatively biased question is being given, that is, that the asker's expectation is wrong.

Even in English, which lacks a special form for this duty, a simple positive answer to a negative question is not fully acceptable. Here English requires an echo answer (see section 4.2.3 immediately below) in addition to the answer word:

(139)   Q: Isn't it raining?
         A: ?Yes
         A: Yes, it is

4.2.3 *Echo systems*

In the third type of answering system, the echo system, no special answer words are used at all. Simple positive and negative responses to questions involve repeating the verb of the question, with or without additional material that varies from language to language. Welsh has such a system (it also has a special negator, *na(c)*, used in short answers instead of the usual negator *ni(d)*):

(140)   Q: A welwch chwi hwy?   'Do you see them?'
            Q see   you them

         A: Gwelaf   '(Yes) I see (them)'
            Na welaf   '(No) I don't see (them)'

An interesting recurrent phenomenon in question-answering systems is that short answers are often peculiar with respect to their phonology; that is, they are often more like paralinguistic utterances than like ordinary morphemes. English *uh-hunh* and *unh-unh* are like this. So is the Yawelmani (Yokuts) affirmative *hɔ·hɔʔ* 'yes', which is pronounced with nasalized vowels: 'nasalized vowels are to be regarded as anomalous phonetic elements having an expressive function rather than as full-fledged phonemes in the Yokuts vowel system' (S. Newman 1944:238).

No language that we know of lacks short answers to questions. Even the echo systems involve reduction of the answers. On the other hand, reduction may be obligatory in some languages, Icelandic for example:

(141)   Q: Ertu ameríkumaður?   'Are you an American?'
         A: Já   'Yes'

         ⎧ ?Já, ég er ameríkumaður ⎫
         ⎨   ⎬ 'Yes, I am (that)'
         ⎩ ?Já, það er ég   ⎭

Here we may be dealing with the grammaticization of a cultural prohibition against undue prolixity (see the next section).

5 Indirect speech acts

5.1 *Conventionality*

It is possible to use nearly any sentence type with the effect of nearly any other, under appropriate circumstances. Thus either of the following could easily function – and be intended to function – as a means of getting an addressee to do something (such as mow a lawn).

(142)   The grass hasn't been mowed in two weeks

(143)   Is it your turn to mow the lawn?

Should these sentences be classed along with imperatives? In this case the answer is no, for three reasons.

First, the success of using (142) or (143) to get the hearer to mow the lawn quite clearly depends on the fact that the form we find in (142) is conventionally associated with the making of statements and that the form of (143) is conventionally used for posing questions.

Second, although (142) and (143) can, on occasion, be used to get across roughly what an imperative does, this fact interacts in no way with the grammar of English. That is, there do not seem to be any features of these sentences used in this way that could properly be called formal. If (142) and (143) were actually ambiguous between an imperative sense and some other sense then we would expect the formal properties of these sentences to reflect their dual nature. For instance, the fact that Chomsky's famous example

(144)   The boy decided on the boat

is ambiguous is amply demonstrated by the fact that the passive

(145)   The boat was decided on by the boy

is unambiguous. But rules of grammar do not seem to be sensitive to the range of uses that (142) and (143) allow. As far as the grammatical conventions of English are concerned, (142) and (143) are the same, regardless of the use to which they are put. So while (142) and (143) might resemble imperatives in *use*, they are not distinct from declaratives and interrogatives (respectively) in *form*.

Third, the means by which uttering (142) or (143) comes to have the contextual import of a request do not seem to be language-specific. Equivalent forms in other languages are likely to be just as effective in getting requests across and would succeed for exactly the same reasons. Thus it seems proper to say that (142) and (143) are respectively a declarative and an interrogative from the point of view of the grammar of English, but their force may be exploited to achieve the kinds of effects that are conventionally associated with imperatives.

The indirect use of one sentence type for effects that properly belong to another can, however, become conventionalized to a greater or lesser extent, and when this happens, a new sentence type can develop. Sometimes, indeed, the historical origins of a sentence type are visible in its synchronic form. For these reasons it is often quite difficult – and sometimes impossible – to tell when a particular indirect form has become conventionalized to a sufficient extent to deserve being called a sentence type. Especially vexing is the fact, stressed by Morgan (1978), that while a *strategy* for obtaining a particular end might be conventional, this is quite a different matter from the case where a particular *form* is arbitrarily connected by convention with a particular effect. Cultures (rather than languages *per se*) may differ in what conventional strategies for indirection are available without there being any strictly grammatical differences between them. For example, the institution of leave-taking in one culture might conventionally require the expression of wishes for long life, happiness, or the like – without specifying exactly what form this sentiment must be cast in. In another culture, the convention might call for an expression of a desire to see the traveler again – also without specifying the words that are to be used in framing this expression.

But the boundaries between culture and language are never precise. Perfect mastery of a language is not really possible without extensive knowledge of the culture in which it is embedded, and, conversely, a culture cannot be fully understood without knowledge of the language in which it is carried on.

5.2 *Some examples of indirection*

Indirection usually serves a purpose in that it avoids – or at least gives the appearance of avoiding – a frank performance of some act that the speaker wishes to perform. For this reason certain sorts of effects are more likely to be targets for indirect accomplishment than others. Most cultures find requests somewhat objectionable socially and these are therefore frequently conveyed by indirect means. Southern Paiute uses the modal of obligation -ɣwa- (roughly 'should') to form 'mild impera-tives'. Numerous languages use some typically subordinate clause form, a free-standing infinitive or subjunctive, for example, as a circumlocu-tion for the imperative. Greenlandic uses one sort of parti-ciple (e.g. 'you who are standing up') for a mild imperative, and so on. Another strategy is to ask a question, the obvious answer to which implies that one of the conditions on the appropriate issuance of requests is met. English has

(146)   Can you do X?

Hebrew has a form meaning approximately 'Are you ready to do X?' and many other languages provide similar examples.

Certain questions and certain assertions may also be considered impolite and may therefore become targets for indirect achievement. In the United States,

(147)   How much do you make?

is an impolite thing for a neighbor (but not the tax man) to ask and would likely be replaced by some circumlocution like

(148)   Do you mind my asking ...?

or

(149)   Would it be too impolite of me to ask ...?

The statement meaning 'I am hungry' is an insulting thing for a guest to say to an Eskimo host. The conventional way to get fed is therefore to use a form that suppresses contrasts of person and means something like 'Someone is hungry', 'There is hunger'.

Often indirect forms become highly specialized. We find that in Maidu '... the intentional ... [I'm/we're going to ...] ... is used with demonstrative or interrogative words to form questions requesting instructions' (Shipley 1964:50). Also in Maidu, the future indicative serves 'as a kind of directive or mild imperative (with the second person only)' (Shipley 1964:47). But notice the English

(150)   You will take out the garbage

is more like an imperious order than a mild imperative.

Sometimes a total replacement of one sentence type by a formerly indirect form takes place. When the historical origins of some sentence type from an indirect form are still clear, it may be difficult to say whether or not the sentence type still exists. In Tzotzil (Cowan 1969), the ordinary yes–no question looks just like an independent *if*-clause, and in Karok, like an elliptical disjunction of indicatives ('It's raining, or ...'). There is some interest in the question of whether or not Tzotzil and Karok should be considered to have a distinct sentence type for yes–no questions. But in any case, the way one gets questions across in these languages deserves mention since this function is indispensable to speakers of the languages.

NOTES

* Our generalizations are based on a survey of the sentence types in a sample of twenty-three languages, chosen because of the availability of usable descriptions and because they represented a wide range of language families and linguistic areas (an asterisk marks languages with which one or both of the authors have first hand acquaintance): Blackfoot, Chrau, Diola-Fogny, Dyirbal, *German, *Greenlandic Eskimo, Hausa, *Hebrew (Modern), Hidatsa, Hopi, Kapampangan, Karok, Lahu, Latin, Maidu, Onondaga, Swahili, Tagalog, Turkish, Tzotzil, *Welsh, Yokuts (Yawelmani), and Yoruba. To this original sample we have added data from *Danish, *English, *French, *Icelandic, Jacaltec, Japanese, Southern Paiute, *Swedish, and *Yiddish, plus references to several other languages in material from existing surveys of topics related to ours. We have followed the transcriptions in our sources, altering only a few opaque or difficult symbols.

We are indebted to the following people for their comments and suggestions on earlier drafts of this chapter: Talmy Givón, Timothy Shopen, Geoffrey Pullum, Edith Moravcsik, Philip Johnson-Laird, Donald Churma, Christopher Longuet-Higgins, Bernard Comrie, Wayles Browne, and Jami Josifek.

1 The statement that no single sentence can simultaneously belong to two sentence types does not exclude the possibility of speech act ambiguity. Thus questions and exclamations are generally distinct – *How pretty is she* versus *How pretty she is* – but can fall together through ellipsis: *How pretty*. But this last example is not *both* a question *and* an exclamation; rather, it is *either* a question *or* an exclamation. Similar situations obtain in other linguistic systems as well. The case system of German, for example, is organized such that no noun phrase is simultaneously nominative and accusative, though there are cases of genuine ambiguity as we find in the phrase *das Mädchen*, which is *either* nominative *or* accusative.

2 In English, the strategy of postposing the subject of a question comes into conflict with the strategy of preposing the question word in an information question (see section 3.3.3) just in case the question word *is* the subject. Here it is the question-word strategy that wins out, the subject remaining before the verb even in the question: *Who shot Bill?*

Echo questions (see section 4.2.3) will also fail to show inversion of verb and subject just in case the utterances they echo were not inverted: *You bought a Cadillac?*

3 'If ... we attempt a *purely notional classification* of utterances, without regard to their grammatical form, it seems natural to divide them into two main classes, according as the speaker does not or does want to exert an influence on the will of the hearer directly through his utterance' (Jespersen 1924:302).

4 While agentivity might not be of much significance elsewhere in the syntax of certain ergative languages, it is always important in the formation of imperatives (see Schachter 1977).

5 Or optatives, as they are sometimes misleadingly called.

6 Again, it is not logically necessary that an interrogative sentence type or types be available in a language. The effect of a yes–no question could be obtained by a declarative sentence meaning 'I want to know: X or not' or by an imperative sentence meaning 'Tell me: X or not' (see section 5.1). As in the case of imperatives, the activity of trying to gain information is so frequent in human social life, and so important to it, that no language (it seems) lacks a form dedicated to it.

7 The negatively biased Latin question is formed with a different particle, *num*, which is sentence initial.

8 Example (110) involves inversion of subject and verb; (111) does not. While it is true that inversion does occur in German information questions in which a constituent other than the subject is questioned, inversion also occurs when *any* item other than the subject occurs sentence initially:

    (i) Was hat Fritz gegessen?
      'What did Fritz eat?'
    (ii) Eine Wurst hat Fritz gegessen
      'It was a sausage that Fritz ate'

9 See Keenan and Hull (1973) for a development of this idea.

10 There are dialects of English in which inversion is allowed in subordinate clauses just in case the clause really represents a question. Thus, many English speakers can say,

    (i) I wonder where did he go

when they mean to ask a question. As far as we know, though, there are no dialects in which the following sentence is grammatical, because it can never be used to ask a question:

    (ii) *I realize where did he go

11 There are also stylistic variants of *yes* and *no*, for instance *yeah*, *nope*, *uh-hunh*, and *unh-unh*.

12 The first two terms are due to Pope (1973), to whom we owe some of the following discussion as well.

4 Negation

JOHN R. PAYNE

0 Introduction

In this chapter we explore the rich variety of forms which negation can take in a variety of languages.

In the first section, we will look at negation primarily in English and establish a basis for typological discussion. We will begin with a review of the criteria for sentential negation (1.0). This distinction is considered to be semantic. The section then outlines the different syntactic forms of sentential negation, namely standard negation (1.1), negated quantifiers (1.2), inherently negative quantifiers (1.3), negated adverbials (1.4) and inherently negative adverbs (1.5).

The second section is the heart of the chapter. It is about the typology of standard negation (2.0). We will show that standard negation may take the form of negative verbs (2.1), negative particles (2.2), morphological negatives (2.3) and negative nouns (2.4). These forms of standard negation may be accompanied by secondary modifications (2.5). Finally, they may associate with focused elements in the sentence (2.6).

In the third section we will look at the negation of quantifiers and adverbials as forms of sentential negation (3.0). We take each of the categories of section 1 in turn, starting with negated quantifiers (3.1) and inherently negative quantifiers (3.2), and concluding with negated adverbials (3.3) and inherently negative adverbs (3.4).

In the fourth and final section we discuss briefly the two types of non-sentential negation which are syntactically distinct from sentential negation: negation in subordinate clauses (4.1), and derivational negation (4.2).

1.0 Sentential negation

The fieldworker who has studied Klima's important treatise on negation in English (Klima 1964) will be familiar with the notions of 'sentential' and 'constituent' negation, and should have no difficulty in applying this distinction to sentences like *John is not happy* (with sentential negation) and *John is unhappy* (with constituent negation of the adjective) or *John is a non-smoker* (with constituent negation of the noun). He may be less aware, however, of the difficulties involved in achieving a satisfactory definition of 'sentential' negation, and of the diversity of syntactic forms which such definitions encompass. Because these issues have important consequences for the analysis of negation in any language, we shall devote this first section to them.

Klima's definition of sentential negation relies on the convergence of a set of diagnostic tests specific to English: sentences with sentential negation are those which permit (i) positive rather than negative tag questions (of the type requesting confirmation), (ii) tags with *neither* rather than the *so* associated with positive sentences, and (iii) continuation with phrases beginning with *not even*.

Similar tests (particularly the *not even* test) can be found for other languages; Kraak (1966) provides a set for Dutch, and Bakir (1970) for Iraqi Arabic. These tests converge, both in English and in other languages, on a diverse range of negation types that include (i) standard negation, (ii) negated quantifiers, (iii) inherently negative quantifiers, (iv) negated adverbials, and (v) inherently negative adverbs. Not all languages possess all these categories. English does, and will therefore serve in this section as the main language of exemplification.

1.1 *Standard negation*

By 'standard' negation, we understand that type of negation that can apply to the most minimal and basic sentences. Such sentences are characteristically main clauses, and consist of a single predicate with as few noun phrases and adverbial modifiers as possible. With this trait as a guide, we can identify standard negation in more complex sentences, for instance sentences with quantifiers, which may permit more than one type of negation. In English, the most minimal sentences are those involving weather predicates of zero valency, but requiring the dummy syntactic subject *it*. Such weather sentences, for example *It does not snow, It is not raining, It doesn't snow, It isn't raining*, are sufficient to fix standard negation in English as either the particle *not* immediately following an obligatory auxiliary verb (i.e. *does not, is not,* etc.), or a specifically negative form, with the bound morpheme *-n't*, of an auxiliary verb (i.e. *doesn't, isn't,* etc.).

When we apply Klima's tests to sentences with standard negation, we get clear results, whether the sentence is minimal as in (1a) or more complex as in (1b):

(1) a.
$$\text{It} \left\{ \begin{array}{l} \text{does}n't \\ \text{does } not \end{array} \right\} \text{rain,} \left\{ \begin{array}{l} \text{does it?} \\ \text{and neither does it snow} \\ \text{not even in Auchtermurphy} \end{array} \right.$$

b.
$$\text{John} \left\{ \begin{array}{l} \text{did}n't \\ \text{did } not \end{array} \right\} \text{kiss Celia in the rain,} \left\{ \begin{array}{l} \text{did he?} \\ \text{and neither did I} \\ \text{not even once} \end{array} \right.$$

In what sense, however, is this negation sentential? Many authors, notably Sgall, Hajičová and Benešová (1973) and Hajičová (1977), have pointed out that what is negated, especially in non-nominal predications like (1b), is often not the whole sentence, but rather a section of it. How we understand a sentence like (1b) depends on what we will call the contextual articulation of the sentence. Two of the most plausible readings of (1b) permit a performative paraphrase as either *I say of John that it is not true that he kissed Celia in the rain*, in which the real scope of negation is the whole verb phrase, or *I say of John's kissing Celia that it is not true that it was in the rain*, in which the real scope of negation is the locative phrase. In both cases, the contextually bound elements are removed from the scope of negation, and what is actually negated is the contextually free portion of the sentence, or perhaps preferably, the relationship between the contextually bound and contextually free portions.

The distribution of elements within the sentence into 'contextually bound' and 'contextually free' is pragmatically determined. Subjects tend to be contextually bound, which often gives the impression that sentential negation might better be described as 'VP negation'. Sentences like *Everyone didn't pass*, which some speakers can interpret as *Not everyone passed*, show however that the subject can be included within the scope of negation. In addition, since negative sentences are most frequently used to deny propositions which are contextually given, rather than to introduce new propositions, they tend to involve contextually bound elements. One reflection of this principle is that there may be blocks against introducing new discourse referents in negative sentences (Givón 1975). Indefinite noun phrases in non-subject position tend to be interpreted non-referentially, while indefinite noun phrases in the primarily referential subject position require extended contexts to be appropriate at all; compare the positive sentences in (2) with their negative counterparts in (3):

(2)   a. I saw an elephant [±referential]

       b. A man [+referential] called yesterday

(3)   a. I did*n't* see an elephant [−referential]

        b. ?A man [+referential] did*n't* call yesterday

In some languages, the non-referential use of the indefinite article may be blocked in object position in negative sentences, rendering sentences like (3a) impossible. Instead, a specifically negative quantifier is used, as in the case of German *kein* (cf. section 3.2).

The foregoing discussion suggests the following principles concerning sentential negation: sentential negation is closely associated with the contextual articulation of the sentence. As the contextual articulation of the sentence varies, so does the apparent scope of negation, and in such a way that what is negated is the contextually free information. In sentential negation, the negative element stands semantically therefore at the boundary between contextually bound and contextually free elements. In addition to Klima's tests, a useful diagnostic is whether a sentence can be given a performative paraphrase of the type *I say of X that it is not true that Y*, where *X* contains the bound elements, *Y* contains the free elements, and the negative relates the two. We will incorporate this notion in a definition and say that among the various kinds of negation, all and only the instances of sentential negation allow this kind of paraphrase. In the case where the whole sentence is contextually bound, *Y* may be zero, and conversely, when the whole sentence is contextually free, *X* may be zero. Sentences like (1a) might plausibly be analyzed in both these ways, for example either as *I say of it's raining that it is not true*, or as *I say that it is not true that it is raining*.

Not all cases of standard negation are necessarily sentential. One motivation for the conception of sentential negation that we have elaborated is that certain cases of standard negation which have long been recognized as creating difficulties for Klima's tests also fail to permit performative paraphrases of the required form. Consider sentence pairs like (4a) and (4b):

(4)   a.   John does*n't* often pay taxes, $\begin{cases} \text{does he?} \\ \text{and neither do I} \\ \text{not even to Malta} \end{cases}$

        b.   ??John often does*n't* pay taxes, $\begin{cases} \text{does he?} \\ \text{and neither do I} \\ \text{not even to Malta} \end{cases}$

As pointed out by Stockwell, Schachter and Partee (1973:248), sentence (4b) has negation in the standard auxiliary position, but the fact that the adverb *often* has higher scope creates a blockage in the applicability of Klima's tests. Turning to the performative paraphrase, we note that (4a) permits a paraphrase of the type *I say of John that it is not true that he often pays taxes*, whereas (4b) must be paraphrased as *I say of John that it is true that he often doesn't pay taxes*, in which both the adverb and the negation are part of the contextually free portion of the sentence. The negative cannot stand at the boundary between the contextually free and contextually bound portions, as is required for sentential negation.

Sentences like (4b) are examples of the non-correspondence between standard and sentential negation. An even greater body of non-correspondences is to be found whenever the rôle of the presumed sentential negative is taken by another form of negation altogether, to which we now turn.

1.2 Negated quantifiers
The second class of sentences on which Klima's tests converge involve negated quantifiers, by which we mean quantifiers which form a syntactic phrase with a negative morpheme, as opposed to quantifiers which happen to occur within the scope of standard negation. Not all languages permit quantifier negation in this sense, and in the languages which do permit it, not all quantifiers can necessarily be negated.

In English, the quantifiers which can be negated by quantifier negation are essentially *many*, *much*, *a lot* (*of*), *all* and *every*, but it is also possible to include the quantifier *any* when negated by the adverbs *scarcely*, *hardly* or *barely*:

(5) a. *Not* many students passed, $\begin{cases} \text{did they?} \\ \text{and neither did I} \\ \text{not even with cribs} \end{cases}$

b. *Scarcely* any students passed, $\begin{cases} \text{did they?} \\ \text{and neither did I} \\ \text{not even with cribs} \end{cases}$

Sentences (5a) and (5b) successfully undergo Klima's tests, and the performative test works with no difficulty for (5a), giving for instance *I say that it is not true that many students passed*. Note that in such a paraphrase of (5a), *many students* cannot be contextually bound, only contextually free, which is to say that there is no paraphrase of (5a) that goes *I say of many students that it is not true that they passed* – this sentence can be a paraphrase of the corresponding sentence with standard negation, *Many students did not pass*. To apply the performative test to (5b), however, we must make a considerable modification replacing *not* with *scarcely* (cf. section 1.5).

Despite the classification of quantifier negation in (5a) and perhaps

(5b) as sentential, we believe it most reasonable to assume that the negative morpheme is a constituent of the quantified noun phrase, and not some displaced form of standard negation. Firstly, we note that *not* occurs in close association with a range of constituents. (Some of these examples have *not* in postverbal position, and such examples have sometimes been ignored in the literature on negation. While such usage is stylistically and sometimes perhaps grammatically constrained, it is a part of error-free spoken and written English):

(6)   a. He went away not very happy
        b. He went away, but not very happy
        c. Not very happy, he went away
                                        (adjective phrase)

(7)   a. He went away not very cheerfully
        b. He went away, but not very cheerfully
        c. Not very cheerfully, he went away
                                        (adverbial phrase)

(8)   a. He went away not in a good humour
        b. He went away, but not in a good humour
        c. Not in a good humour, he went away
                                        (prepositional phrase)

(9)   a. He spent not many weeks deciding what to do
        b. He caught some trout, but not many salmon
        c. Not many weeks could he endure before a decision came
           upon him
                                        (noun phrase)

Although following some theories one might say the *not* has been moved into these constituents from someplace else, its close association with the structure and distribution of these constituents remains, and must be accounted for in any case. What applies to this range of constituents applies *ipso facto* to the subject noun phrase.

Secondly, quantifier negation can co-occur with standard negation (though various dialects of English require at least some instances of such negation to be restricted to subject or presubject position), as in (10) and (11), and in these sentences it would be impossible to say *not* has been moved into the noun phrase from the standard negation position. The *not* in the noun phrase must therefore have some other source, and the noun phrase itself is the best candidate.

(10)   a.   *Not* many students did*n't* pass

      b.   *Murphy did*n't* fail *not* many students

(11)   a.   *Scarcely* any students did*n't* pass

      b.   Murphy did*n't* fail *scarcely* any students

In sentences like (10a) and (11a), it should be noted that it is the quantifier negation which is sentential, rather than the standard negation. Sentence (10a), for instance, would have a performative paraphrase *I say that it is not true that many students didn't pass*, with the standard negation contextually free.

The semantic function of quantifier negation is clear: it serves to differentiate the relative scope of quantifier and negation in sentence pairs like (12) and (13):

(12)   a.   *Not* many students passed

      b.   Many students did*n't* pass

(13)   a.   *Not* every student passed

      b.   Every student did*n't* pass

(12a) and (13a) require the quantifier to be within the scope of negation (so that as opposed to (12b), for instance, (12a) is incompatible with the statement *Many students passed*). The scope of standard negation, on the other hand, is less clear, especially in (13b). Possible readings of (13b) include a reading equivalent to (13a) and a reading equivalent to *No students passed*. It is perhaps because such unambiguous equivalents exist that informant reactions to (13b) are often less than favourable. In (12b), however, the preferred, but perhaps not only interpretation is one in which the quantifier has higher scope (the one that can be continued . . . *but many did*). In contrast to standard negation, then, the semantic function of quantifier negation is unequivocal: the negated quantifier *must* be interpreted as within the scope of negation.

As with standard negation, not all cases of quantifier negation are necessarily sentential. Klima (1964:307) and Stockwell, Schachter and Partee (1973:266) point to minimal pairs like (14a) and (14b), in which the only syntactic indication of sentential negation is the subject–auxiliary inversion characteristic of English:

(14)   a.   In *not* many years will Christmas fall on a Sunday

      b.   In *not* many years Christmas will fall on a Sunday

Using performative paraphrases, (14a) may be analyzed as *I say of Christmas that it is not true that in many years it will fall on a Sunday*, whereas the corresponding analysis for (14b) must be *I say of Christmas that it is true that in not many years it will fall on a Sunday*. Only (14a) is therefore an instance of sentential negation.

1.3 *Inherently negative quantifiers*

Inherently negative quantifiers in English involve the morpheme *no*, bound as in *nothing*, *nobody*, *no-one* and *none*, or free when immediately preceding a nominal expression, as in *no friends*. All these quantifiers possess the characteristics of sentential negation, as we may see with Klima's tests:

(15)   Nothing
         Nobody
         No-one   ⎫ can help us, can {it / they}?
         None   ⎭   and neither can you
         No friends   not even Marmaduke

The performative paraphrase can be made to work by allowing the negative quantifiers to be decomposed (e.g. *nothing → not anything*, *nobody → not anybody*, etc.), so that for instance *Marmaduke cheats nobody* might be paraphrased as *I say of Marmaduke that it is not true that he cheats anybody*.

The inherently negative quantifiers also share some of the properties of the negated quantifiers. In the first place, they may readily co-occur with standard negation when constrained to subject or presubject position. In object position, as in (16b), they are more awkward, though perhaps less unacceptable than a comparable negated quantifier as in (10b).

(16)   a. *None* of the students did*n't* pass

        b. (*) I did*n't* see *none* of the students

In the second place, when in presubject position as a constituent of a preposed adverbial, they trigger subject–auxiliary inversion in precisely those cases where the negation is sentential (compare example (14a) with (14b)):

(17)   a. Under *no* circumstances will I leave today

        b. For *no* reason he threatened to leave today

The two categories do differ, however, in that there are some environments where inherently negative quantifiers may occur postverbally whereas the negated quantifiers may not, or at least not without awkwardness.

(18)   a.   Marmaduke cheats *nobody*

   b. ?*Marmaduke cheats *not* everybody

This is one manifestation of a typological tendency, the details of which are explored in section 3.2, for inherently negative quantifiers to have greater freedom of position than negated quantifiers. It should be noted also that inherently negative quantifiers are negations of the existential quantifier, whereas the negated quantifiers are either universal (*not all*) or express quantitative ideas, like *many*. Inherently negative versions of *not many* and *not much* exist in the quantifiers *few* and *little*, and these pattern syntactically in the same manner as the other inherently negative quantifiers: for instance, *I bought few books* is grammatical, whereas ?**I bought not many books* is either ungrammatical or highly awkward. There appears to be no inherently negative version of the negated universal quantifier *not all*, and indeed we know of no language where such a quantifier may be found. Pragmatic explanations of this restriction on lexicalization are explored in detail in Horn (1978).

1.4 *Negated adverbials*
Just as certain negated quantifiers can produce sentential negation, so can certain negated adverbials. There are just three English adverbs which come into this category: the quantitative and universal quantifiers over time, *often* and *always*, and the universal quantifier over place, *everywhere*. They must occur in sentence-initial position. Cases like *He doesn't often pay taxes* are instances of standard negation containing the adverb within its scope. Like the preposed adverbs containing negated quantifiers and signalling sentential negation, these negated adverbs then trigger subject–auxiliary inversion:

(19)   *Not* often ⎫ do I pay taxes, ⎧ do I?
       Not always ⎭   ⎨ and neither does Murphy
                                 ⎩ not even to Malta

Klima's tests and the performative paraphrase test confirm that these are indeed cases of sentential negation.

   A number of negated adverbial phrases work in a similar way, for instance *not for long, not until Friday, not because I like you, not even on Sundays, not for anything, not for nothing, not in vain* and *not under any circumstances*. These may be contrasted with non-sententially negated adverbials like *not long ago, not far away, not surprisingly* and *not infrequently*, which do not trigger subject-auxiliary inversion and are not restricted to sentence-initial position (Lasnik 1976:16).

1.5 Inherently negative adverbs

There is a small group of inherently negative adverbs which stand in the same relationship to the negated adverbs as the inherently negative quantifiers do to the negated quantifiers. First and foremost in this group are the two adverbs which negate existential quantifiers over time and place, *never* and *nowhere*. Like the inherently negative quantifiers, these are not as syntactically restricted as the negated adverbs and may occur in standard adverbial positions and, in some circumstances, postverbally. In sentence-initial position, however, they trigger the expected subject–auxiliary inversion. For the purposes of the performative paraphrase, they may be decomposed into *not ever* and *not anywhere*. In this group we may also include the adverb *neither*, which decomposes into *not either*.

The next set of inherently negative adverbs consists of *seldom, rarely, hardly, barely* and *scarcely*, which Stockwell, Schachter and Partee (1973:233) term 'incomplete' negatives since they appear not to fulfil all the criteria for sentential negation. There is dialect difference with respect to the acceptability of Klima's tests, and, as we pointed out for *hardly, barely* and *scarcely*, these adverbs require a modification of the performative paraphrase which substitutes an incomplete negative for the full negative *not*, namely, *I say of X that it is scarcely (hardly etc.) true that Y*. With these provisos, however, there can be no doubt that incomplete negatives work in a manner very much akin to full sentential negatives; for instance, like *never, nowhere* and *neither* they all trigger subject–auxiliary inversion:

(20)   Never
       Nowhere
       Neither
       Seldom
       Rarely   } did he say anything about it
       Hardly
       Barely
       Scarcely

2.0 Syntactic typology of standard negation

The fieldworker will usually have no difficulty in recognizing standard negation. Its primary function is the sentential negation of basic sentences, and a good initial test is to negate the most minimal positive sentences such as weather sentences. This in itself may be sufficient, especially when position can be defined in relation to the predicate alone, as in English. In any event, any full analysis of standard negation must at least be consistent with this initial test. We next analyse the negation of basic intransitive and transitive sentence types. Here, however, we may encounter various forms of non-standard negation. We can avoid the most obvious potential confusion, that with quantifier negation, by using definitely referring noun phrases, such as proper names.

Standard negation may take a variety of forms, ranging from fully inflected 'negative verbs' to fully bound derivational morphemes. What these forms have in common is that they all involve the *addition* of a negative morpheme to a corresponding positive sentence. There may be further modifications to the sentence, like a change in word order or in tone pattern, but standard negation never seems to be realized by such modifications alone. The initial categorization of standard negation must therefore be based on the form of the negative morpheme.

2.1 *Negative verbs*

A 'negative verb' always has at least some of the properties of regular verbs, such as occurrence with a verbal complementizer, or inflection for mood, tense, aspect, person or number. A negative verb will always co-occur with the original 'lexical' verb of the corresponding positive sentence. Of major typological interest are then (i) the relationship between the negative and lexical verbs, and (ii) the distribution of secondary markers or inflections between them.

In the first area of interest there appear to be two major groupings. In one, the negative verb seems to have some or all of the characteristics of a higher verb taking a full sentential complement. As such, it is restricted to sentence-initial or sentence-final position, in the configurations *Neg-S* or *S-Neg*, with the natural correlation to verb-initial and verb-final basic word order. It has been pointed out by Mulder (1978) that higher negative verbs appear to be non-existent among verb-medial languages. The second grouping, on the other hand, is rather different: here there is no question of a sentential boundary between the negative verb and the lexical verb. Rather, the negative verb acts as a finite auxiliary to the lexical verb, which in turn typically occurs in some non-finite form. In this second grouping, there are no comparable restrictions on word order, and we will demonstrate verb-medial languages with such negatives.

In practice, the distinction between our two kinds of negative verbs may become blurred as a result of historical evolution. In particular, the sentential boundary between a higher negative verb and its complement may easily be weakened by such processes as topicalization of the subject, or by various manifestations of agreement with the subject of the lower sentence, so that it has become what we should analyse synchronically as an auxiliary negative verb. Nevertheless, clues to its original status invariably survive.

2.1.1 *Higher negative verbs*

Let us consider first some examples of negative verbs in the *Neg-S* configuration, typical in languages of the Polynesian area, here from Tongan (Chung 1970), which illustrates the construction in unweakened form, and from Fijian, which reveals the kinds of weakening which can often occur.

In Tongan, we find positive and negative sentence pairs like (21a) and (21b) (Churchward 1953:56):

(21)   a. Na'e   'alu 'a   Siale
           ASP   go ABSOLUTE Charlie
           'Charlie went'

      b. Na'e   'ikai [$_S$ ke 'alu 'a   Siale]
           ASP   NEG   ASP go ABSOLUTE Charlie
           'Charlie didn't go'

In sentence (21a), the verb *'alu* 'go' is preceded by an aspect particle *na'e*, representing a completed and non-continuing (i.e. simple past) action. *Na'e*, with its variant *na'a* before clitic pronouns, alternates in this position with a full range of aspect particles, for instance *kuo* (completed but continuing, i.e. perfect), *'oku* (non-completed and continuing) and *'e* or *te*, the unmarked or neutral form (non-completed and non-continuing, i.e. mainly habitual or future). All these same particles can modify the negative *'ikai*. In (21b) the same *na'e* precedes *'ikai*, while the aspect particle preceding *'alu* in the complement clause has become *ke*. *Ke* is found solely in embedded clauses with the function of indicating that the action of the negated sentence may someday be accomplished (Chung 1970:8). It alternates with the unmarked *'e*. In these respects then, the negative verb *'ikai* behaves exactly like a main clause verb, and the 'lexical verb' *'alu* behaves like a complement clause verb.

Other features point to the existence of a sentential boundary between the negative verb and its complement. Firstly, the structure of (21b) is identical to that found in the case of other verbs taking full sentential complements, for instance *ngali* 'seem'. Secondly, when the subject of the lexical verb is a pronoun, it is normally placed between the aspect particle and the lexical verb. This pattern is maintained in negative sentences, where subject pronouns obligatorily associate with the complement clause and not the matrix clause (Chung 1970:43–4):

(22)   Na'a ne fai 'a   e   ngauue
        ASP he do ABSOLUTE the work
        'He did the work'

(23)   a. Na'e *'ikai* [$_S$ ke ne fai 'a   e   ngauue]
           ASP   NEG   ASP he do ABSOLUTE the work

        b.*Na'a ne *'ikai* [$_S$ ke fai 'a   e   ngauue]
           ASP   he NEG   ASP do ABSOLUTE the work
        'He didn't do the work'

The negative verbs in Tongan, and generally in Polynesian, do however possess two characteristics which set them apart from other verbs. Firstly, the form of the negative verb may vary according to the aspect of the sentence. For instance, in Tongan, the form *te'eki* is typically used with the *'oku* aspect particle to denote 'not yet', while (and this is a typologically common feature) there is a separate negative *'oua* for negative imperatives. Similarly in Maori (Hohepa 1965) we find, amongst others, the negatives *kiihai* (completed aspect) and *kaahore* (non-completed aspect). Secondly, the Polynesian negative verbs often seem to derive historically from the fusion of an earlier negative with the aspect particles surrounding it. Tongan *'ikai* may well derive from an aspect particle *'i* (still rarely attested) followed by the negative verb **kai*, while *te'eki* may derive from an archaic negative verb *ta'e*, retained in subordinate clauses, and a following aspect particle **ki* (Chung 1970:87). But this does not prevent Tongan negative verbs from combining synchronically with the regular aspect particles like other verbs. The Maori forms *kiihai* and *kaahore*, however, behave synchronically like combinations of a preceding aspect marker and a negative verb, and they do not occur with other aspect markers.

We now turn to Fijian as an example of the ways in which the higher clause status of the negative verb may be weakened. In Fijian, the basic word order is vos, but the subject may be topicalized to initial position:

(24)   a. A   yaco mai ena siga Vakaraubuka ko Jone
           PAST arrive on day Friday   ART John

        b. Ko Jone a   yaco mai ena siga Vakaraubuka
           ART John PAST arrive on day Friday
        'John arrived on Friday'

The negative counterparts to these sentences involve the negative verb *sega*, which like other complementizable verbs, for instance *kila* 'know', appears to take a full sentential complement with the complementizer *ni*. Topicalization may take place as in positive sentences:

(25)   a. A *sega* ni yaco mai ena siga Vakaraubuka ko Jone
            PAST NEG that arrive   on day Friday   ART John

        b. Ko Jone a   *sega* ni yaco mai ena siga Vakaraubuka
            ART John PAST NEG that arrive   on day Friday
            'John didn't arrive on Friday'

From the synchronic point of view, however, two arguments weaken the treatment of *sega* as a higher negative verb. Firstly, we do not observe the same rigidity of tense/aspect marking as in Tongan, where the primary aspectual oppositions are marked solely by the higher negative verb. In Fijian, it is optional whether tense is marked by the negative verb or by the lexical verb. It cannot however be marked by both:

(26)   a. *A*   *sega* ni yaco mai ena siga Vakaraubuka ko Jone
            PAST NEG that arrive   on day Friday   ART John

        b. E *sega* ni *a*   yaco mai ena siga Vakaraubuka ko Jone
            PCL NEG that PAST arrive   on day Friday   ART John

        c.*A   *sega* ni *a*   yaco mai ena siga Vakaraubuka ko Jone
            PAST NEG that PAST arrive   on day Friday   ART John
            'John didn't arrive on Friday'

The particle *e* in (26b) appears in preverbal position when that position is not already occupied by one of a mixed set of morphemes including the past tense *a*, the complementizer *ni* and the first and second person agreement markers. Its function, according to Capell (1957:76), is little more than that of a predicative sign. There is no necessity, therefore, for the supposed higher verb to control the overall tense of the sentence. Rather, it seems that we have a complex verbal group in which tense may be marked either on the auxiliary or on the lexical verb. We may contrast this flexibility of tense assignment with the situation which obtains with verbs like *rogoca* 'hear', which take full sentential complements. In sentence (27), the past tense is obligatorily marked on the *matrix verb*.

(27)   E ratou *a*   rogoca ni sā   yaco mai na waqa
          PCL 3TRIAL PAST hear   that EMPH arrive   ART boat
          'They heard that the boat had arrived'

The second argument against treating *sega* as a higher rather than as an auxiliary negative verb is similar to the second, and concerns verb agreement. Like tense, verb agreement in Fijian is marked by preverbal particles. Indeed, since number is not marked on subject nouns, these preverbal particles serve as the sole indicators of number. In a manner similar to that of the tense particles, it is optional which of the two verbs marks this agreement, although, as before, it is not possible for both verbs to be marked. This holds even when the subject is topicalized, and may be considered as evidence against treating this process as subject-raising:

(28)   a. *Na gone vuli* e   *ra sega* ni   kila   na kena i sau
         ART student PCL 3PL NEG that know ART its   answer

       b. *Na gone vuli* e   *sega* ni   *ra* kila   na kena i sau
         ART student PCL NEG that 3PL know ART its   answer

       c.* *Na gone vuli* e   *ra sega* ni   *ra* kila   na kena i sau
         ART student PCL 3PL NEG that 3PL know ART its   answer
         'The students don't know the answer to it'

We may compare these sentences with sentence (27), in which the trial marker *ratou* obligatorily marks the matrix verb.

In conclusion, although the Fijian negatives are superficially similar to the Tongan ones, they have several properties which suggest an evolutionary process from a higher verb construction to a construction involving a complex verbal group (VG) with an auxiliary negative verb and a lexical verb, either of which may take tense or number agreement. This process of auxiliarization or predicate-raising may be represented schematically as follows (where Comp = Complementizer):

$$[_S V_{neg} [_S \quad Comp \; V_{lexical} \; Obj \; Subj]]$$
$$[_S [_{VG} \; V_{neg} \; Comp \; V_{lexical}] \; Obj \; Subj]$$

Precisely the same kind of processes seem to take place in sov languages with sentence-final higher negative verbs. It is claimed for instance by Munro (1973, 1976, 1977), on the basis of comparative evidence, that the varieties of standard negation currently found in Yuman languages ultimately derive from a structure like

$$[_S [_S \; Subj \; Obj \; V_{lexical}]\text{-}m \; V_{neg}]$$

where the morpheme -*m* intervening between the lexical and negative verbs is a different-subject marker whose presence is required because the subject of the complement is automatically distinct from the subject of the negative verb. Of the Yuman languages, Diegueño appears best to preserve this original structure in negative sentences like (29):

(29)   ?nʸa:-č ?-a:m-x ?-*ma:w*
       I-SUBJ I-go-IRR I-NEG
       'I didn't go'

The different-subject marker has been absorbed into the negative verb
ma:w, and no longer carries its original meaning. In fact, the negative
verb agrees with the subject of the lexïcal verb. Otherwise some
characteristics of the higher verb construction remain: the lexical verb
agrees obligatorily with its subject (thus making agreement in both the
negative and lexical verbs) and it has its own tense marking, although
this is restricted to the irrealis -*x*. The main tense differences are marked
by the negative verb. For instance, the same marker -*x* attached to the
negative verb can indicate futurity (Stenson 1970). In other Yuman
languages, the process of auxiliarization finally results in the negative
becoming merely a suffix on the lexical verb, as in the Mojave sentence:

(30)   ?nʸeč ?-iyem-*mo*-t-m
       I   I-go-NEG-EMPH-TNS
       'I didn't go'

2.1.2 *Auxiliary negative verbs*

We now turn our attention to languages in which the negative verb
originates historically as an auxiliary rather than as a higher verb. In its
purest form, the auxiliary negative verb is marked with all the basic
verbal categories of person, number, tense/aspect and mood (if these
are realized in the language concerned), whereas the lexical verb
assumes an invariant, participial form. There will be no evidence, like
the presence of complementizers, for a full sentential boundary between
the negative verb and the lexical verb, and there may well be evidence
against such a boundary, for instance if the negative has positional
mobility within the sentence. The essence of the construction is captured by the English sentence *John isn't coming*, where *isn't* represents
the negative auxiliary and *coming* the participial form of the lexical
verb. In the languages we shall consider, however, the negative is a verb
stem and not a morphological accretion like English -*n't*.

Consider Evenki, a member of the northern or Siberian subgroup of
the Tungus family (Vasilevič 1934, Gorcevskaja 1941, Konstantinova
1964, 1968). Other members of this northern subgroup, for example
Even (Novikova 1968) and Negidal' (Kolesnikova and Konstantinova
1968), possess similar constructions. In Evenki the stem of the negative
verb is the rather minimal ə- which inflects for person, number, tense
and mood, whereas the lexical verb assumes a participial form which for
the vast majority of verbs ends in the suffix -*ra*/-*rə* (depending on vowel
harmony). Evenki is basically an sov language, and while the lexical

verb typically occurs sentence finally in both positive and negative sentences, the negative auxiliary may either immediately precede it, or occupy the immediate postsubject position. Corresponding to positive sentences like (31a), therefore, we have the two negative sentences (31b) and (31c):

(31)   a. Bi dukuwūn-ma duku-cā-w
          I letter-OBJ   write-PAST-1SG
          'I wrote a letter'

       b. Bi dukuwūn-ma ə-cə̄-w   duku-ra
          I letter-OBJ   NEG-PAST-1SG write-PART

       c. Bi ə-cə̄-w   dukuwūn-ma duku-ra
          I NEG-PAST-1SG letter-OBJ   write-PART
          'I didn't write a letter'

It will be noted that exactly the same inflections as are carried by the lexical verb in the positive sentence are carried by the negative verb in the negative sentences (with variations according to vowel harmony), and this holds for the majority of tenses and moods. We have, for instance, a remote past in -*ŋkī* which gives (32a) and (32b), a conditional in -*mcā* which gives (33a) and (33b), and an imperative in -*kal* which gives (34a) and (34b):

(32)   a. Nuŋan baka-ŋkī-n
          he   find-PAST-3SG
          'He found'

       b. Nuŋan ə-ŋkī-n   baka-ra
          he   NEG-PAST-3SG find-PART
          'He didn't find'

(33)   a. Bi baka-mcā-w
          I find-COND-1SG
          'I wouldn't find'

       b. Bi ə-mcə̄-w   baka-ra
          I NEG-COND-1SG find-PART
          'I wouldn't find'

(34)   a. Baka-kal!
          find-IMP
          'Find!'

       b. ə-kəl   baka-ra!
          NEG-IMP find-PART
          'Don't find!'

In some tenses and moods the correspondence is not quite so exact. For instance, one marker of the future in positive forms is the morpheme -ʒa, in origin a marker of imperfective aspect, giving baka-ʒa-n 'he will find'. The corresponding negative is ə-tə-n baka-ra 'he won't find', using a morpheme tə which has otherwise disappeared from the language. The non-occurrence of -ʒa with the negative verb is certainly due to an aspectual origin, since aspect markers, with the sole exception of the habitual -ŋna, always occur with the lexical verb: for example, the inception marker -l occurs in positive forms like baka-l-cā-tin 'they started to find' and negative forms like ə-cə-tin baka-l-la 'they didn't start to find', but not *ə-l-cə-tin baka-ra. Despite this formal non-correspondence in the future, however, it is clear that the language strives to maintain a functional correspondence between positive and negative forms.

Evenki, Even, and Negidal′ illustrate the Tungus auxiliary negative verb construction in its original form, with all the person, number, tense and mood distinctions marked solely by the negative verb. Other languages of the group reveal a variety of ways in which this construction can develop, the most radical being the reduction of the negative verb to the status of derivational morpheme on the lexical verb, as in the Mojave case. We shall examine this kind of reduction in more detail in section 2.3. For the moment, however, we wish to concentrate on the possibility that the negative verb, while retaining its independent word status, nevertheless loses some of its functions as person, number, tense and mood carrier to the lexical verb.

To a limited extent, this process takes place in Orok, one of the southern group of Tungus languages spoken on Saxalin (Petrova 1967, 1968). Present and future forms of the negative verb carry person and number markings, as in Evenki. There are however two past forms of the negative, illustrated by examples (35a) and (35b):

(35)   a. Si   ə-tci-si   bū-ra
            you NEG-PAST-2SG give-PART

        b. Si   ə-tci-l   bū-rə-si
            you NEG-PAST   give-PART-2SG
            'You didn't give'

In (35a) we have the standard form of the negative verb with the lexical verb as an invariant participle. In (35b) on the other hand the person and number markings are transferred to the lexical verb, leaving the negative with the tense marker. The final -l of the negative verb shows that historically it was a past participle which attained main predicate status, a common process in the Tungus languages. This suffix originally signalled plurality for the participle, but that meaning has now been lost. Amongst the other languages of the southern group, transferral of person and number markings to the lexical verb has also occurred in Oroč (Avrorin and Lebedeva 1968). Here it is restricted to the second person plural of the imperative, with forms like (36b):

(36)   a. ə-ʒi   gun-ə!
          NEG-IMP speak-PART
          'Don't speak!' (singular)

        b. ə-ʒi   gun-ə-su!
          NEG-IMP speak-PART-2PL
          'Don't speak!' (plural)

The basic Tungus pattern is therefore that the negative auxiliary carries tense, mood, person and number markings, whereas other verbal categories such as aspect and voice are indicated by the lexical verb. In the southern group, there is a widespread tendency for the negative verb to fuse with the lexical verb, but where it maintains its independence, there is a limited amount of diffusion of person and number marking to the lexical verb.

More complex patterns of diffusion of verbal categories may be observed in the auxiliary negative verb construction of Uralic languages (Comrie 1976). All the Fennic languages, with the exception of dialects underlying standard Estonian, and all the Samoyed languages, with the exception of Sel'kup, possess auxiliary negative verbs which mark at least some verbal categories. The Estonian negative is an invariant particle *ei* which derives historically from the third person singular of the present form of the negative verb (Collinder 1960:247), while the Sel'kup negative consists of the particles *aśśa* in non-imperative and *yky* in imperative sentences (Tereščenko 1973:82). These two particles may also represent reduced negative verbs, but their precise origin is obscure.

As far as tense distinctions are concerned, the original Uralic contrast between past and non-past is maintained as a feature of the negative verb in the Samoyedic languages: Nenets (Yurak), Enets (Yenisei Samoyed) and Nganasan (Tavgi); in the Permic languages: Udmurt (Votjak), Komi-Zyrjan and Komi-Permjak; in all variants of Mari (Cheremis); in the Mordvin languages: Erzja and Mokša. Further west, the maintenance of the past/non-past distinction in the negative verb is more sporadic, but may be found in some dialects of Lappish and Estonian, and also in Livonian. We illustrate with paradigms of the singular forms from one representative language of each group:

(37)   a. *Nenets* (Ščerbakova 1954:199–200)
Basic word order: sov
Verbs: *xaneś* (trade, hunt), *xajoś* (stay)

Present:	xane-(d)m'		'I trade'
	xane-n		'You trade'
	xane		'He trades'
	ni-(d)m'	xane″	'I don't trade'
	ni-n	xane″	'You don't trade'
	ni	xane″	'He doesn't trade'

Past:	xai-manź		'I stayed'
	xai-naś		'You stayed'
	xai-ś		'He stayed'
	ni-manź	xaju″	'I didn't stay'
	ni-naś	xaju″	'You didn't stay'
	ni-ś	xaju″	'He didn't stay'

(The form of the lexical verb in the negative is here identical to that of the 2nd person singular imperative.)

b. *Komi-Zyrjan* (Lytkin 1966:291–2)
Basic word order: sov
Verb: *gižny* (write)

Present:	giž-a		'I write'
	giž-an		'You write'
	giž-ö		'He writes'
	o-g	giž	'I don't write'
	o-n	giž	'You don't write'
	o-z	giž	'He doesn't write'

Past I:	giž-i		'I wrote'
	giž-in		'You wrote'
	giž-is		'He wrote'
	e-g	giž	'I didn't write'
	e-n	giž	'You didn't write'
	e-z	giž	'He didn't write'

(Here morphological and phonological processes have resulted in a distinct paradigm for the negative verb. Note in particular that the past/present distinction ends up by being a feature of the stem of the negative verb, rather than of its ending.)

c. *Meadow Mari* (Kovedjaeva 1966:231)
   Basic word order: sov
   Verb: *užaš* (see)

Present: už-am   'I see'
          už-at   'You see'
          už-eš   'He sees'
             o-m   už   'I don't see'
             o-t   už   'You don't see'
             og-eš už   'He doesn't see'

Past I: už-ym   'I saw'
         už-yč   'You saw'
         už-o   'He saw'
            š-ym už   'I didn't see'
            š-yč už   'You didn't see'
            yš   už   'He didn't see'

(Here the past/present distinction is a feature of both the stem and the endings of the negative verb. The form *og-eš* derives from an earlier form **o-k*, in which *k* is the original present tense marker, followed by the ending *-eš* taken from the paradigm of regular verbs (Lavrent'ev 1974).)

d. *Erzja* (Feoktistov 1966:187; Serebrennikov 1967)
   Basic word order: svo
   Verb: *kundams* (catch)

Present: kund-an   'I catch'
          kund-at   'You catch'
          kund-y   'He catches'
            a kund-an   'I don't catch'
            a kund-at   'You don't catch'
            a kund-y   'He doesn't catch'

Past I: kund-yn'   'I caught'
         kund-yt'   'You caught'
         kund-as'   'He caught'
            ez-in' kunda(k)   'I didn't catch'
            ez-it' kunda(k)   'You didn't catch'
            ez'   kunda(k)   'He didn't catch'

(Here it will be noted that in the present tense the negative verb has lost all its person/number endings. The resulting invariant particle *a* combines with the regular inflected forms of the lexical verb. The past form of the negative verb preserves all the endings in Erzja, but in some dialects of the related Mokša the past is also generalized to *aš* in conjunction with the regular past forms of the lexical verb. From a historical point of view both *a* and *aš* are third person singular forms (Ščemerova 1972).)

e. *Livonian* (Vääri 1966:145)
   Basic word order: svo
   Verb: *lu'ggə̂* (read)

Present:	lugùB	'I read'
	lugùD	'You read'
	lugùB	'He reads'
	äb lu'G	'I don't read'
	äd lu'G	'You don't read'
	äb lu'G	'He doesn't read'
Past:	lugìz	'I read'
	lugìst	'You read'
	lugìz	'He read'
	iz lu'G	'I didn't read'
	ist lu'G	'You didn't read'
	iz lu'G	'He didn't read'

Livonian is exceptional amongst the Balto-Fennic languages in maintaining a past form of the negative verb. In the majority of these languages, Finnish, Karelian, Veps, Ižor, Vot and Estonian, only a present form is preserved which combines with the past participle to create a negative of the simple past:

(38)   *Veps* (Laanest 1975:91)
       Basic word order: svo (but vso also possible)
       Verb: *lugeda* (read)

Present:	lugen	'I read'
	luged	'You read'
	lugob	'He reads'
	en luge	'I don't read'
	ed luge	'You don't read'
	ī (*ei*) luge	'He doesn't read'

Past:	lugin'	'I read'
	lugid'	'You read'
	lugi	'He read'
	en lugend	'I didn't read'
	ed lugend	'You didn't read'
	ī lugend	'He didn't read'

(In Veps, the negative auxiliary may not only precede the lexical verb, but also follow it (Hämäläinen 1966:96).)

This pattern of combination with the past participle is even found in those Estonian dialects which have the invariant negative *ei*. We have *lugesin* 'I read', but *ei lugenud* 'I didn't read' rather than **ei lugesin* (Kask 1966:49).

Tense distinctions beyond this basic one of past versus non-past are later developments in Uralic, and there is considerable variation amongst individual languages as to the nature of each tense, and as to whether it is the negative verb or the lexical verb, or even both, which serves as the carrier. Both the Samoyedic and the Permic languages have for instance developed morphological futures. Within the Samoyedic group, Nenets keeps the negative verb in its present tense form and attaches the future marker -*ŋgo* (of aspectival origin) to the lexical verb (Ščerbakova 1954:200), whilst Nganasan allows the negative verb itself to take future endings: *nindym midja"* 'I'm not giving up', *nisəmə midja"* 'I didn't give up', *nisyðəmə midja"* 'I won't give up' (Tereščenko 1966:432). Within the Permic group, the Komi languages have morphological futures in positive verb forms only: the non-past negative serves as a negative for both the present and future tenses. In Udmurt, however, the future is marked by the lexical verb, and, in the third person only, by the negative verb as well: *ug myno* 'he does not go' versus *uz myny* 'he will not go' (Comrie 1976:3).

Distinctions of mood in Uralic are similarly language-specific, and the same kind of variation exists as to the distribution of the markings. Mari, for example, has an optative mood formed by the suffix -*ne*, which attaches to the negative verb: *užnem* 'I want to go', *ynem už* 'I don't want to go' (Kovedjaeva 1966:233). This suffix seems to be related to the Balto-Fennic potential mood, whose suffix -*ne* always associates with the lexical verb, as in Finnish *luke-ne-n* 'perhaps I'll read' and its corresponding negative *e-n luke-ne* 'perhaps I won't read'. By contrast, the morphological optative in the Mordvin languages is clearly of more recent origin and transparently derived from the fusion of a participle in -*ks* and the copula *ulems* 'to be'. In Erzja, for instance, we find forms like *kundyksëlin'*. 'I want to catch' based on the participle **kunday-ks* (from the stem *kunday 'catch') and the first singular of the copula *ulejm. The Mokša form kundaləksǝ̂lǝn', with identical meaning, is slightly more complex in structure and appears to contain a second occurrence of the copula whose function is to bear the participial ending. Its source would then be *kunday ule-ks ulejm. Most striking, however, is the difference in the negatives of these forms in the two languages. Whereas in Erzja the negative is simply formed by prefixing the positive with the invariant a, as in example (37d), in Mokša we have a new fully inflected negative verb based on the original negative verb and the same configuration of participial and inflected forms of the copula as in the positive. The Erzja negative is then a kundyksëlin', with invariant negative and fully inflected lexical verb, and the corresponding Mokša negative is afǝ̂lǝksǝ̂lǝn' kunda, with invariant lexical and fully inflected negative verb.

As far as person and number are concerned, it is clear that the original auxiliary negative verb in Uralic was marked for agreement with the subject, while the lexical verb was invariant. The existing languages again however show a more complex distribution. In certain cases, the negative verb has actually gained additional agreement markers. This notably occurs in the Mordvin languages, where the rise of an objective conjugation results in the negative verb agreeing with both subject and object. We have in Erzja kundymik 'you caught me' with its negative ëzimik kunda 'you didn't catch me'. This is restricted however to the past tense, since in the present, the negative is effected as always by simply prefixing the invariant a: a kundasamak 'you don't catch me'.

More usually, person and number distinctions become neutralized in the negative verb, with the result that the lexical verb sometimes gains compensatory markings. In Livonian, for instance, there is an almost total loss of number distinction in the negative verb, but the lexical verb compensates for this: äb lu'G 'I don't read' versus äb lu'ggêm 'we don't read' (Vääri 1966:145). A similar pattern can be found in Udmurt, where only the first person of the negative verb shows a singular/plural distinction. This results in redundant marking of number on both negative and lexical verb in the first person, but number marking solely on the lexical verb elsewhere: ug sylïs'ky 'I don't stand', um sylïs'ke 'we don't stand', ud sylïs'ky 'you (singular) don't stand', ud sylïs'ke 'you (plural) don't stand' (Tepljašina 1966:270). An interesting exception to the compensatory principle is provided by standard Estonian, in which all person and number markings are lost from the negative verb without evoking any change in the original invariant form of the lexical verb. Whereas the positive forms of the lexical verb all agree, there is one negative form for all persons and numbers in the present tense: *loen* 'I read', *loed* 'you read', *loeb* 'he reads', *loeme* 'we read', *loete* 'you (plural) read', *loevad* 'they read', with the negative *ei loe* (Laanest 1975:95–7). This holds equally for the past, in which the positive forms again all mark agreement with the subject in person and number, while the negative forms consist of the invariant *ei* borrowed from the present tense in conjunction with an equally invariant past participle.

The evidence of Uralic, and to a lesser extent the Tungus languages, shows how the basic auxiliary negative verb construction, comprising a negative verb with full inflections and a largely invariant (except for aspectival distinctions) lexical verb, may develop in ways which result in a complex distribution of the categories of person, number, tense and mood between the negative verb and the lexical verb. A limiting case of this development is the total denuding of the negative verb which takes place in Estonian. The sheer variety of possibilities makes generalization difficult, but it is noticeable that categories rarely end up by being redundantly marked on both the negative and lexical verbs, and also that tense and mood distinctions are generally maintained and augmented, wherever they are positioned, whereas person and number distinctions are more easily lost.

We conclude this discussion of auxiliary negative verbs by reverting briefly to questions of word order. In the svo languages we have examined, the negative verb almost invariably occurs immediately before the lexical verb. The only counter-example is Veps, in which the negative verb may also immediately follow. Apart from Veps, which permits vso as a variant order, we have no examples of verb-initial languages with auxiliary negative verbs, although there is no reason why these should not exist with the negative verb in the expected initial position.

In sov languages there seems to be greater freedom of position. The Tungus as well as many of the Uralic languages reveal that the negative verb often immediately precedes the lexical verb, and this may be contrasted with higher negative verbs, which always follow. A further example is provided by the Modern Western Armenian auxiliary negative *tš-*, as in *tš-ɛm sirɛl* 'I don't love' (Helen Haig, p.c.). The northern Tungus languages show in addition that the negative verb may float to postsubject position, as in example (31c). It is equally likely, however, that the negative verb may follow the lexical verb. Indirect evidence for this is provided by those Tungus languages in which the negative verb degenerates into a negative suffix (section 2.3), and direct evidence is provided by the negative verb *an-* (and the more emphatic *mōs-*) in Korean (Martin and Lee 1969:45) and the negative verb *değil* in Turkish.

The origin of negative verbs, both of the higher and the auxiliary variety, is frequently obscure. Nevertheless, some evidence, both direct and circumstantial, exists that in at least some cases the negative verb is simply a negative form of the verb 'be'. Direct evidence may be found, for example, in Fijian, where the (higher) negative verb *sega* may be used on its own to indicate denial of existence (Milner 1956:43): *e sega na wai* 'there is no water'. The Turkish auxiliary negative *değil* and the Armenian *tš-* are also used as simple negatives of 'be', as is, more rarely, the Evenki *ə-* (Gorcevskaja 1941:44). More circumstantial evidence is provided by the Yuman higher negative, which has a parallel construction involving the use of the verb 'be' as a higher verb in positive sentences (Munro 1976). Some cases of negative verbs are however demonstrably not related to the verb 'be'. This commonly occurs when a language has a negative imperative formed by means of a negative verb, whether it uses negative verbs in other moods or not. The Welsh negative imperative is for example based on the verb *peidio* 'to stop', as in *paid â symud* 'don't move!' (Rhys Jones 1977:152), and the Latin negative imperative on the verb *nolle* 'not to want'.

2.2 Negative particles

While negative verbs are without doubt the most interesting of the varied forms of standard negation, the fieldworker is more likely to be faced with some kind of negative particle. The term 'particle' implies invariance, and it is indeed possible to find languages in which the same invariant particle is used no matter what the sentence type, and no matter what the form of the predicate. For example, in Russian the particle *ne* is used with all tenses, aspects and moods, and with verbal, adjectival, nominal and prepositional predicates:

(39)   a. On *ne* igraet   (Verb: imperfective)
             he NEG plays
             'He doesn't play'

        b. On *ne* vyigraet   (Verb: perfective)
             he NEG wins
             'He won't win'

        c. *Ne* igraj!   (Verb: imperative)
             NEG play
             'Don't play!'

        d. On *ne* durak   (Noun)
             he NEC fool
             'He's not a fool'

e. On *ne* molod   (Adjective)
   he NEG young
   'He's not young'

f. On *ne* v komnate   (Prepositional phrase)
   he NEG in room
   'He's not in the room'

It is equally possible, however, for the above factors to be criterial in the selection of the negative particle. Variation of negative particle according to mood is for instance found in Hungarian, where the negative particle for statements is *nem* and for imperatives *ne*. A similar distinction is reconstructable for Indo-European, with **ne* (giving Sanskrit *na*, Gothic *ni* and Slavonic *ne*) for statements and **mē* (giving Sanskrit *mā* and Greek *mē*) for imperatives (Brugmann 1905:818–9, Lehmann 1974:123). Variation according to tense or aspect is equally common, and found for example in many Semitic languages. Among other possible contrasts in standard Arabic, we find *lam naṭṭaliʿ* 'we have not perused' versus *lā naṭṭaliʿu* 'we do/will/can not peruse'. Further negative particles are *mā* and its archaic variant *māʾin*, used with verbs of dynamic aspect (Beeston 1970:99–100). In many cases negative particles which are conditioned in this way by the tense or mood of the predicate turn out to be reduced forms of negative verbs which have lost their person and number inflections. An example of this has already been given (example (37d)) from the Mokša dialect which has generalized the third person singular of the present (*af*) and of the past (*aš*) as otherwise invariant particles combining with the regular inflected forms of the lexical verb.

Finally, the choice of negative particle may depend on the grammatical category of the predicate. Again the Semitic languages provide examples of this, a notable case being Baghdad Arabic (Bakir 1970). In declaratives (the imperative is again different), the particle *ma:/mə* is used with verbal predicates, while the particle *mu:* is used with nominal, adjectival, and prepositional predicates (with definite subjects):

(40) a. ʕəli *ma:* ra:ħ lidda:ʔirə   (Verb)
         Ali NEG went to the office
         'Ali didn't go to the office'

      b. ʔubu:jə *mu:* muħa:mi   (Noun)
         father-my NEG lawyer
         'My father is not a lawyer'

      c. Ha:ðə ʃʃati *mu:* rəmli   (Adjective)
         this   beach NEG sandy
         'This beach is not sandy'

    d. Lməktu:b *mu: ʔili*   (Prepositional phrase)
       the letter NEG for me
       'The letter is not for me'

In terms of position, negative particles are primarily associated with the verb or verb phrase. The most common patterns, in relation to basic word order, strongly resemble those of negative verbs, so that in svo, vso and vos languages the particle precedes the verb, while in sov languages it is equally likely to precede or follow. The main exceptions to these patterns seem to be based on the strong tendency for particle negatives to be emphasized and reinforced, sometimes by addition to the particle itself as in Latin *nōn* (from **ne-oinom* 'not one'), but more frequently by the addition of a further particle elsewhere in the sentence, forming a pair of linked negatives. The classic example of this is the French construction in which the pairs *ne . . . pas* and *ne . . . point* surround the verb and its associated clitics, as in *je ne chante pas* 'I don't sing'. The original French negative is clearly the preverbal *ne* derived from Latin *nōn*; in Old French texts it often occurs without the following *pas* or *point*, and this construction indeed survives to the present day in expressions like *je ne saurais dire* 'I could not say'. From the twelfth century, however, *ne* is reinforced by *pas*, from Latin *passum* 'a step', and *point*, from Latin *punctum* 'a point'. A further such particle, *mie*, from Latin *mica* 'a crumb', has not survived. Originally, these particles must have been full objects of the verbs they were associated with, as for example in *il ne marche pas* 'he does not go (a step)'. Now, they are fully generalized and occur in the presence of other objects (Price 1962, 1971:252). In addition, when the preverbal particle is lost, as in modern colloquial French, we are left with a postverbal particle, an unusual feature in an svo language. The postverbal position of English *not* is explicable in similar terms: the original Old English preverbal *ne* was first reinforced by the postverbal *nawiht* 'nothing', which after the loss of *ne* developed into *not* (Jespersen 1946:427).

It is not always the case that particle pairs of this type immediately surround the verb. Since the object position is the source of the reinforcing particles discussed so far, we might expect that in a vso language, the reinforcing particle would follow the subject, giving the pattern NEG–V–S–NEG–O. The subsequent loss of the preverbal negative would then leave a negative whose position was defined primarily in relation to the subject: V–S–NEG–O. This development is attested in Welsh, where the preverbal particle is *nid*, and the reinforcement particle *ddim* 'thing', which may be omitted (Bowen and Rhys Jones 1960:23):

(41)   *Nid* yw'r bachgen (*ddim*) yn hoffi coffi
       NEG is-the boy   NEG   in like coffee
       'The boy does not like coffee'

In colloquial Welsh, however, *ddim* is retained and the preverbal *nid* disappears, in some circumstances leaving a trace of its former presence. If the following verb is 'be', then the final *d* fuses with the verb giving in effect a negative form of 'be':

(42)   *D*yw'r   bachgen *ddim* yn hoffi coffi
       NEG-be-the boy   NEG   in like coffee
       'The boy does not like coffee'

If the following verb begins with the consonants *g, b, d, c, p, t, m, ll* or *rh*, then this consonant mutates to -, *f, dd, ch, ph, th, f, l* or *r* respectively. Otherwise, there is no reflex of the former *nid*, leaving *ddim* as the sole negative:

(43)   a. Daeth y gath i'r   tŷ
          came the cat into-the house
          'The cat came into the house'

       b. *Dd*aeth y gath *ddim* i'r   tŷ
          came   the cat NEG into the house
          'The cat didn't come into the house'

       c. Eisteddais i yn y gadair
          sat   I in the chair
          'I sat in the chair'

       d. Eisteddais i *ddim* yn y   gadair
          sat   I NEG in the chair
          'I didn't sit in the chair'

In the case of svo languages, it may also happen that the second particle of a negative pair is not immediately next to the verb. The pattern s–NEG–V–O–NEG is an attested one, with a final negative particle. It occurs for example in Hausa (Kraft and Kirk-Greene 1973:310), COMPL = Completive:

(44)   Yārinyà *bà* tà   tàfi gōnā *ba*
       girl   NEG she(COMPL) go   farm NEG
       'The girl did not go to the farm'

The preverbal particle may in some cases fuse with the person–aspect marker, resulting in a form which has a great deal of similarity to negative verbs:

(45)   Mùtûm *bài*   yi   gōnā *ba*
        man   he(NEG COMPL) make farm NEG
        'The man did not make a farm'

According to P. Newman (1971), other Chadic languages, such as Jegu and Sura, have a preverbal particle related to the Hausa one, but a distinct final particle (*dó* and *kás* respectively), while yet others, namely Bolewa, Ngizim, Angas, Ron, Gisiga and Higi, have solely a final marker, giving the pattern s–v–o–NEG. In Tera, which also has this pattern, the negative particle *ɓa* comes at the end of both main and subordinate clauses, so that a sentence like (46) is ambiguous, depending on whether the negative is associated with the matrix or the embedded clause (P. Newman 1970:102):

(46)   Nduk kə   pəz   ndib nə kə ʂugdə a xa   nda *ɓa*
        person SUBJ insult man REL   knife belong him NEG
        'A person should not insult a man who has a knife'
    or 'A person should insult a man who does not have a knife'

Final negative particles in an svo clause may also be found in German sentences like *Ich liebe ihn nicht* 'I don't love him'. In German subordinate clauses however, which have sov order, the negative standardly precedes the verbal group: *weil ich ihn nicht liebe* 'because I don't love him'. There are strong arguments for regarding the main clause order as a transform of the subordinate clause order in which the finite verb is thrown forward to second position, stranding the negative when the finite verb is the only constituent of the verbal group (Zemb 1968).

2.3 *Morphological negatives*

Morphological negation occurs whenever the negative morpheme must be considered to form part of the derivational morphology of the verb. In simple cases, negative prefixes and suffixes transparently derive from the cliticization to the verb of previously independent negative particles. Morphophonemic alternations may show that the particle has become part of the verb, as with the Persian prefix *na-* which umlauts to *ne-* before syllables with a high front vowel. Compare for instance *na-xar-am* 'I may not buy' with *ne-mi-xar-am* 'I am not buying'. Prefixation of this type seems to be more common than suffixation, possibly owing to a reluctance to attach negatives as final suffixes to already inflected verbs. It is striking that most of the English verbs which permit suffixal *-n't* have defective paradigms.

In more complicated cases, the negative morpheme is clearly internal to the verb morphology, preceding such affixes as those of tense, mood, person and number. An extreme example of an internal negative may be found in the Turkish *-me-*, with its variants *-ma-, -mi(y)-* and *-mɪ(y)*, which precedes the above affixes, but follows all of the valency suffixes, i.e. those indicating reflexives, reciprocals, causatives and passives, and itself alternates with a further negative *-eme-*, with variants similar to those of the standard negative, whose function is to express denial of possibility. The agglutinative pattern of all these affixes follows the schema:

$$V + Refl + Recip + Cause + Pass + \begin{Bmatrix} NEG \\ (me) \\ NEG\text{-}Possible \\ (eme) \end{Bmatrix} + \begin{matrix} Possible \\ (ebil) \end{matrix}$$

$$+ \begin{Bmatrix} Tense \\ Mood \end{Bmatrix} + \begin{Bmatrix} Person \\ Number \end{Bmatrix}$$

Lewis (1967:153) cites such forms as *acɪ-n-dɪr-ɪl-ma-dɪ-k* (stem + reflexive + causative + passive + negative + past + 1st plural), meaning 'we were not made to grieve'. Combination of the negative with the possibility marker *ebil* gives the meaning 'possible-not', which then contrasts with the form *-eme-*, as in *gel-miy-ebil-ecek* (stem + negative + possible + future), meaning 'he may not come', and *gel-emiy-ecek* (stem + not possible + future), meaning 'he will not be able to come'.

The position of negation in Turkish is explicable on the grounds that the original negative was a negative verb, inflected for tense, mood, person and number, which fused with an invariant, though possibly derivationally complex, lexical verb in a participial form ending in **-m* (Bang 1923, Menges 1968:144). The original negative verb has not survived as such in Turkic languages. Nevertheless, an identical process of fusion can be demonstrated in the Tungus language Nanai, whose relatives, as we have seen, possess the negative verb *ə-* in a fully independent and inflected form. Positive verb forms in Nanai are based on the principle of adding a possessive pronoun to a participial form of the verb. For the verb *xola* 'read', the present participle ends in *-j* and the past participle in *-xa*, giving the following forms (Avrorin 1961:79):

(47)   a. xola-j-si
        read-PRES-2SG
        'you are reading'

       b. xola-xa-si
        read-PAST-2SG
        'you did read'

In the corresponding negatives, the markers of the present and past participles are quite distinct, and the final vowel of the verb stem is lengthened. This is readily explicable on the grounds that the participial markers are precisely those we would expect to occur with the negative verb, while the lengthening is a reflex of the appropriate form of the stem:

(48)   a. xolā-si-si   (<*xolā ə + si + si)
          read(NEG)-PRES-2SG
          'You aren't reading'

        b. xolā-ci-si   (<*xolā ə + ci + si)
          read(NEG)-PAST-2SG
          'You didn't read'

To conclude this section on morphological negatives, we mention that it is very common to find that a restricted subset of verbs in a language may be subject to morphological negation, even though the majority are not. Undoubtedly the most frequent verb to be negated in this way is 'be', as, for example, in Persian *nist*, Arabic *laysa* and Modern Hebrew *eino*. Other verbs are typically modals, as in the English forms *won't*, *can't*, *mustn't*, *mightn't*, *wouldn't*, *shouldn't*, and Evenki ətə- 'will not'.

2.4 Negative nouns

A rare possibility is that standard negation is realized by means of a negative morpheme which has nominal properties. The only example we have of this is Evenki *ācin*, and similar forms in related languages, whose function is to deny the existence or presence of something. It has a plural form in -*r*, which is the regular plural for nouns ending in -*n*, and agrees with its subject in number (Gorcevskaja 1941:72): *nuŋan ācin* 'he is not here', *nuŋartin ācir* 'they are not here'. In audition it may take case endings, with a meaning something like 'absence':

(49)   nuŋartin *ācir*-du-tin
        they   absence-LOC-their
        'in their absence'

Its use in expressions like *orono ācin bəjə* 'deer-lacking man', in which it agrees in number with the head noun *bəjə* 'man', suggests however a deverbal origin.

2.5 Secondary modifications

It seems that all languages use at least one of the three devices, negative verbs, negative particles and negative derivational morphemes, in order

to effect standard negation. In a few cases, the use of one of these
devices is accompanied by a secondary modification in the sentence to
be negated. The modifications we have observed are: (a) a change in
word order, (b) a change in tone, (c) neutralization of tense distinctions,
(d) the use of supporting verbs, and (e) a change in noun case. Such
modifications on their own, however, are not sufficient to negate any
sentence type in any language. In this respect, negation contrasts with
other features such as tense or mood, which may indeed be realized by
such modifications alone. Dahl (1977), however, mentions a Niger–
Congo language Mano in which negation seems to be carried by tonal
distinctions: *ǹ yídò* 'I know' versus *ń yídò* 'I don't know'.

Change of word order in negative sentences may be found in Kru
(Hyman 1975:125). The svo order of the majority of sentence types is
modified to sov in the corresponding negatives:

(50) a. ɔ́   tè̤ kɔ́
          he(COMPL) buy rice
          'He bought rice'

      b. ɔ́   sé   kɔ̀ tè̤
          he(COMPL) NEG rice buy
          'He didn't buy rice'

This sov order is claimed to be a relic of a stage in Kru prior to the
development of svo order. The negative morpheme *sé* has further
interesting features: in the first and second person singular, the person–
aspect marker is omitted together, and person is marked by the tone of
the negative itself, with a high tone for first person and a low tone for
second person. It also has variants according to tense: *séke* (remote
past: 'long ago'), *sékà* (near past: 'yesterday') and *sémà* (near past: 'two
days ago'). These features give *sé* some verbal status (Rickard 1970).

Change of tone in negative sentences can be observed in many
languages. We cite an example from Igbo, in which the negative particle
is suffixed to the aspect marker within the verbal group. No matter what
the basic tone of the aspect marker, its first syllable always has 'step'
tone when it is negated, so that for instance the incompletive marker *nà*
is modified to *ná* (Welmers and Welmers 1968:107):

(51) Ọ̀ ná-*ghị́*   àsá akwà
      she INCOMPL-NEG do wash
      'She hasn't washed'

Further, more complex, tonal changes take place whenever the morpheme to which the negative is suffixed has more than one syllable.

Neutralization of tense distinctions in negative sentences is a not infrequent phenomenon. It presumably arises out of the failure of negative paradigms to catch up with developments in positive paradigms. We have already mentioned the case of the Permic language, Komi, in which the development of a separate future tense is not reflected in the paradigm of the negative verb, which then serves as the negative form corresponding to both present and future tenses: *gižö* 'he writes', *gižas* 'he will write', *oz giž* 'he doesn't write/he won't write'. Another fascinating example can be found in Logbara, where a negative sentence corresponding to a positive one in the present or future appears in the form of a past tense (Crazzolara 1960:92):

(52)   a. Drùsî   mâ zâ   ɲaa rá
          tomorrow I   meat eat (stress)
          'Tomorrow I shall eat meat'

       b. Drùsî   á ɲaa zá   *kö*
          tomorrow I eat meat NEG
          'Tomorrow I shall not eat meat'

It will be observed that the negative sentence has a totally different construction from that of the positive sentence. Firstly, the negative sentence has svo order corresponding to sov in the positive sentence. Secondly, the negative sentence employs a short form of the subject pronoun (*á*) while the positive sentence employs a long form (*mâ*). Thirdly, the positive sentence has a different tone for the object from that in the negative sentence. All these three features tie the negative sentence into the past tense paradigm, despite its future meaning. Logbara, indeed, combines all three of the secondary modifications discussed so far. The converse phenomenon, in which more distinctions are observed in the negative than in the positive, also sometimes occurs. In written Arabic, for instance, the imperfective verb forms are neutral with respect to tense. The choice of a negative particle, however, distinguishes past, present and future.

The most obvious and immediate example of the fourth type of modification, the use of supportive verbs in negative sentences, is the occurrence of the verb *do* as an inflected verb form in negative paradigms in English. It is however at least arguable that *John doesn't sing* is straightforwardly the negative of *John does sing*, rather than of *John sings*. Just as *John doesn't sing* is used to correct the impression that John sings, so *John does sing* is used to correct the impression that he doesn't. The form *John sings* would then be without a negative, or, alternatively, the distinction between *John sings* and *John does sing* would be neutralized in the negative. Be that as it may, another example of a form such as *do* occurring in negative forms can be found in Nanai where its function is similarly to carry the inflections which cannot be carried by either the invariant negative morpheme or the invariant lexical verb. It will be remembered that the standard verb paradigms of Nanai are based on a participial form to which is added a possessive suffix (example (47)). As shown in (53) the negative of the participle itself is based on three elements: the invariant negative *əm* (a gerund of the original negative verb), an invariant form of the lexical verb, and an inflected form of the verb *ta-* ('do'). Such forms can also be used as full predicates (Avrorin 1961:96):

(53)   a. xola-j
            read-PRES
            'reads/reading'

        b. *əm* xolā *ta*-j
            NEG read do-PRES
            'doesn't read/not reading'

        c. xola-xan
            read-PAST
            'read/having read'

        d. *əm* xolā *ta*-xan
            NEG read do-PAST
            'didn't read/not having read'

Other possible supportive verbs are the verbs 'be' and 'have'. In Chukchee, an invariant negative form of the lexical verb is created by derivational processes, and this is then linked with 'be' or 'have' depending on whether the verb is intransitive or transitive. We have for example *təjkəv-ək* 'to fight', from which is formed the invariant *ə-təjkəv-kə* 'not fighting', which then gives *ə-təjkəv-kə it-ək* 'not to fight' with the verb *it-* 'be' (Skorik 1977: 147).

The final kind of secondary modification we wish to discuss is the change in the case of nouns which may take place in negative sentences. A notable example of this is the choice offered in Russian between the accusative and genitive cases for the direct object, whereas in positive sentences the accusative alone is the general norm. The criteria involved in this choice are complicated, and we refer the reader to Davison (1967) for a full discussion. A typical contrast is given in example (54):

(54)   a. On zabudet   tot   večer
            he will forget that(ACC) evening(ACC)
            'He will forget that evening'

        b. On *ne* zabudet   togo   večera
            he NEG will forget that(GEN) evening(GEN)
            'He won't forget that evening'

2.6 Negation and focus

One well-known feature of standard negation is its tendency to associate with the focused elements in a sentence (Jackendoff 1972). In English, focusing is achieved either through emphatic stress, or through syntactic devices like the cleft construction. These result in contrasts like that between *Hugo didn't shoot **Henry*** and ***Hugo** didn't shoot Henry*, or that between *It wasn't **Henry** that Hugo shot* and *It wasn't **Hugo** that shot Henry*. There is however nothing syntactically special about the form of negation in any of these sentences: they all involve standard negation with the suffix *-n't*. We now wish to discuss briefly languages in which there are special devices for associating negation with focused elements.

The first set of cases arises in languages in which negative particles are freely allowed to associate with any stressed element in the sentence by assuming a position directly adjacent to it. This negative particle may be absolutely identical to the negative particle used in standard negation, as with German *nicht*, giving contrasts like (55):

(55)   a. Er besuchte uns gestern   *nicht*   (standard)
          he visited   us   yesterday NEG
          'He didn't visit us yesterday'

       b. Er besuchte uns *nicht* gestern   (focused)
          he visited   us   NEG yesterday
          'It wasn't yesterday that he visited us'

Sometimes it may be subtly different, as with Persian *na* which is an independent and invariant form in focused negation, but a verb-prefix undergoing umlauting in standard negation. Such particles can usually be linked with adversative conjunctions to give pairs like *nicht ... sondern* and *na ... balke* ('not ... but').

A second set of cases comes from languages which permit a special negative form to be associated with elements which are focused by means of fronting to sentence-initial position. This may be considered as a special negative cleft construction. It occurs for instance in Welsh, where the fronted subject may be preceded either by the particle *nid*, or by the particle *dim* (an unmutated form of the standard negative *ddim*):

(56) $\left.\begin{array}{l} Dim \\ Nid \end{array}\right\}$Blodwen ddaeth (ond Gareth)

       NEG   Blodwen came   (but Gareth)
       'It wasn't Blodwen who came (but Gareth)'

A similar example can be provided from Yoruba, where the special negative particle *kọ́* follows the topic. This negative can indeed co-occur

with the standard preverbal negative *kò* to give a double negative
(Banjo 1974:45):

(57) a. Ade ni   o kọrin
         Ade IDENTIFIER he sang
         'It was Ade who sang'

      b. Ade *kọ́* ni   o kọrin
         Ade NEG IDENTIFIER he sang
         'It wasn't Ade who sang'

      c. Ade *kọ́* ni   kò kọrin
         Ade NEG IDENTIFIER NEG sang
         'It wasn't Ade who didn't sing'

3.0 Syntactic typology of quantifier and adverb negation

It is clear that standard negation is a linguistic universal: all languages
possess at least one of the forms of standard negation presented in
section 2. With the negation of quantifiers and adverbs, however, there
is a considerable degree of variation as to what is permissible. The
fieldworker should bear the following general questions in mind when
working on this topic:

(a)   for any given quantifier, does it possess a specifically negated or
       inherently negative counterpart?
(b)   if it does, then what is its syntactic distribution?
(c)   if it does not, are there any syntactic devices which may be used
       to compensate?

We shall now explore these questions taking in turn each of the
categories of negated quantifiers, inherently negative quantifiers, negated adverbials and inherently negative adverbs.

3.1 *Negated quantifiers*
We have already remarked that specifically negated quantifiers are
generally either quantitative (*many* etc.), or universal (*all* etc.). Not all
languages however permit negatives of the type *not many* and *not all*. In
particular, there would seem to be a correspondence between the lack
of such negatives and morphological forms of standard negation. In
Persian, for example, there is no way of directly negating the quantifier
besyâr 'many' in example (58a). In the only negative version of this
sentence, example (58b), it is the verb which carries the negative
morpheme:

(58) a. Besyâr-i   az danešjuyân javâbrâ midânand
          many-INDEF of students   answer know
          'Many of the students know the answer'

      b. Besyâr-i   az danešjuyân javâbrâ *ne*-midânand
          many-INDEF of students   answer NEG-know
          'Many of the students don't know the answer'

With the quantifier in subject position, as in example (58b), the
overwhelmingly preferred reading is the one in which the quantifier has
higher scope than the negative. The only way of getting the *not many*
reading is to replace *besyâr* by the inherently negative quantifier *kam*
'few'. When the quantifier is in object position, the scope of negation is
ambiguous, as in English, regardless of the difference in linear order in
the two languages:

(59) Man besyâr-i   az danešjuyânrâ *ne*-mišenâsam
      I   many-INDEF of students   NEG-know
      'I don't know many of the students'

Turkish behaves in this respect very similarly to Persian, and it is to
Turkish that we turn for an example of the lack of specific negation of a
universal quantifier. The negative sentence is as before an instance of
standard negation:

(60) a. Herkez   cevab-ı   bil-iyor
          everybody answer-OBJ know-PRES
          'Everybody knows the answer'

      b. Herkez   cevab-ı   bil-*m*-iyor
          everybody answer-OBJ know-NEG-PRES
          'Not everybody knows the answer'
      or 'Everybody doesn't know the answer'

In example (60b), however, even though the quantifier is in subject
position, the preferred reading is one in which the negative has higher
scope, i.e. a reading equivalent to *not everybody*. One factor in the
difference of behaviour between the *many* and *every* quantifiers in this
respect is undoubtedly the fact that for the *everybody not* reading, there
is a universal tendency to prefer a quantifier of the *none* or *not any* type.
In the case of Turkish, this would be the quantifier *hiç* or *hiçbir*.

Despite the similarity in Persian and Turkish in the treatment of
quantitative and universal quantifiers, there is one interesting respect in
which they differ. Whereas Persian has no means of expressing the
double negation in a sentence like *not everyone doesn't know the*

answer, this can be expressed in Turkish simply by adding the negative verb *değil* in sentence-final position:

(61)   Herkez   cevab-ı   bil-*m*-iyor   *değil*
        everybody answer-OBJ know-NEG-PRES NEG
        'Not everybody doesn't know the answer'

Neither of the negatives is of course in itself an instance of specific quantifier negation.

By contrast, languages with negative particles rather than morphological negatives often do permit specific quantifier negation, although the two by no means always go hand in hand. Brandon (1976:38) cites two dialects of Portuguese, one of which permits quantifier negation, and one of which does not:

(62)   a. Muitas flechas *não* acertaram o   alvo
           many   arrows NEG hit   the target
           'Many arrows didn't hit the target'

                                            (Dialect A and dialect B)

        b. *Não* muitas flechas acertaram o   alvo
           NEG many   arrows hit   the target   (Dialect A)

        c.* *Não* muitas flechas acertaram o   alvo
           NEG many   arrows hit   the target   (Dialect B)

        'Not many arrows hit the target'

Dialect A, however, shares with Modern Hebrew the property that the quantifier cannot be negated in a postverbal position. The passive of (62b) is impossible with quantifier negation:

(63)   *O alvo   foi   acertado por *não* muitas flechas
         the target was hit   by NEG many   arrows
         *'The target was hit by not many arrows'

This suggests the general principle that if there is any place a language has quantifier negation it will be in preverbal positions. Languages such as German and Russian, which do permit postverbal quantifier negation, and English, which permits it to a limited extent, also permit it preverbally. It may also be the case that languages which have preverbal quantifier negation without permitting postverbal quantifier negation possess svo word order.

The lack of quantifier negation in a language can often be compensated for by syntactic means. In both dialects of Portuguese, for example, it is possible to make the quantifier *many* into a predicate which is then negated by standard negation:

(64)   *Não* foram muitas as flechas que acertaram o   alvo
     NEG were   many   the arrows that hit   the target
     'The arrows that hit the target were not many'

In Welsh, which has basic word order vso, the problems caused by lack of quantifier negation are reversed. The quantifier in subject position tends to be interpreted as within the scope of standard negation, i.e. with the *not many* reading, whereas syntactic focusing devices are needed to obtain the *many not* reading:

(65)   a. *Nid* oes llawer o bobl   yn gwybod yr ateb
       NEG be many of people in know   the answer
       'Not many people know the answer'

     b. Mae yna   lawer o bobl   *ddim* yn gwybod yr ateb
       be   there many of people NEG in know   the answer
       'There are many people who don't know the answer'

Similar comments apply to the *all* quantifier, with the exception that the *all not* reading is obtainable, as in Turkish, by using a quantifier of the *none* type:

(66)   a. *Nid* yw'r   myfyrywr i gyd yn gwybod yr ateb
       NEG be-the students all   in know   the answer
       'Not all the students know the answer'

     b. *Does   neb* o'r   myfyrywr yn gwybod yr ateb
       NEG-be none of-the students in   know   the answer
       'None of the students know the answer'

3.2 *Inherently negative quantifiers*

Inherently negative quantifiers are, as outlined in section 1.3, primarily negations of the existential quantifier, i.e. quantifiers of the *none*, *no-one*, and *nothing* type. From the typological point of view, these seem to fit into two basic patterns; in one pattern, they obligatorily co-occur with standard negation, while in the other they do not.

The first of these patterns is widely found in the modern Slavonic languages. For instance, the inherently negative quantifiers of Russian are composed of the negative morpheme *ni*, which is distinct from the standard negative particle *ne*, and forms of the interrogative (originally indefinite) pronouns: *kto* 'who'/*nikto* 'nobody', *čto* 'what'/*ničto* 'nothing' etc. One reflex of this origin is the morphological peculiarity that in prepositional occurrences of these pronouns, the negative precedes the preposition, giving for instance *ni o čem* 'about nothing' rather than **o ničem*. All inherently negative quantifiers of this type in Russian (but not *malo* 'little'/'few') obligatorily require the presence of standard negation within the same clause:

(67)   a. *Nikto ne* prišel
           nobody NEG came

        b. *Nikto prišel
           nobody came
           'Nobody came'

This appears to be a secondary development, since clauses like (67b) can be found in earlier forms of the language (Křížková 1968). When the quantifier followed the verb, however, the negative *ne* was present as in the modern language.

One immediate consequence of this conditioned use of standard negation is that it is impossible to make any distinctions of the type *Nobody came* versus *Nobody didn't come*. Furthermore, the use of one quantifier of the *nikto* type within a clause automatically ensures that all subsequent existentially quantified forms are similarly negative:

(68)   *Nikto ni s kem   ni o čem   ne* govoril
        nobody with nobody about nothing NEG spoke
        'Nobody spoke with anybody about anything'

It is therefore impossible to make distinctions of the type *Nobody spoke about anything* versus *Nobody spoke about nothing*. A similar state of affairs holds in Estonian (Rajandi 1967).

The second pattern, which is found for example in English and German, does not require the inherently negative quantifier to be accompanied by standard negation, nor does it require it to be followed by similar negative forms. Existential quantifiers of the *some/any* type are used instead when there is a necessity to express existential quantification within the scope of another negative. In German, for instance, the negative quantifier *kein* is followed by indefinite pronouns like *etwas* 'something':

(69)   *kein*-er   hat etwas   gesagt
        NEG-MASC SG has something said
        'No-one said anything'

In Baghdad Arabic, the negative quantifier *maḥəd* is followed by the indefinite *ʔay-* 'any-' (Ali 1970:71):

(70)   *Maḥəd* raḥ išuf *ʔay-ši*   hnak
        no-one will see any-thing there
        'No-one will see anyone there'

In languages which possess a distinction between quantifiers like *some* and quantifiers like *any*, the precise difference in meaning when they are within the scope of negation can be subtle, and we refer the reader to Lakoff (1969) for a full discussion.

In a large number of languages, inherently negative quantifiers are clearly analysable as a combination of negative particle and indefinite pronoun or article. One interesting exception to this is provided by Fijian, where the negative verb *sega*, with its preceding particle *e*, is apparently prefixed to a determined noun phrase:

(71)   E *sega* na gone vuli e   ra kila   na kena i sau
        PCL NEG ART student   PCL 3PL know ART its   answer
        'No students know the answer to it'

There is some evidence, however, that *sega* has lost some of its verbal status in this role, since it cannot agree in number with the noun phrase. A sentence identical to (71) but beginning *e ra*, with the third person plural marker, is ungrammatical. Furthermore, the sentence can be additionally negated by *sega* in its role of true negative verb:

(72) E *sega* na gone vuli e   ra *sega* ni   kila   na kena i sau
     PCL NEG ART student   PCL 3PL NEG COMP know ART its   answer
     'No students don't know the answer'

As discussed in relation to example (28), the plural marker *ra* can occur either with the negative verb or the lexical verb. In (72) again, however, it cannot occur with the initial *sega*.

In all the languages we have examined, the freedom of occurrence of inherently negative quantifiers has been at least equal to, and in many cases greater than, the freedom of occurrence of negated quantifiers. In extreme cases like Turkish and Persian, inherently negative quantifiers occur in all major syntactic positions, while quantifiers like *many* and *all* cannot be negated in any position. In languages like English and Portuguese, negated quantifiers are restricted to preverbal positions, while inherently negative quantifiers are not. It also appears that inherently negative quantifiers themselves in at least one language are restricted to subject position. According to Osborne (1974:69), the Australian language Tiwi has forms *karəkuwani* 'no-one' and *karəkamini* 'nothing' which are avoided in object position. We would predict therefore that negated quantifiers in this language are at least similarly restricted.

3.3 *Negated adverbials*
In many respects negated adverbs and adverbial expressions possess

similar distributions to negated quantifiers. We have already observed (section 1.4) the fact that in English both negated quantifiers and negated adverbs in their function of sentential negation are restricted to preverbal positions, and, unless a constituent of the subject itself, also trigger subject–auxiliary inversion. In Turkish, which does not permit negated quantifiers at all, there are likewise no negated adverbs of the type *not often* or *not always*. Russian and German on the other hand, vhich do possess negated quantifiers and permit their occurrence in all najor syntactic positions, also permit greater latitude with negated adverbs, for example *nicht oft* 'not often' in German and *ne vsegda* 'not always' in Russian. These forms may occur both preverbally and postverbally. One peculiarity in Russian is that the negative particle, as in the case of the inherently negative quantifiers, precedes any preposition: *ne vo vcex gorodax* lit. 'not in all towns'.

The syntactic device of adverb fronting may be used, in languages which do not possess negated adverbs, to distinguish relative scope of adverb and negation. In Welsh, for instance, the adverbial expression *yn aml* 'often' is interpreted as within the scope of negation when it follows the negative, but as outside the scope of negation when it is fronted:

(73)   a. *Nid* wyf yn aml yn bwyta pisgod
        NEG am I often in eat   fish
        'I don't often eat fish'

      b. Yn aml *nid* wyf yn bwyta pisgod
        often   NEG am I in eat   fish
        'Often I don't eat fish'

This device has the same function as the focusing of the quantified subject in example (65b).

3.4 *Inherently negative adverbs*

As outlined in section 1.5, there are two classes of inherently negative adverbs. The first class, containing adverbs like *never* and *nowhere*, patterns in the same way as the inherently negative quantifiers. In some cases, as with Russian *nikogda* 'never' and *nigde* 'nowhere', the presence of standard negation is simultaneously required, whereas in other cases, as with German *niemals* 'never' and *nirgends* 'nowhere', it is not. The second class contains the incomplete adverbs like *hardly* and *scarcely*. We have scant idea of the typology of such adverbs, but note that in Russian they co-occur with the question particle *li: edva li* 'scarcely'.

4.0 Non-sentential negation

We have already observed the fact that in many cases non-sentential negation assumes a syntactic form which is identical to that of sentential negation. Standard negation can for example be non-sentential when there is a higher occurrence of quantifier or adverb negation, or when it occurs within a subordinate clause. In this section, therefore, we propose to examine briefly all occurrences of negation which are automatically non-sentential because of their syntactic or morphological form. These fall into two classes: (a) occurrences of negation in subordinate clauses, and (b) derivational negation. The term 'constituent negation' may be used as a general term for referring to all occurrences of non-sentential negation, but we prefer the term 'non-sentential' which stresses the fact that the main feature such occurrences share is that they fail the tests for sentential negation: in other respects they are disparate.

4.1 *Negation in subordinate clauses*

In many languages, the devices which are used for negating subordinate clauses are different from those used in main clauses. English provides one instance of this, since the position of the negative particle *not* is preverbal in infinitival and gerundial clauses, as opposed to the postverbal *not* (or *-n't*) in main or other fully tensed clauses. Compare the following examples, in which the negative is bracketed with the verb which defines its position:

(74)   a. He [is *not*] rich
         b. He expects [*not* to be] rich
         c. He likes [*not* being] rich

In certain cases, this dual position of *not* can lead to structural ambiguities. Compare (75a) and (75b):

(75)   a. He [may *not*] come
         b. He may [*not* come]

Example (75a) is an occurrence of sentential negation, and is equivalent to 'he is not permitted to come', while the subordinate negation in (75b) gives the reading 'it is possible that he will not come'.

Yoruba provides a second instance, using a distinct particle rather than a distinct position of the same particle. In Yoruba, the main-clause sentential negative is *kò*, whereas the subordinate negative is *má* (Banjo 1974). This leads to the following contrasts:

(76) a. Ade *kò* lè   korin
         Ade NEG may/can sing
         'Ade cannot sing'

      b. Ade lè   *má* korin
         Ade may/can NEG sing
         'Ade may not sing' (= it is possible he will not)

      c. Ade *kò* lè   *má* korin
         Ade NEG may/can NEG sing
         'Ade cannot not sing'

Similarly in Welsh, the negative particle in subordinate clauses is *na(d)* rather than the *nid* and *ddim* forms found in main clauses.

Special kinds of negation are very often restricted to particular types of subordinate clause. In Russian, for example, the negative particle *ni* (distinct from standard negation *ne*) is used in concessive clauses of the type 'wherever he came, . . .':

(77)   Kuda   by   on *ni*   prišel, . . .
       whither COND he NEG came
       'Wherever he came, . . . '

In French, a wide variety of subordinate clauses require the negative particle *ne* alone (distinct from standard negation *ne . . . pas*). These include complements of verbs of fearing, preventing, and doubt, comparative clauses and clauses beginning with *avant que* 'before' (Grevisse 1955:748–55). Finally, many languages have a special word or form corresponding to English *lest* (= *in order that . . . not*), which is distinct from standard negation. Daga for example has a negative particle *ya* preposed to the verb as standard negation, but a postposed particle *tawa* 'lest' (Murane 1974:128).

4.2 *Derivational negation*
By derivational negation, we understand the use of negative morphemes in the derivation of lexical items. This is a complicated area, and we can only suggest the general line of approach which the fieldworker might take. For further instruction, he should consult the detailed monograph of Zimmer (1964) and the survey of Jespersen (1917).

One important distinction is that negative derivational morphemes can create either contradictory or contrary terms; contradictory terms are mutually exclusive, like *smoker* and *non-smoker*, whereas contrary terms represent opposite poles along a given dimension and leave room for other possibilities in the area between them, as for instance with *intelligent* and *unintelligent*.

Very often, particular derivational morphemes are restricted to certain categories. English *non-*, like French *non-* and German *nicht-*, is restricted to nouns and adjectives, almost invariably in a contradictory sense. English *un-*, like French *in-* and German *un-*, is generally used in the derivation of adjectives in a contrary sense, although there is another prefix *un-*, cognate with German *ent-*, which is used to indicate the reversal of some verbal process, for example *tie* and *untie*. A further common type of affix is one which derives adjectives from nouns in the sense of English *-less*. Like all derivational processes, these may possess varying degrees of productivity, and it is possible that some of the ideas may receive syntactic rather than morphological expression.

5 Passive in the world's languages

EDWARD L. KEENAN

0 Introduction

In this chapter we shall examine the characteristic properties of a construction widespread in the world's languages, the passive. In section 1 below we briefly contrast passives with other foregrounding and backgrounding operations. In section 2 we present the common syntactic and semantic properties of the most widespread types of passives, and in section 3 we consider passives which differ in one or more ways from these. In section 4 we briefly consider differences between languages with regard to the roles passives play in their grammars. Specifically, we show that passives are a more essential part of the grammars of some languages than of others.

1 Passive as a foregrounding and backgrounding operation

Consider the following sentences:

(1)   a. Mary slapped John
        b. John was slapped
        c. John was slapped by Mary

Functionally speaking, passives such as (1b) and (1c) may be considered foregrounding constructions compared with the syntactically less marked and pragmatically more neutral active, (1a): they 'topicalize' ('foreground', 'draw our attention to') an element, *John*, which is not normally presented as topical in the active. To this extent passives are similar to what we shall here call *topicalizations*, (2b) below, and left-dislocations, (3b) below, both prominent foregrounding constructions across the world's languages.

(2)   a. I like beans
        b. Beans I like

(3)   a. Congressmen don't respect the President anymore
       b. As for the President, congressmen don't respect him any-
          more

Functionally, the passives differ from these sentences in at least two
ways. First, by eliminating the subject of the active, as in (1b), or by
relegating it to the status of an oblique NP, as in (1c), they background
the active subject in ways in which the topicalizations or left-dislocations
do not.

Moreover, the passives seem to be weaker foregrounding constructions than either the topicalizations or the left-dislocations. Thus in (3b)
the President is somehow more of a topic than is *congressmen*, the
subject (= unmarked topic) of (3a). But in *John was slapped*, *John*
seems to be a topic only to the same extent that *Mary* is in the
corresponding active, *Mary slapped John*. Notice that it is quite
generally difficult across languages to topicalize or left-dislocate twice
from the same sentence (some exceptions are known). Thus from a
dislocated sentence such as *As for the President I saw him in Chicago a
few days ago* we cannot naturally form *In Chicago as for the President I
saw him a few days ago*. Such examples suggest that it is difficult for a
sentence to present more than one marked topic.

It is however fully natural to topicalize from an already passive
sentence. Thus from *The President was welcomed with open arms in
Chicago* we may naturally form *In Chicago the President was welcomed
with open arms*. It appears then that the foregrounding inherent in
passives does not compete with that expressed by topicalization or
left-dislocation.

Moreover, the fact that we can topicalize or dislocate from a passive
sentence is merely one example of a much broader difference in the
syntactic nature of passive, compared with topicalization and dislocation. It is quite generally the case that the major syntactic operations in
a language, such as nominalizing operations (*I was dismayed at John's
being fired*), relative-clause formation (*the garden in which John was
attacked*), and yes–no question formation (*Was John attacked in the
garden?*), operate freely on passives (with some exceptions, such as
imperative formation); but these processes do not operate freely, often
not at all, on topicalized or dislocated sentences. Thus we cannot say *I
was dismayed at as for John his being fired*, or *the garden in which as for
John Mary attacked him*, and so on. Generally then, basic passives tend
to be well integrated into the rest of the grammar, whereas topicalizations and dislocations tend to be limited to main clauses, only sometimes
being allowed in sentence complements of verbs of thinking and saying.

Furthermore, these basic differences between passives and topicalizations are directly reflected in the observable surface forms of passives.
Thus consider how, as field workers, we can tell if a sentence in a
language is passive or not. What is it about passives that makes them
observably distinct in surface from basic actives? For topicalizations and
dislocations the informal answer is easy. They present NPS in 'unusual'
positions in the sentence, that is, positions in which such NPS would not
occur in basic actives. In addition, in some languages, Lisu (Sino-
Tibetan) and Japanese for example, these NPS may carry a specific
marker, a postposition, of topichood.

But passives are not in general distinct from actives with regard to the
position and case marking of NPS. In particular the foregrounded NP in a
passive, namely the derived subject, is placed and case marked as are
subjects of basic actives. Similarly, 'agent phrases', such as *by Mary* in
John was slapped by Mary, most commonly take the position and case
marking (including choice of pre- and postpositions) of some oblique NP
in active sentences, most usually an instrumental, locative, or genitive.
Thus we cannot recognize a passive in terms of its NPS being marked or
positioned in the sentence in ways different from those used in basic
actives.

Note in particular that this holds for those languages which place the
subject at the end in basic actives (see Keenan 1978 for a more extensive
discussion). Thus in Gilbertese (Micronesia) the basic active order is
Verb + Object (if present) + Subject + Oblique NP. And in the passive,
(4b) below, the derived subject is placed where subjects of intransitive
verbs normally occur in actives, and the agent phrase, constructed with
a preposition, occurs where obliques normally go (the subscripts
indicate agreement on the verb):

(4)   a. E_i kamate-a$_j$ te   naeta$_j$ te moa$_i$
          it kill-it   the snake the chicken
          'The chicken killed the snake'

       b. E_j kamate-aki te   naeta$_j$ (iroun te   moa$_i$)
          it kill-PASS   the snake (by   the chicken)
          'The snake was killed (by the chicken)'

In fact the only way we know that (4b) above is passive is by the
presence of a specifically passive suffix, *-aki*, on the verb. And this
observation turns out to be general across languages.

That is, in general in a language, what is distinctive about the
observable form of passives is localized within the predicate or verb
phrase (understood broadly enough to cover auxiliary verbs). By

contrast, topicalizations and dislocations are not generally marked in the predicate; the VPS in the topicalized and dislocated sentences cited above are identical to the VPS in their untopicalized and undislocated versions. Thus the formation of passives in a language takes place at the level of verb-phrase syntax, whereas topicalization and left-dislocation (as well as right-dislocation: *He's out of work again, my father*) take place at the level of sentence syntax. Stated in generative terms, to form a passive sentence it is sufficient to generate a passive verb phrase; the rules which combine these VPS with NPS to form sentences are rules needed for the formation of simple actives anyway and are not peculiar to passive. In contrast, the rules needed to form topicalizations or dislocations will derive sentences from sentences, and will crucially refer to properties of the sentence as a whole, since they must specify the position to which the topicalized or dislocated element is moved *with respect to the sentence as a whole* – i.e. it is moved to the *front of the sentence* (or to the back in the case of right-dislocations).

Consequently the field worker interested in passives should look for ways of forming verb phrases, not ways of modifying sentences to yield other sentences. And it is this point of view which we adopt in section 2 below in representing the language-general properties of passives.

We might conclude this section by emphasizing that the distinction between sentence-level phenomena and predicate-level ones is deeper and more extensive than simply a difference among foregrounding operations. Thus if passive is thought of as a way of deriving sentences from sentences, as was the case in early forms of generative grammar (Chomsky 1957), we would expect that given a sufficiently large sample of languages, any of the ways in which one sentence could be derived from another would be used in the formation of passives in one or another language. But in fact this is very much not the case. Contrast passive with the formation of yes–no questions, clearly on all accounts a sentence- (or clause-) level derivational process. There are basically two major (not exclusive) means of forming such questions: beginning with a declarative, assign the declarative a distinctively interrogative intonation contour; or insert a particle, where the position of the particle is defined with respect to the (declarative) sentence as a whole, usually at the beginning of the sentence or at the end, more rarely between the subject and the predicate or after the first word or constituent of the sentence. Even such uncommon ways of forming questions as inverting the subject and the predicate or auxiliary verb are essentially sentence-level phenomena, as the smallest linguistic unit which contains the elements mentioned is the sentence. Thus what is distinctive about the observable form of yes–no questions is given by describing properties of the sentence as a whole (intonation contour, position of particle, etc.).

But *passives are never formed in such ways*. No language forms passive sentences by assigning a characteristic intonation contour to an active, or by inserting a sentence-level particle in an active, or by inverting the subject and the auxiliary of an active. Rather, passives are formed by deriving verb phrases in certain ways, ways to which we now turn.

2.0 General properties of basic passives

We shall refer to passives like (1b), *John was slapped*, as 'basic passives'. What makes them distinct from other passives is (i) no agent phrase (e.g. *by Mary*) is present, (ii) the main verb (in its non-passive form) is transitive, and (iii) the main verb expresses an activity, taking agent subjects and patient objects. Our justification for calling such passives 'basic' is that they are the most widespread across the world's languages. More specifically let us note the following generalizations concerning the distribution of passives:

G-1:   Some languages have no passives.
G-2:   If a language has any passives it has ones characterized as basic above; moreover, it may have only basic passives.

In support of G-1 we note that many languages in New Guinea, like Enga (Li and Lang 1978) are cited as having no passives. Similarly Chadic languages are typically passiveless (Hausa being a partial exception here, see Jaggar 1981). Also passiveless are Tamang (Sino-Tibetan; Mazaudon 1976), Isthmus Zapotec (Oto-Manguean; Pickett 1960), Yidiɲ (Australian; Dixon 1977a).

One might wonder whether these languages have a gap in their expressive power. Can they not express 'John was slapped' without committal as to who the agent was? And of course in general they can, but they will use fully active means to do so. If English had no passive, for example, we might give an approximate semantic equivalent by saying *someone slapped John*. It appears however that languages without passives have somewhat more grammaticized means for expressing functional equivalents of basic passives. Perhaps the most common means is to use an active sentence with an 'impersonal' third plural subject. By impersonal here we mean simply that the third plural element is not understood to refer to any specific group of individuals. Example (5b) below from Kru (John Singler, personal communication) is illustrative:

(5)   a. Tò pō slā ná
          Toe build house DEF
          'Toe built the house'

       b. Ī pō slā ná
          3PL build house DEF
          'They built the house' = 'The house was built'

The field worker should note that this functional equivalent to passive is commonly used in languages which have fully productive basic passives. Example (6) below from Russian and (7) from Hebrew are illustrative:

(6)   Včera   ego ubili
       yesterday him killed(3PL)
       'Yesterday they killed him' = 'Yesterday he was killed'

(7)   Ganvu   li   et ha-mexonit
       stole(3PL) to me DO the-car
       'They stole my car' = 'My car was stolen'

A possibly less common alternative to passives is simply to eliminate the subject of the active. This possibility is realized in some ergative languages, such as Tongan, as in example (8):

(8)   a. Na'e tamate'i 'e 'Tevita 'a Koliate
          killed   ERG David ABS Goliath
          'David killed Goliath'

       b. Na'e tamate'i 'a Koliate
          killed   ABS Goliath
          'Goliath was killed'

It is not clear whether we want to consider such cases as (8b) as a 'truncated' active, with perhaps a 3PL pronoun understood (note that Tongan commonly 'pronominalizes by deletion' rather than using an overt pronoun) or as some kind of morphologically degenerate passive in which the verb form is not distinctively marked. We return to this question in section 3.

Note however that, contrary to certain earlier beliefs, it is not the case that ergative languages generally fail to have passives. For example, Gugu Yalanji (Australia), Georgian (Caucasian), Basque (see (9), from Bollenbacher 1977), and Mayan languages generally, for example Jacaltec, are ergative in either case marking, verb agreements, or both; and all present passives, sometimes more than one.

(9)   a. Gizon-a-k   txakurr-a-∅ maluskatu zuan
          man-the-ERG dog-the-ABS beat   AUX(3SG SUBJ 3SG OBJ)
          'The man beat the dog'

b. Gizon-a-k   txakurr-a-$\emptyset$ maluskatu*a* zan
man-the-INSTR dog-the-ABS beat(PASS) AUX(3SG SUBJ)
'The dog was beaten by the man'

The only major difference between the active (9a) and the passive (9b) lies in the form of the verb. In particular, the verb in (9b) is intransitive, taking only subject agreement, not both subject and object agreement as in (9a).

Consider now the distributional claim made in G-2. As formulated it entails G-2.1–G-2.3 below:

G-2.1   If a language has passives with agent phrases then it has them without agent phrases.

G-2.2   If a language has passives of stative verbs (e.g. *lack, have*, etc.) then it has passives of activity verbs.

G-2.3   If a language has passives of intransitive verbs then it has passives of transitive verbs.

G-2.1 is unsurprising, given that agent phrases in passives are typically presented like oblique NPs in actives, and obliques are generally not obligatory. We should note here that Lawler (1977) cites Achenese (Sumatra; Malayo-Polynesian) as having a passive construction requiring an agent phrase. Durie (1981), however, argues with additional data that that construction is in fact an unmarked active. Further, many languages are cited as permitting only agentless passives; Latvian (see Lazdina 1966, from which (10) below is taken), Sonrai (W. African; see Shopen and Konaré 1970), Classical Arabic, Tamazight (Berber), Nandi (Nilo-Saharan; see Creider 1976), Cupeño (Uto-Aztecan), Ute (see Givón 1980), as well as some of the passive constructions in Jacaltec (Mayan; see Craig 1977):

(10)   Es tieku macits (*no mates)
       I   am   taught (by mother)

In addition the field worker should not be surprised to find that agentless passives are preferred even when the language syntactically permits agent phrases. Turkish speakers for example often only accept agent phrases with reluctance. And Kirsner (1976) shows on the basis of text counts in Dutch that agented passives are much less frequent than agentless ones, even though agented ones are fully grammatical.

Regarding G-2.2, the field worker should note that passives are often not formed freely on transitive verbs whose objects are not Patients, that is, not portrayed as being affected. Thus English verbs such as *be, become, lack*, and *have* (in its possessive sense, e.g. *John has a new car*) do not easily passivize (*A new car is had by John*).

On the other hand, it is not the case, as has sometimes been suggested, that highly stative verbs are universally unpassivizable. Whether such verbs passivize or not is in part dependent on the functional role of passive in the rest of the grammar (section 4). Here we note from Kinyarwanda (Bantu; examples from Kimenyi 1980:127–8) that such highly stative verbs as *cost*, *weigh*, and possessive *have* do passivize:

(11) a. Ishaâti i-fit-e   ibifuungo bibiri
         shirt   it-have-ASP buttons   two
         'The shirt has two buttons'

      b. Ibifuungo bibiri bi-fit-w-e   n'îshaâti
         buttons   two   they-have-PASS-ASP by shirt
         'Two buttons are had by the shirt'

Similarly we can form passives in Kinyarwanda which translate as *Four kilos are weighed by this book*, *Much joy is had by the child*, *A bad death was died by the thief*, etc. We note that all such examples cited in Kimenyi (1980) contain agent phrases. And note as well that passives on statives in English often sound better with agent phrases: for example, *These apartments are owned by landlords who live in London* seems more natural than simply *These apartments are owned*. Possibly then there is a greater tendency for passives on statives to present agent phrases, though more languages would have to be investigated before such a generalization could be confirmed.

As regards G-2.3, we note (and discuss in detail in section 3) that many languages with basic passives allow the passive derivational morphology on verbs to apply to intransitive verbs as well.

For example from *amare* 'to love' in Latin we form *amatur* 'he is loved', just as from *currere* 'to run' we form *curritur* 'it is run', in the sense 'there is running going on, running is being done'. And G-2.3 guarantees the field worker that if passives of the *curritur* type are present then so are passives of the *amatur* type. On the other hand, some languages with basic passives, like English, do not permit passives on intransitives.

2.1 The syntactic form of basic passives
In section 1 we noted that what is distinctive about the form of passive sentences is their verb phrase (VP), and passive VPS are naturally expressed in the simplest case as syntactic and morphological modifications of transitive verbs (TVS). More specifically, a passive VP in a language will consist of a strict morphological modification of a TV

together with, in some languages, an auxiliary verb specific to the passive construction.

We understand here that an expression *y* is a strict morphological modification of an expression *x* only where *y* differs from *x* in strictly morphological ways, that is, only by the presence of prefixes, suffixes, ambifixes, or internal vowel change. Note that we do not include tone change and reduplication among the strictly morphological processes, as we know of no language which forms passives by merely reduplicating or changing tonal markings on active transitive verbs. The general syntactic form of passive VPs then may be described by the equation:

(12) $\text{VP}_{+\text{pass}} = \{(\text{Aux}), \ m(\text{TV})\}$ where *m* is a strict morphological function

The use of curly brackets in (12) indicates that the relative order of the Aux, if present, and the modified TV is not specified in the general form of passives; it may occur to the right or the left and may be separated from $m(\text{TV})$ by other material in the clause if that is the way auxiliaries are generally constructed in the language (e.g. German *Franz hat Das Haus verkauft*, lit: *Franz has the house sold = Franz has sold the house*).

Our characterization of passives in (12) allows us to distinguish two broad types of passives: those which use auxiliaries, which we shall call 'periphrastic passives', and those which don't, which we shall call 'strict morphological passives'. The latter have already been illustrated by the examples from Gilbertese (4b), Kinyarwanda (11b), and the Latin cases of the *amatur* type. As an example of a passive with an auxiliary, note the Latin case below (as well as its English translation):

(13)   Dareus (ab Alexandro) victus   est
         Darius (by Alexander) conquered is
         'Darius was conquered (by Alexander)'

This example shows in addition that Latin in fact possesses passives of both types. As we shall see below, it is quite common for a language to have more than one syntactically and semantically distinct type of passive construction.

2.1.1 *Strict morphological passives*

The strict morphological (SM) passives illustrated so far are all formed by suffixing, but this of course is not a general property of SM-passives. Example (14b) below, from Sre (Mön-Khmer; see Manley 1972), illustrates a passive formed by prefixing; (15b) below, from Tagalog, a passive formed by infixing; and (16b) below, from Hebrew, a passive formed by internal vowel change (such forms being characteristic of Semitic languages in general, e.g. Hebrew, Arabic, etc.):

(14)   a. Cal   pa? mpon
            wind open door
            'The wind opened the door'

        b. Mpon gə-pa?   mə cal
            door PASS-open by wind
            'The door was opened by the wind'

(15)   a. S[um]ampal ng lalake ang babae
            [ACTIVE]-slap DO man   TOP woman
            'The woman slapped a man'

        b. S[in]ampal ng babae ang lalake
            [PASS]-slap ACT woman TOP man
            'The man was slapped by the woman'

(16)   a. Ha-saba   gidel   et ha-yeled
            the-grandfather brought up DO the-child
            'The grandfather brought up the child'

        b. Ha-yeled gudal   al yedei ha-saba
            the-child was brought up on hands the-grandfather
            'The child was brought up by the grandfather'

Note that in (15) the root of the verb is *sampal*, *-um-* is an active infix and *-in-* a passive one. In (16) the verbal root is G-D-L, the vowel pattern *i–e* indicates past active, and *u–a* indicates past passive. Other passive patterns in Hebrew are available as well; the above was chosen for simplicity of illustration. The field worker should note then that a given language may present several formally distinct SM-passives. Examples (17b–d) below, from Malagasy, are illustrative:

(17)   a. Man + tsangana (= manangana) ny lai aho
            ACTIVE + put up   the tent I
            'I am putting up the tent'

        b. *A*-tsanga-ko   ny lai
            PASS-put up-by me the tent
            'The tent is put up by me'

        c. *Voa*-tsangana ny lai
            PASS-put up   the tent
            'The tent is put up'

        d. *Tafa*-tsangana ny lai
            PASS-put up   the tent
            'The tent is put up'

Formally, the three passives above differ with respect to the choice of
passive prefix on the verb. In addition the last two do not easily accept
agent phrases, though their presence is perhaps not strictly ungrammatical. Semantically, the three passives are not fully equivalent, however.
(17b) is a neutral passive, being quite paraphrastic with the active in
(17a). The *voa-* passive in (17c), however, is unequivocally perfective
in meaning: the action of putting up the tent is viewed as successfully completed. The meaning of (17d) is somewhat harder to describe, but roughly it suggests that the action of putting up the tent
was almost spontaneous; the conscious activity of the Agent is down-
played. We might almost be tempted to translate (17d) as 'the tent
put itself up', though of course that could not happen literally. See
Randriamasimanana (1981) and Rajaona (1972) for more thorough
discussion.

The existence of multiple SM-passives in a language makes it clear that
(12) does not constitute a formal definition of passive: more than one
passive may satisfy the equation. (Though recall that reduplication and
tone change are excluded from the definition of 'strictly morphological'
and this is a substantive constraint on the form of passives in languages,
since in particular it is not uncommon for verb forms to be derived by
reduplication. Within Malagasy itself, for example, reduplication on
verbs has an imperfectivizing effect: *mandeha* = 'go, walk' whereas
mandehandeha = 'walk around'.)

Moreover, the same types of formal morphological means used in
deriving basic passives are often used to derive VPs which are not
passives. This is particularly true for verbal morphology commonly
associated with reflexives and/or middles (for a good discussion of the
complex relations between passives, reflexives, and middles see Barber
1975). Consider for example the (semantic) reflexive in (18a) from
French and what we shall for the nonce call a (semantic) middle in
(18b):

(18) a. Jean s'-est tué
          Jean self-is killed
          'Jean killed himself'

      b. La porte s'-est ouverte
          the door self-is opened
          'The door opened'

The two sentences seem structurally identical, except for the differences
in lexical items. In both cases the surface subject is the semantic object
of the underlying transitive verb. But (18b) can be true in a situation in
which the door opened spontaneously, that is, there was no external

Agent. On the other hand, the periphrastic passive, (18c) below, implies the existence of an external Agent:

    c. La   porte a   été   ouverte
       'The door has been opened'

If we take the implication of the existence of an Agent as definitional of passives, and the lack of such an implication as definitional of middles, we would say that only (18b) is a middle and not a passive. But there seems to be no way to distinguish middles from passives on purely formal grounds. For example, the same morphology used for reflexives and middles in Russian is also clearly used for passives which may be constructed with agent phrases (note that an agent phrase such as *par Marie* 'by Mary' is not possible in (18b)). Thus compare (19a) and (19b) from Russian:

(19)   a. Doma byli postrojeny raboči mi
       houses were built   workers(INSTR)
       'The houses were built by workers'

       b. Doma strojat-sja raboči mi
       houses build-self workers(INSTR)
       'Houses are built by workers'

(19a) is a straightforward (perfective) periphrastic passive with the agent phrase, as is common, in the instrumental case. (19b) is an imperfective passive, naturally constructed with an agent phrase in the same way as for the periphrastic passives. And even without the overt presence of an agent phrase, as in *New houses are built every year*, we infer the existence of Agents given that houses cannot build themselves. So whether the *-sja* morphology in Russian is interpreted as reflexive, as it would be in *The children are washing themselves*, or as a passive, depends on the semantic characteristics o the verb undergoing the *-sja*-marking. There appear then to be no purely formal grounds for distinguishing passive and reflexive morphology. The distinction between passives and middles or reflexives is made on semantic grounds: the implication of the existence of an Agent.

Note as well that it is not just 'reflexive' morphology which may be interpreted as passive. Thus the *-ka* suffix below in Quechua (Andean-Equatorial; Peru) seems on semantic grounds best glossed as 'middle' in (20), as no Agent is implied (though not of course excluded). But in (21) the social action verb *take* does imply the existence of an Agent, so *-ka* is best glossed as 'passive'.

(20)   Punku kiča-ka-rqa-n
       door open-MID-PAST-3
       'The door opened'

(21)   Čuku apa-ka-rqa-n
         hat   take-PASS-PAST-3
         'The hat was taken'

Finally, there are two further properties of SM-passives which the field worker should be alerted to. First, recall that our definition of strict morphological function only requires that the derived expression differ *at most* from what it is derived from by the presence of affixes or internal vowel change. This allows as a special case that the derived expression not differ at all from what it is derived from. And such 'degenerate' cases of morphological functions are common. For example the function which forms past participles in English (*kicked* from *kick*, *eaten* from *eat*, etc.) is degenerate in certain cases; the past participle of *hit* is simply *hit*, not *hitted* or *hitten*. One might expect, then, to find passive VPS which are identical to the transitive verbs they are derived from. And some few cases seem to exist, though they are not common and usually of restricted distribution in the languages for which we have data. Thus the verb in (22b) from Swahili (Givón 1972) does not differ from its active transitive counterpart in (22a) (except that it shows subject agreement with an NP in a different noun class):

(22)   a. Maji   ya-meenea nchi
            water it-cover   land
            'The water covers the land'

         b. Nchi i-meenea maji
            land it-cover water
            The land is covered by water'

Similar examples are cited for other Bantu languages, e.g. Kinyarwanda (Kimenyi 1980). Kimenyi in particular notes a very large number of constraints both on the formation of such passives as well as on their distribution in various syntactic contexts.

Finally, given that SM-passives are derived VPS, the field worker should be alert to the possibility that other syntactic or morphological processes which operate on VPS may be sensitive as to whether the VP in question is passive or not. We shall illustrate this possibility here with the case of verb (more exactly verb phrase) agreement with subjects. The main point here is that the existence and form of subject agreement affixes on passive verbs differ from those on active verbs. In (i–iv) below we give the principal types of such variation known to us:

(i) *The passive verb may fail to agree with its subject, even though actives do show agreement.* This is the case in Welsh for the SM-passive (there is also a periphrastic passive). Active verbs agree with pronominal subjects, but passive verbs remain invariant: *gwelir di* 'seen you' i.e. 'You are seen', *gwelir fi* 'I am seen', *gwelir ef* 'he is seen', etc.

(ii) More commonly than (i) above, *passive verbs may simply have different agreement affixes from active verbs*. This is the case for example with the sm-passive in Latin. Compare the present indicative actives of *amare* 'to love' with their present indicative passives in Table 5.1. Clearly the variation in person and number in the passive forms is not identical to that of the actives. It is quite common across languages that agreement forms may vary with the other properties which are marked on the verb. Thus person–number endings on verbs in Romance languages may vary with tense, mood, and aspect. So the variation noted above is to be expected as long as passive is a verbal category, not a sentential one. If passive were merely thought of as an operation which topicalized an NP and perhaps backgrounded another, we might expect markings of passive to show up on NPs, but not on the VPs. And in particular we would have no reason to expect that verbs in such 'topicalized' sentences would show different agreement paradigms from their non-topicalized (active) counterparts.

Table 5.1 *Conjugation of Latin* amare

	Present indicative active		Present indicative passive	
	singular	*plural*	*singular*	*plural*
1	amo	amamus	amor	amamur
2	amas	amatis	amaris	amamini
3	amat	amant	amatur	amantur

(iii) *The passive verb may agree with its subject as though it were a direct object of an active verb*. This is the case in Maasai (Nilo-Saharan) and Kimbundu (Bantu; Angola). Example (23) below is from Kimbundu:

(23)   a. A-mu-mono
            they-him-saw
            'They saw him'

        b. Nzua a-mu-mono   kwa meme
            John they-him-saw by   me
            'John was seen by me'

(It is tempting to speculate in this latter case that the passive in (23b) derives historically from an object topicalization from an impersonal third plural active of the sort illustrated in (5b), (6) and (7).)

(iv) *Passive vps may show agreement both with their subject and with the agent phrase*. Example (24) from Kapampangan (Philippines) is illustrative:

(24) a. S*um*ulat   ya ng poesia ing lalaki
         write(ACTIVE) 3SG DO poem SUBJ boy
         'The boy will write a poem'

      b. *I*sulat   na + ya (= ne) ing poesia ning lalaki
         write(PASS) 3SG   3SG   SUBJ poem AG   boy
         'The poem will be written by the boy'

We note that the active verb in (24a) is formed directly from the root *sulat* by infixing *-um-* after the initial consonant. The passive form in (24b) is formed by prefixing the root with *i-*. So the derivational relation between active and passive verb forms is indirect in the sense that each is directly derived from the root, rather than, say, the passive form being derived directly from the active form. This sort of derivational relation is characteristic both of Philippine languages (and Malagasy) and of Semitic languages like Hebrew and Arabic. Dictionaries for these languages normally list items by roots, which may not occur independently as words in the language, and specify in each case the range of affixes they may take to form derived forms.

2.1.2 *Periphrastic passives*

A basic periphrastic passive consists of an auxiliary verb plus a strict morphological function of a transitive verb. These passives fall into natural classes according to the choice of auxiliary verb.

(i) *The auxiliary verb is a verb of being or becoming*. Example (25) below from German and (26) from Persian illustrate the use of 'become' as a passive auxiliary:

(25)   Hans wurde   von seinem Vater bestraft
       Hans became 'by' his   father punished
       'Hans was punished by his father'

(26) a. Ali Ahmed-ra košt
         Ali Ahmed-DO killed
         'Ali killed Ahmed'

      b. Ahmed košté šod
         Ahmed killed become
         'Ahmed was killed'

The use of 'be' as an auxiliary is illustrated by the standard English passive, *John was slapped*, as well as by (13) from Latin, (18c) from

French, and (19a) from Russian. We might note that in the Romance and Germanic cases the morphological form of the transitive verb (e.g. *slapped*, *bestraft*, *victus*, etc.) is identical to that used in active compound past tenses, where it is called a 'past participle'. The auxiliary in these cases is a verb of possession, (e.g. *have*, 'hold' in Portuguese, etc.). Russian, however, does not use such compound past tenses. Furthermore, in several of these cases the past participle in the passive construction behaves like an adjective: for example, it agrees with the subject of the passive VP in number and gender but not person, which is the agreement paradigm for adjectives rather than verbs. In fact certain current approaches to passive in generative grammar have argued that passive should derive adjectives from transitive verbs (see Freidin 1975 for such a proposal; and Wasow 1976, and Bach 1980 for some arguments against).

The field worker should note as well that periphrastic passives of the 'be' sort commonly exhibit a certain ambiguity (or vagueness) according to whether they are interpreted 'dynamically' or purely 'statively'. Thus *The vase was broken* is arguably ambiguous (or vague), according to whether it merely specifies a state of the vase (which might in fact not have been caused by an external Agent) or whether it portrays the result of an activity performed upon the vase. German, by contrast, with its 'become' passive permits two different structures for these cases:

(27)   a. Das Haus wird   verkauft
           the house becomes sold
           'The house is being sold'

        b. Das Haus ist verkauft
           the house is sold
           'The house is sold'

If (27a) obtains you will have a chance to buy the house, whereas if (27b) obtains you are too late. Note that 'get' passives in English (e.g. *The vase got broken*, *John got fired*, etc.) have only the dynamic interpretation.

The field worker should also note that in languages such as Latin, Russian, and Kinyarwanda which present both strict morphological passives and 'be' periphrastic passives, the periphrastic passive is commonly interpreted as stative and perfective. Thus in Latin *amatus sum*, lit: 'loved I + am' is typically glossed as *I have been loved* indicating its highly perfective nature, whereas the strict morphological passive *amor* is not interpreted as specifically perfective.

(ii) *The passive auxiliary is a verb of reception* (e.g. *get*, *receive*, or even *eat*). In such cases it is common that the modification of the transitive verb takes the form of a nominalization, that is, something which occurs independently in the language as a nominal form of some sort. Example (28) below from Welsh and (29) from Tzeltal (Mayan) illustrate this type:

(28) Cafodd Wyn ei rybuddio gan Ifor
      get   Wyn his warning by Ifor
      'Wyn was warned by Ifor'

(29) La y-ich'   'utel   (yu'un s-tat   ) te Ziak-e
      PAST he-receive bawling out (because his-father) ART Ziak-ART
      'Ziak got a bawling out (from his father)'

In fact English constructions like *John got a licking/tongue lashing/beating from Bill* appear to illustrate this sort of passive, though they are highly limited as to which transitive verbs accept them; we cannot say **Bill got a killing/praising, etc. from Harry*.

Note also the rather exotic example of *eat* as an apparent passive auxiliary from Singhalese (Sinhala; Sri Lanka) below:

(30) Kikili   lamajagen   maerun kae:va
      chicken child(INSTR) death eat
      'The chicken was killed by the child'

We should note as well that the nominal source of passives may be more widespread than is generally considered. In particular the highly productive passives of the Philippines and Malagasy, while not constructed with a verb of reception, do present certain nominal characteristics. Specifically, the agent phrases often attach to the modified transitive verb in the same way as do possessors in possessive constructions. Compare (31) and (32) below from Malagasy:

(31) a. ny entana
         the things

      b. ny entan'dRakoto
         the things of Rakoto
         'Rakoto's things'

(32) a. Nosasana ny lamba
         washed   the clothes
         'The clothes were washed'

      b. Nosasan'dRakoto ny lamba
         washed by Rakoto the clothes
         'The clothes were washed by Rakoto'

(iii) *The passive auxiliary is a verb of motion* (e.g. *go, come*). This type seems less well attested than either (i) or (ii) above, but examples (33) below from Hindi and (34) from Persian are suggestive:

(33)   Murgi   mari   gayee
         chicken killed went
         'The chicken was killed'

(34)   a. Ali loget-ra   be kar   bord
            Ali word-DO to work take
            'Ali used the word'

         b. Loget be kar   reft
            word to work   went
            'The word was used'

The Persian example has perhaps the air of an idiom, but we think this not to be the case. In Persian, and many other languages, such as Turkish, transitive verbs are commonly formed from a nominal root plus an 'elementary' verb (e.g. *be, do, go, come*, etc.). And the use of *go* as an appropriate intransitive form of *take*, and *come* as an intransitive form of *bring*, etc. seems quite natural.

(iv) *The passive auxiliary is a verb of experiencing* (e.g. *suffer, touch*, even '*experience pleasantly*'). Example (35) below from Thai and (36) from Vietnamese (diacritics omitted) are illustrative:

(35)   Mary thúuk (John) kóot
         Mary touch (John) embraεe
         'Mary was embraced (by John)'

(36)   Quang bi   (Bao) ghet
         Quang suffer (Bao) detest
         'Quang is detested (by Bao)'

Passives of this sort are widely attested in languages spoken in Southeast Asia, including Mandarin, although their analysis as passives is in fact not obvious. The languages which exhibit them independently are verb-serializing languages: apparently simplex sentences are commonly constructed with multiple verbs and few if any prepositions. For example, a sentence such as 'John took the train to Boston' might be literally rendered as 'John go ride train arrive Boston'. In addition such languages exhibit virtually no bound morphology. And since passive auxiliaries can quite generally (but not always) occur as main verbs in simple sentences, it is plausible to analyze passive sentences in these languages as special cases of serial-verb constructions. We refer the reader for further discussion of these constructions in Vietnamese to

Nguyen Phu Phong (1976), where reasonable evidence is given that the verb of experiencing is functioning as a dependent (that is, auxiliary) verb.

Accepting these structures as passives, the field worker should note that there will commonly be several acceptable choices for passive auxiliaries. Nguyen Phu Phong (1976) cites five such verbs for Vietnamese, among them *duoc*, used when the subject is portrayed as pleasantly affected by the action:

(37)   Quang duoc   Bao thuong
Quang 'enjoy' Bao love
'Quang is loved by Bao'

The use of the auxiliary *bi* 'suffer' is possible in (37) but ironic.

2.2 *The presentation of agent phrases*

We survey here the various ways in which agent phrases may be presented in passives. Let us consider first somewhat more closely what is meant by 'agent phrase'. To say that *by Mary* is the agent phrase of *John was kissed by Mary* is to say that *Mary* functions as the semantic subject but not the syntactic subject of the transitive verb *kiss*, from which the passive VP is derived. In general, an agent phrase will be an NP (with or without adpositions) which functions as the semantic but not syntactic subject of a verb in an expression derived from that verb (or verb phrase). Note that the term 'agent phrase' is misleading in that its thematic role (Agent, Experiencer, etc.) is whatever is required by the verb of which it is the understood subject, and need not be specifically Agent, as in the example *Money is needed by the church*.

Note that agent phrases can occur in structures which are not passives. Consider for example the *-ing* nominals in (38):

(38)   a. The university forbids talking by students during exams
b. Cheating by students is punishable with expulsion

Clearly *students* is the semantic (but not syntactic) subject of the intransitive verbs *talk* and *cheat* in these examples. *By students* then is an agent phrase. And since intransitive verbs in English do not passivize, we infer that agent phrases must be generated independently of the passive construction in English.

A second (non-passive) construction in which agent phrases appear is the causative, especially the indirect as opposed to direct causative. The examples below, (39a) from Japanese (Howard and Niyekawa-Howard 1976) and (39b) from German, are illustrative:

(39)   a. Zyon ga   Biru ni aruk-ase-ta
       John SUBJ Bill AG walk-CAUSE-TNS
       'John had Bill walk'

       b. Seine erste Frau liess sich von ihm scheiden
          his   first wife let   self by him divorced
          'His first wife let herself be divorced by him'

In all the cases above, the agent phrase is marked by the same
adposition as are agent phrases in passives, though in causatives
generally the choice of case or adposition for the understood subject of
the causativized verb may vary as a function of the transitivity of the
underlying verb. Nonetheless, the marking of the agent phrase as in
passives shows up with more than chance frequency. Moreover, the field
worker should be aware that, in addition to the markings on agent
phrases, causatives and passives exhibit more similarities across languages than one might reasonably expect, given that in the most basic
cases, passive eliminates an argument of the verb, deriving an intransitive verb phrase from a transitive one, whereas causative does just the
opposite. Thus, 'cause-cry' will be transitive, formed from the intransitive
'cry'. Nonetheless we find in some languages, such as Korean, illustrated
below (Lee 1973), that the same verbal morphology may sometimes be
interpreted as causative and sometimes as passive:

(40) a. Nuna-ka   emeni-eke ai-lïl   an-*ki*-ess-ta
         sister-SUBJ mother-IO child-DO embrace-CAUSE-PAST-DECLAR
         'Sister had Mother embrace the child'

      b. Ai-ka   emeni-eke caki mom-lil an-*ki*-ess-ta
         child-SUBJ mother-IO self body-DO embrace-CAUSE-PAST-DECLAR
         'The child had Mother embrace him'

      c. Ai-ka   emeni-eke an-*ki*-ess-ta
         child-SUBJ mother-IO embrace-PASS-PAST-DECLAR
         'The child was embraced by Mother'

The examples above make it easy to see how a basically causative
morphology could come to be associated with a passive meaning. Both
(40a) and (40b) are causative. (40c) differs from (40b) by the deletion of
the reflexive direct object, and the reinterpretation of the subject *child*
as an Experiencer rather than an Agent. This is not difficult to
understand, as the causative in (40b) is only an indirect or 'let' type
causative rather than a direct or 'force' type one: the sentence naturally
has a passive meaning with *Mother* interpreted as the Agent of the
complex verb.

It seems to us likely in fact that some such source is the explanation for the existence of 'get' passives in English. Compare the following:

(41)   a. John got Bill fired (Causative)
          b. John got himself fired (Causative)
          c. John got fired (Passive)
          d. The window got broken (Passive)

We note that not all speakers accept 'get' passives like (41d) in which the subject is inanimate, though they are heard often enough for them to be counted as grammatical. Note incidentally that even in (41d) the 'active' nature of *get* is still apparent in that (41d) has only the dynamic interpretation referred to earlier, not the purely stative one in which it only refers to the state of the window regardless of how it got into that state.

Returning now to the discussion of the presence and form of agent phrases, note that we have given three reasons for considering that agent phrases are not in general an integral part of the passive construction itself: (i) they occur in non-passive structures; (ii) many languages present passives which do not permit agent phrases; and (iii) when present, agent phrases most commonly take the form of an independently existing oblique NP in actives. Let us consider (iii) in more detail.

2.2.1 *Agent phrases as active obliques*

Most commonly, agent phrases, whether in passives or other constructions, are presented as (i) instrumentals, (ii) locatives, or (iii) genitives, in active constructions.

(i) *Instrumentals*. Example (19) above from Russian and (9) from Basque illustrate the use of the instrumental case marking on agent phrases, the same case as is used of course for instruments, as in *John cut the bread with a knife*. Similarly in Bantu the agent phrase is marked with the preposition *na* which independently marks instruments in actives, as illustrated in (42) below from Kinyarwanda. Compare with (11):

(42)   Umugabo araandika ibaruwa n-ikaramu
        man   write   letter   with-pen
        'The man is writing a letter with a pen'

(ii) *Locatives*. Agent phrase markers in German, French, and English (among others) are independently used with locative force: for example *He sat by the window and was seen by Mary*; *Il vient de Paris* 'He comes from Paris' and *Il est aimé de ses parents* 'He is loved by his relatives'; *Er wurde von Marie geküsst* 'He was by Mary kissed' and *Er fährt von Stuttgart nach Köln* 'He goes from Stuttgart to Cologne'.

(iii) *Genitives*. The presentation of agent phrases as possessors in Malagasy and the Philippine languages has been illustrated in (32). Equally, both *von* in German and *de* in French have possessive uses (*ein Freund von mir* 'a friend of mine' and *un ami de Pierre* 'a friend of Pierre').

There is however a minority of cases where agent phrases are not presented as instrumentals, locatives, or genitives.

(iv) *The agent phrase has no adposition*. Vietnamese (36) and (37) illustrate this case. Note equally example (43) below from Haya (Bantu: see Duranti and Byarushengo 1977):

(43)   Ebitooke bí-ka-cumb-*w*'   ómukâzi
        bananas   they-PAST-cook-PASS woman
        'The bananas were cooked by the woman'

Note that such examples do not at least obviously violate the claim that agent phrases are presented like active obliques. Many non-subjects and non-objects are commonly presented with no adposition. This is commonly so for temporals, as in *John saw Mary last week*.

(v) *The agent phrase is incorporated into the passive verb*. English illustrates this case for a very limited range of verbs, roughly a subset of those expressing power and authority:

(44)   a. This project is State-controlled/NSF-funded/government-
           regulated
        b. *This project is State-enjoyed/NSF-avoided/government-
           rejected

Such incorporation seems more productive in Quechua, example (45), and Toba Batak, example (46) (Malayo-Polynesian; example from S. Mordechay, personal communication):

(45)   a. Kuru-ø   manzana-ta miku-rqa-n
           bug-SUBJ apple-DO   eat-PAST-3
           'The bug ate the apple'

        b. Kuru miku-sqa-mi   manzana-ø ka-rqa-n
           bug eat-PART-COMMENT apple-SUBJ be-PAST-3
           'The apple was bug eaten'

(46)   a. Manuhor jabu i   ahu
           buy   house DET I
           'I buy the house'

b. Hu-tohor jabu   i
    1SG-buy   house DET
    'The house is bought by me'

Finally, we should note that there m⸱y be a few cases in which agent phrases are introduced by an adposition which does not occur independently in oblique NPs in active structures. For example the agentive preposition *al yedei* in Hebrew (16) is largely limited to agent phrases (though it is closely related to an active oblique preposition *al yad* 'near'). Similarly, the agent preposition *oleh* in Indonesian appears limited to agent phrases.

2.3 *The semantics of basic passives*

There are several correlations between surface forms for passives and their semantic interpretation which the field worker should be sensitive to. (For a formal discussion of these correlations we refer the reader to Keenan 1980, and Keenan and Faltz 1978). Notice first the following very general correlation that holds between form and meaning: *the semantic interpretation of derived structures depends on* (*is a function of*) *the meanings of what they are derived from.* So if we derive the plural *books* from the singular *book* we expect to give the meaning of *books* in terms of that for *book*. Similarly, since we derive passive VPs from active transitive verb phrases (TVPs) we expect to give the interpretation of the former in terms of that of the latter. Specifically, thinking of VPs (not just passive ones) as expressions which are true or false of *individuals* (John, Mary, etc.) and TVPs as expressions which are true or false of pairs of individuals, we may, as a first approximation, give the interpretation of passives as follows: The passive of a TVP is true of an individual x if and only if for some individual y, the TVP is true of the pair (y, x). So *was slapped* holds of John if and only if for some individual y, slap holds of $(y,$ John); that is, someone slapped John.

Notice that this semantic interpretation makes no immediate claim concerning whether passive *sentences* are paraphrases of their actives. Given that NPs like *John* and *Mary* denote individuals, it will claim that *Mary slapped John* entails *John was slapped*. But if the NPs in the sentence are not the sort which denote individuals, then no such entailment paradigm regularly holds. Thus *No student slapped John* will not entail *John was slapped*. Nor will it be the case that passive sentences in general entail the corresponding existential generalization of the active. Thus *Every cake was stolen* does not entail that some individual x stole every cake. Different cakes might have been stolen by different individuals.

The main point we want to notice here, however, is that if passives are treated as ways of deriving VPS from TVPS we can give a basically correct semantic interpretation which is in accordance with the general principle enunciated above. On the other hand, if passive were thought of as a way of deriving sentences from sentences, no regular semantic relationship between the derived structure and what it is derived from could be given. Sometimes an agentless passive is entailed by an active and sometimes it isn't, as we have seen above. Moreover the same disparity exists between agented passives and their actives. Thus while *John was kissed by Mary* is presumably logically equivalent to (has the same truth conditions as) *Mary kissed John*, a sentence like *Each child was kissed by no politician* is clearly not logically equivalent to *No politician kissed each child*. Thus, treating basic passives as a VP derivational process correctly allows us to predict that quantified NPS in passives and actives may exhibit different relative scopes.

There are further, more interesting since less commonly noted, predictions made by our analysis of passives, ones which the field worker should be sensitive to. In particular, since basic passives derive VPS from TVPS, we may expect that the meaning of the derived VP may vary with the semantic properties of the TVP. And this is correct. Although qualifications regarding activities performed by collectives are needed, the semantic interpretation we gave above for passives is a reasonable first approximation for activity TVPS such as *slap*, *kiss*, *hit*, etc.; it is less satisfactory for stative TVPS. Do we want to say that *John is respected* is true just in the case where there is at least one person who respects John? Rather it seems that we should require something stronger, such as that most people respect John. If everyone except John's wife thinks he's an idiot it would seem fair to conclude that John is not respected. Thus the truth conditions for passives derived from stative TVPS will be something closer to a universal quantification over the subject of the TVP rather than the existential quantification used for activity TVPS.

A somewhat subtler case is illustrated by passives of what we can call non-transparent TVPS. The TVP of *Jane kissed a man with a scar on his face* is transparent in that there must have existed a man with a scar on his face. This property is retained in the corresponding passive *A man with a scar on his face was kissed (by Jane)*. But some TVPS are not transparent on their objects. Thus if *The police are looking for (seeking) a man with a scar on his face*, we may not unequivocally infer that such a man exists. And this property is preserved under passive: *A man with a scar on his face is being sought by the police* does not entail the existence of such a man (perhaps the police received an inaccurate description of the man who committed the crime). Thus whether a passive VP is transparent on its subject will depend on whether the TVP it is derived from is transparent on its object. This difference will often show up in other entailments as well. Thus *Mary was kissed in the garden* entails that Mary was in the garden but *Mary was sought in the garden* does not.

The dependencies in interpretation of passive VPs on the TVPs they are derived from are somewhat subtle, but they do show that the precise interpretation of passives may vary with the semantic nature of what they are derived from. Let us turn now to some less subtle dependencies, ones which we are less able to describe formally but which are important in languages with more than one type of basic passive. For the record we note the following generalization:

G-3:   Languages with basic passives commonly have more than one formally distinct passive construction.

Moreover, distinct passives in a language are likely to differ semantically with respect to aspect and/or degree of subject affectedness.

2.3.1 *Aspectual differences*
We note the following generalizations:

G-4:   If a language has any passives it has ones which can be used to cover the perfective range of meaning.
G-5:   If a language has two or more basic passives they are likely to differ semantically with respect to the aspect ranges they cover.

From G-4 we may infer that languages like Russian with a specifically imperfective passive will also present a passive construction which covers the perfective range. Thus no language will have only passives which must be interpreted imperfectively.

G-5 has already been amply illustrated. Recall the three basic passives in Malagasy (example (17)), one of which was semantically rather neutral, the second (the *voa* passive) clearly perfective, and the third (the *tafa-* passive) indicating something like spontaneous action, little intentional involvement of an agent. Recall as well that in languages like Russian, Latin, and Kinyarwanda with a strict morphological passive and also a 'be' type periphrastic passive, the periphrastic form is commonly interpreted as stative or perfective with respect to the SM-passive which is either non-committal as to aspect or else specifically imperfective. And recall finally the distinction between dynamic passives, which focus attention on the action, as opposed to statal or stative passives which focus attention on the state of the object, perhaps regardless of whether an external agent is responsible. Thus the 'get' passives in English are dynamic and the 'be' passives at least ambiguously stative. A similar distinction among SM-passives is illustrated in (47) below from K'ekchi (Mayan; Ava Berenstein, personal communication):

(47)   a. La?in sh-in-sak?-*e*?
        I   PAST-I(ABS)-hit-PASS
        'I was hit' (emphasizes action of hitting)

        b. La?in sak?-*b?il*-in
        I   hit-PASS-I(ABS)
        'I am the one who is hit' (emphasizes the resultant state)

Somewhat more elaborate aspect distinctions are illustrated by the Kapampangan (Philippines; Malayo-Polynesian; see Mulder and Schwartz 1978) examples below. (48a) seems to be inceptive, (48b) progressive, and (48c) past perfective. This complete range of explicit aspect distinctions is apparently present only in the passive and not in the active forms.

(48)   a. *I*-sulat   me   ing   sulat
        PASS-write you   it   SUBJ letter
        'The letter is going to be written by you'

        b. *Su*-sulat   me   ing   sulat
        PASS-write you   it   SUBJ letter
        'The letter is being written by you'

        c. S[*in*]ulat   me   ing   sulat
        [PASS]-write me   it   SUBJ letter
        'The letter was written by you'

Recall from section 2.1.1 that passive verbs in Kapampangan agree with both the derived subject and the agent phrase. The form *me* above (Mirikitani 1972:170) is a contraction or portmanteau form from *mu* 'you, agent' and *ya* 'it, subject'. Example (48b) appears to violate the generalization made earlier that passives are not formed by reduplication. However, it appears from Mirikitani (1972), though more work is needed here, that reduplication derives verbal forms with an imperfective or iterative meaning in the present tense, irrespective of verbal voice. Thus the passive interpretation of (48b) seems due to the interpretation of the root form, not that of the reduplication itself.

2.3.2 Degree of subject affectedness
We note the following generalizations:

G-6:   The subject of a passive VP is never understood to be less affected by the action than when it is presented as the object of an active transitive verb.

G-7: Distinct passives in a language may vary according to degree of affectedness of the subject and whether it is positively or negatively affected, though this variation seems less widely distributed than that of aspect.

Recall in these regards the *bi-* versus *duoc* passives in Vietnamese, (36) and (37), in which the subject of a *bi-* passive is understood to be negatively affected, whereas the subject of a *duoc* passive is understood to be positively affected. In addition Vietnamese may use the passive auxiliary *do* which is semantically neutral as regards subject affectedness, as in (49):

(49)   Thuoc   X *do* Y che   nam 1973
         medicine X PASS Y invent year 1973
         'Medicine X was invented by Y in 1973'

In English, by contrast, passive subjects are often not understood as more affected than the corresponding direct objects of actives. But some cases, however unsystematic, do arise. Examples (50–3) below indicate cases of greater subject affectedness in the passives:

(50)   a. John supports the Democratic Party
         b. The Democratic Party is supported by John

(51)   a. John changed his job
         b. John's job was changed

(52)   a. Someone has slept in this bed
         b. This bed has been slept in

(53)   a. John saw Mary entering the building at 6 o'clock
         b. Mary was seen entering the building at 6 o'clock

(50b) suggests that the existence of the Democratic Party depends in some serious way on John's support, whereas the active does not suggest this, being easily interpreted as a statement concerning John's political allegiance, not his activities. (51a) merely says that John got a new job, whereas (51b) says that he kept his job in some sense but that its nature was changed. (53b), which goes beyond the basic passives proper, somehow implicates that Mary's action will possibly have negative consequences for her. The contrast between *Mary is being watched* and *John is watching Mary* is perhaps clearer in this regard. And in (52b) we are inclined to infer that the bed itself shows visible signs of having been slept in and thus is (visibly) affected by the action, whereas this inference is not so immediate from (52a).

In the languages of Asia, on the other hand, negative effect passives (often called 'adversative passives') seem to be the norm. Thus the common *bei* passive in Mandarin is often interpreted as negatively affecting the subject; similarly for the standard *-are-* passive in Japanese. And as regards Korean, Lee (1973) cites in addition to the *-ki-* passive, a negative effect passive constructed with *tangha* 'to be subjected to', illustrated in (54), and a positive effect passive constructed with *pat* 'to receive' as in (55):

(54)   Pholo-ka   henpjeng-eke kutha-*tangha*-ess-ta
        POW-SUBJ MP-AG   beat-PASS-PAST-DECLAR
        'The prisoner of war was beaten (subjected to a beating) by an MP'

(55)   Ki sensayng-nin haksayng-til-eke conkjeng-*pat*-nin-ta
        the teacher-TOP   student-PL-AG   respect-PASS-PRES-DECLAR
        'The teacher is respected by students'

3.0 Complex (non-basic) passives

In section 2 we considered the syntactic and semantic properties of basic passives, which were defined as ones which lacked agent phrases and were formed from activity transitive verbs. We discussed in addition properties of agent phrases and thus of agented passives, as well as, to some extent, passives formed from non-activity transitive verbs. We shall consider here a variety of less widely distributed passives which differ from basic passives in either of two ways: (i) they are formed from syntactically complex transitive verb phrases, not merely lexical ones; (ii) they are formed from verbs which are not transitive.

3.1 *Passives of internally complex transitive verb phrases*
Most recent treatments of passive which are concerned with an explicit representation of the semantics of passives have treated one or more of (56a–d) below as having the category transitive verb phrase (TVP). Such treatments include those in Keenan (1980), Keenan and Faltz (1978), Bach (1980), Dowty (1978), and Thomason (1976).

(56)   a. John was believed to be an imposter
           believe to be an imposter = TVP

        b. John was persuaded to leave early
           persuade to leave early = TVP

        c. John was robbed and beaten
           rob and beat = TVP

        d. John was seen from the roof
           see from the roof = TVP

Other treatments however, notably Bresnan (1978, 1980), would restrict passive to be a lexical rule, though the lexical entries for verbs like *believe*, *persuade*, etc. are made sufficiently complex so as to contain in effect the information present in the analysis of *believe to be an imposter* as a TVP. We refer the reader to the works cited for arguments, *pro* and *contra*, regarding the domain of passive.

For field workers, it is sufficient to note that they may expect to find passives of the sort illustrated in (56) above, and that it may prove heuristically useful in anticipating the existence of such complex passives to regard the indicated structures above as complex TVPs. In particular the passives of such TVPs differ from the actives by, at most, strict morphological variation and the optional presence of an auxiliary. For example, *be robbed and beaten* differs from *rob and beat* by the presence of the auxiliary *be* and two suffixes, *-ed* and *-en*.

One useful feature of looking at passives in this way is that it may lead to the observation of complex passives whose morphology is not predictable from that used for simple transitive verbs. For example, in some languages, such as Malagasy (Keenan 1976a) and Turkish (Georges and Kornfilt 1977, and Balpinar 1979) it appears that verbs of intent, desire, and aspect can combine directly with transitive verbs to yield complex TVPs (e.g. *intend to kiss*, *want to read*, *begin to kill*, etc.) and these TVPs can passivize in such a way that passive morphology shows up on each part of the complex TVP. Example (57) from Turkish and (58) from Malagasy are illustrative:

(57) a. Ahmet kitab-i   oku-maya   başladi
     Ahmet book-DO read-INF(DAT) begin(PAST)
     'Ahmet began to read the book'

   b. Kitap (Ahmet tarafindan) oku-*n*-may   başla-*n*-di
      book (Ahmet by   ) read-PASS-INF(DAT) begin-PASS-PAST
      'The book was begun to be read (by Ahmet)'

(58) a. /Tia + maN + vono/(= te-*h*amono) ny omby Rabe
      want + ACTIVE + kill(FUT)   the cow Rabe
      'Rabe wants to kill the cow'

   b. Tian-dRabe   hovonoina   ny omby
      wanted-by Rabe (FUT)be killed the cow
      'The cow was wanted (by Rabe) to be killed (by him)'

So both the verb of desire, intent, etc. and the 'main' verb show passive morphology. It is argued in Keenan (1976a) and more particularly in Georges and Kornfilt (1977) that the derivation of such sentences will not proceed satisfactorily if the two verbs are passivized independently.

It rather seems that we want to think of *begin to read* as a complex TVP and form its passive by assigning morphology to each part.

On the other hand the analysis, however informally conceived, of *begin to read* as a complex TVP is clearly not universal, even with respect to its role in passivization. For example, in Kinyarwanda (Kimenyi 1980) it would rather appear that the infinitival clause *to read the book* functions as a kind of object of *begin*. It can in any event passivize to become the subject:

(59) a. Ábáana ba-taangi-ye gu-soma ibitabo
          children they-start-ASP to-read books
          'The children start to read the books'

      b. Gu-soma ibitabo bi-taangi-*w*-e   n'áábáana
          to-read   books it-start-PASS-ASP by children
          'Reading the books is started by the children'

The above examples suggest that whether a given passive is acceptable or not may depend in part on the syntactic nature of the object of the TVP. Roughly speaking, and unsurprisingly, complex 'NPs', like perhaps *to read the books* in Kinyarwanda, function in general less easily as subjects of passive VPs than do lexically simple NPs like *John*. The following generalization for example is likely true:

G-8:   If a language can passivize TVPs taking sentential objects then it can passivize ones taking lexical NP objects.

Finally in this regard we might also note that relations between the subject and object NPs of TVPs may also affect the acceptability of passives. For example the periphrastic passive in Kinyarwanda (see Kimenyi 1980 for examples) is not acceptable if the object of the TVP is animate or the subject is not an agent. More complex restrictions of a chain-of-being sort have been cited for certain American Indian languages such as Navajo. Roughly, humans rate higher on the chain of being than other animals, and animals rate higher in general than inanimates, and it is perhaps unsurprising that passive cannot operate if the object of the TVP is lower on the hierarchy than the subject.

3.2 Passives on non-transitive verbs
The notion of passive we have characterized so far seems very dependent on the notions of intransitive and transitive verb. In fact, however, our notion naturally generalizes in ways which are linguistically enlightening, as they suggest the existence of passives different from those already considered, and languages do in fact present such passives. To see the generalization, let us replace the linguistic notion of 'verb

phrase' with its logical counterpart, that of a 'one-place predicate phrase', namely something which combines with *one* NP to form a sentence. Similarly, the notion of 'transitive verb phrase' may be replaced by that of a 'two-place predicate phrase', something which combines with *two* NPS to form a sentence. In general an *n*-place predicate phrase will combine with *n* NPS to form a sentence. So the standard ditransitive verbs, *give, hand*, etc. might be considered 'three-place predicate phrases'. And the notion of 'sentence' may be treated as the 'zero-place predicate phrase', as they combine with *zero* NPS to form a sentence.

In these terms, passive as we have been characterizing it derives a one-place predicate (phrase) from a two-place predicate (phrase) (we henceforth drop the term 'phrase'). Generalizing over the number of NPS a predicate needs to form a sentence then, we may characterize passive as a way of deriving *n*-place predicates from $n + 1$-place predicates. The case we have treated so far is that for which *n* is 1. Let us consider now the case for $n = 0$. That is, do we find passives in languages which derive zero-place predicates (sentences) from one-place predicates (VPS)? And the answer obviously is yes. We have in fact already cited the Latin examples *currere* 'to run' *curritur* '(it) is run, running is being done'.

As passives on intransitives in the simplest cases will be lacking any NPS, they will of necessity be subjectless, and as such have usually been called 'impersonal passives' in the literature. While their general properties are less well known than the personal passives, we do have several recent studies that make remarks on a variety of languages and on which the remarks below are based. These studies are Comrie (1977), Perlmutter (1978), and to a lesser extent Keenan (1976b). For studies of specific languages we cite: Langacker (1976) for Uto-Aztecan languages generally, Kirsner (1976) for Dutch, Timberlake (1976) for North Russian dialects, Noonan (1978) for Irish, and Givón (1980) for Ute.

Based on these studies, which cover many fewer languages than those considered in our discussion of basic passives, we somewhat tentatively suggest the following general properties of impersonal passives (passives of intransitives).

First, such passives exist and seem to have a reasonable distribution across language areas and genetic families. Thus languages such as the following have basic passives and use the same syntactic and morphological means to derive impersonal passives (sentences) from intransitive verb phrases: Dutch, German, Latin, Classical Greek, North Russian dialects, Shona (Bantu), Turkish, and Taramahua (Uto-Aztecan). For example, in example (60) from German, the impersonal passive is formed from 'become' plus the past participle of the underlying intransitive verb; as are basic passives:

(60)   Gestern wurde getanzt
        yesterday became danced
        'Yesterday there was dancing'

Similarly in the impersonal passive below from Turkish we see the same -n- marking passive as in the basic passive (compare with (57) for example).

(61)   Burada oynanir
        here   played
        'Here it is played/Playing takes place here'

And (62a, b) below from Taramahua clearly illustrate the same bound morphology on the verbs in each case:

(62)   a. Tashi goci-*ru*
           not   sleep-PASS
           'One doesn't sleep'

        b. Gao ne   ʔa-*ru*
           horse I(SUBJ) give-PASS
           'I was given a horse'

Second, the examples also illustrate that impersonal passives may be either of the strict morphological variety, as in Turkish and Taramahua above, or be constructed with an auxiliary, as in Dutch and German. We might note that the impersonal passive in Dutch and German is usually constructed with an overt impersonal subject, *es* 'it' in German, *er* 'there' in Dutch. Thus the untopicalized form of (60) would be:

(63)   Es wurde gestern   getanzt
        it became yesterday danced
        'There was dancing yesterday'

The use of such 'empty' subjects however does not seem general; only Dutch and German present them from the languages in our sample, though we should note that if verbs exhibit agreement with subjects, then in the impersonal passive form they will be third singular (neuter if gender is marked).

Third, impersonal passives using the same verbal morphology as basic passives typically take their agent phrases marked in the same way as in basic passives, if they accept agent phrases at all. Example (64) from Dutch is illustrative:

(64)   Er   wordt   (door de jongens)   gefloten
        there became by   the young men whistled
        'There was some whistling by the young men'

Sometimes, as in Turkish, the passives on intransitives do not accept
agent phrases whereas those transitives do (though only with some
awkwardness in Turkish). For most of the languages where we have
data however, as in Dutch, Latin, North Russian, and Shona, the
impersonals accept agent phrases if the basic passives do.

On the other hand, if the verbal morphology of the impersonals is
different from that of basic passives, as illustrated in (65) below from
Irish, then agent phrases may take different markings:

(65)   a. Bhuail si   e   (Active)
           hit   she him
           'She hit him'

        b. Bhi se buailte   aici   (Basic passive)
           AUX he hit(PART) at her
           'He was hit by her'

        c. Buaileadh (lei)   e   (Impersonal passive)
           hit(IMPRS) (with her) him
           'There was hitting of him (by her)'

Fourth, as is in fact illustrated in (65c), passives of intransitives are
not limited to lexical intransitive verbs. In particular, a transitive verb
together with its NP object will constitute a VP and may be passivized. In
addition to (65c) above, note (66) from North Russian and (67) from
Latin:

(66)   U mena bylo   telenka   zarezano
        at me   was(3SG NEUT) calf(FEM ACC) slaughtered(SG NEUT)
        'By me there was slaughtered a calf'

(67)   a. Boni cives   legibus parent
           good citizens to laws obey
           'Good citizens obey the laws'

        b. Legibus (a   bonis civibus) paretur
           to laws (by good citizens) is obeyed(3SG)
           '(By good citizens) there is obeying laws'

Fifth, it appears in a few languages that 'reflexive' forms come to
function with an impersonal passive meaning, as illustrated in (68) from
Polish and (69) from Spanish:

(68) a. Idzie   sie   szybko (*przez uczniow)
         is walked REFL quickly (by   schoolboys)
         'One walks quickly'

      b. Dokonuje   sie   prace (*przez uczonych)
         is completed REFL works (by   scientists)
         'The works are being completed'

(69) a. No se   habla de musica (*por los estudiantes)
         not REFL. speak of music (by the students)
         'Music isn't spoken of'

      b. En Europa no se   nos conoce (*por los periodistas)
         in Europe not REFL us knows (by the journalists)
         'In Europe we are not known'

And sixth, as indicated by (70) from Irish, a language may have impersonal constructions which are syntactically and morphologically independent of the existence of basic passives. In fact, bogglingly, Noonan (1978) shows that a basic passive in Irish may be further subject to the impersonal construction in that language. Thus the impersonal of (65b) would be:

(70)   Bhiothas   buaitte   (aici)
        AUX(IMPRS) hit(PART) (at her)
        'There was being hit (by her)'

Moreover, given the assumed syntactic and morphological independence, it seems likely that we could find languages with such impersonals but not possessing basic passives. Such at least would appear to be the case in Ute. Thus compare the following:

(71) a. Ta'wá-ci̧ 'u   siváa̧tu-ci 'uwáy pa̧x̂á-qa
         man-SUBJ the(SUBJ) goat-DO   the(DO) kill-ANTERIOR
         'The man killed the goat'

      b. Siváa̧tu-ci 'uway   pa̧x̂á-ta-x̂a
         goat-DO   the(DO) kill-PASS-ANTERIOR
         'Someone killed the goat/The goat was killed'

It appears that the -ta- suffix forms sentences from verb phrases with existential quantification over the subject. If this is considered a passive it would appear that Ute has passive on VPs but not on TVPs; that is, in violation of our first generalization, Ute would have a certain kind of non-basic passive without having the basic passive.

3.3 Passives on ditransitive verb phrases
Among the common three-place or ditransitive verb phrases in a

language will be translations of verbs like *give, show, hand*, etc. Passives of such verbs exhibit the following regularity:

G-9: If a language presents basic passives then it always passivizes 'give', 'show', etc. in such a way that the derived subject is the Patient of the active verb. Passives in which the Recipient is the subject may or may not exist.

Thus a language with any passives may always say *The book was given to Fred*. It may or may not be able to say *Fred was given the book*. French for example does not form such 'Recipient' passives:

(72) a. Jean a donné le livre à Pierre
         Jean has given the book to Pierre
         'Jean gave the book to Pierre'

      b. Le livre a été donné à Pierre
         the book has been given to Pierre
         'The book was given to Pierre'

      c.* Pierre a été donné le livre
          Pierre has been given the book
          'Pierre was given the book'

In addition to the classical three-place predicates such as *give*, languages will commonly have three-place predicators like *put, place* which require a Patient and some sort of Locative in addition to an Agent to form a sentence. And again, the predicate will always have passive forms taking the Patient as the subject if it has any passives at all. It may or may not have passives taking the Locative as subject. English for example by and large does not have locative passives: **The chest was put the jewels in*. We may note that locative passives in some cases are easier if the verb is otherwise intransitive, e.g. *This bed was slept in*.

On the other hand, other languages, such as Kinyarwanda and Chichewa (and commonly in Bantu) as well as Malagasy and the Philippine languages generally, quite productively form passives whose subjects are semantically locatives. There appear to be two general syntactic means for forming such passives. Moreover these means are not specific to Locatives but apply in general to passives which have non-patient subjects.

3.4 Passives with non-patient subjects
One general means of forming such passives is first to modify the n-place predicate ($n > 2$) to a form in which the non-patient is treated like the

(direct) object of simple transitive verbs, and then form a passive as is done generally in the language on transitive verb phrases. Example (73) from Kinyarwanda illustrates this strategy (from Kimenyi 1980):

(73)   a. Úmwáalímu y-oohere-jé igitabo kw-iishuûri
           teacher   he-send-ASP book   to-school
           'The teacher sent the book to school'

        b. Úmwáalímu y-oohere-jé-ho ishuûri igitabo
           teacher   he-send-ASP-to school book
           'The teacher sent the school the book'

        c. Ishuûri ry-oohere-je-w-é-ho   igitabo n-úúmwáalímu
           school it-send-ASP-PASS-ASP-to book   by-teacher
           'The school was sent the book by the teacher'

Note that in (73b) the basic verb 'send' is modified in form by the presence of the goal locative suffix -ho (morphologically related to the goal locative preposition kwa) and 'school' occurs immediately postverbally without a goal locative marker. Kimenyi justifies that this postverbal NP has the properties shared by the sole objects of simple transitive verbs.

In (73c) this complex verb is passivized in the normal way in Kinyarwanda, by the non-final suffix -w-, and 'school' is clearly a derived subject, occurring in subject position, triggering subject agreement on the verb, and in general (as Kimenyi supports in detail) having the characteristic syntactic properties of subjects of basic verbs.

Essentially this sort of analysis has been commonly proposed for recipient passives in English, *Fred was given the book*. In particular, early studies in generative grammar as well as the more recent proposals of relational grammar (see Perlmutter and Postal 1977) proposed to derive such sentences by first deriving something like *X gave Fred the book*, in which *Fred* is a derived direct object, and the ultimate passive form is derived from this intermediate form. The principal differences between Kinyarwanda and English in this regard would be (i) that the form of *give* does not change when the Recipient is made a derived object, and (ii) only a limited class of verbs in English accept such forms. Very roughly the class is limited to commonly occurring 'short' verbs, usually monosyllabic, whereas 'long' verbs like *contribute, dedicate*, etc. do not permit the derived object forms (**John dedicated the soldiers the monument*). For a much more accurate characterization of the verbs which permit the derived object forms see Oehrle (to appear). Whatever the details of the derivation of such complex passives, however, the field worker should be aware that languages can present multiple forms of ditransitive predicates, that these forms may vary with respect to the grammatical status of their non-subject NPS, and that these forms may passivize in otherwise natural ways. In particular we note that Bantu languages such as Kinyarwanda and Chichewa (Trithart 1975) are particularly rich in ways of presenting oblique NPS of actives as derived objects. Essentially any oblique NP in Kinyarwanda can be the surface direct object of some derived form of a verb. See Kimenyi (1980) for detailed support of this claim.

The second general means of forming non-patient passives is to derive passive forms directly from the *n*-place predicate in such a way that the desired NP is the subject. So where such derivational processes are well developed, as in Malayo-Polynesian, we find different morphological forms of ditransitives according to whether their subject is a Patient or non-Patient, and sometimes even we find different morphologies on the verb depending on what sort of non-Patient is the subject. The basic pattern is illustrated below from Malagasy:

(74)   a. Nanasa ny lamba amin'ny savony Rasoa
           washed the clothes with-the soap   Rasoa
           'Rasoa washed the clothes with the soap'

        b. Nosasan-dRasoa amin'ny savony ny lamba
           washed-by Rasoa with-the soap   the clothes
           'The clothes were washed with the soap by Rasoa'

        c. Nanasan-dRasoa   ny lamba ny savony
           washed with-by Rasoa the clothes the soap
           'The soap was washed the clothes with by Rasoa'

Note in particular that the verb forms in (74b) and (74c) are different. The form in (74b) tells us that the Patient is the subject, and that in (74c) some non-Patient (finer distinctions can be made) is the subject. Philippine languages are particularly rich in the variety of verbal forms they present according to the thematic role of their subject. Example (75) below from Kalagan (Collins 1970) is a relatively simple case; six different verbal forms are cited for Kapampangan in Mirikitani (1972) and up to twelve for Tagalog by Schachter and Otanes (1972), though not all verbs accept all forms.

(75)   a. K[um]amang aku   sa tubig na lata adti balkon
           [ACTIVE]-get I(SUBJ) DO water with can on porch
           'I'll get the water on the porch with the can'

        b. Kamang-in   ku   ya tubig na lata adti balkon
           get-PASS(PATIENT) I(AG) SUBJ water with can on porch
           'The water will be got by me with the can on the porch'

    c. Pag-kamang   ku   ya   lata sa tubig adti balkon
       PASS(INSTR)-get I(AG) SUBJ can DO water on   porch
       'The can will be got water with by me on the porch'

    d. Kamang-an   ku   ya   balkon sa tubig na   lata
       get-PASS(LOC) I(AG) SUBJ porch   DO water with can
       'The porch will be got water on by me with a can'

4 The functional load of passive in grammars

We began this study by considering the functional role of passives in terms of foregrounding and backgrounding elements relative to actives. Passives certainly do have these functions, though they effect them in a rather specific way: namely, by forming derived predicates whose argument structure differs in the ways we have considered from those they are derived from.

We have seen as well that languages vary considerably with regard to the productivity of their passives. Some languages have no passives at all; others present passives on a limited class of transitive and ditransitive verbs, those with Patient objects, and not applying to intransitive verbs at all. Other languages on the other hand, such as many among the Bantu and Malayo-Polynesian groups, essentially allow all verbs to passivize, and commonly a given verb will have several different passive forms according, for example, to the aspect of the derived structure or the thematic role of its derived subject. Given the productivity of passive in these languages it would be surprising if passive formation did not interact with other rules of the grammar in regular ways. One way to assess the importance of passive relative to other rules of grammar in a language is to ask what other syntactic/morphological operations can apply to passive structures, and what such operations effectively require that the structures they apply to be passive. As we mentioned earlier, passives, where they exist, are normally well integrated in the grammar, in the sense that major operations such as relative-clause formation and nominalizations typically can apply to passive structures. Some operations however, such as imperative formation, often cannot. English is in this sense a typical language with passives.

In the languages with highly productive passives, however, we find that the possibility of forming structures which are in principle independent of passives often depends on the existence of specific passives. Thus if in English we lost the possibility of forming passives, we would not be obliged to change the way relative clauses are formed, or questions, or nominalizations, or reflexives; for in fact no major syntactic operation in English ever requires that the structure it operates on be passive. However, in Malagasy and the languages of the Philippines, by and large only main clause subjects can be relativized. That is, while we can literally say 'the man who washed the clothes', relativizing on the subject of 'washed', in Malagasy or Tagalog, we cannot literally say 'the clothes that the man washed' (*ny lamba izay nanasa ny lehilahy*). The expected structure can only mean 'the clothes which washed the man' – which doesn't make much sense. In any event, a relative clause is always understood in such a way that the head noun is the semantic subject of the main vp of the subordinate clause. Thus to refer to the clothes that John washed we must formally construe clothes as the subject of the subordinate clause. That is, we must say 'the clothes that were washed by John' using an appropriate passive form of 'wash' (in this case the one in which the Patient is the subject). And to say 'the soap with which Mary washed the clothes' we must again use the passive form which presents the instrumental as the subject; literally, 'the soap which was washed + with by Mary the clothes'. Hence in Malagasy and the Philippine languages, if we lost all passives, we would have to make very significant changes in the way relative clauses were formed. Similarly, the formation of constituent questions and 'clefts' ('it was Mary who John kissed') are not independent of passives in these languages. Thus many major syntactic processes in effect require in certain contexts that what they operate on be passive. (See Keenan 1972 for a much more thorough discussion of this point.)

Similarly in Bantu languages like Kinyarwanda we find that certain major processes such as relative-clause formation by and large (see Kimenyi 1980 for much discussion) operate only on subjects or direct objects. Thus to say 'the knife with which John killed the chicken' we must construe the subordinate clause as one in which 'knife' is either a subject or an object; it cannot be directly relativized as an oblique NP. So again, major syntactic operations depend on the existence of ways of forming derived objects and subjects in a way quite unlike English.

The field worker then should be alert to the fact that if passives are highly productive in the language(s) he or she is working with, then other syntactic processes may require the structures they operate on, in various cases, to be passive.

6 Information packaging in the clause*

WILLIAM A. FOLEY and
ROBERT D. VAN VALIN, Jr

0 Introduction

This chapter will deal with constructions such as passive, dative-shift
and topicalization which present the arguments of a predicate in a
variety of ways. Language serves a number of important functions:
transmitting and requesting information, requesting and ordering actions, expressing social relationships and many others. These constructions afford different possibilities for 'packaging' information.

To take a simple example from English, consider the following
sentences:

(1)   a. The boy hit the ball

        b. The ball was hit by the boy

These two sentences contain the same basic information, namely the
hitting of the ball by the boy, but the NPs *the boy* and *the ball* have
different kinds of 'prominence'. In the first sentence the subject NP
refers to the doer of the action and the direct object NP refers to the
entity affected by the action. In the second it is the NP denoting the
affected entity which is the grammatical subject, while the NP denoting
the doer of the action occurs in a postverbal prepositional phrase. We
ordinarily understand each of the sentences in (1) as being about their
subjects: about *the boy* (1a) and about *the ball* (1b). The same event is
reported in each sentence, but from a different perspective. The same
information is expressed in each sentence, but it is 'packaged' in
different ways.

When people interact verbally, they do so within a context or setting
that can include previous speech. This context is the background against
which people interpret the meaning and relevance of new utterances so
that the utterances go together to make up a discourse. A discourse is
not merely a set of sentences randomly strung together, but is rather a
structural series, the development of which constitutes a coherent whole
and is recognized as such by speakers of a language. A context is a

situation defined by the interlocutors: a set of circumstances given a cultural interpretation. Within this framework a particular speech activity is carried out and interpreted.

The shared knowledge and experience of the interlocutors is a very important component in the construction and interpretation of a coherent discourse, as in this example (Haviland and Clark 1974):

'The procedure is actually quite simple. First you arrange things into different groups depending on their makeup. Of course, one pile may be sufficient depending on how much there is to do. If you have to go somewhere else due to lack of facilities that is the next step, otherwise you are pretty well set. It is important not to overdo any particular endeavour. That is, it is better to do too few things at once than too many ...'

This example is probably totally opaque to the reader. If one knows, however, that the topic of this discourse is washing clothes, then it immediately becomes intelligible. This illustrates nicely the importance of background knowledge for the interpretation of speech.

1 The status of NPs

1.1 *Discourse prominence of NPs*
In the examples in (1) above, two ways of packaging in English the idea of a boy hitting a ball were illustrated. This idea can be expressed in two different clause types, active or passive. Note that a primary difference between the English active and passive concerns the syntax of the NP arguments. Two clauses which are packaging variants of the same information often show different syntactic behaviour for NPs.

NPs refer to the participants and accessories of actions and states. In the development of a discourse these participants are introduced, discussed, set aside, and possibly reintroduced with different statuses for the NPs which refer to them. These differences in status often constitute the variable determining which clause type or packaging variant will be used. There are three sets of contextual factors which are relevant to the status of an NP in a discourse. The first factor is whether an NP in a clause actually refers to an entity in the world. NPs which refer in this way are called referential NPs: we say they have a referent.

Another difference in status is illustrated in:

(2)   a. The boy saw the wombat

        b. A boy saw a wombat

While all NPs in (2) are referential, there is still a meaning difference between them. The NPs in (2a) are both introduced by *the* and are *definite*. A speaker marks an NP as definite when he assumes that the hearer can uniquely identify the referent of the NP. Suppose a friend comes up to you and says 'Fred bought the car'. He is assuming that you know which car he is talking about. If you do not know the referent of *the car*, you would ask 'which car?' If, on the other hand, he says 'Fred bought a car', then he is referring to a particular car, but is not assuming that you know which car he is talking about. Note that in both cases, the speaker is referring to a particular car (*car* is a referential NP), but when the NP is marked with *the*, the speaker assumes that the hearer can identify the referent, while he makes no such assumption when the NP is marked with *a*. Referential NPs marked by *a* in English, as in (2b), are *indefinite*. Indefinite NPs are those for which the speaker does not assume that the hearer can identify the referent.

In many languages the definiteness of a particular NP is the critical factor determining which particular packaging variant will be used. In Chinese (Li and Thompson 1976), a definite NP precedes the verb, while an indefinite one follows:

(3)   a. Sǐ rén   le
          die person PERF
          'A man has died'

       b. Rén   sǐ le
          person die PERF
          'The man has died'

Other languages in which the definiteness of an NP plays a crucial role in determining clause structure are Hindi (Tunbridge 1980), Hebrew (Berman 1978), Tagalog (Schachter 1976) and various Bantu languages (Moralong and Hyman 1977; Kimenyi 1980).

NPs are not necessarily referential, as the following examples show:

(4)   a. The wombat is a marsupial

       b. A wombat is a marsupial

       c. Wombats are marsupial

The subjects of these examples refer not to particular wombats, but to the entire class of wombats. Such NPs are called *generics*. In English there is no specific grammatical indicator of generic NPs, as witnessed by the examples in (4) in which the NPs are marked by *the*, *a* and zero.

Generics are not the only non-referential NPs:

(5)   Mary hasn't received a letter this week

In this example *letter* does not refer to anything; no letter exists such that Mary received it. *Letter* is not generic nor does it refer to the entire class of letters. The NP *a letter* is not referential.

Like definiteness, the generic status of an NP, especially a direct object, will determine the clause type in which a proposition will be expressed. Perhaps the most common kind of construction of this type is the incorporated-object construction, in which a generic direct object becomes an adverbial-like modifier of the verb and the whole clause is formally intransitive, as in Fijian (Foley 1976):

(6)   a. E   ra   sogo-t-a   na kātuba
         CLAUSE MARKER 3PL(SUBJ) close-TRANS-3SG(OBJ) ART door
         'They close the door'

      b. E   ra   sogo kātuba
         CLAUSE MARKER 3PL(SUBJ) close door
         'They close doors'

(6a) is a normal Fijian transitive clause. The verb takes a suffix *-t* which indicates that it is transitive, and a pronominal concord suffix *-a* which indicates that the direct object is third person singular. In such a clause, the direct object is necessarily referential. This contrasts with (6b), in which the object is generic in the incorporated-object form. The clause is formally intransitive; the verb may not occur with the transitive suffix or object concord suffix. The verb and the object are inseparable: no morphemes may be inserted between them. Clearly, in Fijian the difference between referential and generic direct objects is crucial in determining clause patterns. Other languages of this type include Chukchee (Comrie 1978), Tongan (Green 1979) and Kusaiean (Sugita 1973).

The indefinite article in English can mark both referential and non-referential indefinite NPs. There are sentences in English which are ambiguous between the referential indefinite meaning ('specific') and the non-referential indefinite meaning:

(7)   I'm looking for a snake

This can mean either 'I'm looking for a particular snake' or 'I'm looking for any snake', as exemplified in (8):

(8)   a. I'm looking for a snake. It is 4 feet long and has red stripes

      b. I'm looking for a snake; any one will do

A snake in (8a) is a referential indefinite NP; it is clear from the description that the speaker means a certain snake with particular features. In (8b), however, *a snake* is a non-referential indefinite NP, as any snake will satisfy the speaker's desires. We can see then that definiteness and referentiality are independent notions, although clearly related.

The final contextual factor affecting the status of an NP is whether it refers to a participant being introduced into the discourse (new information) or to a participant already established in the discourse (given information). This is illustrated in (9):

(9)   a. A boy went for a walk in the woods

       b. He saw a snake

       c. It wasn't poisonous

       d. He took it home

In this mini-discourse, the first sentence, (9a), introduces a boy into the context, as new information. In (9b) he is now given information and is referred to by the pronoun *he*; this sentence also introduces a new participant, a snake. The snake is referred to again in (9c), where it is given information and is therefore denoted by the pronoun *it*. In the final sentence, both the boy and the snake are given information and are referred to with pronouns. It would also be appropriate in this context to say 'the boy took the snake home'. In these sentences new information is expressed in indefinite NPs and given information in definite pronouns or NPs.

While this correlation is very common, others are possible:

(10)   A boy was riding his horse through the mountains near Santa Barbara when he saw the President of the United States standing by a creek

In this example, the new participant, the President of the United States, is definite, despite being new information, because he is a unique individual whom the speaker assumes the hearer can easily identify by virtue of his extralinguistic knowledge. NPs bearing new information may also be treated as definite if they are part of the immediate physical setting of the interaction, as in (11) (lecturer to students in a classroom):

(11)   Let us now turn our attention to the map

The map is part of the immediate physical setting of a classroom interaction and visible to all participants, and is, therefore, treated as definite.

The differences between given and new information may also play a role in determining the packaging of a sentence. In some languages with relatively free word order, for example Russian (Comrie 1979), given information will precede new information; and even in languages with more rigid word order, like English, the distinction between given and new information will play some role in determining word order (Halliday 1967–8).

The contextual factors we have discussed may be summarized as in Table 6.1.

Table 6.1 *Typology of contextual factors*

1	NP has unique referent
	a. + = referential
	b. − = non-referential
2	Speaker assumes hearer can identify referent
	a. + = definite
	b. − = indefinite
3	Referent has previously been introduced into context
	a. + = given information
	b. − = new information

1.2 *Animacy hierarchy*

In the previous section we have discussed the information status of NPS as established by the discourse context. We now turn to the information status of NPS as determined by inherent properties of their referents, the most significant of which properties is being one of the immediate speech act participants: the speaker or the addressee. Speaker and addressee generally correspond to the personal pronouns *I* and *you*. The traditional definition of a pronoun as a word which stands for a noun is inaccurate in the case of *I* and *you* in that there is no possible NP for which they stand. The referents *I* and *you* are not constant, but rather they change in the course of an interaction, depending on who is doing the speaking and who is being spoken to. This interplay of the shifting referents of *I* and *you* in the ongoing speech act is a fundamental fact of language.

The elements which do fit the traditional definition of pronouns as the forms which take the place of nouns are the third person pronouns: in English *he, she, it, they*. These are fundamentally different from *I* and *you*. Whereas *I* and *you* have the present speech participants as referents, a third person pronoun may refer to any referent, other than the speech act participants. The Arab grammarians referred to it as 'the one who is absent'. The third person is in fact a non-person, its possible referents being restricted to non-participants in the speech act. The

non-participant status of the third person as opposed to the first and
second is reflected in the fact that while all languages have overt
morphemes for first and second persons, many have a zero morpheme
for the third.

There is a fundamental principle of salience in the system of persons.
The speech act participants, speaker and addressee, are more salient
than the absent participants of the third person (Silverstein 1976). In
some languages (e.g. Algonquian, see Wolfart 1973), the addressee is
more salient than the speaker. In other languages (e.g. Bantu, see
Duranti 1979), the speaker is more salient than the addressee. And, in
still other languages (e.g. Dyirbal, see Dixon 1972), speaker and
addressee have equal salience. Many languages make further distinctions between different types of third person NPS. NPS with animate
referents are more salient than those with inanimate referents, and
among animates, human referents are the most salient. Some languages
make a further distinction among NPS with human referents, with proper
nouns more salient than common nouns. Finally, third person pronouns
are generally more salient than full NPS. We may set up a hierarchy of
inherent salience as:

> speaker/addressee > 3rd person pronouns > human proper
> nouns > human common nouns > other animate nouns >
> inanimate nouns

The inherent salience of an NP often determines the packaging of a
particular expression. NPS higher on the inherent salience hierarchy tend
to occupy more prominent syntactic positions than NPS lower on it.
Many languages have grammatical systems which are sensitive to the
distinctions along this hierarchy. Navajo (Hale 1972), Dyirbal (Dixon
1972), Cree (Wolfart 1973) and Shona (Hawkinson and Hyman 1974)
are all languages in which this hierarchy plays a central role. We will
investigate the functioning of this hierarchy in Tlahuitoltepec Mixe (S.
Lyon 1967), a language of the Mixe-Zoque family of Mexico. The Mixe
version of the above hierarchy is:

> speaker > addressee > human proper > human common >
> other animate > inanimate

In Mixe, speaker is more salient than addressee, and third person
pronouns are not distinguished as a class from full NPS. Third person
NPS, whether pronominal or full NPS, are differentiated along semantic
lines such as proper or common, animate or inanimate. In a Mixe clause
with subject and object NPS, the higher ranked NP along the hierarchy
controls verb agreement. There are two sets of verbal agreement

morphemes: one set indicates that the subject is the higher ranked NP, while the other indicates that the object is the higher ranked. Table 6.2 presents these forms.

Table 6.2 *Mixe verbal agreement morphemes*

	Subject higher (SH)	Object higher (OH)
1st person	n-	š-
2nd person	s-	m- . . . -ə
3rd person	t-	y- ~ -y- . . . -ə

(12) a. Tə paat ha həyuhk t-wopy
        ART Peter ART animal SH:3-hit
        'Peter hit the animal'

      b. Tə paat ha həyuhk w[y]opy-ə
        ART Peter ART animal [OH:3]-hit-OH
        'The animal hit Peter'

In the examples in (12) we have two NPs, *tə paat* 'Peter', a human proper NP, and *ha həyuhk*, 'animal', a non-human animate NP. The human proper NP is higher on the hierarchy than the non-human animate NP, so *tə paat* 'Peter' will always control verb agreement. In (12a), *tə paat* 'Peter' is functioning as the subject, and so the verb is prefixed with the subject higher, third person form *t-*; in (12b) it is the object and so the verb is infixed with *-y-*, the object higher, third person morpheme, and suffixed with an additional morpheme *-ə*, which is used as a further indicator of a higher ranking object.

(13)   a. Tə paat ha hɔɔʔy t-wopy
          ART Peter ART person SH:3-hit
          'Peter hit the person'

        b. Tə paat ha hɔɔʔy w[y]opy-ə
          ART Peter ART person [OH:3]-hit-OH
          'The person hit Peter'

In (13) we again have the proper human noun *tə paat* 'Peter', but this time in combination with *ha hɔɔʔy* 'the person', a common human NP. Again *tə paat* 'Peter' is the higher ranking NP on the hierarchy. Consequently, in (13a), in which it is the subject, the verb is prefixed with the subject higher, third person prefix *t-*, but in (13b), in which it is the object, the verb is infixed with *-y-* and suffixed with *-ə*, indicating a higher ranking object in the third person.

(14)   a. Tə   mehc ha   hɔɔʔy s-wopy
           PAST you   ART person SH:2-hit
           'You hit this person'

        b. Tə   mehc ha   hɔɔʔy m-wopy-ə
           PAST you   ART person 2-hit-OH
           'The person hit you'

In (14) there is a second person NP, *mehc* 'you', with the addressee as
referent, and a common human noun. The addressee is higher on the
inherent salience hierarchy than a common human noun, and will
therefore be the NP indexed by the verb agreement. In (14a) the second
person NP is the subject, and the verb is prefixed with the subject higher,
second person prefix *s-*. If the second person NP is the object, the verb is
prefixed with *m-*, indicating second person, and suffixed with -ə,
indicating a higher ranking object, as is exemplified by (14b). Clauses
involving a first person NP, having the speaker as referent, and a third
person NP follow the same pattern but do not employ the object higher
suffix -ə:

(15)   a. Tə   əhc ha   hɔɔʔy n-wopy
           PAST I   ART person SH:1-hit
           'I hit the person'

        b. Tə   əhc ha   hɔɔʔy s-wopy
           PAST I   ART person OH:1-hit
           'The person hit me'

As noted above, Mixe is a language in which the speaker ranks above
the addressee, so in the transitive clause with first person and second
person participants, the verbal prefix is always that of first person:

(16)   a. Tə   əhc mehc n-coky
           PAST I   you   SH:1-want
           'I wanted you'

        b. Tə   əhc mehc s-coky
           PAST I   you   OH:1-want
           'You wanted me'

In (16a) the first person pronoun is the subject, and therefore the verb is
prefixed with the subject higher, first person prefix *n-*. In (16b) it is the
object, so the verbal prefix is *s-*, the object higher, first person prefix.

In Mixe, this hierarchy is crucially important in determining the
structuring, that is the packaging, of the clause. The basic word order of
the clause, as well as the pattern ɔf verb agreement, is determined by
the inherent salience hierarcɧy. We have shown in sections 1.1 and 1.2
how the packaging of a clause may be determined by the information

status of an NP, whether from its inherent salience or its discourse acquired prominence.

2.0 Lexical and morphological packaging variants

In the previous section we demonstrated how a feature of NPS, their information status, can determine the syntactic structure of a clause. NPS which are most topical due to their information status occupy the topical grammatical slot, the subject position. A radical rearrangement of the syntactic structure of the clause, such as a passive construction, may be necessary to meet this target. This is an example of a *syntactic* packaging device, but there are at least two other types of packaging devices: morphological and lexical. We will discuss these in turn, starting with lexical.

2.1 *Converse predications: lexical*
In most languages there is more than one predicate to describe a given state, event or action. For example, a commercial transaction involving two participants and an object can be expressed either as in (17a) or (17b):

(17)   a. Doug bought a sheep from Malcolm

b. Malcolm sold a sheep to Doug

In both of these sentences the same event is captured, namely the purchase of a sheep by Doug from Malcolm, but the two sentences are packaged differently around the verbs *buy* and *sell*. With *buy* the recipient of the sheep is the subject, whereas with *sell* the vendor of the sheep is the subject. In English, as in many other languages, the subject is the most topical NP, so *buy* makes the recipient the topic, while *sell* indicates that the vendor is more topical. More examples of this kind of packaging alternation are given below:

(18)   a. The sun emits radiation

b. Radiation emanates from the sun

(19)   a. Bruce gave the ring to Sheila

b. Sheila took the ring from Bruce

(20)   a. Malaria killed Colin

b. Colin died from malaria

(21)   a. Tony lent the book to Ken

b. Ken borrowed the book from Tony

Since these packaging differences depend on the lexical choice of the predicate, we refer to them as *lexical* packaging devices.

Tagalog (22) and German (23) also have lexical packaging variants of this kind. The basic system of Tagalog grammatical relations is discussed by Andrews in the second chapter of this volume (1.2), and we assume familiarity with it here. Our analysis sometimes leads us to use terms somewhat different from those employed by Schachter and Otanes (1972) and by Andrews. What they call 'object' we call 'patient' and what they call 'directional' we call 'locative'. We share with them the terms 'actor' and 'focus'. In the Tagalog examples here, AF = actor focus, P = patient and LOC = locative.

(22) a. K[um]uha ng gulay   sa lalake ang   bata
         [AF]-take P vegetables LOC man   FOCUS child
         'The child took vegetables from the man'

      b. Nag-bigay ng gulay   sa bata ang   lalake
         AF-give   P vegetables LOC child FOCUS man
         'The man gave vegetables to the child'

(23) a. Das   Kind nimmt dem   Mann die   Gemüse
         the(NOM) child take the(DAT) man the(ACC) vegetables
         'The child takes the vegetables from the man'

      b. Der   Mann gibt dem   Kind die   Gemüse
         the(NOM) man give the(DAT) child the(ACC) vegetables
         'The man gives the vegetables to the child'

There is a semantic difference between the two sentences in each of the pairs of examples, that parallels the difference in topic status for the recipient and vendor NPs. It concerns the choice of the initiating and controlling participant in the event. If in the sheep transaction between Doug and Malcolm, Doug is considered by the speaker to be the primary performer and initiator of the action, then (17a) with *buy* is appropriate. If, on the other hand, Malcolm is taken to be the initiating and controlling participant, then (17b) with *sell* is appropriate. The same distinction obtains in (18–23). The NP referring to the initiating and controlling participant in an event or action we term the *actor*, which in an active sentence is always the most topical NP, and hence the subject. Our notion of actor is equivalent for all practical purposes to Andrews' (1.2) notion of *subject* as a primitive grammatical relation. Thus in (17a) *Doug* is the actor, while in (17b) *Malcolm* is the actor. In passive sentences the actor and subject are different NPs, as a passive signals that an NP other than the actor is the topic:

(24)　a. Doug was sold a sheep by Malcolm　(cf. 17)

　　　b. Sheila was given the ring by Bruce　(cf. 19)

Doug is the subject in both (17a) and (24a), but only in (17a) is he the actor. Similarly, *Sheila* is subject in both (19b) and (24b), but she is the actor only in (19b). The difference between predicates like *buy* and *sell* or *give* and *take* reflect different choices of participant as the actor.

Just as there are variations in the lexical choice of predicates, which signal different choices for the actor, there is a similar pattern of lexical variation with regard to the selection of the participant affected by the action or event expressed by the predicate. A clear example of this can be found in the pair of English verbs *rob* and *steal*:

(25)　a. Howard robbed Frank of $50

　　　b. Howard stole $50 from Frank

Syntactically, these sentences differ in the selection of the direct object. In (25a) *Frank* is the direct object, while in (25b), *$50* is the direct object. The schematic difference between these two sentences relates to degree of involvement of Frank in the action. In the example with *rob* he is more directly involved in and affected by the action than is the case in the example with *steal*. Note that (26a) is plausible, but (26b) is decidedly odd:

(26)　a.　Howard stole $50 from Frank, but Frank didn't know it

　　　b.　?Howard robbed Frank of $50, but Frank didn't know it

The oddity of (26b) illustrates that with *rob*, Frank must be central in the action (in this case he must be aware of its result), whereas *steal* does not carry this interpretation. The central affected participant in a situation we will refer to as the *undergoer*. This notion of undergoer corresponds to Andrews' (1.2) usage of the term *object*; like actor, it refers to a primitive syntactico-semantic relation which may appear in different syntactic forms and is not equivalent to the notion of *direct object*, although that is probably the most common grammatical slot in English for the undergoer to fill. However, undergoers can function as grammatical subjects in passive constructions. Compare (27) with (25):

(27)　a.　Frank was robbed of $50 by Howard

　　　b.　$50 was stolen from Frank by Howard

Thus, a single transitive clause in any language has two essential basic syntactico-semantic relations, an actor and an undergoer. Languages, then, may possess packaging devices like active and passive, or lexical pairs of predicates such as *buy/sell*, *rob/steal*, which present different possibilities for the grammatical treatment of these two relations.

2.2 Converse predications: morphological

Another way in which these packaging variations can be achieved is through morphological means. Morphological packaging devices are of two kinds. One concerns the semantics of actor and undergoer choice, and the other expresses the information status of arguments as determined by discourse factors or inherent properties (see section 1).

The variation in the status of actor is coded lexically in English and may be expressed by morphological means in other languages. Consider these Tagalog sentences:

(28)   a. B[*um*]ili   ng isda sa bata ang   lalake
             [AF]-transact P fish LOC child FOCUS man
             'The man bought fish from the child'

        b. *Nag*-bili   ng isda sa   bata ang   lalake
             AF-transact P fish LOC child FOCUS man
             'The man sold fish to the child'

(29)   a. *Um*-abot ng gulay   ang   lalake
             AF-transfer P vegetables FOCUS man
             'The man reached out for vegetables'

        b. *Nag*-abot ng gulay   ang   lalake
             AF-transfer P vegetables FOCUS man
             'The man passed vegetables'

Bili simply means 'to transfer goods in a commercial event', and *abot* 'to transfer from hand to hand'. The semantics of the actor, whether the point of origin of the transfer or its point of termination, is supplied by the verbal affixes *-um-*, which means 'actor is point of termination of the transfer' or *nag-*, which means 'actor is point of origin of transfer'. Thus, when *-um-* is infixed to *bili*, the resulting meaning is 'buy', but when *nag-* is added, the result is 'sell'. In parallel fashion *um-abot* means 'reach out for', but *nag-abot* means 'pass to'.

There is a similar situation in German with respect to the verbs 'buy', 'sell' and 'rent (to/from)', as shown in (30) and (31):

(30)   a. Jürgen kaufte   zwei Bücher   von Almuth
             Jurgen buy(PAST) two book(ACC PL) from Almuth
             'Jurgen bought two books from Almuth'

        b. Almuth verkaufte zwei Bücher   an Jürgen
             Almuth sell(PAST) two book(ACC PL) to Jurgen
             'Almuth sold two books to Jurgen'

(31) a. Die   Studenten mieteten   das   Haus
the(NOM PL) student(PL) rent(PAST PL) the(ACC) house

von der   alten   Frau
from the(DAT) old(DAT) woman
'The students rented the house from the old woman'

b. Die   alte   Frau   vermeitete das   Haus an
the(NOM) old(NOM) woman rent(PAST) the(ACC) house to

die   Studenten
the(ACC PL) student(PL)
'The old woman rented the house to the students'

In German the morphologically unmarked members of each pair are *kaufen* 'buy (from)' and *mieten* 'rent (from)'; they take the recipient of the transfer as the actor. The addition of *ver-* to these verbs signals that the source of the transfer is the actor. With these verbs ϕ- and *ver-* function in German analogously to *-um-* and *mag-* in Tagalog in expressing different choices of the actor with a verb.

An analogous situation exists in English with the verb *rent*, but the choice of actor is signalled not by a verbal affix but rather by a preposition occurring with a non-actor argument of the verb. Note that (32a) is ambiguous:

(32) a. Michael rented the apartment

b. Michael rented the apartment to Jennifer

c. Michael rented the apartment from Jennifer

The English verb *rent* is ambiguous between the meanings of German *mieten* and *vermieten*; (32a) can mean either that Michael rented the apartment to someone, or from someone. The overt expression of a third argument with the preposition *to* or *from*, as in (32b) and (32c), disambiguates *rent*. Thus the prepositions *to* and *from* signal the different choices of the actor, analogous to the verbal affixes in Tagalog and German. There are few examples of this type in English, because most alternations of this kind are lexicalized as two different verbs as in (17–21). In Tagalog, on the other hand, there are few examples of lexicalized actor choice, along the lines of 'give' and 'take' (see (22)), as perspective choices of the actor are usually signalled by morphological means, as in (28–9).

In the foregoing, we have discussed morphological means for signalling the semantics of the actor. This is an example of morphological signalling of packaging variations. We mentioned earlier that morphological means of encoding packaging variations concern the expression either of different meanings for the NPs in perspective, or of the information status of NPs according to discourse argument or inherent properties. A very clear-cut example of this second function is found in Lisu (Hope 1974), a Tibeto–Burman language of Southeast Asia, with its clitics *nya* and *xə*. An NP whose referent is given and salient as determined by the discourse is marked by *nya*:

(33)   a. Làma *nya* ánà khų̀-ą̇
             tiger   dog bite-DECLAR
             'Dogs bite tigers' *or* 'Tigers bite dogs'

         b. Ánà *nya* làma kyų̀-ą̇
             dog   tiger bite-DECLAR
             'Dogs bite tigers' *or* 'Tigers bite dogs'

In these examples Lisu does not distinguish actors from undergoers, so these sentences are ambiguous as to the roles of 'tigers' or 'dogs'. An NP may be explicitly marked as undergoer by the postposition *læ* as in (34a). There is another clitic to indicate salience, *xə*, and its difference from *nya* is brought out in this sequence:

(34)   a. Làma *nya* ánà læ khų̀ ɤə-ą̇
             tiger   dog to bite give-DECLAR
             'A tiger bit a dog'

         b. Yí *nya* na   le-ą̇
             he   sore become-DECLAR
             'He (the tiger) got hurt'

         c. Yí *xə* na   le-ą̇
             he   sore become-DECLAR
             'He (the dog) got hurt'

The tiger is the topic of (34a), in which he bites a dog. *Yí* 'he' in (34b) is marked with *nya* and necessarily has the tiger as its referent, the same topic as in (34a), while in (34c) *yí* 'he' is marked with *xə* and must refer to the dog. *Nya* signals that the topic of this clause is the same as that of the previous clause, while *xə* indicates a change in topic.

A different type of system for signalling the discourse status of an argument is found in Algonquian languages. It combines both an animacy hierarchy of the kind discussed in section 1.2, and discourse salience factors of the type discussed for Lisu. The basic Algonquian animacy hierarchy (for singular arguments) is 2nd person > 1st person > 3rd person. Moreover, there is a further distinction in the third person between what Algonquianists call *proximate* and *obviative*. If there is only one third person argument in a clause, it must be proximate, which is morphologically unmarked on full NPs. If there are two third persons, however, one must be proximate and the other obviative. The choice of proximate argument is apparently determined by discourse conditions: 'The proximate third person represents the topic of discourse, the person nearest the speaker's point of view, or the person earlier spoken of and already known' (Bloomfield 1962:38). Within the animacy hierarchy, proximate third persons outrank obviative. Accordingly, the animacy hierarchy is 2nd person > 1st person > 3rd person PROX > 3rd person OBV.

This animacy hierarchy is an essential part of the means by which actor and undergoer are expressed in a clause. In Algonquian languages both actor and undergoer are coded on the verb, but the order of the affixes on the verb reflects the animacy hierarchy and not whether the affix is actor or undergoer. Thus, for example, if the two arguments of a verb are first and second person, then they will occur in the verb in the order second–first person, regardless of which is actor and which is undergoer. This is illustrated in (35); the examples are from Plains Cree (Wolfart 1973), an Algonquian language spoken in Canada:

(35)   a. Ki-tasam-i-n
            2-feed-DCT-1
            'You feed me'

        b. Ki-tasam-iti-n
            2-feed-INV-1
            'I feed you'

The second person affix *ki-* occurs as a prefix in both forms, even though it is the actor in (35a) and the undergoer in (35b). Similarly, the first person affix *-n* is a suffix in both sentences, despite its different function in the two sentences. The specification of actor and undergoer in a clause is achieved by what is usually called the *direction* marker, *-i-* in (35a) and *-iti-* in (35b). The affix *-i-* indicates that in terms of the animacy hierarchy the actor is higher ranking than the undergoer: in (35a) second person > first person. In such a situation the action of the verb is said to be *direct*, and consequently *-i-* signals direct (DCT) action. If, on the other hand, the actor is lower ranking on the animacy hierarchy than the undergoer, as in (35b) where first person > second person, then the affix *-iti-* is used to signal this. In such a case the action of the verb is said to be *inverse* (INV). The affixes expressing the argument of a verb do not express their function by themselves; rather, the choice of the actor and undergoer is indicated by the direction marker.

Further Plains Cree examples to illustrate this system of discourse salience marking and actor/undergoer coding are given below:

(36)   a. Ki-tasam-ā-w atim-∅   (DIRECT)
          2-feed-DCT-3 dog-PROX
          'You feed the dog'

       b. Ki-tasam-ik   napew-∅   (INVERSE)
          (ki-tasam-ekw-w)
          2-feed-INV-3   man-PROX
          'The man feeds you'

       c. Ki-tasam-ā-w   (DIRECT)
          2-feed-DCT-3
          'You feed him'

(37)   a. Ni-tasam-ā-w atim-∅   (DIRECT)
          I-feed-DCT-3 dog-PROX
          'I feed the dog'

       b. Ni-tasam-ik   napew-∅   (INVERSE)
          (ni-tasam-ekw-w)
          I-feed-INV-3   man-PROX
          'The man feeds me'

(38)   a. Asam-ē-w napew-∅ atim-wa   (DIRECT)
          feed-DCT-3 man-PROX dog-OBV
          'The man feeds the dog'

       b. Asam-ik   napew-a   atim-∅   (INVERSE)
          (asam-ekw-w) (napew-wa)
          feed-INV-3   man-OBV   dog-PROX
          'The man feeds the dog'

(39)   a. Asam-ē-w atim-wa   (DIRECT)
          feed-DCT-3 dog-OBV
          'He feeds the dog'

       b. Asam-ik   atim-∅   (INVERSE)
          (asam-ekw-w)
          feed-INV-3   dog-PROX
          'He feeds the dog'

(The -t- in (36–7) is the result of a morphophonemic process by which
/t/ is inserted between a prefix ending with a vowel and a stem
beginning in a vowel.)

The examples in (36) and (37) involve a third person and a non-third
person. Those in (38) and (39) involve two third persons, one proximate
and one obviative; obviative NPS are not directly coded in the verb in
Plains Cree. The two possible choices for which NP is proximate and

which is obviative yield two different ways of saying the same thing, in this case 'The man feeds the dog'. When the actor (man) is proximate, as in (38a, 39a), then the action is direct. When, on the other hand, the object (dog) is proximate, as in (38b, 39b), then the action is inverse. The actual choice of the proximate argument in discourse would depend on a number of factors, including which argument was established as given, and what is being talked about. This choice has implications, not only for the signalling of the status of the arguments in discourse, but also for the expression of actor and object in the clause.

3.0 Syntactic packaging: clause-internal

In addition to lexical and morphological devices, languages also possess several types of syntactic devices to express variations in the packaging of information. The most widely known of these are passives, but other types of constructions are also widespread. In this section we will discuss a wide variety of syntactic information packaging options: passives, antipassives, left-dislocations, topicalizations and others. We intend to examine these constructions in terms of both their structures and their functions.

3.1 *Passives*

Passives are constructions which characteristically present the undergoer argument as subject, as in (40):

(40)   a. The sandwich was eaten by the boy

       b. The man was kissed by the woman

In (40) the undergoer argument of the verb is the subject of the clause, and the actor is marked with the preposition *by*. These contrast with the corresponding active constructions in which the actor is subject, and the undergoer is a direct object:

(41)   a. The boy ate the sandwich

       b. The woman kissed the man

Traditionally, the subject has been described as the constituent which specifies what the sentence is about, so that the passives are generally understood to be about the undergoer rather than the actor. Generally, it is the subject which occupies sentence-initial position, in both active and passive constructions, but there are other constructions, which place an NP other than a subject in sentence-initial position. These are known as topicalizations or left-dislocations:

(42)   a. Teheran, I don't care for much

b. Trevor, I haven't seen today

c. As for Alan's car, he tried to drive it today

d. That paper, it was a total loss

e. As for the wombat, it eats roots, shoots and leaves

(42) presents examples of both types of construction. (42a,b) are topicalizations and (42c,d,e) are left-dislocations. The difference is that in left-dislocations but not in topicalizations there is a pronoun in the clause which refers to the clause-initial NP. This non-subject clause-initial NP we will term the *external topic*.

Passives, then, present undergoer arguments as the subject, while topicalizations and left-dislocations present undergoers and other constituents as the external topic. It is quite clear that subject and topic must be distinguished because they can both occur in the same clause:

(43)   a. With a sword, the prisoner was quickly despatched

b. To John, the book was given by the king

These examples establish subject and external topic as different, but what is the nature of this difference?

Subjects and external topic are both constituents which present as topical constituents NPs which are prominent because of their information status. However, the syntactic status of these two NPs is radically different. The subject is a basic NP constituent of the clause. Semantically, it must correspond to an argument of the verb. Topics are *not* constituents of the clause, but rather are external to it, in juxtaposition to the clause as a whole (see also Andrews, 1.2). They do not necessarily bear any semantic relationship to the predicate or its arguments:

(44)   a. As for food, let's drive into town to MacDonald's

b. As for elephants, their noses are long and their skin is thick

In both of these examples the external topics are not arguments of the predicates, and are clearly in apposition to the clause as a whole. Of course external topics may be arguments, but still they are only in apposition to the clause:

(45)   a. As for John, he is such a fool

b. For Mary, John bought a dozen roses

c. Tokyo, I can't visit

Subjects in all cases are internal constituents of the clause, and must be an argument of the predicate. Among the NP constituents of the clause we must recognize a fundamental distinction between core constituents and peripheral constituents. The distinction between core and periphery is recognized by other writers, for example Dixon (1977a:402–4) and Andrews (1.2), who terms them core and oblique. For English, core constituents are the actor and the undergoer, for any simple transitive verb. These are the core arguments for a transitive verb, the arguments entered in its lexical entry. Clearly, they are necessary for a clause to form a conceptual whole.

Peripheral constituents are those filled by circumstantial arguments like instruments, benefactives, or causes; or locative arguments like goals, sources or paths. Peripheral constituents are generally marked in some way, by a case marker or an adposition, whereas core constituents are more likely to be unmarked. In some languages, core constituents are cross-referenced on the verb, but peripheral constituents are not. For example, in English, actor and undergoer in a normal active transitive clause are unmarked, and furthermore, a third singular actor is cross-referenced on the verb (*he sings*). Peripheral constituents in English are always marked with a preposition: *with a knife, near the sea, out of love, for his wife*; and they are never cross-referenced on the verb. Other differences between core and peripheral constituents will be noted later.

As we will show, passive in most languages is restricted to core constituents, while topicalization and left-dislocation are not so restricted. In English, instruments and locatives, which are peripheral constituents, may be external topics, but not passive subjects:

(46) a. Fred sliced the bread with the knife
       b. With the knife Fred sliced the bread
       c. *The knife was sliced the bread with by Fred

(47) a. The hunter shot a bear in the woods
       b. In the woods the hunter shot a bear
       c. *The woods were shot a bear in by the hunter

In (46) and (47) we have peripheral instrument and locative constituents *with a knife* and *in the woods*. In the (a) active sentences they occur as postverbal peripheral constituents. In the (b) sentences they are topicalized and occur in the clause-initial topic position. The (c) passive sentences, however, are ungrammatical because instrument and locative constituents are peripheral, and are not possible subjects of passive constructions. Thus, these peripheral constituents freely occur as external topics, but not as passive subjects, which are part of the core.

While all languages have a fundamental distinction between core and periphery, it is possible in many languages for certain NP types to appear as either core or peripheral constituents. There is a common process of periphery-to-core promotion that many languages have. In English, benefactives, unlike locatives or instruments, may be either core or peripheral constituents, as in (48):

(48)   a. Craig Claiborne cooked a four course dinner for Mary

        b. Craig Claiborne cooked Mary a four course dinner

In (48a), *Mary* is a peripheral argument and is marked with the preposition *for*. In (48b) it is a core argument and appears as the direct object. The shift from peripheral to core status for Mary in (48a,b) entails a semantic change. (48) can mean either 'C.C. cooked for Mary's benefit', or 'in place of Mary', in a situation where Mary was supposed to cook dinner for someone but fell ill, and so C.C. stepped in and cooked in her place. (48b), however, is not ambiguous in this regard; it can mean only 'for Mary's benefit'. The meaning change reflects the shift from the periphery to the core because in (48b), but not in (48a), Mary is the undergoer of *cook*, which entails that she is directly affected by the action of the verb. She is directly affected by an action done to benefit her but not by an action done by someone in her place. The semantic difference between (48a) and (48b) indicates that the NP *Mary* is the undergoer in (48b) and hence part of the core of the clause.

There are also syntactic differences between (48a) and (48b) in terms of their behaviour with respect to passivization, topicalization and left-dislocation.

(49)   a. For Mary, Craig Claiborne cooked a four course dinner

        b. ?Mary, Craig Claiborne cooked four course dinner for her

        c. *Mary, Craig Claiborne cooked a four course dinner

        d. Mary, Craig Claiborne cooked her a four course dinner

(50)   a. *Mary was cooked a four course dinner for by Craig Claiborne

        b. Mary was cooked a four course dinner by Craig Claiborne

(49a,b) present topicalized and left-dislocated versions of (48a) with a peripheral benefactive, while (49c,d) give the topicalized and left-dislocated form of (48b) with a core benefactive. (49c), in which the promoted core benefactive is topicalized, is ungrammatical due to a general constraint in English which disallows promoted core benefactives or recipients to be topics via topicalization rather than left-dislocation. This is probably due to a problem of grammatical inconsistency. Because no trace remains in the direct object position after topicalization, there is no indication of the promotion of the former peripheral benefactive to core status. However, the topic is unmarked by a preposition, and would normally be taken as a core constituent. The sentence could be interpreted as having two undergoers, a possibility not allowed in English; and thus, such sentences are ruled out by English grammar. If the core benefactive is made the topic by left-dislocation then a pronoun is left in the direct object position, so no ambiguity arises. Such sentences, as in (49d), are perfectly grammatical. (49b) is of questionable grammaticality because a peripheral constituent has become an external topic as an unmarked NP, a feature of core constituents. The corresponding (49a) is much better because the peripheral benefactive external topic is still marked as a peripheral with a preposition.

The possibilities for passivization for core and peripheral benefactives are quite different: (50a), the passive version of (48a), is ungrammatical, whereas (50b), the passive variant of (48b), is fine. Passivization is possible only when the beneficiary is in the core, as in (48b).

These differences in behaviour of passivization and topicalization with respect to the peripheral arguments, instruments and locatives, versus the core argument of undergoer, is evidence for a basic distinction between core and periphery. The fact that direct object benefactives passivize, but oblique ones do not, is further evidence for this distinction, as direct object benefactives are core arguments, but oblique ones are peripheral. In summary, passive is a syntactic device which only affects core arguments, but topicalization and left-dislocation affect both core and peripheral arguments.

Passive is signalled by various means across languages, but there is always some mark in the core, usually on the predicate, which signals the passive; there is no such marker for topicalization and left-dislocation. In (40a) the passive form is indicated by the use of the *be*-auxiliary, the past particulate form of the verb, and by the use of the preposition *by* with the actor. There is no comparable alteration in the core in (41a). With the topicalization of core arguments there is simply a gap in the clause, and with left-dislocation there is a pronoun which refers to the sentence-initial NP. Since topics are outside of the core, it is not surprising that no explicit marker of them in the core is necessary. On the other hand, because passive involves a change in the syntactic status of core constituents, it is to be expected that it would be overtly indicated in the core in some way.

So far in our presentation we have employed the notion of subject with little comment. We have simply pointed out the contrast between it and the notion of external topic. The most notable feature of the notion of subject in English and many other languages is the number of grammatical processes sensitive to it. For example, it is always the target of deletion in complements:

(51)   a. Fred wants to go to the movies

          b. Fred wants to see Marsha

          c. *Fred wants Marsha to see [him]

          d. Fred wants to be seen by Marsha

In (51a,b) *Fred* is the subject of the complement and the matrix verb, and is deleted in the complement. In (51c) *Fred* is the object in the complement and may not be deleted. Rather, the complement must be passivized, making *Fred* the subject, which is then deleted.

The subject is also the pivotal NP of many other grammatical constructions in English:

(52)   Participial relativization:

          a. The woman scolding the policeman is my mother

          b. *The policeman the woman scolding is my father

          c. The policeman being scolded by the woman is my father

(53)   Raising-to-subject:

          a. It seems that Paul caught the wombat

          b. Paul seems to have caught the wombat

          c. *The wombat seems Paul to have caught

          d. The wombat seems to have been caught by Paul

(54)   Deletion in coordinate structures:

          a. Oscar went to the store and bought some milk

          b. *Oscar went to the store and Bill spoke to [him]

          c. Oscar went to the store and was spoken to by Bill

In all these constructions the affected NP in the embedded or second clause is the subject. In participial relative clauses only the subject may be relativized. Hence (52a,c) are grammatical, while (52b) is not. Similarly, in (53) only the subject of the embedded clause may occur as the subject of the matrix verb *seem*. Hence, (53c) is ungrammatical because *wombat* is the object. The passivized (53d) is necessary to raise *wombat*. Finally, in (54), only subjects may be deleted in the second of two conjoined clauses. (54b) is ungrammatical if the goal of speaking,

Oscar, is deleted; instead, a pronoun must occur. However, if the sentence is passivized, making *Oscar* the subject, then it may be deleted. Clearly, in all these constructions the subject is the pivotal NP.

We now introduce the technical term *pivot*. A *pivot* is any NP type to which a particular grammatical process is sensitive, either as controller or as target. The English subject is the pivot for all of the above constructions, although there are a few constructions in English to be discussed later for which the undergoer is the pivot. This is the general notion of pivot. However, we will operate with a more specific usage of the term. Many languages like English have a particular NP type which is privileged in controlling a great deal of the language's syntax. In other languages, such as Archi or Yimas, this does not appear to be the case. For most languages which have a special privileged pivotal NP, it is the subject, as in English. In others such as Dyirbal (Dixon 1972), it is the object. It is always limited to a choice between these two. No language has a benefactive (or a location) nominal as its pivot. We will refer to this special privileged NP as the *pivot* in the language, employing this henceforth in place of the term subject, which has a confusing usage in the literature and is best avoided.

A further distinction between types of pivots must be made (see Andrews, 1.2). In many languages, like Warlpiri, Enga or Choctaw (Van Valin and Foley 1980), the pivot is always crucially associated with a semantic role. In Enga and Warlpiri the actor is always the pivot. In Choctaw (Heath 1977) the actor, if present, is always the pivot. If the clause does not contain an actor, then another NP may be the pivot. Pragmatic notions of discourse topicality do not interfere in the choice of pivot in these languages. It is determined strictly on semantic lines, according to a semantic hierarchy. The pivots of such languages are *semantic pivots* (SmP).

In other languages, like English or Tagalog, the pivot is crucially associated with pragmatic notions of discourse topicality. The choice of pivot is not determined solely by semantic considerations, but notions of discourse topicality also govern its choice. In many of these languages one NP type will be the preferable choice for pivot. In English it is the actor. However, for reasons of discourse topicality and other pragmatic considerations, an alternative choice can be made, that of the undergoer. Thus, voice distinctions of the type active–passive are a common feature of languages of this type, although, as we shall see below, they are not restricted to these languages. Pivots in languages of this type, in which pragmatic notions play an important role in their selection, will here be referred to as *pragmatic pivots* (PrP). Pragmatic pivots can be distinguished from semantic pivots primarily in that their selection is not strictly semantically determined, but is in part discourse determined. Furthermore, notions of definiteness play an important role in the selection of pivots in many languages with pragmatic pivots.

A good grammatical frame of reference for distinguishing pragmatic from semantic pivots is in constructions requiring zero anaphora in subordinate or coordinate sentences, as in (54) above. Zero anaphora is only permitted of highly topical referents, and the control of this process by an NP type is a good diagnostic indicator that it is a pragmatic pivot; provided, of course, that its selection is not predictable in purely semantic terms. That is, if we find a language like Enga in which zero anaphora is always restricted to actors, then the pivot is a semantic one. However, in English, as (54) shows, both actors and undergoers may be subject to zero anaphora, proving that the English pivot is a pragmatic one, rather than a semantic one.

Semantic and pragmatic pivots are not mutually exclusive. There are languages such as Tagalog or Yidiɲ (Dixon 1977a) which possess both types, each of them controlling or being the target of different grammatical processes. Tagalog (Schachter 1976, 1977) is an especially good example of a language of this type. The actor is a semantic pivot controlling a few clause-internal grammatical processes, like reflexivization, while what is referred to in Tagalog grammar as the topic, the NP marked by the preposition *ang*, is the pragmatic pivot, controlling most of the cross-clausal grammatical processes and the maintenance of discourse cohesion. In this sense, we can view the pragmatic pivot as a specialized topic notion, one operating inside the clause, rather than external to it.

3.1.1 *Foregrounding passives*

The passive construction is a packaging variant in which a non-actor argument occurs as the pivot of a transitive verb. Languages differ as to what non-actor arguments may occur as the pivot. Languages like German and Italian (Duranti and Ochs 1979) are quite restrictive and only allow undergoers as pivots in passive constructions:

(55)   a. Der   Junge hat   das   Butterbrot gegessen
           the(NOM) boy   have(3SG) the(ACC) sandwich   eaten

       'The boy ate the sandwich'

       b. Das   Butterbrot wurde   von dem
           the(NOM) sandwich   became(3SG) by the(DAT)

Jungen gegessen
boy   eaten
'The sandwich was eaten by the boy'

The pivot in German is signalled by the nominative case. In (55) the actor *der Junge* 'the boy' is the pivot, while in (55b) the object *das Butterbrot* 'the sandwich' is the pivot. The pivot in German is a pragmatic one. Zubin (1979) has shown the importance of the nominative case to topicality and maintenance of discourse cohesion. Furthermore, as in English, the nominative NP is the target for zero anaphora in conjoined clauses.

One of the main functions of nominative NPS is to control zero pronominalization across clauses. This is illustrated in (56).

(56)   a. Der   Junge hat   das   Butterbrot gegessen
          the(NOM) boy   have(3SG) the(ACC) sandwich   eaten

          und ist   dann ins Kino gegangen
          and be(3SG) then into movie gone
          'The boy ate the sandwich and then went to the movie'

       b. Die   Frau   sah   den   Mann und __
          the(NOM) woman saw(3SG) the(ACC) man   and

          schlug   ihn
          hit(3SG) him(ACC)
          'The woman saw the man and hit him'

       c. Er   wurde   zusammengeschlagen und __
          he(NOM) became(3SG) beaten up   and

          ging   dann ins Krankenhaus
          went(3SG) then into hospital
          'He was beaten up and then went to the hospital'

       d. Die   Frau   sah   den   Mann und __
          the(NOM) woman saw(3SG) the(ACC) man   and

          wurde   gekidnappt
          became(3SG) kidnapped
          'The woman saw the man and was kidnapped'

In all of these sentences the pragmatic pivot (PrP) in the first clause is controlling the zero pronominalization, i.e. deletion, of the PrP of the second clause. It is important to note that whether the PrP is the actor or the undergoer semantically is irrelevant to this control of coreferential deletion. In (56a,b) the PrPs in both clauses are actors, while in (56c,d) one is an actor and the other an undergoer in each sentence. That it is the PrP which is both the controlling and target NP for this deletion can be seen from the ungrammaticality of the following sentences:

(57)   a. *Die   Frau   sah   den   Mann und er
          the(NOM) woman saw(3SG) the(ACC) man   and he
          schlug   __
          hit(3SG) [her]
          'The woman saw the man and he hit [her]'

       b. *Die   Frau   sah   den   Mann und __
          the(NOM) woman saw(3SG) the(ACC) man   and [he]
          schlug   sie
          hit(3SG) her
          'The woman saw the man and [he] hit her'

       c. *Die   Frau   sah den Mann und __ wurde
          the(NOM) woman saw the man and [he] became(3SG)
          gekidnappt
          kidnapped
          'The woman saw the man, and [he] was kidnapped'

       d. *Die   Mann wurde   von der   Frau
          the(NOM) man became(3SG) by the(DAT) woman
          gesehen und __ schlug ihn
          seen   and [she] hit(3SG) him(ACC)
          'The man was seen by the woman and [she] hit him'

In (57a) the accusative undergoer in the second clause is deleted under coreference with the PrP of the first, rendering the sentence ungrammatical. In (57b) the PrP of the second clause is deleted under coreference with the accusative undergoer in the first, again yielding an ungrammatical sentence. (57c) is formally identical with (56d), but is ungrammatical if the deleted PrP of the second clause is understood to be the same as the accusative undergoer of the previous clause. Even though both the controlling and target NPs are undergoers, the sentence is still ungrammatical. Finally, in (57d) the demoted actor in a passive construction in the first clause is coreferential with the deleted PrP in the second, resulting in ungrammaticality. Note that the actors and under-goers are the same in (56b) and (57d) but the PrPs are not; and only (56b) is grammatical. This shows first that the controller and target of zero pronominalization in German is the PrP, and second that the PrP of a passive construction has the same properties in this regard as the PrP of an active construction. English has the same constraint on zero pro-nominalization as German; the English glosses for the German sentences in (56) and (57) show the same pattern of the PrP as controller and target of zero pronominalization in both active and passive constructions.

NPs which are not case marked accusatively may not be promoted to PrP status in a passive; in particular, dative arguments do not become the PrP in a passive, regardless of whether they are the direct object of a verb which takes only dative objects, like *helfen* 'help' or *danken* 'thank', or the indirect object of a transitive verb:

(58) a. Der   alte   Herr   hat   mir
        the(NOM) old(NOM) gentleman have(3SG) me(DAT)
        geholfen
        helped
        'The old gentleman helped me'

     b. Das   Mädchen hat   mir   ein   Buch
        the(NOM) girl   have(3SG) me(DAT) a(ACC) book
        geschenkt
        give (as present)
        'The girl gave me a book'

(59) a. Mir   wurde   von dem   alten
        me(DAT) became(3SG) by the(DAT) old(DAT)
        Herrn   geholfen
        gentleman(DAT) helped
        'I was helped by the old gentleman'

     b. *Ich   wurde   von dem   alten
         I(NOM) became(3SG) by the(DAT) old(DAT)
         Herrn   geholfen
         gentleman(DAT) helped
         'I was helped by the old gentleman'

     c. Mir   wurde   ein   Buch geschenkt
        me(DAT) became(3SG) a(NOM) book given (as gift)
        'I was given a book'

     d. *Ich   wurde   ein   Buch geschenkt
         I(NOM) became(3SG) a(ACC) book given (as gift)
         'I was given a book'

What appears to be the derived subject of the passive sentence is in the dative rather than the nominative case, just as it is in the corresponding active sentence. Since they are not in the nominative case, we would expect that they are not PrPs, and this is borne out by their inability to be the controller or target of zero pronominalization:

(60) a. *Mir   wurde   von dem   alten
          me(DAT) became(3SG) by the(DAT) old(DAT)

          Herrn   geholfen und __ dankte
          gentleman(DAT) helped   and   thank(1SG PAST)

          ihm   deswegen herzlich
          him(DAT) therefore heartily
          'I was helped by the old gentleman and therefore thanked him heartily'

      b. *Mir   wurde   ein   Buch von dem
          me(DAT) became(3SG) a(NOM) book by the(DAT)

          Mädchen geschenkt   und habe   __   es
          girl   given (as gift) and have(1SG)   it(ACC)

          sofort   verloren
          immediately lost
          'I was given a book by the girl and immediately lost it'

      c. *Ich   bin   zu der   Bank gegangen und __
          I(NOM) be(1SG) to the(DAT)   bank gone   and

          wurde   von einem   alten   Herrn
          became (1SG) by   an(DAT) old(DAT) gentleman(DAT)

          geholfen
          helped
          'I went to the bank and was helped by an old gentleman'

      d. *Ich   bin   zu der   Bank gegangen und __
          I(NOM) be(1SG) to the(DAT) bank gone   and

          wurde   viel Geld   gegeben
          became(3SG) much money given
          'I went to the bank and was given a lot of money'

These sentences are ungrammatical because in each of them a dative subject of a passive is either a controller or a target of zero pronominalization. This shows that they are not PrPs. Thus in German, only accusative NPS may occur as the PrP in passive constructions.

   Other languages are not so restrictive as German in what arguments are allowed as the PrP in passive clauses. Some languages, like English or those of western Indonesia such as Indonesian/Malay, Javanese, Sundanese, Madurese and Balinese, allow other non-actor core arguments in addition to the object to occur as PrP. In Indonesian, as in

English, recipient or benefactive may become core arguments, and may be PrPs in passive sentences. A verbal extension suffix (EXT) *-kan* indicates that the normally peripheral constituent has become core:

(61)　a.　Ali meng-(k)irim surat itu　kepada Hasan
　　　　　Ali ACTIVE-send　letter DEF to　　　Hasan
　　　　　'Ali sent the letter to Hasan'

　　　　b.　Ali meng-(k)irim-*kan* Hasan surat itu
　　　　　Ali ACTIVE-send-EXT　Hasan letter DEF
　　　　　'Ali sent Hasan the letter'

(62)　a.　Ali mem-beli　ayam　　itu　untuk Hasan
　　　　　Ali ACTIVE-buy chicken DEF for　　Hasan
　　　　　'Ali bought the chicken for Hasan'

　　　　b.　Ali mem-beli-*kan*　Hasan ayam　　itu
　　　　　Ali ACTIVE-buy-EXT Hasan chicken DEF
　　　　　'Ali bought Hasan the chicken'

These active verbs are all prefixed with the suffix *meN-* which undergoes assimilation with the following stop, and, if the following stop is voiceless as in (61), undergoes further cluster simplification to the plain nasal. Thus, *meN-kirim* becomes *mengirim*. In the (a) examples, the recipient and benefactive NPs are peripheral and this status is reflected by their being preceded by the prepositions *kepada* 'to' and *untuk* 'for'. In the (b) examples, these arguments have become core. This is indicated by their immediate postverbal position and the suffix *-kan* on the verb. As peripheral NPs, recipients and benefactives are not possible PrPs, but, as core, they are:

(63)　a.　*Hasan di-kirim　surat itu　(kepada) oleh Ali
　　　　　Hasan PASS-send letter DEF to　　　by　Ali
　　　　　'Hasan was sent the letter (to) by Ali'

　　　　b.　Hasan di-kirim-*kan*　surat itu oleh Ali
　　　　　Hasan PASS-send-EXT letter DEF by　Ali
　　　　　'Hasan was sent the letter by Ali'

(64)　a.　*Hasan di-beli　ayam　　itu　(untuk) oleh Ali
　　　　　Hasan PASS-buy chicken DEF for　　by　Ali
　　　　　'Hasan was bought the chicken (for) by Ali'

　　　　b.　Hasan di-beli-*kan*　　ayam　itu oleh Ali
　　　　　Hasan PASS-buy-EXT chicken DEF by　Ali
　　　　　'Hasan was bought the chicken by Ali'

The (a) sentences are ungrammatical because regardless of whether the prepositions are present or not, there is no -*kan* suffix on the verb, and consequently the recipient and benefactive NPs must be peripheral. As peripheral constituents they are not potential PrPs, and so these passive sentences are ungrammatical. However, in the (b) sentences with the -*kan* suffix indicating their core status, they are possible PrPs, and so these passives with benefactive and recipient PrPs are grammatical. Thus, Indonesian has a less restricted range of options for possible PrPs than German.

Passives are not restricted to morphologically accusative languages, but are also found in ergative languages. Tzotzil, a Mayan language of Mexico, is a language with verbal inflection on a completely ergative pattern (John Haviland, personal communication):

(65)   a. Bat-em-ø
          go-PERF-3SG(ABS)
          'He's gone'

       b. S-max-ox-ø
          3SG(ERG)-hit-PAST-3SG(ABS)
          'He hit him'

This is verb agreement on an ergative pattern. The actor of the intransitive verb in (65a) and the object of the transitive verb in (65b) are both indicated by a zero suffix, the suffix for third singular absolutive, while the actor of the transitive verb in (65b) is the prefix *s-*, the morpheme for third singular ergative. However, whereas Tzotzil is ergative morphologically, its selection for PrP is like German, an accusative language. The actor is the PrP for an active verb, and therefore, unlike German, there is no consistent morphological marking for the PrP. It is absolutive for an intransitive verb, but ergative for a transitive verb. The PrP is always clause final in Tzotzil. But regardless of the morphology, the notion of PrP in Tzotzil is like that in German. So when an undergoer is needed as PrP in order to meet a coreferentiality constraint as the target for deletion in a subsequent clause, Tzotzil, like German, uses a passive to meet this constraint (John Haviland, personal communication):

(66)   a. S-mil-ox-ø   Xan li Petal e
          3SG(ERG)-kill-PAST-3SG(ABS) John ART Peter
          'Peter killed John'

       b. Mil-bil-ø   yuʔun Petal li   Xan e
          kill-PASS-3SG(ABS) by   Peter ART John
          'John was killed by Peter'

c. A li Petal e bat-em-ø   ta xobel
    TOP ART Peter go-PERF-3SG(ABS) to town

    s-max-ox-ø   li   Anton e
    3SG(ERG)-hit-PAST-3SG(ABS) ART Anton
    'Peter went to town and hit Anton'

d. A li Petal bat-em-ø   ta xobel max-bil-ø
    TOP ART Peter go-PERF-3SG(ABS) to town hit-PASS

    yuʔun li Anton
    by   ART Anton
    'Peter went to town and got hit by Anton'

(66a,b) correspond as an active and passive pair. The passive is formed by marking the actor as an oblique NP with the preposition *yuʔun* 'by', dropping the ergative prefix from the verb and suffixing the verb with the passive suffix *-bil*. In (66c), 'Peter' is the actor for both the first verb and the second verb and, as the PrP, can be the target for deletion in the second clause with no further restructuring. But in (66d), 'Peter' is the undergoer of the second verb, and, in order to be the target for deletion, it must be the PrP. Consequently, a passive construction must be used to present the undergoer as PrP, exactly as in German. Thus, German and Tzotzil, although they are contrasting types morphologically along the lines of accusative versus ergative, both make use of the same notion of PrP.

There are still other languages, notably those of the Philippines, which allow peripheral arguments to be PrPs. These are among the least restrictive languages with regard to selection for PrP. In Tagalog, NPS bearing a wide range of semantic roles can be PrP (marked by *ang*), and the semantic properties of the NP functioning as PrP are indicated by a verbal affix, the focus affix. (See the detailed discussion in Andrews, 1.2, concerning the focus system and its function in Tagalog.) Tagalog has actor focus, patient focus, instrumental focus, etc. constructions.

The non-actor focus constructions may be viewed as passives, in which different non-actor NPS, both core and peripheral, may be PrP, as illustrated below:

(67)   a. Actor focus:
          B[*um*]ili   *ang* lalake ng isda ng   pera   sa
          [*PrP=ACT*]-buy PrP   man   P fish INSTR money LOC
          tindahan
          store

          'The man bought fish with money in the store'

    b. Patient focus:

       B[in]ili-∅   ng lalake *ang* isda ng   pera   sa
       [PERF]-buy-*PrP=P* ACT man   *PrP* fish INSTR money LOC

       tindahan

       store

       'The man bought the fish with money in the store'

    c. Locative focus:

       B[in]ilh-*an*   ng lalake ng isda ng   pera   *ang*
       [PERF]-buy-*PrP=LOC* ACT man   P fish INTR money *PrP*

       tindahan

       store

       'The man bought fish with money in the store'

    d. Instrumental focus:

       Ip[in]*am*-bili   ng lalake ng isda *ang* pera   sa
       [PERF]-*PrP=INSTR*-buy ACT man   P fish *PrP* money LOC

       tindahan

       store

       'The man bought fish with the money in the store'

The actor focus construction in (67a) in which the actor is the PrP corresponds to an active clause in other languages, while the non-actor focus constructions in (67b,c) correspond to passives. In the patient focus passive construction (67b), it is a core constituent which is the PrP, while in the locative and instrumental focus (67c,d), it is clear that peripheral NPS are PrPs. When non-focused these NPS always occur with the oblique peripheral preposition *sa*. Instrumental and locative NPS with a verb like 'buy' are clearly peripheral in that they need not be specified and yet the clause is still semantically complete; this is not the case if the actor or undergoer is omitted. A patient of 'buy' is always understood if not specified, and this reflects its core status. Thus, Tagalog and other Philippine languages have a wider range of choices for PrP than English, German, or Indonesian, allowing both core and peripheral NPS to assume this status.

    However, having claimed that peripheral NPS may be PrPs, several caveats are in order. First, it must be pointed out that passives with peripheral NPS are extremely rare, while passives with core patient NPS are extremely common, being more common than active clauses. Naylor (1975) found no examples of clauses with instrument PrPs and only four with locative PrPs in her entire large corpus of texts and conversations. Furthermore, the range of arguments that a given verb can take as its associated PrP is heavily constrained by the semantics of the verb and its core arguments. For example, a verb with three core arguments, like 'give', cannot have a peripheral locative as its PrP, but an intransitive verb like 'go', with only one core argument, can:

(68) a. *B[in]igy-*an*   ng lalake ng isda sa   bata *ang*
          [PERF]-give-*PrP=LOC* ACT man   P fish LOC child *PrP*
          tindahan
          store
          'The man gave fish to the child in the store'

      b. P[in]untah-*an*   ng lalake *ang* tindahan
          [PERF]-go-*PrP=LOC* ACT man   *PrP* store
          'The man went to the store'

For more details concerning these points, see Ramos (1974) and Naylor (1975).

The parameters which determine PrP choice in Tagalog are exclusively contextually based, and this is a strong diagnostic indicator that the pivot is a pragmatic one. PrPs must be referential and are normally definite. Passive clauses are required in many contexts in Tagalog. For example, relativization in Tagalog is constrained so that the NP head of the relative clause must be coreferential with the PrP of the relative clause, and so a passive construction must be used when the head is coreferential with a non-actor argument:

(69) a. libro-ng *i*-b[in]igay   ng lalake sa bata
          book-REL *PrP=P*-[PERF]-give ACT man LOC child
          'the book which was given to the child by the man'

      b. bata-ng b[in]igy-*an*   ng lalake ng libro
          child-REL [PERF]-give-*PrP=LOC* ACT man   P book
          'the child which was given the book by the man'

      c. *libro-ng *nag*-bigay   *ang* lalake sa   bata
          book-REL *PrP=ACT*-give *PrP* man   LOC child
          'the book which was given to the child by the man'

      d. *libro-ng b[in]igy-*an*   ng lalake *ang* bata
          book-REL [PERF]-give-*PrP=LOC* ACT man   *PrP* child
          'the child which was given the book by the man'

(69a,b) are grammatical because the heads of the relative clauses are coreferential with the patient NP in (69a) and the recipient/locative NP in (69b), and the verbs are inflected for the focus affixes indicating PrP=P and PrP=LOC. The coreferential NP in the relative clause (the PrP) is deleted. (69c,d) are ungrammatical because the head of the relative clause is coreferential with the patient of the relative clauses, but the

PrPs of these clauses are the actor in (69c) and the recipient/locative in (69d).

As noted above, the parameters which determine PrP choice in Tagalog are exclusively contextual. A PrP must be referential and is generally given information. The discourse orientation of the PrP in Tagalog is much greater than that of the English PrP. English subjects, for example, may be non-referential (*it's raining*) and are often new information. In many ways, the Tagalog PrP partakes of many of the features of extended topics, for example in its strong discourse orientation and accessibility to peripheral constituents. In fact, one useful way to view the Tagalog PrP is as a hybrid notion, a topic which is internal to the clause. Tagalog has external topics as well, so topic and PrP are not equivalent. A given clause can have both an external topic and a PrP:

(70) a. Sa babae, *i*-b[in]igay   ng lalake *ang* libro
         LOC woman PrP=P-[PERF]-give ACT man   PrP book
         'To the woman, the man gave the book'

      b. Sa tindahan, b[in]ili-∅   ng lalake *ang* isda
         LOC store   [PERF]-buy-PrP=P ACT man   PrP fish
         'At the store the man bought the fish'

In these examples, the topic is the preverbal NP and the PrP is the NP marked with *ang*. PrPs are also possible topics:

(71) Ang libro 'y *i*-b[in]igay   ng lalake sa babae
      PrP book TOP PrP=P-[PERF]-give ACT man   LOC woman
      'The book, the man gave (it) to the woman'

The correlation between PrP and topic in Austronesian languages is even more apparent in Palauan, a western Austronesian language of Micronesia. In this language, there is a basic passive construction in which all NPs, whether core or peripheral, are potential PrPs. In Palauan, like Tagalog, relativization is restricted to coreferential PrPs and, thus, the passive is necessary to the formation of relative clauses on non-actor arguments. The Palauan passive is marked by a special set of verb prefixes which agree with the actor and a pronoun or verb suffix which agrees with the PrP. The position of the PrP is clause initial:

(72) a. A ?ad a mos-terir   a ngalek
         ART man see-3PL(HUMAN) ART child
         'The man saw the children'

      b. A ngalek a le-bos-terir   a ?ad
         ART child   PASS 3SG-see-3PL(HUMAN) ART men
         'The children were seen by the men'

c. A ngelek-ek a s[m]e?er   er   a   tereter
   ART child-my   [INTRANS]-sick with ART cold
   'My child is sick with a cold'

d. A tereter a l-se?er   er ngiy a ngelek-ek
   ART cold   PASS 3SG-sick with 3SG ART child-my
   'With a cold is being sick by my child'

In (72) there are active and passive pairs. In (72b) a core argument is the PrP, but in (72d) a peripheral argument has this status.

Note the strong similarity of Palauan passive constructions to left-dislocations. A trace pronoun of the PrP is left in its normal position in the clause, exactly as in a left-dislocation. These Palauan passives cannot be simply dismissed as left-dislocations, however, because they result in major rearrangement of the clause structure as well as requiring special verbal prefixes agreeing with the passive actor (see Keenan, 1.5). Furthermore, they are required in the formation of relative clauses. The following examples illustrate the role of the passive in relativization:

(73) a. a le-bos-terir   a ?ad el ngalek
          ART PASS 3SG-see-3PL(HUMAN) ART man REL child
          'the children which were seen by the man'

      b. *a ?ad a mos-terir   el ngalek
          ART man see-3PL(HUMAN) REL child
          'the children which were seen by the man'

      c. a l-se?er   er ngiy a ngelek-ek el tereter
          ART PASS 3SG-sick with 3SG   child-my REL cold
          'the cold that my child is sick with'

      d. *a ngelek-ek a s[m]e?er   (er ngiy) el tereter
          ART child-my   [INTRANS]-sick with it   REL cold
          'the cold that my child is sick with'

In (73) we have relative clauses in which the head is coreferential with a non-actor argument which is core in (73a) and peripheral in (73c). In both cases the passive must be used. Failure to use the passive in (73b) and (73d) results in ungrammaticality.

The explanation for these Palauan data seems to be that a left-dislocation or topicalization construction began to be used in relative clauses to meet the constraint that only topical NPs were relativizable. The topic position in Palauan is preverbal, but normally only actors occur in topic position. However, this odd left-dislocation construction was innovated to allow other NP types, core object NPs as well as peripheral NPs, to occur there, leaving pronominal traces in their normal position in the clause. This accounts for the strong similarity of the PrP in Palauan to the notion of external topic. It may also explain somewhat the situation in Tagalog and other Philippine languages. The focus systems in these languages may have evolved in a similar way to meet a similar need, but generally the topic became the pivot for more and more of the syntactic processes of the languages and became part of the internal structural of the clause – a PrP. This would explain why the Tagalog PrP shares features of topics, and would account for some of the unique features of Philippine focus systems in contrast to Indo-European voice systems. The moral of the story seems to be that it may be inadvisable to draw too sharp a distinction between 'internal topicalization' constructions like passive and 'external topicalization' constructions like left-dislocations.

3.1.2 Backgrounding passives

We have discussed passives thus far in terms of their function of permitting non-actors to occur as PrP. In promoting the non-actor to PrP status the actor is necessarily displaced. It may occur as the object of a pre/postposition as in German, English, Tzotzil and Indonesian; it may change its case marking as in Russian, where the actor is in the nominative case in an active clause but is in the instrumental case in a passive; or it may be eliminated altogether. Generally, with passives, the actor may be eliminated in a passive construction, and in many languages it must be. For example, English and German permit the passive actor either to be expressed or omitted, while Ulcha (Manchu-Tungus, Siberia; Nichols 1979) does not allow the actor to be mentioned in a passive. Another important difference in passive constructions among languages concerns the case-marking or coding properties (see Andrews, 1.2) of the non-actor pivot NP. Compare German, (74a,b), with Ulcha, (74c):

(74)   a. Das   Butterbrot wurde   gegessen   (cf. (55b))
          the(NOM) sandwich   became(3SG) eaten
          'The sandwich was eaten'

       b. Die   Frau   wurde   gekidnappt   (cf. (56d))
          the(NOM) woman became(3SG) kidnapped
          'The woman was kidnapped'

       c. Ti   dūse-we hōn-da ta-wuri?
          DEM tiger-ACC how-PCL do-PASS
          'What's to be done about that tiger?'

The German examples follow the usual pattern in that the undergoer is in the nominative case as a PrP. In Ulcha, the undergoer remains in the accusative case. The difference in case marking for the undergoer in Ulcha and German brings up an important question. While the undergoer in passive clauses in German is a PrP (in the nominative) in that it controls and is the target for zero anaphora, can the same be claimed of this accusatively marked NP in Ulcha? Nichols (1979) demonstrates that it is, in fact, nominative NPs, not accusatives, which control and are the target for zero anaphora:

(75) Ti dūse-ø ilzu-mi   erke herelu-mi   nantiti
      DEM tiger-NOM stand-SG SIM slowly turn-SG SIM at them
      iceheni
      (he) looked
      'The tiger, standing up, slowly turning around, looked at them'

Here the actor, nominatively case-marked *dūse* 'tiger' behaves like a PrP in controlling zero anaphora in the conjoined clauses. This zero anaphora is indicated by the suffix -*mi* on the verbs, which signals that the actions of the two verbs are simultaneous(SIM). Nichols (1979) claims that an accusative NP, as in the passive in (74c), does not have this syntactic property, and it cannot therefore be a PrP.

If the accusative in (74c) is not a PrP, then, as there is no other possible candidate, we must conclude that this clause does not have a PrP. The fact that passive clauses in Ulcha are PrP-less while those in German do have a PrP points to an important difference between the two languages.

In order to understand this difference it is necessary to go back to the general notion of pivot introduced in 3.1, as an NP type of crucial importance in controlling or being the target of many of the syntactic processes in the language. We further distinguished two types of pivots: semantic pivots (SmP) and pragmatic pivots (PrP). When the choice of pivot in a clause is motivated by considerations of discourse topicality (section 1.1) and is not automatically determined by semantic rule, i.e. by whether an NP is actor or undergoer, then the pivot is a pragmatic one. In German the selection of the PrP with a transitive verb is not determined by the semantic functions of the arguments of the verb, but rather by their salience and importance in the ongoing discourse. Thus, German has a pragmatic pivot, as do the other languages discussed so far.

In many other languages, however, this is not the case; the choice of the pivot in a clause is not affected by the information status of NPs in discourse, but rather by their semantic function. In such languages the actor is the pivot of a transitive verb, and this choice cannot be overridden for the purpose of expressing that a particular NP is more salient than the actor in a particular discourse. This is the case in Ulcha, where the actor is only one possible choice for the pivot of a verb; the pivot may be deleted in a passive, but no other NP may assume pivot status (see Nichols 1979).

While the actor controls zero anaphora in Ulcha, as in (75), and consequently is the pivot for this construction, it is a semantic pivot (smP), because pivot selection is strictly semantically determined: no other NP type may ever be the pivot in this construction. Zero anaphora is the diagnostic test for pragmatic pivots only when more than one NP type, for example both actor and undergoer, is accessible to pivot status, proving that the pivot choice is in fact sensitive to discourse and pragmatic factors, and is not an automatic consequence of the presence of a particular semantic role, such as actor.

The contrast between PrP and smP can be illustrated in the following data from German, (76), and Choctaw, (77) (Muskogean, North America; Heath 1977) (U = Undergoer):

(76)　　a. Die　　　　Hausfrau　hat　　　zwei　Bücher
　　　　　　the(NOM) housewife have(3SG) two　book(ACC PL)

　　　　　　gekauft
　　　　　　bought
　　　　　　'The housewife bought two books'

　　　　　b. Zwei Bücher　　　　　wurden　　　von der
　　　　　　two　books(NOM PL) became(3PL) by　the(DAT)

　　　　　　Hausfrau　gekauft
　　　　　　housewife bought
　　　　　　'Two books were bought by the housewife'

(77)　　a. Hattak at　　ø-iya-h
　　　　　　man　　smP 3(ACT)-go-PRES
　　　　　　'The man goes'

　　　　　b. Hattak at　　ø-abi:ka-h
　　　　　　man　　smP 3(U)-be sick-PRES
　　　　　　'The man is sick'

　　　　　c. Hattak at　　oho:yoh (a:)　　ø-ø-pisa-h
　　　　　　man　　smP woman　(OBL)　3(ACT)-3(U)-see-PRES
　　　　　　'The man sees the woman'

　　　　　d. Hattak at　　oho:yoh (a:)　　i:-ø-nokso:pa-h
　　　　　　man　　smP woman　(OBL)　3(DAT)-3(U)-be afraid-PRES
　　　　　　'The man is afraid of the woman'

In the German sentences in (76) the verb *kaufen* 'buy' has two arguments, *die Hausfrau* 'the housewife', the actor, and *zwei Bücher* 'two books', the undergoer. Either argument may appear as PrP in the nominative case, the choice being governed by discourse factors (Zubin 1979).

Choctaw, as illustrated in (77), has both nominal and verbal case marking. The affixes on the verb indicate the semantic functions (actor, undergoer, locative) of its arguments, while the nominal marking (by means of articles + suffix) signals only a binary smP/non-smP or oblique distinction. The choice of the NP marked by *a-t* 'the-smP' is fixed by the semantics of the predicate and is not affected by the discourse topicality or salience of the arguments. There is a semantic function hierarchy of actor > undergoer > locative such that the highest ranking NP in the clause is marked by *at*. In (77a,b) there is only one NP in the clause, and it receives *at*. In (77c) *hattak* 'man' is the actor and hence is marked by *at*, whereas *oho:yah* 'woman' is the undergoer and takes the optional oblique marker *a:* (<*a-n* 'the-OBL'). The person who is afraid is coded as an undergoer with the verb *nokso:pa* 'be afraid of', and the cause of the fear is expressed as a locative argument; consequently *hattak* 'man', the undergoer who is afraid, receives *at* marking and *oho:yoh* 'woman', the locative argument, gets oblique marking. These NP case-marking possibilities are thus determined by the semantic functions of the arguments, and not by their salience in discourse.

There is no passive construction in Choctaw analogous to that in German which would allow the undergoer of *pisa* 'see' or the dative argument of *nokso:pa* 'be afraid of', to occur as pivot with *at* marking. Thus the NP marked by *at* is not a PrP analogous to the nominative case NP in German, and we may conclude that Choctaw is a language which has semantically determined pivots (smP) rather than pragmatically determined pivots (PrP). Choctaw is similar to Ulcha in that the smP controls a type of zero anaphora across clauses. Choctaw has an elaborate system of switch-reference, with a verb taking a suffix which indicates whether its smP is the same as or different from the smP of the next clause (Heath 1977).

We began this discussion of smPs versus PrPs with a comparison of passive constructions in German and Ulcha. The characteristic feature of the Ulcha passive is the elimination of the smP without changing the syntactic status of the undergoer-accusative NP. Such constructions are also found in Nanai, (78a) (Manchu-Tungus, Siberia; Nichols 1979) and Finnish, (78b) (Comrie 1977):

(78)   a. Ej dansa-wa tej erinčie xola-o-xan   bičin
           DEM book-ACC DEM time   read-PASS-PAST AUX(PAST)
           'The book had already been read by that time'

        b. Han-et jätettiin kotiin
           he-ACC was left at home
           'He was left at home'

These examples, along with the one from Ulcha, illustrate the second
major function of passive constructions: the removal of the actor from
the core of the clause. This is accomplished in either of two ways: (i) the
actor is demoted to the periphery of the clause, or (ii) it is not expressed
at all. Both of these options are available in some languages, like
English, German, and Tzotzil, while others, such as Nanai and Finnish,
have only the second option. We thus have two different major
functions which passives may serve. Passives which serve to permit a
non-actor to occur as PrP we will label *foregrounding passives*.

Foregrounding passives are features of languages with pragmatic
pivots. The foregrounding passive functions to allow the non-actor core
argument to occupy the PrP position in place of the actor. Foregrounding
passives may also be called *pragmatic passives* by virtue of their
association with accessibility to pragmatic pivots or perhaps *rearranging
passives*, as they function to rearrange the normal choice for pivot of the
clause. Those passives which function to eliminate the actor from the
core of the clause we will call *backgrounding passives*.

In some languages, one construction may have both of these functions. In German and English, as we have seen, the passive construction
both allows a non-actor to occur as PrP and removes the actor from the
core, with optional deletion. However, as is clear from the definitions of
these two types of passives, the two functions are logically independent
of each other and consequently need not co-occur in the same general
constructions.

A very common type of semantic passive which does not allow the
expression of an actor is a construction in which a transitive verb has
been detransitivized, and often stativized, and only the undergoer is
present. This stativization is a very common effect of the backgrounding
passive. Such constructions are often called *mediopassives* or *middle
voice* (MID) rather than passives. The following examples are from
Choctaw, (79) (Nicklas 1974) and Chichewa, (80) (Bantu, Africa;
Watkins 1937):

(79)   a. Bill at   okhisa an tiwwih
           Bill smP door   OBL he opens it
           'Bill is opening the door'

b. Okhisa at   tinwah
   door   smP open(MID)
   'The door is open'

(80) a. Chifußá chámunthi chirumi-ka
         chest   of-person bite-MID
         'The man's chest is (being) bitten'

      b. Mwaná wáŋgá wapandí-ka
         child   my   beat-MID
         'My child has been beaten'

These constructions differ from the German (74a,b) in two ways. First, although the undergoer is now the pivot, it is not a PrP, but an smP, as these languages lack PrPs. Second, there is no implication of any kind of actor in them; this is particularly clear in (79b). These constructions differ from those in Nanai, Ulcha and Finnish in allowing the undergoer to occur as smP. Such constructions are also found in languages with PrPs, such as German, (81), and Spanish, (82):

(81) a. Mein   Wagen wird   (von dem   Mechaniker
         my(NOM) car   become(3SG) by the(DAT) mechanic

         repariert
         repaired
         'My car is (being) fixed (by the mechanic)'

      b. Mein   Wagen ist   (*von dem   Mechaniker)
         my(NOM) car   be(3SG)   by the(DAT) mechanic

         repariert
         repaired
         'My car is fixed (*by the mechanic)'

      c. Das   macht   sich leicht
         that(NOM) make(3SG)   REFL easily
         'That is easily done'

(82) a. Se   abre   la puerta
         REFL   open(3SG)   the door
         'The door is open'

      b. Se   quemaron   las   casas
         REFL   burn(3PL PAST) the(PL) house(PL)
         'The houses burned down'

German has two different constructions for the total suppression of the actor. The regular German foregrounding passive uses *werden* 'become' as its auxiliary, and it can take an overt peripheral actor phrase, as in (81a). German passives may also be formed with *sein* 'be' as the auxiliary, and in such forms, as in (81b), no actor can be expressed, and the sentence has a stative meaning. This is a background-ing passive. German also has a construction involving the reflexive pronoun *sich* which serves to allow the object as PrP with no expression of an actor. It is illustrated in (81c). Spanish has a similar reflexive-mediopassive form as in (82). These German and Spanish reflexive-mediopassives are also backgrounding passives.

Other languages possess passives which, although they totally sup-press the actor, do not detransitivize or stativize the clause. Fijian (Austronesian) is a language of this type:

(83)   a. E   ∅   a   kau-ti   ira   na gone
           CLAUSE MARKER 3SG(ACT) PAST carry-TRANS 3PL(U) ART child

           na tūraga
           ART chief
           'The chief carried the children'

        b. E   ra   a   kau-ti   na gone
           CLAUSE MARKER 3PL(SUBJ) PAST carry-TRANS ART child

           (*e na tūraga)
           (by the chief)
           'The children were carried'

In Fijian a verb in a transitive clause is marked by a proclitic indicating the person and number of the actor, a verbal suffix which indicates transitivity, and an enclitic for the person and number of the object. The actor is the normal SMP for a transitive clause. In (83a), an active transitive clause, the actor proclitic is ∅ for '3SG' and the object enclitic is *ira* for '3PL'. (83b) is a passive clause, and the actor may not be expressed. It is clearly a passive in that the object now agrees as an SMP, like the actor in a normal transitive clause, with the pronominal proclitic *ra* for '3PL' SMP. The verb, although passive, still retains the transitive suffix and is semantically active, not stative. This contrasts with the detransitivizing, stativizing mediopassives of Choctaw, Chichewa, German and Spanish.

We previously saw backgrounding passives which were pivotless, in which no NP took up the pivot position of the actor. These were passive constructions in Ulcha, (74c), Nanai, (78a), and Finnish, (78b), all languages without PrPs. Most languages with PrPs seem to require a new core argument to take up the PrP functions, but there are some languages of this type which allow the demotion of the actor, but do not require another NP to take up the PrP position. Dutch, (84), and other

Germanic languages make use of this possibility with their so-called impersonal passives (Kirsner 1976):

(84)   a. Er   wordt   door de jongens gefloten
          there become(3SG) by   the boys   whistled
          'There is whistling by the boys'

       b. Er   wordt   door de studenten gestaakt
          there become(3SG) by   the students struck
          'There is a strike by the students'

       c. Er   woorden   daar huizen gebouwd
          there became(3PL) there houses built
          'There were houses built there'

These constructions are possible with both intransitive (84a,b) and transitive (84c) verbs; the (c) example is from John Verhaar (personal communication). With a transitive verb the undergoer remains the direct object; it does not become PrP. These sentences are PrP-less. The actor is no longer PrP, as indicated by its oblique status, as well as by the fact that it no longer controls, nor is it the target for, typical PrP functions like zero anaphora across clauses (Kirsner 1976):

(85   a.   De vrouwen lachten en huilden
           the women   laughed and cried
           'The women laughed and cried'

      b. *Er   werd   door de vrouwen gelachen en
           there became(3SG) by   the women   laughed and
           __ huilden
              cried
           '*There was laughing by the women and cried'

The *er* is just a dummy pivot holder; it is non-referential and not a PrP.

Earlier we defined backgrounding passives as those constructions which remove the actor from the core, either presenting it as an oblique NP or deleting it entirely, and foregrounding passives as those in which a non-actor occurs as PrP. These two functions are independent of each other, and there are four possible types of passives which result from their interaction. We can have a backgrounding passive which demotes the actor, but does not promote a non-actor to SmP/PrP. The Dutch impersonal passive, as well as those in Nanai, Ulcha and Finnish, are examples of this type. On the other hand, there are backgrounding passives which demote the actor, but also promote a non-actor argument to SmP status. Choctaw, Chichewa, and Fijian are languages of this type. Foregrounding passives promote a non-actor to PrP status. One type of foregrounding passive, exemplified by German and English, promotes a non-actor to PrP and, secondarily, removes the actor from the core, as in a backgrounding passive. Other languages do not require this backgrounding passive-like side effect with their foregrounding passives. These languages promote a non-actor NP to PrP, but allow the actor to remain a core argument. This type of foregrounding passive is found in Lango, a Nilo-Saharan language of East Africa (Noonan and Bavin Woock 1978) and in Philippine languages.

In Lango, the PrP is always the leftmost NP in the clause. The actor normally occupies this PrP position. Lango has a foregrounding passive which places the non-actor core argument before the actor argument, but no other change is effected in the clause:

(86)   a. Dákó   ò-jwát-ò   lócà
            woman 3SG(ACT)-hit-3SG(U) man
            'The woman hit the man'

        b. Lócà dákó   ò-jwát-ò
            man woman 3SG(ACT)-hit-3SG(U)
            'The man was hit by the woman'

(87)   a. Lócà ò-mí-ɔ̀   mɔ̀t bɔ̀t àtín
            man 3SG(ACT)-gave-3SG(U) gift to   child
            'The man gave the gift to the child'

        b. Àtín lócà ò-mí-ɔ̀   mɔt bɔt-ɛ
            child man 3SG(ACT)-gave-3SG(U) gift to(3SG)
            'The child was given the gift by the man'

The passive is restricted to core arguments, as in the examples in (86) and (87). The passive PrP occurs first and the remainder of the clause follows it. There are no changes in verbal morphology or case marking associated with the passive. This is clearly a foregrounding passive, in that the fronted NP controls the cross-clausal properties in a manner typical of PrPs.

(88)   a. Dákó   ò-nén-ò   lócà tè   jwâtt-ò
            woman 3SG(ACT)-see-3SG(U) man and then hit-3SG(U)
            'The woman saw the man and then *she* hit *him*'

        b. Lócà dákó   ò-nén-ò   tè   jwâtt-ò
            man woman 3SG(ACT)-see-3SG(U) and then hit-3SG(U)
            'The man was seen by the woman and then *he* hit *her*'

In (88) the actor and PrP of the second clause with *jwâtt-ò* 'hit her' is determined by coreferentiality with the PrP of the first clause. In (88a) in which the first clause is active and the PrP is the actor *dákó* 'woman', then the PrP and actor of the second clause must also be *dákó* 'woman'. However, in (88b) the first clause is passive and the PrP is *lócà* 'man'. Therefore, the PrP and actor of the second clause must be *lócà* 'man'. Thus, as is typical with PrPs, the first NP both controls and is the target for zero anaphora under coreference.

In contrast to languages like English or German, however, all evidence seems to indicate that in Lango the actor in a passive construction is not a peripheral but a core argument. We employ here some of the general diagnostic tests for core versus peripheral constituents in Andrews (1.2). As a core argument, the actor may still function as a pivot (smP) for certain actor-linked grammatical constructions. Peripheral arguments never function significantly as pivots in a language. First, the actor continues to control verb agreement in passives (see examples above), a feature of core arguments. Actors in English passive clauses no longer control verb agreement:

(89)   a. The woman is kissing me

      b. I am/*is being kissed by the woman

But there are stronger bits of evidence as well. Actors, whether in active or passive clauses, are the controllers of reflexivization.

(90)   a. Lócà ò-kwá-ò   dákó   pìr-έ   kὲnὲ
        man 3SG(ACT)-ask-3SG(U) woman about-3SG self
        'The man asked the woman about *herself/*himself*'

      b. Dákó lócà ò-kwá-ò   pìr-έ   kὲnὲ
        woman man 3SG(ACT)-ask-3SG(U) about-3SG self
        'The woman was asked by the man about *herself/*himself*'

Whether the actor *lócà* 'man' is PrP or not, the reflexive is always coreferential with it. In English the actor in a passive clause may never be coreferential with a reflexive:

(91)   a. John talked to Mary about himself

      b. *Mary was talked to by John about himself

The fact that actors in passive clauses can control reflexivization in Lango, but not in English, is due to the fact that in Lango they are core constituents, while in English they are peripheral.

Addressee of imperatives is another actor-controlled property:

(92)   a. Jwât-á   (án)!
        hit-1SG(U) me
        'Hit me!'

b. Án jwât-á!
   me hit-1SG(U)
   'Hit me!'

Here the second person addressee is actor in both the active and passive clauses. But in English, actors in passives are not possible addressees in imperatives:

(93)   a.   Close the door!

       b.   *Be the door closed (by you)!

This difference in behaviour between passive actors in Lango and English reflects their core status in Lango, but peripheral status in English.

The foregrounding passives in Philippine languages, traditionally known as the focus types and discussed earlier, are exactly parallel to Lango. They are foregrounding passives in which the actor remains a core argument. Actors in passive clauses control reflexivization and are the addressee of imperatives, as these Tagalog examples illustrate:

(94)   a.   B[um]ili   ng isda para sa   kaniyang sarili *ang* lalake
            [PrP=ACT]-buy P   fish BEN LOC his   self   PrP man
            'The man bought some fish for himself'

       b.   *I*-b[in]ili   ng lalake ng isda *ang* kaniyang
            PrP=BEN-[PERF]-buy ACT man   P   fish PrP his
            sarili
            self
            'The man bought some fish for himself'

       c.   *B[um]ili   ng isda para sa   lalake *ang* kaniya sarili
            [PrP=ACT]-buy ACT fish BEN LOC man   PrP his   self
            'The man bought some fish for himself'

       d.   *I*-b[in]ili   ng kaniyang sarili ng isda *ang* lalake
            PrP=BEN-[PERF]-buy ACT his   self   P fish PrP man
            'The man bought himself some fish'

(95)   a.   B[um]ili   ka   ng isda sa   bata
            [PrP=ACT]-buy you(PrP) P   fish LOC child
            'Buy some fish from the child'

       b.   Bi[in]ili-ø   mo   *ang* isda sa   bata
            [PERF]-buy-PrP=P you(ACT) PrP fish LOC child
            'Buy the fish from the child'

The actor is the only controller of reflexivization. In (94a,b) the actor controls reflexivization of the benefactive, regardless of whether it is the PrP (as in (94a)) or not (as in (94b)). (94c,d) are ungrammatical because the benefactive is controlling reflexivization of the actor. Whether the benefactive is the PrP (as in (94d)) or not (as in (94c)) is irrelevant. Both sentences are ungrammatical. (95a,b) show the actor as addressee of the imperative, regardless of its status as PrP. In (95a) the actor is PrP, and in (95b) it is not, but both sentences are perfectly grammatical. These facts exactly parallel Lango and demonstrate that the actor in passive clauses in Tagalog is a core argument, in contrast to English in which it is peripheral.

We mentioned earlier that verb agreement is a general feature of core arguments. While Tagalog does not have verb agreement for any of its verbal arguments, Kapampangan, another Philippine language (Miriki-tani 1972), does have verbal agreement for actors, whether they are PrP or not.

(96)   a. S[*um*]ulat   *ya*   ng poesia *ing* lalaki
          [*PrP=ACT*]-write *3SG(PrP)* P   poem PrP man
          'The man will write a poem'

      b. *I*-sulat   na   *ya*   *ing* poesia ning lalaki
          PrP=P-write 3SG(ACT) *3SG(PrP)* PrP poem ACT man
          'The man will write the poem'

That the actor in passive clauses in Kapampangan continues to control verb agreement is further evidence of its core status.

Bantu languages present a passive construction different in certain crucial respects from any discussed thus far. Bantu languages have passive constructions with expressed actors, which are superficially similar to the corresponding English or German sentences. Note these Chichewa examples (Trithart 1979):

(97)   a. Jóni a-ná-meny-a   m-ái   w-áŋgá
          John 3SG(ACT)-PAST-hit-INDIC mother my
          'John hit my mother'

      b. M-ái   w-áŋgá a-na-meny-*edw*-a   ndí Joní
          mother my   3SG(ACT)-PAST-hit-*PASS*-INDIC by John
          'My mother was hit by John'

In Chichewa, as in other Bantu languages, subjects always show agreement in gender class and number, with a verbal prefix, for example *a*- in (97). In an active construction such as (97a) the actor controls verb agreement and appears as the preverbal NP. In a passive like (97b) the undergoer appears before the verb and controls verb agreement, while the actor appears in an oblique phrase after the verb. The verb is inflected with the passive suffix -edw as well. This construction shows a striking similarity to the English passive, and has often been analysed in a similar way. This would suggest that the Bantu passive, represented here by Chichewa, is a foregrounding passive. But there are several problems with this analysis which suggest that it is not correct.

Unlike other foregrounding passives, which are only present in languages with PrPs in which the choice of which NP is the PrP is determined by discourse contextual factors, Bantu passives are basically sensitive to inherent semantic factors of the NP arguments of the verbs, such as person and animacy (section 1.2). Trithart (1979) argues that passive is favoured when the NP to become subject is higher on the inherent pivot hierarchy, discussed earlier:

> 1st person > 2nd person > proper human > common human > animate > inanimate

or on the following role hierarchy:

> recipient/benefactive > patient > instrument

The role hierarchy is simply another version of the inherent salience hierarchy, because benefactives and recipients are generally human, patients may be animate or inanimate, and instrumentals are generally inanimate. The Bantu passive simply operates to put higher ranking NPs on this hierarchy in pivot position. In one sense, it is not really like a passive at all; it is rather more like the inverse person-marking system of Algonquian discussed in section 1.2. Since it does, however, demote the actor to a peripheral constituent, it has the function of a backgrounding passive. The Bantu passive may be profitably viewed as a type of backgrounding passive demoting the actor combined with an Amerindian-like inverse person-marking system. The passive operates to place as pivot an NP more salient than the actor in terms of inherent salience (the inverse person-marking function) and to place the lower ranking actor in an oblique peripheral phrase (the backgrounding passive function).

A possible alternative would be to claim that these Bantu passives are in fact foregrounding passives with the normal corresponding backgrounding passive side-effects. However, this is somewhat problematic in that they would be the only known cases of foregrounding passives operating in PrP-less languages, functioning to place non-actor core arguments in SmP position, rather than PrP. The Bantu pivots do seem to be smPs in that their selection is semantically determined by role and person/animacy considerations, and they do not function as discourse topics in the maintenance of discourse cohesion through coreference systems, such as zero anaphora. Rather, the coreference monitoring functions of PrPs are handled in Bantu by the elaborate nominal class-concord system. These examples are from Chichewa (Watkins 1937):

(98)   a. Mwará   wá-ŋgá u-kú   phi chifukwá mɔtɔ
          stone(CL2a) CL2a-my CL2a-become hot reason   fire(CL2a)

          wá-úkúrú u-wu-tɛ:nth-a
          CL2a-big CL2a(ACT)-CL2a(U)-burn-INDIC
          'My stone is becoming hot because the big fire is burning it'

       b. Chámkɔlέ   chá-nú   cháchí-kú·rú chí-tha:ß-a
          hostage(CL6) CL6-your CL6-valuable CL6(ACT)-run away-INDIC

          á-chí-gwir-á   ni mu·nthu
          CLI(ACT)-CL6(U)-catch-INDIC   is person(CLI)
          'Your valuable hostage is running away and the man is catching him'

In these examples the coreference of actor and undergoer across the clauses is indicated by the verbal concord prefixes. There is no passive used, as would be the case in languages with foregrounding passives. Note that the verb agreement in the second clause of (98b) clearly identifies the person *mu·nthu* (class I) as the actor with the class I prefix in the actor slot and the hostagé *chámkɔlέ* (class 6) as the undergoer, as the class 6 prefix is in the undergoer slot. The undergoer of the second clause is coreferential with the actor of the first clause, as indicated by the class 6 subject agreement in the first clause, but a passive is not used. In a language with PrPs and foregrounding passives like Tzotzil or Indonesian, a passive construction with zero pronominalization of the PrP would be used in the second clause of an example like (98b). Chichewa seems to lack a PrP, and the passive is best analysed as a backgrounding one, performing a function parallel to inverse person marking.

3.1.3 *Summary of passive constructions*

Our discussion of passives may be summarized as follows. Passives may be divided into two general types according to their function. Passives which serve to remove the actor from the core of the clause are backgrounding passives, whereas those which function to permit a non-actor to occur as pivot are foregrounding passives. Foregrounding passives are found only in languages which have PrPs (with the possible exception of Bantu), that is, in languages in which the choice of pivot is governed by salience of an argument in discourse (cf. section 3.1). Backgrounding passives, on the other hand, are not so constrained and occur both in PrP and smP languages. Table 6.3 presents the various backgrounding and foregrounding passives we have discussed.

There are two kinds of backgrounding passives found in smP languages. The first type, exemplified in (74c) for Ulcha, (78a) for Nanai and (78b) for Finnish, involves the elimination of the actor from the clause without any other NP assuming smP status. The second type, illustrated with the mediopassive constructions from Choctaw in (79) and Chichewa in (80), again entails the removal of the actor from the clause, but in this case the undergoer takes over smP status.

Both backgrounding and foregrounding passives are found in PrP languages. There are two kinds of backgrounding passives. In both, the actor is removed from the core of the clause, but they differ as to whether a non-actor becomes the PrP. In the impersonal passives from Dutch in (84–5) the non-active does not become the PrP; whereas in Spanish mediopassives with *se* in (82), and German *sein*-passives and *sich*-mediopassives in (81), the non-actor does assume PrP status. There are likewise two types of foregrounding passives, both of which allow a non-actor to occur as PrP. They are distinguished by the status of the actor. In Philippine languages and Lango (cf. 86–95) it is still a core argument of the verb, while in German (*werden*-passives), English, Tzotzil and Indonesian it is peripheral (cf. 55–66).

The effects which semantic and pragmatic passives have on the meaning of a sentence have often been characterized in terms of the notions of *foregrounding* and *backgrounding*: hence the cover terms we have used for the two types. They are based on the spatial metaphor of looking at a sentence as being somehow analogous to a landscape or photograph, such that elements in the foreground are more salient and important than those in the background. The foreground of a sentence is constituted by the PrP or smP and, to a lesser extent, the verb and the other core argument. The background consists of the non-topicalized peripheral elements of the sentence. Given this characterization, it is easy to see how the promotion to PrP status of a non-actor can be viewed as a kind of foregrounding, and how the removal of the actor from the core of the clause can be interpreted as backgrounding. However, these terms are used more generally to describe any kind of enhancing or demoting operation. For example, it has been argued by some linguists

Table 6.3 *Summary of passive constructions*

SmP languages	PrP languages	
Backgrounding passives	Backgrounding passives	Foregrounding passives
1 ACT=X(-ACT≠SmP) Nanai Ulcha Finnish	1 ACT=X(-ACT≠PrP) Dutch (impersonal)	1 -ACT=PrP(ACT≠X) Tagalog Lango
2 ACT=X(-ACT=SmP) Choctaw Chichewa	2 ACT=X(-ACT=PrP) Spanish (*se*-mediopassive) German (*sich*-mediopassive, *sein*-passive)	2 -ACT=PrP(ACT=X) German (*werden*-passive) English Tzotzil Indonesian

Note: X = 'non-core'

that the kind of backgrounding passive found in Nanai and Finnish involves foregrounding of the undergoer, because the removal of the actor makes it the only core argument, and hence more salient.

This general sense of foregrounding and backgrounding is useful in that it renders intelligible the kinds of constructions which certain languages use to approximate the functions of backgrounding and foregrounding passives. There are many languages which lack all of the constructions summarized in Table 6.3. Nevertheless, they do have means of expressing that a non-actor is more important than the actor. The most common way of doing this is to use a construction in which the verb is not specified for a particular actor but rather is indefinite as to who is doing the action, analogous to English 'they are painting the house', or 'someone is painting the house'. The following examples are from Lakhota (Siouan, North America):

(99)   a. Wičháša ki   hená matho ki   ∅-kté-pi
           men   the those bear   the 3SG(U)-kill-3PL(ACT)
           'The men killed the bear'
        b. Mathó ki   ∅-kté-pi
           bear   the 3SG(U)-kill-3PL(ACT)
           'They killed the bear' or 'The bear was killed'

The Lakhota sentences in (99) illustrate the contrast between a specified third person plural subject, as in (99a), and an indefinite subject, as in (99b). In both sentences the actor is still part of the core, but it is backgrounded in (99b) because of its unspecified reference. Moreover, *mathó ki* 'the bear' can be said to be foregrounded, as it is now the only NP in the sentence, but its syntactic status in the clause is unchanged, as it is still the object of *kté* 'kill'. Thus, languages which lack formal passive constructions of both types can employ other devices to achieve the foregrounding and backgrounding effects of backgrounding and foregrounding passives.

The backgrounding and foregrounding passives given in Table 6.3 reflect different packaging options which languages have. Foregrounding passives are concerned primarily with the packaging of the undergoer, and in most cases this will also have consequences for the expression of the actor. Backgrounding passives, on the other hand, affect the actor primarily, very often eliminating it from the clause entirely. In many languages this has implications for the presentation of the undergoer, which may assume the case marking and syntactic status of the actor, becoming an SMP. In short, both backgrounding and foregrounding passives afford the speakers of the languages in which they occur a number of options for expressing lexical material in a clause.

3.2 *Antipassive*
3.2.1 *Foregrounding antipassives*
In our discussion of passives in 3.1.1 we mentioned that foregrounding passives are found in ergative languages, and gave Tzotzil as an example. Some ergative languages also have a type of construction which is functionally parallel to foregrounding passives in accusative languages like German, English and Indonesian. In these ergative languages the PrP is signalled by the absolutive case, as in the following examples from Dyirbal (Australia; Dixon 1972):

(100) a. Balan   dyugumbil   bani-nyu
          CL(ABS) woman(ABS ACT) come-TNS
          'Woman came'

       b. Balan   dyugumbil   bangul yaṛangu   buṛa-n
          CL(ABS) woman(ABS U) CL(ERG) man(ERG ACT) see-TNS
          'Man saw woman'

That the absolutive NP is the PrP can be seen from the following sentences:

(101) a. Balan   dyugumbil   bani-nyu __ bangul
          CL(ABS) woman(ABS ACT) come-TNS   CL(ERG)

          yaṛangu   buṛa-n
          man(ERG ACT) see-TNS
          'Woman came and man saw [her]'

       b. *Bayi   yaṛa   bani-nyu balan   dyugumbil   __
          CL(ABS) man(ABS ACT) come-TNS CL(ABS) woman(ABS U)

          buṛa-n
          see-TNS
          'Man came and saw woman'

       c. Balan   dyugumbil   bangul yaṛangu   buṛa-n __
          CL(ABS) woman(ABS U) CL(ERG) man(ERG ACT) see-TNS

          waynydyi-n
          go uphill-TNS
          'Man saw woman and [she] went uphill'
          (*'Man saw woman and went uphill')

These sentences illustrate that the NP in the absolutive case is the controller and target for zero anaphora, and thus is the PrP. In (101a) *balan dyugumbil* 'woman' is omitted in the second clause under coreference with the absolutive NP in the first clause; note that it is the undergoer in the second clause. In (101b) the ergative NP *baŋgul yaṛangu* 'man' is omitted under coreference with the absolutive NP in the first clause, and the result is ungrammatical. This shows that an ergative NP cannot be realized by zero anaphora. The omitted NP in the second clause in (101c) would have been in the absolutive case because it is the single argument of an intransitive verb, and it can be deleted only if it is coreferential with the absolutive case NP in the preceding clause. Consequently (101c) can be interpreted only as '... and the woman went uphill' and not as '... and the man went uphill', and this shows that only the absolutive NP can be the controller of zero anaphora. Thus we may conclude that the absolutive NP is the PrP in Dyirbal.

In a simple transitive clause in Dyirbal such as (100b), the absolutive case NP is the undergoer. If one wanted to say 'man came and saw woman' as in (101b), then the actor of *buṛan* 'see' would have to be the PrP in the absolutive case before it could be deleted. In order to have the actor occur as PrP, an *antipassive* construction must be used. In Dyirbal, this involves adding the suffix -*ŋay* to the verb and changing the tense suffix from transitive to intransitive; the actor occurs in the absolutive case and the undergoer in the dative.

(102) a. Bayi   yaṛa   bagun   dyugumbilgu
           CL(ABS) man(ABS ACT) CL(DAT) woman(DAT U)

           buṛal-ŋa-nyu
           see-ANTIPASS-TNS
           'Man saw woman'

       b. Bayi   yaṛa   bani-nyu ___ bagun   dyugumbilgu
           CL(ABS) man(ABS ACT) come-TNS   CL(DAT) woman(DAT U)

           buṛal-ŋa-nyu
           see-ANTIPASS-TNS
           'Man came and saw woman'

       c. Bayi   yaṛa   bagun   dyugumbilgu
           CL(ABS) man(ABS ACT) CL(DAT) woman(DAT U)

           buṛal-ŋa-nyu   ___ waynydyi-n
           see-ANTIPASS-TNS   go uphill-TNS
           'Man saw woman and went uphill' (*... and [she] went
           uphill)

The antipassive version of (100b) is presented in (102a), and in (102b,c) the actor-PrP is the target and controller of zero anaphora (cf. (102b,c)). Thus the antipassive construction in Dyirbal performs the same basic function as the foregrounding passives in German and English (cf.

(55–8)) of allowing alternative choices for PrP status. In German and English the actor is the PrP in a simple transitive clause, while in Dyirbal it is the undergoer. Foregrounding passives allow non-actors to occur as the PrP, and Dyirbal antipassive permits non-undergoers to be the PrP. Hence they are functionally parallel constructions. This is illustrated in Table 6.4.

Table 6.4 *Foregrounding passive and antipassive*

		I	II
1 Basic pattern:	intransitive transitive	single argument = PrP ACT = PrP	single argument = PrP U = PrP
2 Altered pattern:		Passive -ACT = PrP	Antipassive -U = PrP

In a system of type I the choices for the PrP in the basic pattern follow the morphological case-marking pattern of a language like German: the actor and the single argument of an intransitive verb are treated alike as the PrP, to the exclusion of the undergoer of a transitive verb. This morphological pattern is usually termed *accusative*, and we will extend this term to refer to pivot systems of type I in which the actor is the PrP in the basic pattern. Similarly, the choices of the PrP in the basic pattern in systems of type II parallels ergative case-marking patterns: the undergoer of a transitive verb and the single argument of an intransitive verb are PrPs to the exclusion of the actor of a transitive verb. Accordingly, type II pivot systems will be called *ergative*. Thus, in a language in which the pivot system is accusative, the foregrounding passive functions to allow non-actors to occur as PrP, whereas in ergative languages the *foregrounding antipassive* serves to permit non-undergoers to occur as PrP. It must be noted that the pivot choice and morphological patterns of a PrP language need not coincide. It is possible for a language to be morphologically ergative and yet for its pivot system to be accusative. Tzotzil, as we saw in section 3.1.1, is an example of this.

Languages with PrP selection following an ergative pattern possess foregrounding antipassives which allow the ergatively case-marked actor NP to occur as the absolutively case-marked PrP, in order to meet the general coreference constraints associated with PrPs. They are parallel to foregrounding passives. They differ from foregrounding passives in that some accusative languages, like Tagalog or Lango, arguments other than the undergoer are potential PrPs, but with the foregrounding antipassive only actors, case marked as ergative NPs, can become PrPs. In Dyirbal (example (102) above), the antipassive marks the actor as the PrP, and the undergoer is demoted to peripheral status, marked by the dative (or ergative) case. Foregrounding antipassives of this kind also occur in Yidiɲ, (103) (Australia; Dixon 1977a) and Eskimo, (104) (A. C. Woodbury 1977):

(103)   a. Wagudya-ngu bunya-ɸ   giba:l
            man-ERG(ACT) woman-ABS(U) scratch(PAST)
            'The man scratched the woman'

        b. Wagu:dya-ɸ   giba-:dyi-nyu   bunya:-nda
            man-ABS(ACT) scratch-ANTIPASS-PAST woman-DAT(U)
            'The man scratched the woman'

(104)   a. Arna-p   niqi-ɸ   niri-vaa
            woman-ERG(ACT) meat-ABS(U) eat-INDIC(3SG)
            'The woman ate the meat'

        b. Arnaq-ɸ   niqi-mik   niri-NNig-puq
            woman-ABS(ACT) meat-INSTR(U) eat-ANTIPASS-INDIC(3SG)
            'The woman ate some of the meat'

In these examples the (a) sentences are simple ergatively marked basic clauses. The actor is in the ergative case and the undergoer in the absolutive. The (b) examples are antipassive constructions. The actor is now case marked as absolutive, and the undergoer is marked as a peripheral case, dative in Yidiɲ (parallel to Dyirbal) and instrumental in Eskimo. In both Yidiɲ and Eskimo the antipassive allows the actor to occur as PrP, in contrast to the basic choice of undergoer, and the undergoer occurs as a peripheral constituent. We have been unable to find any examples of foregrounding antipassives in which the undergoer remains a core argument, analogous to the foregrounding passives in Lango and Tagalog.

3.2.2 Backgrounding antipassives

In addition to foregrounding antipassives, many languages also possess *backgrounding antipassives*. Backgrounding antipassives function to demote the undergoer to peripheral status, and in this way they parallel backgrounding passives in which the actor is made peripheral. With a backgrounding antipassive, the actor normally appears in the absolutive case because the clause is intransitive. As with backgrounding passives, languages have a range of backgrounding antipassive constructions. The most typical construction is that in which the undergoer is suppressed entirely and removed from the clause. This again parallels the widespread actorless backgrounding passive construction. Example (105) is from Yidiɲ (Dixon 1977a) and (106) is from Bandjalang (Crowley 1978):

(105) a. Yinydyu:-n bunya:-n   mayi-ɸ   buga-ŋ
           this-ERG   woman-ERG(ACT) vegetables-ABS(U) eat-PRES
           'This woman is eating vegetables'

       b. Yinu-ɸ bunya-ɸ   buga:-dyi-ŋ
           this-ABS woman-ABS(ACT) eat-ANTIPASS-PRES
           'This woman is eating'

(106) a. Mali-yu dya:dyam-bu mala-ɸ   bulan-ø   dya-ila
           that-ERG child-ERG(ACT) that-ABS(U) meat-ABS(U) eat-PRES
           'The child is eating meat'

       b. Mala-ɸ dya:dyam-ɸ   dya-le-ila
           that-ABS child-ABS(ACT) eat-ANTIPASS-PRES
           'That child is eating'

These examples illustrate the basic semantic antipassive function of undergoer suppression. In the basic transitive clause of the (a) examples, we have the normal transitive pattern, with the verb having both the actor argument in the ergative and the undergoer in the absolutive. In the (b) examples, the backgrounding antipassive is applied as indicated by the antipassive suffix in the verb. The undergoer is deleted from the clause, and the actor becomes PrP, case marked as absolutive.

This type of undergoer suppression antipassive has an interesting specialization in many languages: it often serves as the means of reflexivization. The undergoer is removed from the clause under coreference with the actor, and this is indicated by the antipassive affix in the verb in Yidiɲ, (107) (Dixon 1977a) and Dyirbal, (108) (Dixon 1972):

(107) a. Wagu:dya-ɸ bambi:-dyi-nyu
           man-ABS(ACT) cover-ANTIPASS-PAST
           'The man has covered himself'

(108) b. Bayi yaṛa   buybayi-ri-nyu
           CL(ABS) man(ABS ACT) hide-ANTIPASS-TNS
           'The man hid himself'

In these reflexive examples, the undergoer has been suppressed under coreferentiality with the actor, and this is signalled by the antipassive suffix on the verb. This is a backgrounding antipassive function. In Yidiɲ all antipassives, whether backgrounding or foregrounding, are marked with the suffix -:*dyi*, but in Dyirbal, foregrounding antipassives are generally marked -ŋay (see (102) above) and backgrounding anti-passives with -riy.

While the languages discussed so far have all exhibited PrP selection on ergative lines, backgrounding antipassives, unlike foregrounding ones, are not restricted to this type of language. Languages with PrP selection on an accusative pattern, that is, where the normal PrP of a transitive clause is the actor, as well as SmP languages without PrPs, also have backgrounding antipassives. Of course, they never have fore-grounding antipassives, as the basic PrP in transitive clauses in such languages will always be the actor. These ergative languages with actor/PrP may have foregrounding *passives*, for example Tzotzil. Thus, languages with foregrounding passives and backgrounding antipassives are possible, and examples are found in the Mayan language family.

We have already seen in our discussion of Tzotzil above that while it is morphologically ergative, it is syntactically accusative with a basic selection of actor as PrP and foregrounding passive which places the undergoer as PrP. But Tzotzil and other Mayan languages also have backgrounding antipassives which remove the undergoer from the core; the Tzotzil example in (109) is from John Haviland (personal com-munication) and the Jacaltec one in (110) from Craig (1977) and Datz (1980).

(109) a. S-mil-ox-∅   li   Anton e
          3SG(ERG)-kill-PAST-3SG(ABS) ART Anton
          'Someone killed Anton' or 'Anton killed someone'

       b. Mil-∅-wan   li   Anton e
          kill-3SG(ABS)-ANTIPASS ART Anton
          'Anton killed [someone]'

(110) a. X-∅-s-mak   naj ix
          ASP-3SG(ABS)-3SG(ERG)-hit he she
          'He hit her'

       b. X-∅-mak-wa   naj y-iñ   ix
          ASP-3SG(ABS)-hit-ANTIPASS he 3SG(ERG)-on she
          'He hit on her'

The Tzotzil sentence in (109a) is ambiguous as to whether the post-verbal NP *li Anton e* 'Anton' is the actor or undergoer, as the verb is inflected for both third person singular actor and undergoer. In (109b), however, the occurrence of the suffix -*wan* indicates that the undergoer has been eliminated, and consequently *li Anton e* can only be inter-preted as the actor. Thus the -*wan* construction in Tzotzil is a back-grounding antipassive which removes the undergoer from the clause. A similar situation can be found in Jacaltec. The addition of the *-wa* suffix to a transitive verb signals the removal of the undergoer from the core of the clause. It may still occur as a peripheral oblique NP as in (110b), and its peripheral status is confirmed by the fact that it may not be questioned, clefted or relativized upon, as it could be in (110a). The undergoer may also be deleted altogether, as in Tzotzil, yielding *x-ø-mak-wa* 'he hit [something]'. There is also a construction in Jacaltec in which the undergoer is incorporated into the predicate, losing its status as an independent argument; it is illustrated from Datz (1980):

(111)   X-ø-mak-wi   ix   naj
        ASP-3SG(ABS)-HIT-ANTIPASS woman he
        'He hits women (women-hits)'

The incorporated undergoer *ix* 'woman' must be generic, and it cannot be modified by noun classifiers, benefactives or demonstratives; these features are diagnostic of noun incorporation. Mayan languages, then, are morphologically ergative but syntactically accusative languages which have two types of backgrounding antipassive.

Backgrounding antipassives, as we have seen, are found in ergative languages with both accusative PrP selection (Tzotzil) and ergative PrP selection (Dyirbal). But the large majority of ergative languages do not fall into either of these types. Most ergative languages have no pragmatic pivots at all; they are like the SmP languages such as Choctaw discussed in 3.1.2, in which pivot selection is determined strictly on semantic lines and pragmatic notions of contextual salience play no role. These ergative languages also have antipassives, but only background-ing antipassives. Live syntactically ergative languages such as Yidiɲ, and morphologically ergative but syntactically accusative languages such as Jacaltec, these SmP ergative languages have back-grounding anti-passives which suppress or incorporate undergoers. These examples are from Tongan (Polynesian; Green 1979) and Chukchee (Palaeo-Siberian, Siberia; Ard 1978, Comrie 1978):

(112)   a. 'Oku ta 'a   Sione 'e   Mele
           PRES hit ABS(U) John ERG(ACT) Mary
           'Mary is hitting John'

        b. 'Oku ta a   Mele
           PRES hit ABS(ACT) Mary
           'Mary is playing (a musical instrument)/batting (in cricket)'

(113)   a. Na'e tō   a   e   talo 'e   he tangata
           PAST plant ABS(U) ART taro ERG(ACT) ART man
           'The man planted the taro'

    b. Nale tō   talo   'a   he tangata
       PAST plant taro(u) ABS(ACT) ART man
       'The man was taro-planting'

(114) a. Morg-ə-man mət-wiriŋərkən-ət   tumg-ət
       we-ERG(ACT) we-are defending-them friends-ABS(u)
       'We are defending the friends'

    b. Muri   mət-ine-wiriŋərkən
       we(ABS ACT) we-ANTIPASS-are defending
       'We are defending (someone/something)'

(115) a. Tumg-e   nantəwatən kupre-n
       friend-ERG(ACT) they set it   net-ABS(u)
       'The friends set the net'

    b. Tumg-ət   kupra-ntəwatg'at
       friend-ABS(ACT) net-they set
       'The friends engaged in net setting'

The first set of examples for Tongan and Chukchee, (112) and (114), show a backgrounding antipassive which completely eliminates an undergoer from the clause. The (a) examples are normal, transitive, ergatively case-marked clauses. The (b) examples exhibit the backgrounding antipassive. The undergoer is deleted from the clause, and as the clause is formally intransitive, the actor is case marked as an absolutive NP, as the single argument of an intransitive clause. Note the semantic specialization in Tongan in (112b) in which the normal transitive verb *hit* has undergone a semantic antipassivization. Semantic effects like this are a common feature of backgrounding antipassives, just as they were with the backgrounding passives discussed earlier.

The second set of examples in (113) for Tongan and (115) for Chukchee exhibit semantic antipassives with the function of incorporating the NP undergoer into this verb. Again, the clause becomes intransitive with the backgrounding antipassive, as in the (b) examples, and the actor is absolutely case marked.

There is yet another type of backgrounding antipassive commonly found in these smP ergative languages, in which the undergoer is still present but is demoted from the core and marked as oblique. These backgrounding antipassive constructions contrast with the normal ergative construction in expressing the incompleteness of the action as it affects the object. Note these semantic antipassive examples, (116) from Kabardian (Northwest Caucasian, USSR; Catford 1976) and (117) from West Circassian (Northwest Caucasian, USSR; Comrie 1978).

(116) a. fie-m   qʷipŝfire-r   jedzaq'e
          dog-ERG(ACT) bone-ABS(U) bite
          'The dog bites the bone (through to the marrow)'

       b. fie-r   qʷipŝfire-m je[w]dzaq'e
          dog-ABS(ACT) bone-ERG [ANTIPASS]-bite
          'The dog is gnawing the bone'

(117) a. Pisásá-m   chəy-ər   yada
          girl-ERG(ACT) cherkesska-ABS(U) she sews it(TRANS)
          'The girl is sewing the cherkesska'

       b. Pisásá-r   chəy-əm   yadə
          girl-ABS(ACT) cherkesska-ERG she sews it(INTRANS)
          'The girl is sewing away at the cherkesska'

In both of these examples, the ergative construction in (a) means that
the undergoer is completely affected and, in the case of (117a), the
undergoer is brought into being. In the antipassive constructions in (b),
the undergoer is only partially or superficially affected by the action.
The change effected by the backgrounding antipassive is from a normal
transitive clause with ergative case marking to the antipassive intransitive clause in which the actor is case-marked as absolutive, and the
undergoer as ergative–instrumental, in this instance reflecting a
peripheral constituent. There is a change in verbal inflection in (117)
from transitive (117a) to intransitive (117b).

Languages with accusative case marking also have backgrounding
antipassives, just as ergative languages have backgrounding passives.
For example, Tongan, a morphologically ergative language, in addition
to having backgrounding antipassives (see examples (112–13 above))
also has a backgrounding passive (Green 1979):

(118) a. Nale 'ilo   'e   Sione 'a   Mele
          PAST recognize ERG(ACT) John ABS(U) Mary
          'John recognized Mary'

       b. Nale 'ilo-a   'a   Mele
          PAST recognize-PASS ABS(U) Mary
          'Mary was well known'

The suffix -*a* indicates a backgrounding passive, the actor is deleted and
the verb takes on a stative meaning. The semantic backgrounding
construction is intransitive, and consequently, there is no case-marking
change for the object.

Accusatively case-marked languages with backgrounding antipassives
are quite widespread. Backgrounding antipassives in accusative lan-

guages are restricted to the functions of suppression and incorporation of undergoers. Kusaiean and other Micronesian languages have backgrounding antipassives which incorporate undergoers (Sugita 1973):

(119)   a. Nga ɔl-læ   nuknuk ɛ
           I   wash-PERF clothes the
           'I washed the clothes'

        b. Nga owo nuknuk læ
           I   wash clothes PERF
           'I washed clothes'

        c. Nga owo læ
           I   wash PERF
           'I washed'

In (119b), the undergoer is clearly incorporated, as the aspect particle follows it. Normally aspect particles immediately follow the verb, as in (119a). Incorporation in Kusaiean and other languages is restricted to generic undergoers. A clause with a backgrounding antipassive of incorporation is, of course, intransitive, as the undergoer is no longer an independent constituent, but more like an adverbial modifier of the verb. This intransitivity is demonstrated by the intransitive form of the verb 'wash': *owo* in (119b) (compare (c)) in contrast with the transitive form *ɔl* in (119a).

Several languages of North and Middle America also exhibit noun incorporation as a type of backgrounding antipassive. The following examples are from two Uto-Aztecan languages, Tubatulabal in (120a) and Classical Nahuatl in (120b) (Langacker 1977):

(120)   a. Punẓi-gaa'aẓa-t
           seed-boil-PRES
           'He is boiling mush'

        b. Ni-naka-kʷa
           I-meat-eat
           'I eat meat'

In both of these examples, the undergoer occurs as part of the verb and not as an independent element. Noun incorporation is also found in Lakhota (Siouan; Boas and Deloria 1941), Onondaga (Iroquoian; H. Woodbury 1975), and Plains Cree (Algonquian; Wolfart 1973) (see also Sapir 1911). Another type of backgrounding antipassive found in North American languages involves the suppression of the undergoer and is signalled by what is often called an 'indefinite object' marker. The following examples are taken from Lakhota (Boas and Deloria 1941):

(121)   a. Wičháša ki   wa-ɸ-kté
        man   the ANTIPASS-3SG(ACT)-kill
        'The man killed [something]'

    b. Wičháša ki   mathó wą ɸ-ɸ-kté
        man   the bear a 3SG(U)-3SG(ACT)-kill
        'The man killed a bear'

The (b) example is a normal Lakhota transitive clause, and (a) is
the backgrounding antipassive construction in which no object may be
present and the verb is prefixed with *wa-*, the indefinite object marker.

English, a morphologically and syntactically accusative language, has
backgrounding antipassives which are analogous to the noun incorporation constructions mentioned above:

(122)   a. John went to hunt the tiger

    b. John went tiger-hunting

That *tiger* is incorporated in (122b) is indicated by its preverbal position,
the occurrence of only one main stress in the compound, and its generic
interpretation. It also cannot be inflected for plural and rejects any
other normal NP modifiers, such as adjectives.

3.2.2 *Summary of antipassive constructions*
This typology of antipassivization is summarized in Table 6.5.

In SMP languages the effects of the backgrounding antipassive differ
according to whether the language is morphologically ergative or
accusative. In morphologically ergative languages the actor occurs in the
absolute case as a result of the suppression or incorporation of the
undergoer. In languages without ergative morphology the case marking
of the actor is unaffected. The languages of the top group exhibit
undergoer suppression and undergoer incorporation constructions:
Tongan (112–13), Kusaiean, (119), Chukchee, (114–15), Uto-Aztecan,
(120a,b), and Lakhota, (121b). Caucasian languages exhibit another
variety of this type of backgrounding antipassive, namely, the expression of differences in object affectedness, as in (116–17).

Backgrounding antipassives are well attested in PRP languages. They
are found in three types of languages: morphologically and syntactically
ergative (e.g. Dyirbal, Yidiɲ, Bandjalang), morphologically ergative
and syntactically accusative (e.g. Tzotzil), and morphologically and
syntactically accusative (e.g. English). The first two groups have backgrounding antipassives which suppress the undergoer, as in Bandjalang,
(106), and Yidiɲ, (105). In Yidiɲ, (107), and Dyirbal, (108), these
antipassives which suppress the undergoer also have a specialized

Table 6.5 Typology of antipassive constructions

smp languages	PrP languages	
Backgrounding antipassives	Backgrounding antipassives	Foregrounding antipassives
1 $U=X(ACT \neq smP)$ No known examples	1 $U=X(ACT \neq PrP)$ No known examples	1 $-ACT=PrP(U \neq X)$ No known examples
2 $U=X(ACT=smP)$ Tongan Kusaiean Chukchee Uto-Aztecan Lakhota Caucasian	2 $U=X(ACT=PrP)$ Bandjalang Dyirbal Yidiɲ Tzotzil Jacaltec English	2 $-U=PrP(U=X)$ Dyirbal Yidiɲ Eskimo Bandjalang

Note: X = 'non-core'

function as reflexive constructions in which the object is suppressed
under coreference with the actor. In Mayan languages, e.g. Tzotzil,
(109), and Jacaltec, (110), the object is removed from the core of the
clause. It must be deleted in Tzotzil, but may occur as an oblique
peripheral NP in Jacaltec. This language also has an undergoer-
incorporation antipassive, as shown in (111). Finally, English has
undergoer incorporation as in (122).

It must be pointed out that we have been unable to find any
backgrounding antipassives in which the actor does not assume pivot
status. Note that with backgrounding passives in some languages, for
example Ulcha, (74c), it is possible for the undergoer not to assume
pivot position. For the corresponding backgrounding antipassive this
does not seem to be attested; the actor always assumes pivot status.

There are two possible types of foregrounding antipassives, parallel to
the difference in foregrounding passives as to whether the actor is
removed from the core or not. The two types of foregrounding
antipassives differ only in their side-effect on the undergoer. We have
been unable to find an example of a foregrounding antipassive in which
the undergoer remains a core argument. In Dyirbal, (102), Yidiɲ, (103),
and Eskimo, (104), the undergoer becomes a peripheral NP which may
be freely deleted.

These antipassive constructions are intimately involved in the packaging of information in the clause. The foregrounding antipassive affects
the packaging of the actor and of the undergoer as well. Backgrounding
antipassives are primarily concerned with the expression or non-
expression of the undergoer, and in morphologically ergative languages
this always has repercussions for the packaging of the actor as well.

3.3 *Dative shift*

Backgrounding antipassives, as we have seen, are constructions which
remove undergoers from the core and either delete them entirely or
mark them as oblique peripheral constituents. Many languages also
have a rule which takes non-undergoer arguments and makes them
undergoers. In some cases this may involve other core arguments; in
other cases it may involve peripheral arguments. This construction is
generally referred to as *dative shift* or *dative movement*. The English
examples with the verb *give* are the generally cited cases of this rule:

(123)   a. Ulysses gave the flowers to Circe at the wedding

       b. Ulysses gave Circe the flowers at the wedding

Give is a verb with three core arguments: actor, undergoer, and
recipient; and it allows two different ways of packaging the non-actor

core arguments. In (123a) the undergoer occurs in the immediate postverbal slot in the clause, and the recipient argument follows it, marked by the preposition *to*. In (123b), on the other hand, the recipient argument supplants *flowers* as the undergoer, and appears without a preposition in the immediate postverbal position. The NP referring to the gift follows it.

This type of alternation with recipient NPs is not restricted to English, but is found in other languages as well. However, all known languages with this alternation have actor-verb-undergoer (SVO) word order, with no nominal case marking for actor and undergoer, as in these examples from Nengone, (124) (Austronesian, New Caledonia; Tryon 1967), Acooli, (125) (Nilotic, Uganda; Crazzolara 1955) and Lango, (126) (Nilotic, Uganda; Noonan and Bavin Woock 1978):

(124)   a. Inu či   kanon ɔre tusi   du bɔn
           I   PRES give   the book to him
           'I give the book to him'

        b. Inu či   kanon bɔn re   tusi
           I   PRES give   him the book
           'I give him the book'

(125)   a. Dáakó òmììò càak ki làtëënɛ
           woman gave   milk to her child
           'The woman gave milk to her child'

        b. Dáakó òmììò làtëënɛ càak
           woman gave   her child milk
           'The woman gave her child milk'

(126)   a. Lócà òmíɔ mɔt bɔ àtín
           man gave gift to child
           'The man gave a gift to the child'

        b. Lócà òmíɔ àtín mɔt
           man gave child gift
           'The man gave the child a gift'

There are also constructions in which a peripheral NP becomes the undergoer; in such a construction an otherwise non-core NP becomes a core argument. This is illustrated for English in (127) and Hungarian in (128).

(127)   a. The men loaded the plane with marijuana

        b. The men loaded marijuana on the plane

        c. Michael sprayed the window with red paint

    d. Michael sprayed red paint on the window

    e. Fred hit the door with his fist

    f. Fred hit his fist against the door

(128)   a. Megrakta a   szekeret szénával
            he put it the cart(ACC) with hay
            'He loaded the cart with hay'

        b. Rárakta   a   szénat   a   székerre
            he put it onto the hay(ACC) the onto cart
            'He loaded the hay onto the cart'

        c. János bemázolta   a   falat   festékkel
            John he smeared it on the wall(ACC) with paint
            'John smeared the wall with paint'

        d. János rámázolta   a   festéket   a   falra
            John he smeared it onto the paint(ACC) the onto wall
            'John smeared paint on the wall'

(The Hungarian sentences are from Moravcsik 1978.) In (127a,c,e) there is a peripheral instrument marked by *with*, whereas in (127b,d,f) these NPS occur as undergoers in the immediate postverbal position, with the objects of (127a,c,e) in prepositional phrases. A similar alternation between accusative and locative objects is found in the Hungarian sentences in (128). There is an important semantic difference between the sentences in (127a,b), (127c,d), (128a,b) and (128c,d): in the first sentence of each pair the window, plane, cart, and wall are fully affected by the action of the verb, whereas in the second sentence they are not so affected. Thus in (127a) and (128a) the plane and the cart are interpreted as being filled up, while there is no such implication in (127b) and (128b). Similarly, in (127c) and (128c) the window and the wall are understood as being fully covered with paint, but not in (127d) and (128d). This semantic distinction correlates with the occurrence of these NPS as undergoer and non-undergoer: when the NP is fully affected, it occurs as undergoer and hence as direct object, and when it is only partially affected, it is an object of a preposition.

    These alternations differ from the more classic dative shift alternations involving 'give' in (123–6) in two ways. First of all, 'give' is a ditransitive verb with three core arguments, so there is no promotion of a peripheral constituent to core status: there is, rather, a rearranging of which core argument is the undergoer. However, these examples in (127–8) involve the promotion of a normally peripheral constituent to core and assigning it undergoer status. Also, the alternations with 'give' involve a rearrangement of constituents for purely pragmatic reasons (see Erteschik-Shir 1979); no meaning change is effected by it. However, the alternations with *load* and *spray* do involve a meaning change: when the NP is peripheral, it is partially affected, but when it is the undergoer, it is totally affected. It might be objected that the alternation involving *load* and *spray* should not be treated as a type of dative shift at all, but as a completely different rule. To some extent, the answer revolves around the personal preference of the analyst, but a few points supporting the position taken here can be advanced.

From a structural point of view, both the alternations with *give* and those with *load* or *spray* involve the constituent normally occurring as a prepositional phrase, functioning as direct object. For both types of alternations, they are lexically governed by certain verbs. Not all verbs in English allow alternations of this type: they are restricted to verbs of transfer or verbs of impact. In fact, some verbs closely related to *give* semantically, have an alternation pattern like that of *load*:

(129)   a. John presented the gift to Mary

         b. John presented Mary *with* the gift

Present is semantically close to *give*, but note that unlike *give* it requires the gift to occur in a prepositional phrase with *with* when not functioning as the direct object. This is parallel to the examples with *load* in which the object loaded must also appear in a prepositional phrase with *with* when not functioning as direct object (see (127a)). This suggests that the constructions with *load* and *give* are not too dissimilar.

Finally, there are some alternations with verbs of the *load* class which do not seem to involve a meaning change of the partially-affected to totally-affected type, but seem more to involve differences in topicality or speakers' viewpoint, similar to the alternations with *give*. (127e,f) illustrate this. In these examples, neither *the fist* nor *the door* seems more affected in one example than the other. Rather the example in which *the door* is direct object is concerned with the door and its role in the action, whereas the example in which *the fist* is direct object is concerned with the fist. This is basically a pragmatic difference between the two sentences, and the alternation is like that involving *give*. We may conclude, then, that treating these alternation types as different subtypes of a unified dative shift rule is warranted.

Several Mayan languages (Huastec, Chorti, Chol, Tzotzil and Tzeltal) have a construction which permits a peripheral recipient, i.e. a benefactive or malefactive argument, or the possessor of the undergoer, to occur as the undergoer in the absolutive case. This is illustrated for Chol from Dayley (1980) (INCOMPL = incompletive):

(130) a. Mi-j-kájti-b'e-n-et
       TNS-1SG(ERG)-ask-DAT-INCOMPL-2SG(ABS)
       'I ask you it/it of you'

   b. Woli-j-k'el-b'e-n-ø
       TNS-1SG(ERG)-see-DAT-INCOMPL-3SG(ABS)
       'I am watching him for him'

Indonesian also presents pairs of sentences parallel to (127) (Dard-jowidjojo 1971):

(131) a. Dia mengalir-*i*   sawah-nya dengan air   itu
       he flow-U=LOC ricefield-his with   water DEF
       'He flooded his rice field with water'

   b. Dia mengalir-*kan* air   itu ke sawah-nya
       he flow-U=INSTR water DEF to ricefield-his
       'He made water flow into his rice field'

The behaviour of *mengalir* 'flow' parallels that of 'load' and 'spray' in (127). In (131a) in which the locative is undergoer (marked by the suffix *-i*), the undergoer is completely affected: in this case, flooded. In (131b), in which the instrument is undergoer (marked by the extension marker *-kan*), the locative is only partially affected. Thus, (131a) is parallel to (127a,c), while (131b) is parallel to (127b,d). Indonesian also has other types of dative shift constructions like those of English (Dardjowidjojo 1971):

(132) a. Dia mem-beli ayam   itu untuk Hasan
       he ACTIVE-buy chicken DEF for   Hasan
       'He bought the chicken for Hasan'

   b. Dia mem-beli-*kan* Hasan ayam   itu
       he ACTIVE-buy-EXT Hasan chicken DEF
       'He bought Hasan chicken'

(133) a. Dia meng-ajar-*kan*   Inggris kepada saya
       he ACTIVE-teach-EXT English to   me
       'He taught English to me'

   b. Dia meng-ajar   saya Inggris
       he ACTIVE-teach me   English
       'He taught me English'

The semantics of *-kan* varies for verb classes (compare (132) with (133) to note this variability) but in each pair of sentences, one verb has the suffix *-kan* and the other is unmarked. The (a) sentences are the basic form, and the (b) examples are dative shift constructions.

The universal dative shift rule can be summarized as in (134):

(134)   a. $[\text{ACT V }_u[\text{NP}_i]_u]_{\text{core}}\ \text{NP}_j$
        b. $\text{NP}_j = \text{U}$
        c. $\text{NP}_i = \text{-U} \sim \text{NP}_i = \text{X}$

(134a) represents the basic form of a sentence with two core arguments and one peripheral argument as in (127a,c) and (128a,c). The alternative form is captured in (134b,c): NP_j occurs as the undergoer, and NP_i is no longer the undergoer. In most languages NP_i becomes a peripheral argument, although there are some in which it may remain core. English and several other svo languages have a restricted type of dative shift which affects the choice of the undergoer with ditransitive verbs of giving. It is schematized in (135):

(135)   a. $[\text{ACT V}_u[\text{NP}_i]_u\text{ to NP}_j]_{\text{core}}$
        b. $\text{NP}_j = \text{U}$
        c. $\text{NP}_i = \text{-U}$

Here again (a) represents the basic form of a sentence with a ditransitive verb of giving as in (123a), (124a), (125a), and (126a), and the alternative form is captured in (b) and (c). NP_j occurs as undergoer and hence as the direct object and NP_i is no longer the undergoer but is still a core argument. (135) differs from (134) in two respects: first NP_j is peripheral in (134a) but core in (135a), and second, NP_i does not become peripheral in (135), while it normally does in (134). It should be emphasized that the rule in (135) is limited to ditransitive verbs of giving, while that in (134) is rather more general and not restricted to one type of verb.

The side-effect of the dative shift rule given in (134) for most languages is '$\text{NP}_i = \text{X}$', and since NP_i is the undergoer in (134a), it may be rephrased as '$\text{U} = \text{X}$'. This is, of course, the backgrounding antipassive rule discussed in section 3.2.2. Thus the side-effect of dative shift is backgrounding antipassive (cf. Table 6.5). This can be seen clearly in a comparison of the Hungarian sentences in (128) and the Caucasian semantic antipassive examples in (116–17). In the Caucasian sentences, the removal of an NP from undergoer to the periphery changes the meaning in exactly the same way that the meaning of NP_i is affected when it is supplanted as the undergoer by NP_j; that is, it goes from being totally to partially affected. Furthermore, the English morphological alternations below can be viewed as a type of backgrounding antipassive which is the same as (135c), in that NP_i is stripped of its undergoer status, but does not become peripheral:

(136) a. The tiger clawed the hunter

      b. The tiger clawed at the hunter

      c. Leroy hacked the wood

      d. Leroy hacked at the wood

In the first sentence of each pair, the postverbal NP is an undergoer and fully affected by the action, whereas in the second it is not an undergoer and is only partially affected. They are still core arguments, however, as they readily occur as the PrP in a passive.

(137) a. The hunter was clawed at by the tiger

      b. The wood was hacked at by Leroy

      c. The mountain was climbed up by Jacques

Thus English has a restricted type of backgrounding antipassive of the form 'NP$_i$ = -U', which has the same semantic import as the 'U = X' antipassives of Caucasian languages.

The relationship between dative shift and backgrounding antipassive can be represented as in Figure 6.1.

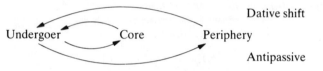

Figure 6.1 Dative shift and semantic antipassive

Periphery-to-undergoer dative shift is captured in (134) and core-to-undergoer dative shift in (135). The first type of dative shift is found in English, Hungarian, Indonesian, and Chol, while the second type occurs in English, Nengone, Lango, and Acooli. The antipassive side-effects differ in different constructions across languages. In English *give* alternations the undergoer is shifted to a non-undergoer core argument, whereas in *load* alternations and in Indonesian and Hungarian the undergoer shifts to the periphery.

The intimate interrelationship between dative shift and antipassive can be seen clearly in the instrumental verb forms in Dyirbal (Dixon 1972). The following sentence presents a Dyirbal clause containing two core arguments and a peripheral instrument:

(138) Balan dyugumbil   bangul yaṟangu   bangu
      CL(ABS) woman(ABS U) CL(ERG) man(ERG ACT) CL(INSTR)

      yugungu   balga-n
      stick(INSTR) hit-TNS
      'The man is hitting the woman with the stick'

The peripheral instrument argument occurs in the instrumental case. It is possible to have *yugu* 'stick' as a core argument, by making it the undergoer in the absolute case, putting *dyugumbil* 'woman' in the dative case, and adding the suffix *-mal* to the verb.

(139) Bala   yugu   baŋgul yaɽaŋgu   balgal-ma-n
       CL(ABS) stick(ABS U) CL(ERG) man(ERG ACT) hit-INSTR-TNS

       bagu   dyugumbilgu
       CL(DAT) woman(DAT)
       'The man is using the stick to hit the woman'

The dative shift of *yugu* 'stick' into the core results in the removal of *dyugumbil* 'woman' from the core to the periphery, which is the backgrounding antipassive. Notice that this is not a foregrounding antipassive, as the actor is still the PrP in the absolutive case, and the verb still takes the transitive tense suffix *-n*; rather it is a dative shift construction in which the undergoer NP has changed, but an undergoer is still present.

Dative shift constructions are summarized in Table 6.6.

Table 6.6 *Summary of dative shift constructions*

Basic construction	Restricted case
1 a. $[\text{ACT V }_U[\text{NP}_i]_U]_{core}\text{NP}_j$	2 a. $[\text{ACT V }_U[\text{NP}_i]_U \text{ NP}_j]_{core}$
b. $\text{NP}_j = \text{U}$	b. $\text{NP}_j = \text{U}$
c. $\text{NP}_i = \text{-U} (\text{-U} = X)$	c. $\text{NP}_i = \text{-U}$

3.4 *Summary of clause-internal packaging devices*

We may summarize the discussion of passive, antipassive, and dative shift as in Table 6.7.

Table 6.7 *Summary of core packaging options*

	Passive	Antipassive	Dative shift
Foregrounding	-ACT = PrP	ACT = PrP	-U = U
Backgrounding	ACT = X	U = X	

The interactions among these rules are complex. Foregrounding passives and antipassives normally have their backgrounding counterparts as side-effects, and the reverse is very often the case as well. Backgrounding antipassive and dative shift are virtual mirror images of each other, as in most constructions -U means non-core. Moreover, dative shift has backgrounding antipassive as its side-effect. Finally, foregrounding passive and dative shift are linked in languages in which the undergoer is the exclusive or preferred derived PrP of a passive, in that dative shift allows non-undergoer (usually peripheral) arguments to become undergoer in order to become accessible to passivization.

4.0 Syntactic packaging: clause-external

In section 3.1 we discussed and motivated a distinction between clause-internal pivot and clause-external topic, and in doing so we contrasted passive constructions with topicalizations and left-dislocations, constructions which involve clause-external topics. Like foregrounding passives and antipassives, they are foregrounding constructions, and in this section we will discuss them along with another foregrounding device, the cleft construction.

4.1 *Topicalization and left-dislocation*

As pointed out in section 3.1, topicalization and left-dislocation involve the occurrence of an external topic NP followed by a sentence which relates to it in some way. In most cases the external topic corresponds to some NP constituent in the clause in which the external topic has some function. The two constructions are distinguished formally by the existence of a pronominal element in left-dislocations which refers to the topic; it is lacking in topicalization. The following examples from English illustrate this distinction:

(140) a. That man, I saw *him* running away from the scene of the robbery yesterday

      b. My car, *it* couldn't make it to Queanbeyan without overheating

      c. John's knife, I accidentally cut myself with *it*

(141) a. That dump Bill wouldn't live in __ for anything

      b. Fred I can't stand __ but Ursula I get on with __ quite well

      c. This cheese we haven't touched __ yet

The sentences in (140) are left-dislocations, and the anaphoric element referring to the external topic is italicized. Those in (141) are topicalizations, with the line indicating the gap left in the following sentence.

Although these constructions have foregrounding effects like foregrounding passives and antipassives, their discourse function is rather different from the clause-internal constructions. According to Keenan and Schieffelin (1976), who investigated these constructions in English discourse, and Duranti and Ochs (1979), who examined them in Italian conversation, the primary functions of these constructions are to introduce new referents into a discourse or to reintroduce a referent which was previously introduced but which has not been mentioned in the immediately preceding discourse. Keenan and Schieffelin (1976) present the following example:

(142)   a. An' I got a red sweater, an' a white one, an' a blue one, an' a yellow one, an' a couple other sweaters, you know, and uh my sister *loves* borrowing my sweaters because they're pullovers, you know, an' she c'n wear a blouse under'em an' she thinks 'well this is great'
(pause)

b. An' so my *red* sweater, I haven't seen it since I got it

There are a couple of significant features in this example. First, *red sweater* is introduced in the first sentence and then not mentioned again for several sentences. When it is reintroduced, it is first presented as an external topic followed by a sentence which contains two pronouns referring to it. The left-dislocation construction serves to reintroduce a referent, in this case *red sweater*, into the discourse. Second, there is a contrastive meaning here as well, in that the *red* sweater is picked out of the group of sweaters mentioned in the first sentence. The contrastive meaning of these constructions is evident in (142b) in which the comparison is made explicit. These functions of topicalization and left-dislocation are sharply opposed to those of foregrounding passives and antipassives, which are involved in the presentation of alternative choices for the pivot of a clause.

It must be noted that because topics are outside of the clause rather than within it, whether a language has a PrP or SmP for its pivot is irrelevant to the presence or absence of external topics. They are found in both PrP and SmP languages. For example, of the languages cited below, Tagalog, Italian, and Jacaltec are PrP languages, while Lakhota and Kinyarwanda are SmP languages. The following examples of topicalizations are from Tagalog:

(143)   a. Nag-bigay   ng libro sa   babae   ang lalake
PrP=ACT-give P   book LOC woman PrP man
'The man gave a book to the woman'

b. Ang lalake ay nag-bigay   ng libro sa   babae
PrP   man   TOP PrP=ACT-give P book LOC woman
'The man, [he] gave a book to the woman'

    c. Sa babae, nag-bigay   ng libro ang lalake
      LOC woman PrP=ACT-give P book PrP man
      'The woman, the man gave __ a book'

(143a) is the unmarked clause pattern, without any topicalized NPS. (143b) is an example in which the pivot of the clause has been topicalized. In such constructions an obligatory *ay* must occur between the external topic and the predicate. The other topicalization construction is illustrated in (143c). This construction is limited to peripheral constituents. No *ay* may occur between the external topic and the predicate, and the external topic preserves its oblique case marker *sa*. Tagalog does not permit the topicalization of non-pivot core arguments: an actor or patient may not be topicalized if it is not the pivot.

(144)   *Ng libro nag-bigay   ang lalake sa babae
       P book PrP=ACT-give PrP man LOC woman
       'The book, the man gave (it) to the woman'

Left dislocations are found in a wide range of languages. The following examples are from Italian, (145) (Duranti and Ochs 1979), Kinyarwanda, (146) (Kimenyi 1980), Jacaltec, (147) (Craig 1977) and Lakhota, (148):

(145) a. Ho   fatto a Roberto aspetta' un 'ora
        have-I made to Roberto wait   an hour
        'I made Roberto wait for an hour'

      b. A Roberto l'ho   fatto aspetta' un 'ora
        to Roberto him have-I made wait   an hour
        'Roberto, I made him wait for an hour'

(146) a. Umugóre y-a-boon-ye   umugabo
        woman   3SG(ACT)-PAST-see-ASP man
        'The woman saw the man'

      b. Umugabo, umugóre y-a-mu-boon-ye
        man   woman   3SG(ACT)-PAST-3SG(U)-see-ASP
        'The man, the woman saw him'

(147) a. X-ϕ-s-mak   naj Pel ix Malin
        ASP-3SG(ABS)-3SG(ERG)-hit CL Peter CL Mary
        'Peter hit Mary'

      b. Naj Pel x-ϕ-s-mak   naj   ix Malin
        CL Peter ASP-3SG(ABS)-3SG(ERG)-hit CL(he) CL Mary
        'Peter, he hit Mary'

c. Ix Malin x-∅-s-mak   naj Pel   ix
   CL Mary ASP-3SG(ABS)-3SG(ERG)-hit CL Peter CL(she)
   'Mary, Peter hit her'

(148) a. Wičháša ki ∅-nuwá-he   k'éyaš hokšíla ki
          man   the 3SG(ACT)-swim-PROG but   boy   the

          wą-∅-∅-yáke-šni
          see-3SG(U)-3SG(ACT)-NEG
          'The man was swimming, but the boy didn't see him'

       b. Hokšíla ki wičháša ki ∅-nuwá-he   k-éyaš
          boy   the man   the the 3SG(ACT)-swim-PROG but

          wą-∅-∅-yáke-šni
          see-3SG(U)-3SG(ACT)-NEG
          'The boy, the man was swimming but he didn't see him'

In all of the sentences in (144–7) which have external topics, there is a
pronoun in the following sentence which references the topic. In
Kinyarwanda, Jacaltec and Lakhota it is a verbal affix, while in Italian it
is a preverbal clitic pronoun.

In sum, topicalization and left-dislocations are clause-external packaging devices which contrast with internal devices like foregrounding
passives and antipassives, both in form and discourse function.

4.2 Clefts and pseudo-clefts

The final information-packaging device to be discussed is the cleft
construction. English has two types of cleft constructions, pseudo- or
wh-clefts and it-clefts. These are illustrated in (149):

(149) a. Ron ate a sandwich
       b. What Ron ate was a sandwich
       c. The one who ate a sandwich was Ron
       d. It was a sandwich (that) Ron ate
       e. It was Ron who ate a sandwich

(149b,c) are examples of wh- or pseudo-cleft constructions, and
(149d,e) are both it-clefts. Both core arguments may be clefted in
English, as well as most peripheral arguments:

(150) a. It was with a hammer that Frank broke the vase
       b. What Frank broke the vase with was a hammer
       c. It was at the grocery store that Hank ran into Margaret
       c. Where Hank ran into Margaret was at the grocery store

The clefted constituent in (150a,b) is a peripheral instrument and in (150c,d) a peripheral locative.

The two types of clefts differ both formally and functionally. A pseudo-cleft in English is characterized by the following form:

Who/What/Where + clause − argument$_i$ + copula + argument$_i$

That is, a *wh*-word followed by a clause minus an argument constitutes the 'subject' of the construction, with the copula *be* as predicate and the argument from the *wh*-clause as a predicate nominal. *It*-clefts have the form:

It + copula + predicate nominal + relative clause

While all the sentences in (149) could be said to mean 'the same thing' because they all refer to the eating of the sandwich by Ron, they nevertheless have very different discourse functions. Prince (1978) shows that the *wh*-clause in a pseudo-cleft normally expresses what the speaker assumes the hearer to be thinking about. This assumption may be based on previous discourse, inferences from previous discourse, or aspects of the speech event and situation. Prince presents the following examples (clefts are italicized):

(151) a. There is no question what they$_i$ are after. *What the commit-tee$_i$ is after* is somebody at the White House. They$_i$ would like to get Haldeman or Colson, Ehrlichman

   b. Nikki Caine, 19, doesn't want to be a movie star. *What she hopes to do* is be a star on the horse-show circuit

   c. Nixon: I knew there was something going on, but I didn't know it was Hunt.

      Dean: *What really troubles me* is: one, will this thing not break some day and the whole thing – domino situation – everything starts crumbling, fingers will be pointing . . .

In each of these examples the *wh*-clause in the pseudo-cleft relates to what the speaker assumes the hearer has in his/her mind at that moment; in the first two examples it is derived from the immediately preceding discourse, while in the third it is a function of the general topic of the speech event and situation.

It-clefts, according to Prince, have rather different functions. On the one hand, the relative clause in the cleft may represent information which the speaker does not assume the hearer to be thinking about but which he/she feels the hearer knows or can readily deduce. On the other hand, the relative clause may contain information which the speaker believes that the hearer knows but is not thinking about at that time. Examples of the first type of *it*-cleft are given in (152) and of the second type in (153), again from Prince (1978):

(152) a. So I learned to sew books. They're really good books. *It's just the covers that are rotten*

  b. A: So who's Barbara?
    B: Let me put it this way. When you last saw me with anyone, *it was Barbara I was with*

(153) a. *It was just about 50 years ago that Henry Ford gave us the weekend.* On September 25, 1926, in a somewhat shocking move for that time, he decided to establish a 40-hour week, giving his employees two days off instead of one

  b. *It is through these conquests that the peasantry became absorbed into a single form of lord–tenant relationship*

In the first pair of examples, the *it*-cleft does not represent information which is directly given in the preceding discourse, as in *wh*-clefts, but rather expresses information which the speaker assumes the hearer can link up through either prior knowledge or deduction. In the second pair the cleft represents information which the speaker believes the hearer to be aware of but not thinking of at the time of the interaction. The information is contextually new but known to the hearer. Thus the two types of clefts, pseudo-(*wh*-)clefts and *it*-clefts differ in both their form and discourse function.

Both types of cleft construction are found in other languages, but there is no detailed functional study of their uses in these languages, along the lines of Prince's (1978) study of English. Kihung'an, a Bantu language of Zaire (Takizala 1972) has both types of cleft construction:

(154) a. Kipes   ka-swiim-in kit   zoono
       Kipese 3SG-buy-PAST chair yesterday
       'Kipese bought a chair yesterday'

  b. (Kwe) kit   Kipes ka-swiim-in zoono
     (it's) chair Kipese 3SG-buy-PAST yesterday
     'It's a/the chair that Kipese bought yesterday'

  c. (Kwe) Kipes a-swiim-in   kit   zoono
     (it's) Kipese PRO-buy-PAST chair yesterday
     'It's Kipese who bought a/the chair yesterday'

d. (Kiim) ki a-swiim-in Kipes zoono (kwe) kit
(thing) that PRO-buy-PAST Kipese yesterday (is) chair
'What Kipese bought yesterday is a/the chair'

e. (Muut) wu a-swiim-in kit zoono (kwe) Kipes
(person) that PRO-buy-PAST chair yesterday (is) Kipese
'The one who bought a/the chair yesterday is Kipese'

The Kihung'an examples are quite similar to the corresponding constructions in English. *It*-clefts are indicated by an optional copula at the beginning of the sentence, followed by the predicative nominal modified by the relative clause. *Wh*-clefts are found with an optional head noun for the relative clause, followed by the relative clause, then an optional copula, and finally the predicative nominal.

Jacaltec (Craig 1977) also has cleft constructions, but only those corresponding to English *it*-clefts.

(155) a. X-∅-s-lok naj Pel no' cheh
ASP-3SG(ABS)-3SG(ERG)-bought CL Peter CL(the) horse

c'ej'in
black
'Peter bought the black horse'

b. Naj Pel x-∅-lokni no' cheh c'ej'in
CL Peter ASP-3SG(ABS)-buy CL(the) horse black
'It's Peter who bought the black horse'

c. No' cheh c'ej'in x-∅-s-lok naj
CL(the) horse black ASP-3SG(ABS)-3SG(ERG)-buy CL

Pel
Peter
'It's the black horse that Peter bought'

In Jacaltec a special suffix -*ni* must be used when relativizing and clefting an ergative NP. Also in these constructions the ergative NP ceases to be cross-referenced on the verb. The structure of Jacaltec clefts is: clefted NP followed by the modifying relative clause.

Tagalog at first glance appears to have one construction corresponding to English *it*-clefts and another to English *wh*-clefts (Naylor 1975):

(156) a. Si Juan ang l[um]akad
PrP John PrP [PrP=ACT]-walk
'It was John who walked'

b. Ang l[um]akad   ay si Juan
   PrP [PrP=ACT]-walk TOP PrP John
   'The one who walked was John'

c. Si Juan ang k[um]ain   ng isda
   PrP John PrP [PrP=ACT]-eat P fish
   'It was John who ate the fish'

d. Ang k[um]ain   ng isda'y si Juan
   PrP [PrP=ACT]-eat P fish-TOP PrP John
   'The one who ate the fish was John'

The Tagalog equivalent of an *it*-cleft consists of a predicate nominal
followed by a headless relative clause, as in (156a,c). The *wh*-cleft is
basically this same construction, except that inversion of the predicate
nominal and headless relative clause occurs by topicalizing the relative
clause. Note the presence of *ay*, the topicalization marker, in (156b,d).
This is because a pivot NP occurs before the predicate. These Tagalog
data show the close interrelations of the two types of clefts.

Finally, in some languages, clefts and left-dislocations seem to be the
same construction. This is not surprising in that these constructions
selectively foreground just one NP, and, furthermore, these constructions are features of the clause exterior. Duala, a Bantu language of
Cameroun in West Africa (Epée 1976) exhibits this pattern:

(157)   a. Kuo a bodi nu motu kalati kiele
           Kuo he give that man book yesterday
           'Kuo gave a book to that man yesterday'

        b. Kuo nde a bodi nu moto kalati kiele
           Kuo TOP he give that man book yesterday
           'It's Kuo who gave a book to that man yesterday'

        c. Nu moto nde Kuo a bodi *no* kalati kiele
           that man TOP kuo he give PRO book yesterday
           'It's that man that Kuo gave a book to yesterday'

        d. Kiele   nde Kuo a bodi *no* nu   moto kalati
           yesterday TOP Kuo he give PRO that man book
           'It's yesterday that Kuo gave that man a book'

In Duala, clefts and left-dislocations are identical. To foreground a
constituent in Duala, it is simply moved to the clause-initial position and
followed by the topic marker *nde*. If the foregrounded constituent is
actor, there is no further change in the clause; the actor concord marker
remains preceding the verb. If it is any other NP type, then a special
pronominal-like morpheme *no* must appear enclitic to the verb. That

these left-dislocations are structurally identical to clefts is demonstrated by the fact that this pattern also obtains in relative clauses:

(158)   a. Muto   nu tondi mba
           woman REL love me
           'The woman who loves me'

        b. Muto   na tondi *no*
           woman I   love PRO
           'The woman I love'

The portion of the examples in (157) which follows *nde* is structurally like a relative clause, and consequently, in Duala, left-dislocations and clefts must be viewed as the same construction.

5 Summary[1]

In this chapter we have dealt with a wide range of information-packaging devices in the clause, which include lexical, morphological, and syntactic structures. Our main focus has been on syntactic devices, especially those which rearrange core arguments of the clause. We have pointed out the difference between such clause-internal constructions and those which function outside the clause. Internal constructions have both foregrounding and backgrounding effects (e.g. foregrounding passives foreground non-actors, while backgrounding passives background actors), while external constructions are exclusively foregrounding. These constructions can be summarized as in Table 6.8.

Table 6.8 *Summary of syntactic packaging devices*

Internal constructions
 1 passive – foregrounding and backgrounding
 2 antipassive – foregrounding and backgrounding
 3 dative shift

External constructions
 1 topicalization
 2 left-dislocation
 3 clefts

NOTES

* We would like to thank the following people for useful comments on earlier versions of this paper: Ken Whistler, Bob Dixon, Tim Shopen, Anna Wierzbicka, Linda Schwartz, Alessandro Duranti, John Verhaar, David Wilkins.

1 Some suggestions for further reading: two useful books in the general area are Cole and Sadock (1977), particularly the articles by Comrie, Fillmore, Gary and Keenan, Kisseberth and Abasheikh, and Schachter; and Li (1976), particularly the articles by Chafe, Givón, Keenan, Kirsner, Li and Thompson, Schachter, and Timberlake. Other general works of interest include Anderson (1971), Blake (1976), Dixon (1972, 1979), Erteschik-Shir (1979), Foley and Van Valin (1977), Heath (1976), Hopper and Thompson (1980), Perlmutter and Postal (1977), Prince (1978), Trithart (1979), and Van Valin (1980).

Bibliography

Adams, K. L. and N. F. Conklin. 1974. On the numeral classifier in Thai. Paper presented at the Seventh International Conference on Sino-Tibetan Language and Linguistic Studies, Atlanta, Georgia

Ali, L. H. 1970. Some aspects of negation in English and Baghdad Arabic. *Archivum Linguisticum* 1(n.s.):67–83

Anderson, J. 1971. On the role of deep structure in semantic interpretation. *Foundations of Language* 7:387–96

Anderson, S. R. 1976. On the notion of Subject in ergative languages. In Li 1976:1–23

Andrews, A. D. 1982. The representation of case in modern Icelandic. In Bresnan 1982a:427–503

Ard, J. 1978. Subject-based and absolutive-based syntactic processes in Kamchadal. *Lingua* 45:193–231

Austin, P. K. 1981a. *A grammar of Diyari, South Australia*. Cambridge, Cambridge University Press

Austin, P. K. 1981b. Switch-reference in Australia. *Language* 57:309–33

Avrorin, V. A. 1961. *Grammatika Nanajskogo jazyka II*. Moscow, Nauka

Avrorin, V. A. and E. P. Lebedeva. 1968. Oročskij jazyk. In Vinogradov 1968:191–209

Bach, E. 1980. In defense of passive. *Linguistics and Philosophy* 3:297–341

Bach, E. and R. T. Harms, eds. 1968. *Universals in linguistic theory*. New York, Holt, Rinehart and Winston

Bakir, M. J. 1970. An account of negation in colloquial Iraqi Arabic. Unpublished M.A. thesis, Bangor

Balpinar, Z. 1979. Some aspects of Turkish passivization. Unpublished manuscript, LSA Institute, University of Salzburg, Austria

Bamgboṣe, A. 1966. *A grammar of Yoruba*. Cambridge, Cambridge University Press

Bang, W. 1923. Das negative Verbum der Turksprachen. *Abhandlungen der Preussischen Akademie der Wissenschaften, Philosophisch-historische Klasse* 17:114–31

Banjo, A. 1974. Sentence negation in Yoruba. *Studies in African Linguistics*, Supplement 5:35–47

Barber, E. J. W. 1975. Voice – beyond the passive. *Berkeley Linguistics Society* 1:16–24

Bateson, M. C. 1967. *Arabic language handbook*. Washington, Center for Applied Linguistics

Bavin, E. L. 1980. On the grammatical notion, Subject. Unpublished Ph.D. dissertation, State University of New York, Buffalo

Beeston, A.F.L. 1970. *The Arabic language today*. London, Hutchinson

Bell, S. J. 1976. Cebuano subjects in two frameworks. Unpublished Ph.D. dissertation, M.I.T. (Distributed by Indiana University Linguistics Club, 1979)

Berman, R. 1978. *Modern Hebrew structure*. Tel Aviv, Tel Aviv University Press

Binh, D. T. 1971. *A tagmemic comparison of the structure of English and Vietnamese sentences*. The Hague, Mouton

Blake, B. J. 1976. On ergativity and the notion of subject. *Lingua* 39:281–300

Blake, B. J. 1977. *Case marking in Australian languages*. Canberra, Australian Institute of Aboriginal Studies

Bloomfield, L. 1933. *Language*. New York, Holt

Bloomfield, L. 1962. *The Menomini language*. New Haven, Conn., Yale University Press

Boas, F. and E. Deloria. 1941. *Dakota grammar*. Washington, DC, Government Printing Office. (Memoirs of the National Academy of Science, 23)

Bollenbacher, J. 1977. The Basque passive. Unpublished manuscript, Department of Linguistics, University of California at San Diego

Bowen, J. T. and T. J. Rhys Jones. 1960. *Welsh*. London, English Universities Press. (Teach Yourself Books)

Brain, J. L. 1960. *Basic structure of Swahili*. Syracuse, N.Y., Eastern African Studies Program, Syracuse University

Brandon, F. R. 1976. Quantification, negation and the semantic isolation of sentence. *Working Papers on Language Universals* 20:19–42

Bresnan, J. 1978. A realistic transformational grammar. In Halle *et al.* 1978:1–59

Bresnan, J. 1980. *The passive in lexical theory*. Cambridge, Mass., M.I.T. Center for Cognitive Science. (Occasional Paper, 7)

Bresnan, J., ed. 1982a. *The mental representation of grammatical relations*. Cambridge, Mass., M.I.T. Press

Bresnan, J. 1982b. Control and complementation. In Bresnan 1982a:282–390

Bright, W. 1957. *The Karok language*. Berkeley, University of California Press

Brugmann, K. 1905. *Abrégé de grammaire comparée des langues Indo-Européenes*. Paris

Burzio, L. 1981. Intransitive verbs and Italian auxiliaries. Unpublished Ph.D. dissertation, M.I.T.

Capell, A. 1957. *A new Fijian dictionary*. Glasgow, W. Guthrie

Carden, G. 1972. Multiple dialects in multiple negation. *Chicago Linguistic Society* 8:32–40

Catford, J. C. 1976. Ergativity in Caucasian languages. *North Eastern Linguistic Society* 6. (Recherches Linguistiques à Montréal, 6)

Cena, R. M. 1977. Patient primacy in Tagalog. Paper read at the Winter Meeting of the Linguistic Society of America, Chicago

Chafe, W. L. 1970a. *A semantically based sketch of Onondaga*. Bloomington, Indiana University Press

Chafe, W. L. 1970b. *Meaning and the structure of language*. Chicago, Chicago University Press

Chafe, W. L. 1976. Givenness, contrastiveness, definiteness, subjects, topics, and point of view. In Li 1976:25–55

Chao, Y.-R. 1968. *A grammar of spoken Chinese.* Berkeley, University of California Press

Chomsky, A. N. 1957. Syntactic structures. The Hague, Mouton

Chomsky, A. N. 1965. *Aspects of the theory of syntax*. Cambridge, Mass., M.I.T. Press

Chomsky, A. N. 1981. *Lectures on government and binding*. Dordrecht, Foris

Christaller, J. G. 1875 (1964). *A grammar of the Asante and Fante language called Tshi*. Ridgewood, N.J., Gregg Press

Chung, S. 1970. Negative verbs in Polynesian. Unpublished senior honours thesis, Harvard University

Chung, S. 1976. An object creating rule in Bahasa Indonesia. *Linguistic Inquiry* 7:41–87

Chung, S. 1978. *Case marking and grammatical relations in Polynesian languages*. Austin, University of Texas Press

Churchward, C. M. 1953. *Tongan grammar*. London, Oxford University Press

Cinque, G. 1977. The movement nature of left dislocation. *Linguistic Inquiry* 8:397–412

Cole, P. and G. Hermon. 1981. Subjecthood and islandhood, evidence from Quechua. *Linguistic Inquiry* 12:1–30

Cole, P. and J. M. Sadock, eds. 1977. *Syntax and semantics 8: Grammatical relations*. New York, Academic Press

Collinder, B. 1960. *Comparative grammar of the Uralic languages*. Stockholm, Almqvist and Wiksell

Collins, G. 1970. Two views of Kalagan grammar. Unpublished Ph.D. dissertation, University of Indiana

Comrie, B. 1975. The antiergative: Finland's answer to Basque. *Chicago Linguistic Society* 11:112–21

Comrie, B. 1976. The negative auxiliary. Unpublished mimeo

Comrie, B. 1977. In defense of spontaneous demotion: the impersonal passive. In Cole and Sadock 1977:47–58

Comrie, B. 1978. Ergativity. In Lehmann 1978:329–94

Comrie, B. 1979. Russian. In T. Shopen, ed. *Languages and their speakers*. Cambridge, Mass., Winthrop: 91–151

Comrie, B. 1981. Ergativity in Kala Lagaw Ya. *Australian Journal of Linguistics* 1:1–42

Corum, C., T. C. Smith-Stark and A. Weiser, eds. 1973. *You take the high node and I'll take the low node*. Chicago, Chicago Linguistic Society

Courtenay, K. 1976. Ideophones defined as a phonological class: the case of Yoruba. *Studies in African Linguistics*, Supplement 6:13–26

Cowan, M. M. 1969. *Tzotzil grammar*. Norman, University of Oklahoma, Summer Institute of Linguistics

Craig, C. G. 1977. *The structure of Jacaltec*. Austin, University of Texas Press

Crazzolara, J. 1955. *A study of the Acooli language*. London, Oxford University Press

Crazzolara, J. 1960. *A study of the Logbara (Ma'di) language*. London, Dawson

Creider, C. 1976. A typological sketch of Nandi. Unpublished manuscript, Department of Anthropology, University of Western Ontario

Crowley, T. 1978. *The middle Clarence dialects of Bandjalang*. Canberra, Australian Institute of Aboriginal Studies

Curme, G. O. 1935. Parts of speech and accidence. Vol. 2 of G. O. Curme and H. Kurath, eds. *A grammar of the English language*. Boston, D. C. Heath and Co.

Dahl, Ö. 1977. *Negation in universal grammar*. Gothenburg, Gothenburg Papers in Theoretical Linguistics

Dardjowidjojo, S. 1971. The *men-*, *men-kan* and *men-i* verbs in Indonesian. *Philippine Journal of Linguistics* 2:71–84

Datz, M. 1980. Jacaltec syntactic structures and the demands of discourse. Unpublished Ph.D. dissertation, University of Colorado

Davies, W. D. 1981. Choctaw clause structure. Unpublished Ph.D. dissertation, University of California at San Diego

Davison, R. M. 1967. *The use of the genitive in negative constructions*. Cambridge, Cambridge University Press. (Studies in the Modern Russian Language, 2)

Dayley, J. 1980. Voice and ergativity in Mayan languages. Unpublished manuscript, University of California, Berkeley

Dixon, R. M. W. 1972. *The Dyirbal language of North Queensland*. Cambridge, Cambridge University Press

Dixon, R. M. W., ed. 1976a. *Grammatical categories in Australian languages*. Canberra, Australian Institute of Aboriginal Studies

Dixon, R. M. W. 1976b. The syntactic development of Australian languages. In Li 1977:365–415

Dixon, R. M. W. 1977a. *A grammar of Yidiɲ*. Cambridge, Cambridge University Press

Dixon, R. M. W. 1977b. Where have all the adjectives gone? *Studies in Language* 1:19–80

Dixon, R. M. W. 1979. Ergativity. *Language* 55:59–138

Doke, C.M. 1935. *Bantu linguistic terminology*. London, Longmans, Green

Dowty, D. 1978. Governed transformations as lexical rules in a Montague grammar. *Linguistic Inquiry* 9:393–426

Dowty, D. 1982. Grammatical relations and Montague grammar. In Pullum and Jacobson 1982

Duranti, A. 1979. Object, clitic pronouns in Bantu, and the topicality hierarchy. *Studies in African Linguistics* 10:31–46

Duranti, A. and E. Byarushengo. 1977. On the notion of 'direct object' in

Haya. In E. Byarushengo, A. Duranti and L. M. Hyman, eds. *Haya grammatical structures. Southern California Occasional Papers in Linguistics* 6:45–71

Duranti, A. and E. Ochs. 1979. Left-dislocation in Italian conversation. In Givón 1979b:377–416

Durie, M. 1981. Verbal agreement in Acehnese. Talk delivered to the Australian Linguistic Society, Canberra

Elliott, D. 1971. The grammar of emotive and exclamatory sentences in English. *Ohio State University Working Papers in Linguistics*, 8

Epée, R. 1976. On some rules that are not successive cyclic in Duala. *Linguistic Inquiry* 7:193–8

Erteschik-Shir, N. 1979. Discourse constraints on dative movement. In Givón 1979b:441–67

Faltz, L. M. 1977. Reflexivization: a study in universal syntax. Unpublished Ph.D. dissertation, University of California, Berkeley

Faltz, L. M. 1978. On indirect objects in universal grammar. *Chicago Linguistic Society* 14:76–87

Feoktistov, A. P. 1966. Erzjanskij jazyk. In Vinogradov 1966:177–98

Fillmore, C. J. 1965. *Indirect object constructions in English and the ordering of transformations*. The Hague, Mouton

Fillmore, C. J. 1968. The case for case. In Bach and Harms 1968:1–88

Fillmore, C. J. 1977. The case for case reopened. In Cole and Sadock 1977:59–82

Foley, W. A. 1976. Comparative syntax in Austronesian. Unpublished Ph.D. dissertation, University of California, Berkeley

Foley, W. A. and M. Olson. 1985. Clausehood and verb serialization. In J. Nichols and A. C. Woodbury, eds. *Grammar inside and outside the clause*. Cambridge, Cambridge University Press

Foley, W. A. and R. D. Van Valin, Jr. 1977. On the viability of the notion of 'subject' in universal grammar. *Berkeley Linguistics Society* 3:293–320

Frantz, D. G. 1971. *Toward a generative grammar of Blackfoot (with particular attention to selected stem formation processes)*. Norman, University of Oklahoma, Summer Institute of Linguistics

Freidin, R. 1975. The analysis of passives. *Language* 51:384–405

Fries, C. 1952. *The structure of English*. New York, Harcourt Brace

Gary, J. O. and E. L. Keenan. 1977. On collapsing grammatical relations in universal grammar. In Cole and Sadock 1977:83–120

Georges, L. and J. Kornfilt. 1977. Infinitival double passives in Turkish. *North Eastern Linguistics Society*, 7

Givón, T. 1972. Review of *Some problems in transitivity in Swahili* by W. H. Whitely. *African Studies* 31:273–7

Givón, T. 1975. Negation in language: pragmatics, function, ontology. *Working Papers on Language Universals* 18:59–116

Givón, T. 1976. Topic, pronoun and grammatical agreement. In Li 1976:149–88

Givón, T. 1979a. *On understanding grammar*. New York, Academic Press

Givón, T. 1979b. *Syntax and semantics 12: Discourse and syntax*. New York, Academic Press

Givón, T. 1980. The Ute impersonal passive: topicality, agency, transitivity. Unpublished manuscript, Department of Linguistics, University of California, Los Angeles

Gorcevskaja, V. A. 1941. *Formy otricanija v Èvenkijskom jazyke.* Leningrad, Nauka

Granites, R. J. 1976. Short essays in Warlpiri linguistics (in Warlpiri and English). Cambridge, Mass., M.I.T. (mimeo)·

Green, I. 1979. Arguments against the Proto-Polynesian passive – semantic versus pragmatic properties of the -Cia suffix. Unpublished manuscript, Australian National University

Greenberg, J. H. 1963. Some universals of grammar with particular reference to the order of meaningful elements. In J. H. Greenberg, ed. *Universals of language.* Cambridge, Mass., M.I.T. press: 73–113

Greenberg, J. H., C. A. Ferguson and E. A. Moravcsik. 1978. *Universals of human language. Vol. 4: Syntax.* Palo Alto, Calif., Stanford University Press

Grevisse, M. 1955. *Le bon usage.* 6th edn. Paris, P. Geuthner

Gruber, J. S. 1965. *Studies in lexical relations.* Bloomington, Indiana University Linguistics Club

Gruber, J. S. 1976. *Lexical structures in syntax and semantics.* Amsterdam, North-Holland

Haiman, J. 1978. Conditionals are topics. *Language* 54:564–89

Hajičová, E. 1977. Focus and negation. In A. Zampolli, ed. *Linguistic structures processing.* Amsterdam, North-Holland: 83–115

Hale, K. L. 1972. A note on subject–object inversion in Navajo. In B. B. Kachru *et al.*, eds. *Papers in linguistics in honor of Henry and Renee Kahane*

Hale, K. L. 1973. Person marking in Walbiri. In S. R. Anderson and P. Kiparsky, eds. *A Festschrift for Morris Halle.* New York, Holt, Rinehart and Winston

Hale, K. L. 1976. The adjoined relative clause in Australia. In Dixon 1976a:78–105

Hale, K. L. 1978. The essentials of Walbiri main clauses. Unpublished manuscript, M.I.T.

Hale, K. L. 1979. *On the position of Walbiri in a typology of the base.* Bloomington, Indiana University Linguistics Club

Hale, K. L. 1982. Some essential features of Warlpiri verbal clauses. In S. Swartz, ed. *Papers in Warlpiri grammar in honour of Lothar Jagst.* Darwin, Summer Institute of Linguistics. (Work Papers of SIL-AAB, A.6)

Hale, W. G. and C. D. Buck. 1966. *A Latin grammar.* University of Alabama Press. (Reprint of 1903 edition)

Halle, M., J. Bresnan and G. Miller, eds. 1978. *Linguistic theory and psychological reality.* Cambridge, Mass., M.I.T. Press

Halliday, M. A. K. 1967–8. Notes on transitivity and theme in English. *Journal of Linguistics* 3:37–81,199–244; 4:179–215

Hämäläinen, A. 1966. Okinukke Inkerin vuotuisjuhlissa. *Kalevalaseuran Vuosikirja* 56:276–93

Harper, K. 1974. Some aspects of the grammar of the Eskimo dialects of

Cumberland Peninsula and North Baffin Island. *National Museum of Canada, Ethnology Division Paper*, 15

Harris, A. C. 1981. *Georgian syntax: a study in relational grammar*. Cambridge, Cambridge University Press

Haviland, S. and H. Clark. 1974. What's new? *Journal of Verbal Learning and Verbal Behavior* 13:512–21

Hawkinson, A. K. and L. M. Hyman. 1974. Hierarchies of natural topic in Shona. *Studies in African Linguistics* 5:147–70

Heath, J: 1976. Antipassivization: a functional typology. *Berkeley Linguistics Society* 2:202–11

Heath, J. 1977. Choctaw cases. *Berkeley Linguistics Society* 3:204–13

Hohepa, P. 1965. A profile-generative grammar of Maori. Unpublished thesis, Indiana University

Hoijer, H. *et al.*, eds. 1946. *Linguistic structures of native America*. New York, Viking Fund

Hope, E. R. 1974. *The deep syntax of Lisu sentences: a transformational case grammar*. Canberra, Australian National University, Research School of Pacific Studies, Department of Linguistics. (Pacific Linguistics, B.34)

Hopper, P. J. and S. A. Thompson. 1980. Transitivity in grammar and discourse. *Language* 56:251–399

Horn, L. R. 1978. Some aspects of negation. In Greenberg *et al.* 1978:127–210

Howard, I. and A. Niyekawa-Howard. 1976. Passivization. In M. Shibatani, ed. *Syntax and semantics 5: Japanese Generative Grammar*. New York, Academic Press: 201–37

Hyman, L. M. 1975. On the change from SOV to SVO: evidence from Niger–Congo. In Li 1975:113–47

Jackendoff, R. 1969. An interpretive theory of negation. *Foundations of Language* 5:218–41

Jackendoff, R. 1972. *Semantic interpretation in generative grammar*. Cambridge, Mass., M.I.T. Press

Jackendoff, R. 1976. Toward an explanatory semantic representation. *Linguistic Inquiry* 7:89–150

Jackendoff, R. 1978. Grammar as evidence for conceptual structure. In Halle *et al.* 1978:201–28

Jacobsen, W. H., Jr. 1976. Noun and verb in Nootkan. Paper presented at the Victoria Conference on Northwestern Languages. Published 1979 in Efrat, ed. *The Victoria Conference on Northwestern Languages*. Victoria, British Columbia Provincial Museum: 83–153

Jaggar, P. 1981. Some unusual lexical passives in Hausa. Unpublished M.A. dissertation, Department of Linguistics, University of California, Los Angeles

Jespersen, O. 1917. Negation in English and other languages. *Kgl. Danske Videnskabernes Selskab, Historisk-Filologiske Meddelelser* 1, no. 5

Jespersen, O. 1924. *The philosophy of grammar*. London, Allen and Unwin

Jespersen, O. 1946. *A modern English grammar on historical principles*. Vol. 6. London, Allen and Unwin

Johnson, D. E. 1977. On relational constraints on grammars. In Cole and Sadock 1977:151–78

Johnson, D. E. and P. M. Postal. 1980. *Arc pair grammar*. Princeton, N.J., Princeton University Press

Johnson, M. R. 1980. *Ergativity in Inuktitut (Eskimo) and in relational grammar*. Bloomington, Indiana University Linguistics Club

Kachru, Y., B. B. Kachru and T. K. Bhatia. 1976. The notion 'Subject', a note on Hindi-Urdu, Kashmiri and Panjabi. In Verma 1976

Kask, A. 1966. Eesti kirjakeele arenemisest noukogude perioodil. *Emakeele Seltsi Aastaraamat* 11:3–22

Keach, C. M. B. 1980. *The syntax and interpretation of the relative clause construction in Swahili*. Ph.D. dissertation, University of Massachusetts at Amherst. Reproduced by University of Massachusetts Graduate Student Linguistic Association, Amherst, Mass.

Keenan, E. L. 1972. Relative clause formation in Malagasy (and some related and some not so related languages). In P. M. Peranteau, J. N. Levi and G. C. Phares, eds. *The Chicago which hunt*. Chicago Linguistic Society: 169–89

Keenan, E. L. 1976a. Remarkable subjects in Malagasy. In Li 1976:247–301

Keenan, E. L. 1976b. Some universals of passive in relational grammar. *Chicago Linguistic Society* 11:340–52

Keenan, E. L. 1976c. Towards a universal definition of Subject. In Li 1976:303–33

Keenan, E. L. 1978. The syntax of subject-final languages. In Lehmann 1978:267–327

Keenan, E. L. 1980. Passive is phrasal, not sentential or lexical. In T. Hoekstra, H. Hulst and M. Moorgat, eds. *Lexical grammar*. Dordrecht, Foris

Keenan, E. L. and B. Comrie. 1977. NP accessibility and universal grammar. *Linguistic Inquiry* 8:63–100

Keenan, E. L. and L. Faltz. 1978. *Logical types for natural language*. Los Angeles, University of California. (U.C.L.A. Occasional Papers in Linguistics, 3)

Keenan, E. L. and R. D. Hull. 1973. The logical syntax of direct and indirect questions. In Corum *et al.* 1973:348–71

Keenan, E. O. and B. Schieffelin. 1976. Topic as a discourse notion: a study of topics in the conversations of children and adults. In Li 1976:335–84

Kibrik, A. E. 1979. Canonical ergativity and Daghestan languages. In Plank 1979:61–77

Kimenyi, A. 1980. *A relational grammar of Kinyarwanda*. Berkeley, University of California Press. (University of California Publications in Linguistics, 91)

Kirsner, R. 1976. On the subjectless pseudo-passive in standard Dutch and the semantics of background agents. In Li 1976:385–415

Kisseberth, C. and M. Abasheikh. 1977. The object relationship in Chi-Mwi:ni, a Bantu language. In Cole and Sadock 1977:179–218

Klaiman, M. H. 1980. Bengali dative subjects. *Lingua* 51:275–95

Klaiman, M. H. 1981a. Towards a universal semantics of indirect subject constructions. *Berkeley Linguistics Society* 7:123–35

Klaiman, M.H. 1981b. *Volitionality and subject in Bengali*. Bloomington, Indiana University Linguistics Club

Kleinschmidt, S. 1968. *Grammatik der Gronlandischen Sprache, mit teilweisem Einschluss des Labradordialekts*. Hildesheim, G. Olm

Klima, E. S. 1964. Negation in English. In J. A. Fodor and J. J. Katz, eds. *The structure of language*. Englewood Cliffs, N.J., Prentice-Hall: 246–323

Kolesnikova, V. D. and O. A. Konstantinova. 1968. Negidal'skij jazyk. In Vinogradov 1968:109–28

Konstantinova, O. A. 1964. *Èvenkijskij jazyk*. Moscow, Nauka

Konstantinova, O. A. 1968. Èvenkijskij jazyk. In Vinogradov 1968:68–87

Kovedjaeva, E. I. 1966. Lugovo-Vostocnyj Marijskij jazyk. In Vinogradov 1966:221–40

Kraak, A. 1966. *Negatieve zinnen*. Hilversum, W. de Haan

Kraft, C. H. and A. H. M. Kirk-Greene. 1973. *Hausa*. London, English Universities Press. (Teach Yourself Books)

Křížková, H. 1968. K voprosu o tak nazyvaemoj dvojnoj negacii v Slavjanskix jazykaz. *Slavia* 37:21–39

Kuno, S. 1971. The position of locatives in existential sentences. *Linguistic Inquiry* 2:333–78

Kuno, S. 1973. *The structure of the Japanese language*. Cambridge, Mass., M.I.T. Press

Laanest, A. 1975. Pribaltijskie-Finskie jazyki. In V. I. Lytkin, K. E. Majtijskaja and K. Redei, eds. *Osnovy Finno-Ugorskogo jazykoznanija: Pribaltijsko-Finskie, Saamskie i Mordovskie jazyki*. Moscow, Nauka: 5–122

Lakoff, R. 1969. Some reasons why there can't be any some–any rule. *Language* 45:608–15

Langacker, R. 1976. *Non-distinct arguments in Uto-Aztecan*. Berkeley, University of California Press. (University of California Papers in Linguistics, 82)

Langacker, R. 1977. *An overview of Uto-Aztecan grammar*. Dallas, Summer Institute of Linguistics. (Summer Institute of Linguistics Publications in Linguistics and Related Fields, S6)

Lasnik, H. 1975. On the semantics of negation. In D. Hockney, W. Harper and B. Freed, eds. *Contemporary research in philosophical logic and linguistic semantics*. Dordrecht, Reidel: 279–311

Lasnik, H. 1976. *Analyses of negation in English*. Bloomington, Indiana University Linguistics Club

Lavrent'ev, G. I. 1974. Otricatel'nye glagol'nye formy nastojašče-buduščego vremeni v Marijskix dialektax. *Sovetskoe Finno-Ugrovedenija* 10:241–6

Lawler, J. 1977. *A* agrees with *B* in Achenese: a problem for relational grammar. In Cole and Sadock 1977:219–48

Lazdina, T. 1966. *Latvian*. London, English Universities Press. (Teach Yourself Books)

Lee, C. M. 1973. *Abstract syntax and Korean with reference to English*. Seoul, Pan Korea Book Corporation

Lehmann, W. P. 1974. *Proto-Indo-European syntax*. Austin, University of Texas Press

Lehmann, W. P., ed. 1978. *Syntactic typology*. Austin, University of Texas Press

Levin, L. and J. Simpson. 1981. Quirky case and the structure of lexical entries. *Chicago Linguistic Society* 17:185–96

Lewis, G. L. 1967. *Turkish grammar*. Oxford, Clarendon Press

Li, C. N., ed. 1975. *Word order and word order change*. Austin, University of Texas Press

Li, C. N., ed. 1976. *Subject and topic*. New York, Academic Press

Li, C. N., ed. 1977. *Mechanisms of syntactic change*. New York, Academic Press

Li, C. N. and R. Lang. 1978. Ergativity in Enga and other Papuan languages. Unpublished manuscript, Linguistics Program, University of California at Santa Barbara

Li, C. N. and R. Lang. 1979. The syntactic irrelevance of an ergative case in Enga and other Papuan languages. In Plank 1979:307–24

Li, C. N. and S. A. Thompson. 1975. The semantic function of word order: a case study of Mandarin. In Li 1975:163–95

Li, C. N. and S. A. Thompson. 1976. Subject and topic: a new typology of language. In Li 1976:457–89

Li, C. N. and S. A. Thompson. 1978. An exploration of Mandarin Chinese. In Lehmann 1978:223–66

Li, C. N. and S. A. Thompson. 1981. *Mandarin Chinese: a functional reference grammar*. Berkeley, University of California Press

Longacre, R. E. 1976a. *An anatomy of speech notions*. Lisse, Peter de Ridder

Longacre, R. E. 1976b. 'Mystery' particles and affixes. *Chicago Linguistic Society* 12:468–75

Lyon, S. 1967. Tlahuitoltepec Mixe clause structure. *International Journal of American Linguistics* 23:25–45

Lyons, J. 1968. *Introduction to theoretical linguistics*. Cambridge, Cambridge University Press

Lyons, J. 1977. *Semantics*. Vol. 2. Cambridge, Cambridge University Press

Lytkin, V. I. 1966. Komi-Zyrjanskij jazyk. In Vinogradov 1966:281–99

Maling, J. M. 1980. Inversion in embedded clauses in modern Icelandic. *Islenkst Mal og Almenn Malfraedi* 2:175–94

Manley, T. 1972. *Outline of Sre structure*. Honolulu, University of Hawaii Press. (Oceanic Linguistics Special Publications, 12)

Martin, S. E. and Y.-S. Lee. 1969. *Beginning Korean*. New Haven, Conn., Yale University Press

Matisoff, J. 1973. *The grammar of Lahu*. Los Angeles, University of California Press

Matthews, G. H. 1965. *Hidatsa syntax*. The Hague, Mouton

Matthews, P. H. 1981. *Syntax*. Cambridge, Cambridge University Press

Mazaudon, M. 1976. La formation des propositions relatives en tibétain. *Bulletin de la Société de Linguistique de Paris* 73:401–14

McCawley, J. D. 1970. On the deep structure of negative clauses. *Eigo Kyōiku* 19.6:72–5. (Reprinted in McCawley 1976b:277–84)

McCawley, J. D. 1976a. A note on multiple negatives. In McCawley 1976b:206–10

McCawley, J. D. 1976b. *Grammar and meaning*. New York, Academic Press

McCawley, J. D. 1977. Remarks on the lexicography of performative verbs. In Rogers *et al.* 1977:13–25

McCawley, N. A. 1973. Boy! Is syntax easy! *Chicago Linguistic Society* 9:369–77

McClendon, S. 1978. Ergativity, case, and transitivity in Eastern Pomo. *International Journal of American Linguistics* 44:1–9

Menges, K. 1968. *The Turkic languages and peoples*. Wiesbaden, Harrassowitz

Milner, G. B. 1956. *Fijian grammar*. Suva, Fiji Government Press

Mirikitani, L. 1972. *Kapampangan syntax*. Honolulu, University of Hawaii Press. (Oceanic Linguistics Special Publications, 10)

Mohanan, K. P. 1982. Grammatical relations and clause structure in Malayalam. In Bresnan 1982a:504–89

Moralong, M. and L. Hyman. 1977. Animacy, objects and clitics in Sesotho. *Studies in African Linguistics* 8:199–217

Moravcsik, E. A. 1971. Some cross-linguistic generalizations about yes–no questions and their answers. *Stanford University Working Papers on Language Universals* 7:45–193

Moravcsik, E. A. 1978. On the case marking of objects. In Greenberg *et al.* 1978:249–89

Moravcsik, E. A. and J. R. Wirth, eds. 1980. *Syntax and semantics 13: Current approaches to syntax*. New York, Academic Press

Morgan, J. L. 1978. Two types of convention in indirect speech acts. In P. Cole, ed. *Syntax and semantics 9: Pragmatics*. New York, Academic Press: 261–80

Mulder, J. G. 1978. Universal grammar and diachronic syntax. The case of the Finnish negative. Unpublished M.A. thesis, University of California, Los Angeles

Mulder, J. and A. Schwartz. 1978. On the subject of passives in the Philippine languages. Unpublished manuscript, Department of Linguistics, University of California, Los Angeles

Munro, P. 1973. Reanalysis and elaboration in Yuman negatives. *Linguistic Notes from La Jolla, University of California, San Diego* 5:36–62

Munro, P. 1976. Subject copying, auxiliarization and predicate raising: the Mojave evidence. *International Journal of American Linguistics* 42:99–112

Munro, P. 1977. From existential to copula: the history of Yuman *be*. In Li 1977:445–90

Murane, E. 1974. *Daga grammar*. Norman, University of Oklahoma, Summer Institute of Linguistics

Nash, D. G. 1980. Topics in Warlpiri grammar. Unpublished Ph.D. dissertation, M.I.T.

Naylor, P. 1975. Topic, focus, and emphasis in the Tagalog verbal clause. *Oceanic Linguistics* 14:12–79

Newman, P. 1970. *A grammar of Tera*. Berkeley, University of California Press. (University of California Publications in Linguistics, 57)

Newman, P. 1971. The Hausa negative markers. *Studies in African Linguistics* 2:183–95

Newman, R. M. 1971. A case grammar of Ga'anda. Unpublished Ph.D. dissertation, University of California, Los Angeles

Newman, S. 1944. *Yokuts language of California.* New York, Viking Fund

Nichols, J. 1979. Syntax and pragmatics in Manchu-Tungus languages. In *The elements: a parasession on linguistic units and levels, including papers from the conference on Non-Slavic languages of the USSR.* Chicago Linguistic Society:420–28

Nichols, J. 1980. Control and ergativity in Chechen. *Chicago Linguistic Society* 16:259–68

Nicklas, T. 1974. The elements of Choctaw. Unpublished Ph.D. dissertation, University of Michigan

Noonan, M. 1978. Impersonal constructions: some evidence from Irish. Unpublished manuscript, Department of Linguistics, State University of New York, Buffalo

Noonan, M. and E. Bavin Woock. 1978. The passive analog in Lango. *Berkeley Linguistics Society* 4:128–39

Novikova, K. A. 1968. Èvenskij jazyk. In Vinogradov 1968:88–108

Oehrle, R. 1975. The dative alternation in English. Unpublished Ph.D. dissertation, M.I.T.

Oehrle, R. To appear. *The English 'dative' constructions: grammatical form and interpretation.* Dordrecht, Reidel. (Synthèse Language Library Series)

Osborne, C. R. 1974. *The Tiwi Language.* Canberra, Australian Institute of Aboriginal Studies

Ostler, N. D. M. 1979. *Case linking: a theory of case and verb diathesis applied to Classical Sanskrit.* Bloomington, Indiana University Linguistics Club

Pandaripande, R. and Y. Kachru. 1976. *Relational grammar, ergativity, and Hindi-Urdu.* Urbana, University of Illinois. (Studies in the Linguistic Sciences, 6)

Payne, T. E. 1982. Role and reference related subject properties and ergativity in Yup'ik Eskimo and Tagalog. *Studies in Language* 6:75–106

Perlmutter, D. 1971. *Deep and surface structure constraints in syntax.* New York, Holt, Rinehart and Winston

Perlmutter, D. 1978. Impersonal passives and the unaccusative hypothesis. *Berkeley Linguistics Society* 4:157–89

Perlmutter, D. 1980. Relational grammar. In Moravcsik and Wirth 1980:195–229

Perlmutter, D. and P. Postal. 1977. Toward a universal characterization of, passivization. *Berkeley Linguistics Society* 3:394–417

Petrova, T. I. 1967. *Jazyk Orokov (Ul'ta).* Leningrad, Nauka

Petrova, T. I. 1968. Orokskij jazyk. In Vinogradov 1968:172–90

Phong, N. P. 1976. *Le syntagme verbal en vietnamien.* Paris, Mouton

Pickett, V. 1960. *The grammatical hierarchy of Isthmus Zapotec.* Baltimore, Linguistic Society of America. (Language Dissertation, 56)

Plank, F. ed. 1979. *Ergativity.* New York, Academic Press

Polomé, E. C. 1967. *Swahili language handbook.* Washington, DC, Center for Applied Linguistics

Pope, E. 1973. Question-answering systems. *Chicago Linguistic Society* 9:482–92

Postal, P. M. 1982. Some arc-pair grammar descriptions. In Pullum and Jacobson 1982

Price, G. 1962. The negative particles *pas, mie* and *point* in French. *Archivum Linguisticum* 14:14–34

Price, G. 1971. *The French language, present and past*. London, Edward Arnold

Prince, E. F. 1978. A comparison of WH-clefts and It-clefts in discourse. *Language* 54:883–906

Prince, E. F. 1979. Towards a taxonomy of given/new information. *Chicago Linguistic Society* 15:267–78

Prince, E. F. 1981. Topicalization, focus-movement and Yiddish-movement: a pragmatic differentiation. *Berkeley Linguistics Society* 7:249–64

Pullum, G. K. and P. Jacobson, eds. 1982. *The nature of syntactic representation*. Dordrecht, Reidel

Rajandi, H. 1967. Some general properties of the Estonian negation system. *Sovetskoe Finno-Ugrovedenija* 3.1:11–21

Rajaona, S. 1972. *Structure du Malgache*. Fianarantsoa, Madagascar, Ambozontany

Ramos, T. 1974. *The case system of Tagalog verbs*. Canberra, Australian National University, Research School of Pacific Studies, Department of Linguistics. (Pacific Linguistics, B.27)

Randriamasimanana, C. 1981. A study of the causative construction in Malagasy. Unpublished Ph.D. dissertation, University of Southern California

Rhys Jones, T. J. 1977. *Living Welsh*. London, Hodder and Stoughton

Rickard, D. T. 1970. *Kru grammar*. Monrovia

Robins, R. H. 1964. *General linguistics: an introductory survey*. London, Longmans, Green

Rogers, A. R., R. Wall and J. P. Murphy, eds. 1977. *Proceedings of the Texas Conference on Performatives, Presuppositions, and Implicatures*. Washington, DC, Center for Applied Linguistics

Rognvaldsson, E. 1982. We need (some kind of a) rule of conjunction reduction. *Linguistic Inquiry* 13:557–61

Rosen, C. 1982. The interface between semantic roles and initial grammatical relations. In Zaenen 1982

Ruhlen, M. 1976. *A guide to the languages of the world*. Palo Alto, Stanford University, Language Universals Project

Sadock, J. M. 1970. Whimperatives. In Sadock and Vanek 1970:223–38

Sadock, J. M. and A. Vanek, eds. 1970. *Studies presented to Robert B. Lees by his students*. Edmonton, Linguistic Research

Sapir, E. 1911. The problem of noun-incorporation. *American Anthropologist* 13:250–83

Sapir, E. 1921. *Language*. New York, Harcourt Brace

Sapir, E. 1930. Southern Paiute, a Shoshonean language. *Proceedings of the American Academy of Arts and Sciences* 65:1–296

Sapir, E. and M. Swadesh. 1960. *Yana dictionary*. Berkeley, University of California Press

Sapir, J. D. 1965. *A grammar of Diola-Fogny*. Cambridge, Cambridge University Press

Ščemerova, V. S. 1972. K voprosu ob a-ovoj osnove glagol'nogo otricanija v Mordovskix jazykax. *Sovetskoe Finno-Ugrovedenija* 8:173–80

Ščerbakova, A. M. 1954. Formy otricanija v Neneckom jazyke. *Učenye Zapiski Leningradskogo Gospedinstituta imeni Gercena* 101:181–231

Schachter, P. 1974. A non-transformational account of serial verbs. *Studies in African Linguistics*, Supplement 5:253–70

Schachter, P. 1976. The subject in Philippine languages: topic, actor, actor-topic, or none of the above. In Li 1976:491–518

Schachter, P. 1977. Reference-related and role-related properties of subjects. In Cole and Sadock 1977:279–306

Schachter, P. 1978. English propreciates. *Linguistic Analysis* 4:187–224

Schachter, P. and F. T. Otanes. 1972. *Tagalog reference grammar*. Berkeley, University of California Press

Schultz-Lorenzen, C. W. 1969. *Det vestgrønlandske sprog i grammatisk fremstilling*. Copenhagen, Anden Udgave, Ministeriet for Grønland

Schwartz, A. 1976. On the universality of subjects: the Ilocano case. In Li 1976:516–43

Searle, J. R. 1977. A classification of illocutionary acts. In Rogers *et al.* 1977:27–45

Serebrennikov, S. A. 1967. *Istoričeskaja morfologija Mordovskix jazykov*. Moscow, Nauka

Sgall, P., E. Hajičová and E. Benešová. 1973. *Topic, focus and generative semantics*. Kronborg Taunus, Scriptor Verlag

Shipley, W. F. 1964. *Maidu grammar*. Berkeley, University of California Press

Shopen, T. and M. Konaré. 1970. Sonrai causatives and passives: transformational versus lexical derivations for propositional heads. *Studies in African Linguistics* 1:211–54

Silverstein, M. 1976. Hierarchy of features and ergativity. In Dixon 1976a:112–71

Skorik, P. J. 1977. *Grammatika Čukotskogo jazyka* II. Leningrad, Nauka

Stenson, N. 1970. Negation in Diegueño. *Linguistic Notes from La Jolla, University of San Diego* 4:17–28

Stockwell, R. P., P. Schachter and B. Partee. 1973. *The major syntactic structures of English*. New York, Holt, Rinehart and Winston

Sugita, H. 1973. Semitransitive verbs and object incorporation in Micronesian languages. *Oceanic Linguistics* 12:393–406

Swadesh, M. 1939. Nootka internal syntax. *International Journal of American Linguistics* 9:77–102

Takizala, A. 1972. Focus and relativization: the case of Kihung'an. *Studies in African Linguistics* 3:259–88

Tepljašina, D. I. 1966. Udmurtskij jazyk. In Vinogradov 1966:261–80

Tereščenko, N. M. 1966. Nganasanskij jazyk. In Vinogradov 1966:416–37

Tereščenko, N. M. 1973. *Sintaksis samodijskix jazykov*. Leningrad, Nauka

Thomas, D. D. 1971. *Chrau grammar*. Honolulu, University of Hawaii Press

Thomason, R. 1976. Some extensions of Montague grammar. In B. Partee, ed. *Montague grammar*. New York, Academic Press: 77–117

Thrainsson, H. 1979. *On complementation in Icelandic*. New York, Garland

Timberlake, A. 1976. Subject properties in the North Russian passive. In Li 1976:545–57

Trithart, L. 1975. Relational grammar and Chichewa subjectivization rules. *Chicago Linguistic Society* 11:615–24

Trithart, L. 1977. *Relational grammar and Chichewa subjectivization rules*. Bloomington, Indiana University Linguistics Club

Trithart, L. 1979. Topicality: an alternative to the relational view of Bantu passives. *Studies in African Linguistics* 10:1–30

Tryon, D. 1967. *Nengone grammar*. Canberra, Australian National University, Research School of Pacific Studies, Department of Linguistics. (Pacific Lingustics, B.6)

Tunbridge, D. 1980. Hindi-Urdu: a case study. Unpublished Honours thesis, Australian National University

Ultan, R. 1969. Some general characteristics of interrogative systems. *Stanford University Working Papers on Language Universals* 1:41–63

Upadhyaya, U. P. and N. D. Krishnamurthy. 1972. *Conversational Kannada*. Dharwar, India, Lakshmibai Gurunath Joshi

Vääri, E. E. 1966. Livskij jazyk. In Vinogradov 1966:138–54

Van Valin, R. D. 1977. Ergativity and the universality of subjects. *Chicago Linguistic Society* 13:689–705

Van Valin, R. D. 1980. On the distribution of passive and antipassive constructions in universal grammar. *Lingua* 50:303–27

Van Valin, R. D. 1985. Case marking and the structure of the Lakhota clause. In J. Nichols and A. Woodbury, eds. *Grammar inside and outside the clause*. Cambridge, Cambridge University Press

Van Valin, R. D. and W. A. Foley. 1980. Role and reference grammar. In Moravcsik and Wirth 1980:329–52

Vasilevič, G. M. 1934. *Učebnik Évenkijskogo (Tungusskogo) jazyka*. Leningrad, Nauka

Verma, M. K., ed. 1976. *The notion of subject in South Asian languages*. Madison, University of Wisconsin. (University of Wisconsin Publication Series, 2)

Vinogradov, V. V., ed. 1966. *Jazyki narodov S.S.S.R.*, Vol. 3. Moscow, Nauka

Vinogradov, V. V., ed. 1968. *Jazyki narodov S.S.S.R.*, Vol. 5. Leningrad, Nauka

Voegelin, C. F. and F. M. Voegelin. 1973. *Index of the world's languages*. Washington, DC, Department of Health, Education and Welfare, Office of Education, Bureau of Research

Warotamasikkhadit, U. 1972. *Thai syntax*. The Hague, Mouton

Wasow, T. 1976. Transformations and the lexicon. In P. Culicover, T. Wasow and A. Akmajian, eds. *Formal syntax*. New York, Academic Press: 327–60

Watkins, M. 1937. *A grammar of Hichewa*. Philadelphia, Linguistic Society of America. (Language Dissertation, 24)

Weber, D. 1976. *Suffix-as-operator analysis and the grammar of successive encoding in Llacon (Huanuco) Quechua.* Yarinacocha, Peru, Instituto Linguístico de Verano

Welmers, W. E. and B. F. Welmers. 1968. *Igbo: a learner's dictionary.* Los Angeles, University of California, African Studies Centre

Welmers, W. E. and B. F. Welmers. 1969. Noun modifiers in Igbo. *International Journal of American Linguistics* 35:315–22

Whitman, R. 1971. *Order of accessibility: variables in negation.* Honolulu, University of Hawaii. (Working Papers in Linguistics)

Whorf, B. L. 1938. Some verbal categories of Hopi. *Language* 14:275–86 (Reprinted in Whorf 1956:112–24)

Whorf, B. L. 1956. *Language, thought, and reality: selected writings of Benjamin Lee Whorf.* Ed. by J. B. Carroll. Cambridge, Mass., M.I.T. Press

Wickman, B. 1955. The form of the object in the Uralic languages. *Uppsala Universitets Arsskrift,* 6

Wierzbicka, A. 1981. Case marking and human nature. *Australian Journal of Linguistics* 1:43–80

Winstedt, R. O. 1914. *Malay grammar.* Oxford, Clarendon Press

Wolfart, C. 1973. Plains Cree: a grammatical study. *Transactions of the American Philosophical Society* 63, 5

Woodbury, A. C. 1977. Greenlandic Eskimo, ergativity, and relational grammar. In Cole and Sadock 1977: 307–36

Woodbury, H. 1975. Onondaga noun incorporation: some notes on the interdependence of syntax and semantics. *International Journal of American Linguistics* 41:10–20

Woodcock, E. C. 1959. *A new Latin syntax.* Cambridge, Mass., Harvard University Press

Zaenen, A. 1980. Extraction rules in Icelandic. Unpublished Ph.D. dissertation, Harvard University

Zaenen, A., ed. 1982. *Subjects and other subjects: proceedings of the Harvard Conference on the Representation of Grammatical Relations.* Bloomington, Indiana University Linguistics Club

Zemb, J. M. 1968. *Les structures logiques de la proposition allemande.* Paris, O.C.D.L.

Zimmer, K. 1964. Affixal negation in English and other languages: an investigation of restricted productivity. *Word* 20.2, Supplement. (Word Monograph, 5)

Ziv, Y. and G. Sheintuch. 1979. Indirect objects—reconsidered. *Chicago Linguistic Society* 15:390–403

Zubin, D. 1979. Discourse function of morphology: the focus system in German. In Givón 1979b:469–504

Zwicky, A. M. 1974. Hey, whatsyourname! *Chicago Linguistic Society* 10:787–801

Index

Note: References in this index are to all three volumes of *Language typology and syntactic description*. For ease of reference volume numbers are shown in bold type.